D0014009

READINGS IN

FINANCIAL INSTITUTIONS

Edited by

Marshall D. Ketchum

UNIVERSITY OF CHICAGO

and Leon T. Kendall

UNITED STATES SAVINGS AND LOAN LEAGUE

Readings in Financial Institutions

Houghton Mifflin Company • *Boston*

NEW YORK   ATLANTA   GENEVA, ILL.   DALLAS   PALO ALTO

HG
2481
.K53

Copyright © 1965 by Marshall D. Ketchum and Leon T. Kendall. All rights reserved including the right to reproduce this book or parts thereof in any form.

Printed in the U. S. A.

PREFACE

THIS IS A BOOK of readings that it is hoped will be found useful in courses in financial institutions, money and banking, investment, the capital markets, and real estate.

THE READINGS CONSIST of papers presented at meetings of the Conference on Savings and Residential Financing. This conference was established in 1958 under the sponsorship of the United States Savings and Loan League. It has been held each year since 1958, with each conference session two days in length. The programs of the conference have focused on significant problems in the areas of financial institutions and the capital markets. Those invited to present papers are economists of national reputation. The conference programs have been planned by an Executive Committee consisting of Edward Edwards of Indiana University, Harry Guthmann of Northwestern University, Leon Kendall of the United States Savings and Loan League, Marshall Ketchum of the University of Chicago, and Paul Van Arsdell of the University of Illinois.

THE PROCEEDINGS of the six conferences held since 1958 have been published under the co-editorship of Marshall Ketchum, director of the conference, and Leon Kendall, economist of the United States Savings and Loan League. Extensive use has been made of the Proceedings by university teachers as supplementary readings in relevant courses. However, the printings of the Proceedings were limited, and the Proceedings are (or soon will be) out of print and will not be reprinted. This book of readings is presented in the belief that the papers included will continue to be valuable to students, and will become used more extensively because of their ready availability within the covers of one volume.

THIS BOOK will be found most useful at the advanced undergraduate and graduate levels. It is assumed that the student has some familiarity with the organization and functions of the principal financial institutions, and with the sources and uses of funds of these institutions. This knowledge will presumably have been acquired in courses prerequisite to those in which this book will be employed.

v

93382

AN IMPORTANT FEATURE of this volume is that it makes it possible for instructors to convey to their students the principal elements of theoretical and practical controversies in the field of financial institutions without requiring them to refer to more comprehensive publications. This book permits the student to acquire the essentials in concise form from a single source. He may then, if he wishes, undertake study in greater depth by going back to a more extensive treatment that the economist has presented elsewhere. If, for example, interest is aroused in Milton Friedman's ideas on monetary policy, the student can refer to Friedman's *A Program for Monetary Stability* and to Friedman and Schwartz, *A Monetary History of the United States, 1867–1960.* If he wishes to learn more of Denison's views of economic growth, he can proceed to Denison's *The Sources of Economic Growth in the United States and the Alternatives Before Us.*

THE SELECTIONS IN THIS VOLUME have been made without prejudice to other papers that have been presented at annual sessions of the conference. It has been necessary to limit selection to the few that appear most appropriate in terms of the particular topics involved.

LEON T. KENDALL
United States Savings and Loan League

MARSHALL D. KETCHUM
University of Chicago

CONFEREES

Following is a list of all conferees contributing to this book, together with their institutional affiliations at the time they were conferees.

Allan Anderson, Federal Home Loan Bank of Chicago, Chicago, Ill.

Carl T. Arlt, Oberlin College

Nathaniel A. Bailey, School of Business Administration, American University

B. Haggott Beckhart, Graduate School of Business, Columbia University

Glenn H. Beyer, Housing Research Center, Cornell University

Harry Blythe, College of Business Administration, Arizona State University

Jules I. Bogen, Graduate School of Business Administration, New York University

John W. Bowyer, Jr., Graduate School of Business Administration, Washington University

Martin Bronfenbrenner, Department of Economics, University of Minnesota

Lester V. Chandler, Department of Economics, Princeton University

John C. Clendenin, Graduate School of Business Administration, University of California at Los Angeles

Miles Colean, Consultant on Building Finance and Construction, Washington, D. C.

Gerhard Colm, National Planning Association, Washington, D. C.

Paul G. Darling, Department of Economics, Bowdoin College

Edward F. Denison, The Brookings Institution, Washington, D. C.

James S. Duesenberry, Harvard University

James S. Earley, Department of Economics, University of Wisconsin

Theodore R. Eck, School of Business Administration, Southern Methodist University

Edward E. Edwards, Graduate School of Business, Indiana University

David I. Fand, Department of Economics, Southern Methodist University

Harold Feldman, School of Business Administration, Fairleigh Dickinson College

Robert M. Fisher, Board of Governors, Federal Reserve System, Washington, D.C.

Harold G. Fraine, School of Commerce, University of Wisconsin

Milton Friedman, Department of Economics, University of Chicago

Sylvester M. Frizol, College of Commerce, Loyola University

James Gillies, Graduate School of Business Administration, University of California at Los Angeles

Raymond W. Goldsmith, National Bureau of Economic Research, New York, N. Y.

Richard Goode, The Brookings Institution, Washington, D. C.

Howard S. Gordman, School of Business Administration, Georgia State College

H. Peter Gray, College of Liberal Arts, Wayne State University

Leo Grebler, Graduate School of Business Administration, University of California at Los Angeles

Donald Grunewald, School of Business, Rutgers — The State University, Newark, N. J.

John G. Gurley, The Brookings Institution, Washington, D. C.

Harry G. Guthmann, School of Business, Northwestern University

George Hanc, National Association of Mutual Savings Banks, New York, N. Y.

Douglas A. Hayes, School of Business Administration, University of Michigan

Warren Hill, New Jersey Savings and Loan League, Newark, N. J.

Walter E. Hoadley, Armstrong Cork Company, Lancaster, Penn.

Bion B. Howard, School of Business, Northwestern University

Marshall Kaplan, President's Council of Economic Advisers, Washington, D. C.

Leon T. Kendall, United States Savings and Loan League, Chicago, Ill.

John W. Kendrick, George Washington University

Reuben A. Kessel, Graduate School of Business, University of Chicago

Marshall D. Ketchum, Graduate School of Business, University of Chicago

Saul B. Klaman, National Association of Mutual Savings Banks, New York, N. Y.

Clifton H. Kreps, School of Business Administration, University of North Carolina

Eric W. Lawson, College of Business Administration, Syracuse University

James W. Leonard, College of Commerce and Business Administration, University of Illinois

Abba P. Lerner, School of Business and Public Service, Michigan State University

Eugene Lerner, School of Business and Public Administration, City College of New York

Richard W. Lindholm, School of Business Administration, University of Oregon

Shaw Livermore, College of Business and Public Administration, University of Arizona

James Longstreet, School of Business Administration, University of California

Lester B. McAllister, Department of Economics and Business, Beloit College

Gordon W. McKinley, Prudential Insurance Company, Newark, N. J.

Hugh Macaulay, Graduate School, Clemson College

Sherman J. Maisel, School of Business Administration, University of California

Preston Martin, Graduate School of Business Administration, University of Southern California

Arthur C. Meyers, Jr., Department of Economics, Saint Louis University

George W. Mitchell, Federal Reserve Bank of Chicago, Chicago, Ill.

Eugene M. Mortlock, First Federal Savings and Loan Association, New York, N. Y.

Walter A. Morton, Department of Economics, University of Wisconsin

G. Warren Nutter, Department of Economics, University of Virginia

John L. O'Donnell, Graduate School of Business Administration, Michigan State University

J. Charles Partee, Division of Research and Statistics, Board of Governors, Federal Reserve System, Washington, D. C.

John K. Pfahl, College of Commerce and Administration, Ohio State University

Leland J. Pritchard, Department of Economics, University of Kansas

Chester Rapkin, Wharton School of Finance and Commerce, University of Pennsylvania

Richard U. Ratcliff, School of Commerce, University of Wisconsin

Sidney M. Robbins, Graduate School of Business, Columbia University

Nathaniel H. Rogg, National Association of Home Builders, Washington, D. C.

William D. Ross, College of Commerce, Louisiana State University

Paul A. Samuelson, Department of Economics and Social Science, Massachusetts Institute of Technology

R. Duane Saunders, Office of Debt Analysis, United States Treasury Department, Washington, D. C.

Leon M. Schur, Department of Economics, Louisiana State University

Harry S. Schwartz, Federal Home Loan Bank Board, Washington, D. C.

Eli Shapiro, Graduate School of Business Administration, Harvard University

Sherman Shapiro, College of Business Administration, University of Notre Dame

Theodore H. Smith, School of Business Administration, University of Montana

Ezra Solomon, Graduate School of Business, University of Chicago

Robert M. Solow, School of Industrial Management, Massachusetts Institute of Technology

John Stafford, United States Savings and Loan League, Chicago, Ill.

Roland Stucki, College of Business, University of Utah

Lawrence E. Thompson, Graduate School of Business Administration, Harvard University

Robert C. Turner, School of Business, Indiana University

Ernest W. Walker, Department of Finance, University of Texas

Arthur M. Weimer, School of Business, Indiana University

Paul F. Wendt, Graduate School of Business Administration, University of California

Elmus R. Wicker, College of Arts and Sciences, Indiana University

Louis Winnick, The Ford Foundation, New York, N. Y.

Thomas W. Wolfe, United States Treasury Department, Washington, D. C.

CONTENTS

PART ONE

Savings and Institutions

PART TWO

Economic Growth

PART SIX

Focusing on Institutions

READINGS IN

FINANCIAL INSTITUTIONS

Savings and Institutions

Some of the series of lectures in this book have features of a debate, even though the topic of the session is not stated in the form of a resolution. Two, and sometimes three, economists appear on a particular topic. One of the lecturers is a protagonist for a position, and another is an antagonist, or at least is one who is not yet convinced of the validity of the views set forth by the protagonist.

The first selection in Part One is a series of two lectures on "Financial Institutions in the Saving-Investment Process" by John G. Gurley and Ezra Solomon, both now (1964) at Stanford University. The lectures dealt with the "Gurley-Shaw thesis" as set forth in *Money in a Theory of Finance* by John G. Gurley and Edward S. Shaw and published by the Brookings Institution in 1960. The thesis is "a theory of finance that encompasses the theory of money." Financial institutions other than commercial banks are viewed as a possible source of weakness in an economy in which the Federal Reserve authorities are confined to monetary, as distinct from financial, control. This theory holds that commercial banks and other financial institutions alike can increase the supply of loanable funds. A logical extension of the theory is the imposition of reserve requirements for non-bank financial institutions similar to those that commercial banks are now required to keep on their deposits.

The second set of lectures poses the question: "Should Commercial Banks Accept Savings Deposits?" This problem has to do with the similarities and dissimilarities between commercial banks and non-banks as repositories of the savings of individuals. It asks further whether a profit-maximizing institution such as a commercial bank should "seek" time and savings deposits or, as Pritchard asks, whether commercial banks should "incur interest, advertising and other expenses in order to induce their customers to transfer their demand deposits into time deposits." Different views are presented by Leland Pritchard, Edward Edwards, and Lester Chandler. Readers of these lectures may be stimulated to study Pritchard's position in greater detail in Chapters 32 and 33 of his *Money and Banking* (2nd edition) published by Houghton Mifflin Company in 1964. The problem was treated also in a panel in the *Proceedings of the First Annual Conference*, 1958, pp. 166–70, and in the Discussion, pp. 186–93.

Part One concludes with a paper by Haggott Beckhart entitled "Criteria of a Well-Functioning Financial System." This paper represents an extension of work done by Professor Beckhart for the Commission on Money and Credit. The criteria considered relate to the structure of a financial system, to the sources and uses of funds, to credit availability and credit costs, to the payments mechanism, and to the problems of stability and growth.

1

Financial Institutions in the
Saving-Investment Process–I*

John G. Gurley was, in 1959, a senior staff member of the Brookings Institution and associate professor of economics at the University of Maryland. He has written numerous articles for professional journals and, as co-author with E. S. Shaw, has prepared a number of monographs for the Brookings Institution. Dr. Gurley earned his bachelor of arts and doctorate degrees at Stanford University. He formerly served on the faculties of Stanford and Princeton universities.

THIS MORNING I SHALL TRY to strip away some of the layers of confusion about financial intermediaries.[1] I propose to examine, from both an historical and analytical standpoint, the role played by financial assets and financial institutions in economic activity. After that, I shall look at some of the alleged differences between commercial banks and other financial institutions. This will prepare the way for a few remarks on monetary controls in our present financial environment.

AN ECONOMY WITHOUT FINANCIAL ASSETS

Suppose that there were an economic system that had no financial assets at all. There are at least two things that one could say about such

* Proceedings of the Second Annual Conference, 1959, pp. 12–28.
[1] This paper is an offshoot of work done with E. S. Shaw for the Brookings Institution. Several parts of my paper are much improved for my having read James Tobin's paper, "Financial Intermediaries and the Effectiveness of Monetary Controls" (Cowles Foundation Discussion Paper No. 63, Jan. 13, 1959).

an economy. First, without money, the economy would be subject to all the inefficiencies of a barter system. Second, without money or other financial assets, the economy would probably have a relatively low level of investment and would tend to misallocate whatever investment it had.

The second point requires elaboration. An economy without financial assets would require each economic unit to invest in real goods whatever part of its current income was not consumed, which is its saving. I neglect for the moment trading in existing real assets. No unit could invest more than its saving because there would be no way to finance the excess expenditures. And no unit could invest less than its saving because there would be no financial assets in which to put the excess saving. Each economic unit would be forced into a balanced budget position, with saving equal to investment. This sort of arrangement would quite likely lead to a relatively low level of investment and saving and hence tend to retard the rate of growth of national output.

The absence of financial assets, moreover, would bring about an inefficient allocation of resources. An ordering of investment opportunities by their expected rates of return would almost always imply investment by some economic units that exceeded their saving (that is, deficits) and investment by others that fell short of their saving (that is, surpluses). But without financial assets, this efficient ordering of investment could not be achieved. Relatively inferior investment projects would be undertaken and many of the superior ones would go by the boards, simply because there would be no way to distribute investment projects among economic units in a way that differed from the distribution of saving among them.

Money Increases Investment and Saving

Let us now introduce paper money into the economy; the government issues it when it purchases goods and services. A means of payment will, of course, allow the economy to get rid of the inefficiences due to barter. But money will do more than that: it will increase the efficiency of resource allocation and it will most likely lead to a higher level of investment.

Consider, first, the new possibilities for private investment. Private economic units that have highly promising investment opportunities may now make investment expenditures in excess of their current saving by drawing down previously accumulated money balances. Others that do not have such promising investment opportunities can save in excess of their real investment by accumulating money balances. Thus, some promising investment projects can be undertaken that otherwise would not have seen the light of day; and other, inferior investments that otherwise might have been undertaken can now give way. Money allows investment spending to be distributed among economic units in a different way from saving. In allowing some specialization among economic units in investment and saving, it opens up the possibility for a more efficient ordering of investment throughout the economy.

Consider, next, the investment opportunities for government, the issuer of money. As private economic units increase their demand for money balances during output growth, the government can satisfy this demand by new issues of money. Since this money is issued by governmental purchases of goods and services, a rising private demand for money means that economic resources are turned over for government's use. These resources can be used to increase social capital or, through transfer payments, to finance private investment. The way is clearly opened up for an increase in investment and saving.

ELEMENTARY INNOVATIONS IN FINANCE

A financial system restrains growth if it ties the distribution of spending too rigidly to the distribution of income among economic units and if it does not make institutional provision for selective matching of budget surpluses in some sectors with budget deficits in others. Economic units can be expected to look for ways around such restraints. Indeed, in any economy, the financial structure is continually reshaped by the efforts of economic units to break out of the confines of existing financial arrangements. Before moving on to the more sophisticated efforts involving new financial assets, markets and institutions, let us look at a few elementary innovations in finance. For this purpose, the early economic history of this country offers interesting illustrations.

Our economy in its early stages approximated the economy I have just pictured. Its leading financial asset was money; it had few, if any, financial institutions; and its markets for other financial assets were hardly developed. There were definitely financial restraints on real growth, and these were hurdled in very elementary ways.

For example, the formation of partnerships was a common device for mobilizing savings in the American colonies, before the emergence of corporate organization and of private markets in corporate securities. The merging of business budgets by partnership arrangements widened the range of investment opportunities for any given dollar of saving.

Another popular technique for raising funds in colonial times was the lottery, which has a long tradition the world over as a substitute for borrowing. The colonial governments used lotteries not only to gain funds for themselves, but also to extend grants to private individuals and business firms. The colonies — and the states later on — also permitted individuals to conduct lotteries to finance designated investments. The lottery ticket may not be a perfect substitute for a bond or a stock certificate, but in many countries it has been one of the first steps along the road of financial development.

Governments have gained economic resources not only by issues of money and by lotteries, but also by taxation, by sale of goods produced under government auspices, by direct appropriation of private output, and in other ways. They have used these resources for government investment projects and they have released some to private enterprise through numerous techniques of transfer. In our own colonies, these transfer techniques included bounties to encourage investment in preferred categories, premiums for output of exceptional quality, and subsidies for desired enterprise that was slow to gain momentum.

All governments, both in primitive and advanced societies, have tried to increase private demand for money balances for the purpose of obtaining economic resources. Money was early made receivable for taxes in this country and elsewhere, and usually receivable for payment of debts, with penalties provided for creditors who preferred other means of settlement. In physical appearance, in denomination, in provisions for convertibility, and in other ways, efforts were made to increase demand for money. Primitive price controls and rationing cannot be omitted from this list of devices.

Tangible assets may serve the same purpose as money balances. Any existing asset that a sector is willing to acquire as an alternative to spending on current output releases that output for other uses, including new investment. Public lands served admirably in this country, both in colonial times and later, to secure funds for development purposes. The most famous instances were the land grants to canal and railroad companies. To the extent that the companies sold the land, their need to obtain external funds by other means, including security sales, was reduced. Many savers certainly preferred to accumulate land instead of securities in those years, and the saving they released clearly was allocable to new investment.

PRIMARY SECURITIES

These elementary innovations, however, can carry us only so far. To make further progress, we must allow our economic units to issue securities of their own. These are primary securities, or claims against nonfinancial economic units. In the early stages of development, they usually take the form of face-to-face loans. An economic unit that wishes to borrow seeks out another that wants to lend, and a loan is negotiated on the spot. We may think of primary securities as initially taking this form.

The ability of economic units to borrow directly from one another affords those with highly productive investment projects more scope than before to bid away resources from others with less productive projects. Primary securities stimulate real growth by increasing the probability that alternative investments will be exploited in order of their productivity. They also more fully exploit financial incentives to saving and thereby make it more likely that the level of saving and investment will be raised.

DISTRIBUTIVE TECHNIQUES

Face-to-face loans, however, are not a good way of getting primary securities distributed from borrowers to lenders. Therefore the next step must be the development of distributive techniques. These include the broadcast of information to borrowers regarding the asset preferences of lenders and to lenders regarding the issues of borrowers. They include, too, a widespread network of communication that tends to overcome regional market barriers. Facilities for rapid contract and settlement of loan transactions — security exchanges — increase the resemblance of security markets to competitive commodity exchanges. Facilities for brokerage, for market support and seasoning of new issues, for dealer inventories and for future as well as spot deliveries are other familiar distributive techniques. The guaranty of private primary securities by governments and the issuance of government securities themselves in place of private securities are still other examples.

The effect of distributive techniques in widening security markets is to permit each borrower and lender a higher degree of diversification in his debt and financial assets. Investing in primary securities alone, each lender can spread his budget of financial assets over a greater variety of claims than he could acquire on local markets. He can enrich the packet of advantages associated with the marginal dollar's worth of "consumption" of primary securities. And each borrower can diversify the form of his debts, reducing the real disadvantages associated with the marginal dollar's worth of indebtedness.

The development of distributive techniques, then, tends to raise the level of investment and saving by increasing the marginal utility of the last dollar's worth of financial assets to the lender and reducing the marginal disutility of the last dollar's worth of debt to the borrower. At the same time, such development tends to increase the efficiency of resource allocation by pitting more and more investment opportunities against one another for lenders to look over.

INTERMEDIATIVE TECHNIQUES

Distributive techniques get primary securities distributed efficiently from borrower to lender and from lender to lender. But no matter how efficient this process is, lenders still end up with primary securities. And the fact is that, although these securities may be tied with a red ribbon and sprayed with perfume, there has always been a conflict between borrowers and lenders, between the types of securities that borrowers can best issue and the types of securities that lenders desire to accumulate.

This is where financial intermediaries come in. These institutions place themselves between ultimate borrowers and lenders, purchasing the primary securities of the borrowers and issuing claims against themselves (indirect securities) for the portfolios of lenders. Financial intermediaries resolve, in part, the long-standing conflict between borrowers and lenders by "turning" primary securities into the types of financial assets that lenders want, at prices that do not inhibit growth unduly.

Intermediative techniques give lenders a wide variety of financial assets particularly suited to them and, at the same time, make it less necessary for borrowers to issue types of securities that are ill-adapted to their businesses. Like distributive techniques, then, intermediative techniques raise the marginal utility of the last dollar's worth of financial assets to the lenders and reduce the marginal disutility of the last dollar's worth of debt to the borrowers. In these ways, they tend to raise investment and saving and to allocate scarce savings optimally among investment alternatives.

FINANCIAL TECHNIQUES SUMMARIZED

All of the things I have mentioned are financial techniques for raising levels of saving and investment and allocating resources efficiently. The role of financial intermediaries in the saving-investment process, then, is essentially the same as the earlier role of lotteries, public land sales, Jay Cooke's distributive techniques during the Civil War, and so on. The financial development of our country can be thought of as a rather steady progression from the cruder to the more sophisticated techniques for solving a common economic problem, with the colonial governments' paper money issues at one end and modern intermediative techniques at the other.

COMMERCIAL BANKS AND OTHER INTERMEDIARIES

So far I have suggested that intermediative techniques should be thought of as being on the same footing as any of a number of other techniques designed to improve the saving-investment process. I now want to focus more sharply on financial intermediaries themselves. Here I shall contend that commercial banks, or more properly the monetary system, are essentially on the same footing as other financial intermediaries in the role they play in the saving-investment process.

The generally held opinion about this, I believe, is the opposite. It is alleged that commercial banks are a different animal because they create money, because the creation process is one of multiple expansion, and because there are inflationary consequences of such creation. I want to examine each of these, but first I shall say a few things about the act of creation in general.

There is nothing strange in the fact that commercial banks create something. All financial assets in the economy are created. Corporate bonds are created by corporations, mortgages by individuals and others, savings and loan shares by savings and loan associations, and so on.

But *how* are these financial assets created? Money is created when the monetary system purchases nonmonetary assets, mainly primary securities. Other financial assets are created when their issuers purchase money — yes, *purchase* money, because money is also a claim, though generally a noninterest-bearing one. With few exceptions, each financial asset is created when its issuer purchases another financial asset. In this respect, the difference between savings and loan associations and commercial banks is that the former create savings and loan shares by purchasing money while the latter create money by purchasing, say, bonds. And the difference, in this regard, between nonfinancial corporations and commercial banks is that the former create bonds by purchasing money while the latter create money by purchasing bonds. But there is nothing in these processes of creation to suggest that we should stand in awe of one at the expense of the others.

MONEY VERSUS OTHER FINANCIAL ASSETS

"But money is different," you might say. It is true that money is different from other financial assets, for it is a means of payment. But corporate stocks are different from other financial assets, too, for they carry ownership rights. And policyholders' equities in insurance companies are different because they are linked to insurance attributes. What is inherently more important about financial assets that are means of payment than financial assets that give people the opportunity to participate in private enterprise or financial assets that protect one's family against a myriad of catastrophes? These last two attributes make money look puny in comparison. On the other hand, the means-of-payment attribute of money makes many other financial assets look puny. The fact is that there is differentiation of financial assets throughout our economy, and it is not obvious at all that one kind of differentiation should be singled out for special analytical treatment.

MULTIPLE CREATION IN THE GENERAL SENSE

It has been said that commercial banks are different from other financial institutions in that they can engage in multiple creation or expansion of deposits while the others cannot. In analyzing this statement we have to distinguish carefully between multiple creation in the general sense and multiple creation in the legal reserve sense.

In the general sense, multiple creation is found almost everywhere. Take automobiles. Suppose that the production process calls for 10 cents' worth of rubber inputs and 90 cents' worth of other inputs to produce a dollar of automobiles. Then automobiles are produced or created in a ratio of 10 to 1 to rubber inputs — a dollar's worth of automobiles for every 10 cents' worth of rubber. This is multiple creation of automobiles. Housewives create omelettes by some multiple of cream inputs. Laundries create laundry services by some multiple of their starch inputs. Farmers create agricultural products by some multiple of their land inputs. There is multiple creation in each of these examples because the value of the output exceeds the value of any one of the inputs with which the output is being compared.

Let us apply these notions to commercial banks. Since I want to stick to multiple creation in the general sense, I assume to begin with that commercial banks are not subject to quantitative controls. I further assume that they purchase assets of various types, mostly primary securities, and create demand deposits; and I abstract from time deposits and capital accounts. Now suppose that some commercial bank creates $100 of demand deposits by purchasing $100 of corporate bonds, which are claims on corporations; or $100 of paper money, which are claims on, say, the Treasury; or $100 of checks, which are claims on other commercial banks. In any of these cases, we may say that our bank has purchased $100 of some input to produce $100 of demand-deposit output. If the demand deposits are compared to this input, whatever it might be, we would have to say that there has been no multiple creation of demand deposits — the ratio is one to one.

Suppose, however, that our commercial bank creates $100 of demand deposits by purchasing $100 of a mixture of inputs, either initially or by later exchanging some of its first input for other inputs. For example, the bank may create $100 of demand deposits by purchasing $100 of paper money and then selling some of the paper money for other claims, such as bonds or mortgages. If the demand deposits are compared to any one of the bank's inputs, it is clear that demand deposits are a multiple of this, or any other, input. And since demand deposits have been created, there has clearly been multiple creation of demand deposits.

Let us switch now to savings and loan associations, as an example of other financial intermediaries. An association, we shall suppose, creates $100 of savings and loan shares by purchasing $100 of paper money, which again are claims on the Treasury, or $100 of checks, which are claims on commercial banks. At this point, just as in the case of commercial banks, there is no multiple creation: the money inputs of the association are exactly equal to its share outputs. Suppose, however, that the association creates $100 of shares by purchasing $100 of a mixture of inputs, either initially or by later selling some of its first input for other inputs. It may, for example, create $100 of shares by purchasing $100 of claims on commercial banks and then selling some of these claims for mortgages. If the shares are now compared to any one of the association's inputs, it is clear that shares are a multiple of this, or any other, input. And since the shares have been created, there has clearly been multiple creation of shares. You will notice that I have described the association's transactions in the same way as the bank's.

We conclude, therefore, that there is multiple creation, in the general sense, almost everywhere. This is simply a way of saying that it generally takes more than one ingredient to make a cake, the value of the cake being a multiple of the value of any one of the ingredients.

MULTIPLE CREATION IN THE LEGAL RESERVE SENSE

Next, I want to talk about multiple creation in the legal reserve sense, and I shall start with commercial banks, which are assumed to be subject to quantitative controls. Commercial banks are no longer free to purchase any combination of inputs they desire. We require that they purchase special claims on a central bank, which are their legal reserves, equal to at least 20% of their demand deposits. However, their other inputs may be in any form desired. Let us say that our bank purchases $100 of claims on the Treasury (that is, paper money), and creates $100 of demand deposits. It must then sell $20 of paper money to the central bank in exchange for an equivalent amount of legal reserves. It may then sell all or any part of the remainder of its paper money for other claims, as it sees fit. After these transactions, the bank's demand deposits are five times its legal reserves; there has been creation of demand deposits in a multiple of five to legal reserves.

Some of you might prefer to look at this process in another way. Alternatively, then, suppose our bank creates $100 of demand deposits by purchasing $100 of paper money, which it sells to the central bank for an equivalent amount of special claims — reserves. Our bank now has $100 of total reserves and $80 of excess reserves. Next, it purchases $80 of bonds or mortgages, creating this amount of demand deposits. These demand deposits are checked out to other banks, and our bank loses $80 of demand deposits and $80 of reserves. What is left? It has $20 of reserves, $80 of primary securities, and $100 of demand deposits. Again, its demand deposits are five times its reserves, so that there has been multiple creation of demand deposits, the ratio to legal reserves being five to one. As this process continues, reserves are distributed throughout the system of banks in accordance with depositors' preferences among banks. At the end of the process, we find that each bank has created demand deposits in a multiple of five to the reserves it has left and that the system of banks has created demand deposits in a multiple of five to the reserves *it* has left.

We shall now impose quantitative controls on savings and loan associations by forcing them to purchase a special type of input in an amount that is at least 20% of their share outputs, the supply of these special claims being under strict control of a central association. Suppose, then, that an association purchases $100 of money and creates $100 of shares. It must now, with the central association's consent, sell $20 of money to the central association in exchange for an equivalent amount of reserves. It may then sell all or any part of the remainder of its money for other claims. At this point our association has created shares in a multiple of five to its legal reserves. And it can expand no further unless the central association permits it to purchase additional reserves. That is, our association cannot legally purchase any more money to create additional shares; it is "monied up" in the same way that a commercial bank in a similar situation would be "loaned up."

Imagine, next, that the central association permits our association to purchase an additional $10 of reserves. With these additional reserves, our association can now purchase an additional $50 of money and create an additional $50 of shares. It can create shares in a multiple of five to its new reserves — unlike a single bank but like the system of banks. Finally, it is clear that a reduction in reserve requirements will allow further multiple creation of shares.

But this is surely enough to establish the point I want to make. The point is that, in the legal reserve sense, only commercial banks engage in multiple creation because only commercial banks are subject to quantitative controls. If other intermediaries were subject to the same controls, they too would create liabilities in some multiple of their legal reserves. In brief, if there is anything different about commercial banks in this respect, it is because they are controlled; they are not controlled because they are different.

Volatility of Intermediaries

Some people evidently feel that commercial banks are inherently different from other financial institutions in that they are more unstable or more volatile — that they are capable of expanding and contracting violently. This, I think, is largely though not entirely an illusion that arises from the fact that commercial banks are subject to quantitative controls while other intermediaries are not. Again I believe it is fair to say that if banks are different in this regard, it is because they are controlled; they are not controlled because they are different.

Commercial bankers often have a profit incentive to produce more money output than the central bank wants them to produce. To limit production, the central bank imposes direct controls by rationing one of the banks' inputs and specifying how much of this input is to be used per unit of the banks' output. The imposition of these direct controls, along with restrictions on free entry, creates a disequilibrium system in the banking industry — an excess of the money supply that banks would like to produce over the money supply that they are forced to produce. As in any disequilibrium system, pressures are created that tend to make the industry look quite volatile.

In this situation of strain, an increase in total reserves or a reduction in reserve requirements would naturally bring about a rapid and almost explosive expansion of output to the new legal limit. And, of course, a tightening of controls would cause banks to contract output rapidly — for that is the law. Thus, when controls are first eased and then tightened and then eased on an industry in a disequilibrium position, an illusion is created from the responses of the industry that there is something inherently unstable about it.

I am reasonably sure that the savings and loan business would exhibit the same tendencies if it were subject to similar quantitative controls. The business would then be producing at a level short of its competitive level and there would be competitive pressures for expansion. A relaxation of controls would cause the business to "explode" to the higher legal limit, and a tightening of controls would, by law, force it to contract rapidly. In the meantime, an uncontrolled commercial banking system would have reached some sort of an equilibrium level of output, thereafter expanding with increases in the demand for money and contracting with decreases in the demand for money.

Money and Inflation

It has often been said that commercial banks are different from other financial institutions in that an increase in the money supply is inflationary, while an increase in claims on other intermediaries is not.

I shall define inflationary pressure as an excess supply of money over the demand for it, at given levels of interest rates, commodity prices and output. Inflationary pressure may be created, therefore, by an increase in the supply of money or by a decrease in the demand for money, or both. In quantity-theory terms, inflationary pressure may be created by an increase in M or an increase in V, or both.

There is no question, then, that the monetary system can add to inflationary pressure by increasing the money supply, given the demand for it. But nonmonetary intermediaries can also add to inflationary pressure, not by increasing the money supply, to be sure, but by reducing the demand for money, that is, by raising V. This comes about when anyone is induced to give up money balances to purchase claims on nonmonetary intermediaries. Assuming the transaction is for $100, the demand for money is initially reduced by $100. The intermediaries will ordinarily increase their demand for money by a small fraction of this sum, purchasing primary securities with the remainder. Therefore the demand for money is reduced by something less than $100 while the supply of money is unchanged. This creates an excess supply of money in the economy, which shows up as excess demands in security and commodity markets. Thus the activities of nonmonetary intermediaries can lead to an excess of ex-ante investment over ex-ante saving, to excess demands in commodity markets.

This numerical example, of course, is just one possibility. The extent of the inflationary pressure created by the expansion of nonmonetary intermediaries depends, in general, on the absolute amount of their expansion over any period of time, the degree of substitutability between money and the various claims on other intermediaries, and the incremental demand for money by intermediaries as they expand.

CREATION OF LOANABLE FUNDS

Closely related to the previous point is the allegation that commercial banks can create loanable funds while other intermediaries cannot. Now if by loanable funds we mean money, then the statement is obviously true and we are back where we started. The orthodox meaning of loanable funds, however, is different.

The supply of loanable funds is defined as:

Planned saving by economic units
plus
Increase in stock of money
minus
Increase in demand for money (hoarding).

Planned saving by economic units is their increase in demand for primary securities, money and nonmonetary indirect assets (i.e., claims on nonmonetary intermediaries). Hence, the supply of loanable funds is equal to:

Economic units' increase in demand for primary securities
plus
Economic units' increase in demand for nonmonetary
indirect assets
plus
Increase in stock of money.

Finally, we note that economic units' increase in demand for non-monetary indirect assets is equal to nonmonetary intermediaries' increase in demand for primary securities, neglecting the small amount of money held by these intermediaries. And the increase in the stock of money is equal to the monetary system's increase in demand for primary securities. So the supply of loanable funds boils down to:

> Economic units' increase in demand for primary securities
> plus
> Nonmonetary intermediaries' increase in demand for primary securities
> plus
> Monetary system's increase in demand for primary securities.

Consequently, the supply of loanable funds is simply the incremental demand for primary securities by economic units, nonmonetary intermediaries, and the monetary system. All three are on the same footing; all three can create loanable funds.

THE ARGUMENT SUMMARIZED

The main points of this section on commercial banks and other intermediaries are these:

1. The mere act of creating financial assets does not distinguish commercial banks from other intermediaries or from other creators of financial assets, for each financial asset is quite clearly created by someone.

2. There is a great deal of differentiation of financial assets in our economy; each type differs in some respect from all others. Money is a very important financial asset, but so are many others, judging by the demands for them. It is not obvious that one kind of differentiation should be considered holy, to the neglect of others.

3. In the general sense, multiple creation is found throughout the economy — in commercial banks, in other financial intermediaries, in business firms, and so on. This does not set commercial banks apart from other creators of financial assets. In the legal reserve sense, there is multiple creation of money because commercial banks are subject to quantitative controls. In the same sense, there would be multiple creation in nonmonetary intermediaries if they were subject to the same controls.

4. Commercial banks appear to be inherently more volatile than other financial intermediaries, but this appearance is largely due to the fact that banks are subject to quantitative controls and other intermediaries are not. The tables would be turned to a large extent if controls were placed on nonmonetary intermediaries and commercial banks were not subject to them.

5. Both commercial banks and nonmonetary intermediaries can add to inflationary pressure. Both can create an excess supply of money; both can create loanable funds, in the orthodox definition of the term.

QUANTITATIVE CONTROLS AND FINANCIAL INTERMEDIARIES

I have attempted to show that in no important respect is it legitimate to single out commercial banks and money for special analytical treatment. The question now arises whether it is legitimate to single them out for special legal treatment, in the form of quantitative controls.

Why should there be any quantitative controls at all on financial intermediaries, including commercial banks? Suppose there were none. Then commercial banks would expand by purchasing primary securities and creating demand deposits. As they expanded, interest rates on primary securities, including loans, would fall and competition among banks would raise their deposit rates to their depositors. Eventually the banking system would reach an equilibrium level of output, at which there would be no further incentive for any existing bank to expand or for further entry into the industry. At the same time, nonmonetary intermediaries would expand toward an equilibrium level of output in the way they now do.

There would be some rate of interest on primary securities associated with these equilibrium output levels. This rate of interest, however, might be so low as to bring about a level of aggregate demand for goods that exceeded the aggregate supply of goods at current prices. If so, there would be inflationary pressure, due partly to an excessive amount of financial intermediation.

Presumably there is some level of federal government expenditures and taxes that could remove this pressure, so that fiscal policy could carry the entire brunt of an anti-inflationary program. Leaving this aside, inflationary pressure could be reduced by reducing the size of financial intermediaries through the imposition of quantitative controls. The purpose of the quantitative controls is to create an excess demand for money — a demand for money that exceeds the supply of money — at the current levels of interest rates and commodity prices. This excess demand for money will translate itself into excess supplies of primary securities and goods. In particular, the controls will compel financial intermediaries to reduce their liabilities and sell primary securities. The public will consent to hold more primary securities and less indirect securities only at a higher interest rate on primary securities. This higher interest rate will reduce the level of aggregate demand and take some of the steam out of inflation.

If the controls were placed on commercial banks alone, the supply of money would be reduced and this would tend to create the desired excess demand for money. However, this policy would tend to increase the public's demand for claims on nonmonetary intermediaries as interest rates rose and as these intermediaries competed for additional funds. To some extent this would water down the excess demand for money, although it could be compensated for by further tightening of controls on commercial banks.

If the controls were placed on nonmonetary intermediaries alone, the supply of claims on these intermediaries would be reduced, which would tend to increase the public's demand for money and to bring about the desired excess demand for money. As the interest rate on primary securities rose, however, uncontrolled commercial banks would have an incentive to compete for funds and increase the supply of money. This would water down the excess demand for money, but it could be compensated for by tightening on nonmonetary intermediaries.

The controls would be more effective if they were imposed on both commercial banks and nonmonetary intermediaries. Then a reduction in the supply of money and an accompanying increase in the interest rate on primary securities could not lead to an increase in the supply of claims on nonmonetary intermediaries and hence could not lead to a watering down of the excess demand for money. Alternatively, a reduction in the supply of claims on nonmonetary intermediaries and the accompanying increase in the rate of interest on primary securities could not lead to an increase in the supply of money. And again the excess demand for money could not be watered down.

The controls are more effective in this case in the sense that a given reduction in the supply of money or a given reduction in the supply of claims on nonmonetary intermediaries would raise the interest rate on primary securities by more than it otherwise would have been raised. If the controls were either on commercial banks alone or on nonmonetary intermediaries alone, it would require a greater amount of tightening on the sector controlled to bring about the higher interest rate, due to leaks through the uncontrolled sector. But the additional tightening could presumably be done in either case.

CHANGING TAX RATES AS A STABILIZATION MEASURE

In choosing among these alternative patterns of control, there are many more questions to consider than I have had time for this morning. I can, however, suggest the scope of these questions by looking at a hypothetical problem in the area of fiscal policy that is very similar to our problem in the area of monetary policy. In this hypothetical problem in the fiscal area, changing tax rates is the counterpart of changing reserves and reserve requirements in the monetary area; they are both key stabilization measures.

Suppose, then, that for stabilization purposes an income tax is imposed on one important group in the economy, all other groups escaping the tax. The discriminated group might be farmers, corporations producing specified products, or some other group. The counterpart of this in the monetary area is the imposition of quantitative controls on commercial banks only. Now it could be argued that this tax system is perfectly adequate. If there is excessive spending in the economy, the policy is to raise tax rates on the taxed group; if there is deficient spending, the policy is to lower tax rates. The tax rates might have to go very high at times, or very low at other times to achieve the policy goals, but presumably this could be done if the discriminated group were important enough.

And now the arguments begin. Some economists claim that the whole system is inequitable, that there is no justification for singling out this one group for special legal treatment when there is really no basic difference among the various groups of income receivers and spenders. Others, however, say there is a difference. The taxed group, they claim, is (let us say) farmers, and there is no other group just like it. After all, they ask, what other group creates agricultural products?

Another argument is advanced against this tax system. During periods of sustained inflationary pressure, it is said, tax rates on the discriminated group would have to be very high indeed to achieve policy goals. This would lower the rate of return on capital in the discriminated area and capital would gradually leave, until what was left was earning a return comparable to that earned in other areas. The discriminated area would fail to attract the best people, and the vitality of the area would gradually be sapped. This would then require countermeasures by the government if it wanted to support the area against possible future catastrophes, to keep the area viable, or to maintain the quality of its output. But from the other side of the fence we hear that these people are doing pretty well as it is. No need to worry about those plutocrats. Besides, if they are hurt to some extent during periods of high tax rates, there are periods of low tax rates when they can recoup. And from the sidelines a few voices say that if the area is really in such a mess, then nationalize it.

Other economists think the system is not efficient in achieving policy goals. They argue that there are too many possible leaks in the system — that when tax rates are, say, raised on the discriminated group, other groups may increase their spending for one reason or another and there is no way to predict this or to control it. Also, it is claimed, it may be politically impossible to raise tax rates on the discriminated group high enough to achieve policy goals when inflationary pressures are especially severe. But this prompts the reply that the spending habits of the untaxed groups are really quite reliable. It is true that at times these groups will increase or decrease their spending when the opposite is wanted; but there is nothing erratic about this and it can, in any case, be offset by appropriate measures on the taxed group. And don't worry about the politics: we have "independent" policy-makers who are really running the show.

There are further arguments about the tax system's inability to bring about a desirable allocation of resources, but proponents of the system reply that tax rates on just one group interfere less with resource allocation than would tax rates on all groups. "Do you want to slap controls on the whole economy?" they ask. They also appeal to the administrative simplicity of the present system, arguing that any extension of tax rates to other groups would involve an almost insurmountable administrative problem. And so it goes.

It must be clear to you that all these arguments and counterarguments apply equally well to the question in the monetary area of whether to extend quantitative controls to other financial institutions. And there are, of course, other arguments that can be brought to bear on each side. I do not want to minimize the importance of the arguments that can be used to support the status quo, for a pretty good case can be made for that position. But, as I have no doubt indicated, I think that the better case lies on the other side. The important thing about this problem of controls, however, is that the discussion of it is bound to improve our theory and understanding of finance. And that is surely the first step.

2

Financial Institutions in the

Saving-Investment Process–II*

Ezra Solomon was, in 1959, professor of finance in the Graduate School of Business at the University of Chicago. He is a consultant to government and private organizations and is the author of *The Economy of Metropolitan Chicago,* and the editor and author of a number of works in the field of monetary economics, capital budgeting, and economic forecasting. Dr. Solomon received his bachelor of arts degree from the University of Rangoon (Burma) and his doctorate from the University of Chicago. He was formerly the editor of the *Journal of Business* of the University of Chicago.

My talk has the same general title as John Gurley's, but the subheadings are a little different. I shall begin with a minute or two on monetary policy in general. My personal feelings are that the record of monetary policy and the economy it seeks to stabilize has probably been better since 1951 than in any other eight-year period in our history. Oddly enough, this has led to more diversified controversy today over monetary policy than we have had in decades — and more committees, too, I think.

The first and most important controversy is the active re-emergence of the ancient problem of growth versus price stability. I say "ancient" because I think the entire economic history of the United States could plausibly be written in terms of this basic conflict. But this controversy

* Proceedings of the Second Annual Conference, 1959, pp. 30–41.

is essentially one of social goals. It always generates a great deal of oratory but very little genuine argument.

The second controversy is a narrower one. Given our economic goals, what should be the operating goal of Federal Reserve policy? Milton Friedman, for example, thinks the Fed would do much better to concentrate on keeping the money supply growing at a constant rate and abandon its present concentration on the reserve position of the banking system. The Fed does not agree. This controversy involves financial intermediaries directly, because it can be argued — and indeed has already been argued — that we should keep total liquid assets growing at a constant rate, and this would imply control over all financial intermediaries.

A third set of controversies involves the implementation of policy. This includes questions of timing; whether open-market operations should be restricted to the short end of the market; whether changes in reserve requirements might not be a better instrument than open-market operations; and so on.

Finally, the fourth issue encompasses the first three issues, yet has a life all its own aside from the other three. This is the issue of financial intermediaries and whether they should be brought under the direct network of quantitative control. I do not know the name of this argument; parts of it are called the Gurley-Shaw thesis, but in a sense it is broader than the direct statements John and Ed have made. I shall summarize the argument as I see it.

THE GURLEY-SHAW ARGUMENT

POINT 1: The size and variety of financial intermediaries has grown rapidly since 1900. As a consequence the oldest intermediaries of all, commercial banks, have declined in relative importance.

POINT 2: In spite of this decline in the relative importance of banks, the mainstream both of theory and of control is directed exclusively at the banking system.

POINT 3: This procedure is ineffective because banks are simply one variant form of intermediary, and their liabilities — demand deposits — are simply one variant form of financial assets. To single out demand deposits for special analytical treatment or to single out banks for special control makes very little sense.

POINT 4: Effective control would cover the assets of all financial intermediaries, not of commercial banks alone. This particular line of argument has given rise to more academic controversy than have the other three — and also to more theoretical confusion.

My own position is that much of this controversy and confusion is due to two factors. First, the heated and prolonged debates on monetary theory which raged in the late 1930s were never resolved but were shelved when people got tired of trying to unsnarl semantic tangles and when the war diverted attention to other things. Now these unresolved differences in viewpoint are re-emerging. And second, the present controversy has gotten itself ensnarled in new semantic confusions and definitional difficulties and will not be resolved if these persist. Incidentally, I think the jumble of semantics in the 1930s was partially excusable because of the many genuine differences which existed at that time. By contrast, some of the present confusion seems to be at least partly deliberate!

But everything has a bright side, including muddled semantics. In the late 1930s, a virtuous by-product was two delightful articles by Dennis Robertson on "Words and Things." And today we are being treated to a mixture of metaphors, analogies and figures of speech. If you look at the literature on the subject, you will find it is rich in all of these things.

Goldsmith's Asset/Wealth Data Examined

Let me run through the four or five major elements in the broad financial intermediaries argument. The first point is that financial intermediaries have grown extremely rapidly since the turn of the century, based on Goldsmith's data on assets and wealth, and particularly on the ratio between total assets of intermediaries and total national wealth defined in one of the various ways that Goldsmith defines it. Being a careful scholar, he has at least three or four definitions.

I think this ratio is a little deceptive. Goldsmith's standard definition of financial intermediaries includes the Federal Reserve System, all the federal lending agencies, Old Age and Survivors Insurance and all other federal trust funds, and state and local retirement funds. It also includes the assets of fire and casualty insurance companies, finance companies, and a number of other institutions which are not generally used as a depository for personal savings — or certainly not for voluntary personal savings. A very big part of the great growth in financial assets as defined by Goldsmith has taken place in these sectors.

The definition of financial intermediaries that we usually have in mind includes essentially those institutions which serve as an outlet for voluntary liquid savings. By these I mean banks, savings and loan associations, life insurance companies, postal savings and credit unions. And I suppose if we wanted to broaden it, private pension plans and mutual investment companies could also be included.

To avoid confusion, I shall call these institutions savings intermediaries;

and these are the ones I am going to be talking about, rather than the broader classification Goldsmith uses. Now, these savings intermediaries have not been growing nearly so rapidly as total financial assets.

Goldsmith's denominator is one measure or the other of total wealth, presumably at current market values. The possible range of error in this statistic is obviously fairly large.

An alternative approach is to take the ratio of assets of savings intermediaries to gross national product. If we do this, there appears to be no startling growth at all. These savings assets grew 666% from 1900 to 1929, when gross national product grew about 460%. But from 1929 to 1955, savings assets grew less than gross national product, 250% as compared to 285%. In other words, the really rapid growth of the savings intermediaries ended over 30 years ago. Since then they have been growing more slowly than the economy.

It is interesting to note that two important factors have been operating which should have led to a rising ratio between savings assets and current output. (Of course there are other factors at work in the opposite direction.) The first factor is the pace of urbanization. Obviously, an urban society needs financial assets more than a rural society does.

The second factor is the rapid rate at which post-retirement longevity has been growing. This we tend to underestimate. We all recognize that once a person reaches the age of 60, his chances of reaching age 70, for example, are only slightly higher than they were 50 years ago. But the slightest difference here makes big differences in the amount of assets required. If his retirement age is 65 and longevity 66, he has to provide for one year of retirement income. If his retirement age is 65 and longevity is increased to 68, however, he has to provide for three years, and he needs three times as much in the way of financial assets.

What I am suggesting is that, if anything, the forces at work since 1929 should indicate a fairly rapid growth in savings assets and that, if anything, there should be concern not that they have been growing too fast but that they are not growing fast enough! Possibly savings intermediaries need encouragement rather than control.

Anyway, so much for the first point: Defined in this narrower way, there is no startling growth of savings intermediaries.

BANK VERSUS NONBANK GROWTH

The second broad point made is that the nonbank savings intermediaries have been growing much faster than the commercial banks. The facts, however, do not support such a sweeping statement. The measurement problem here is difficult. First, there is a question of what to include in the commercial banking sector. Demand deposits?

Demand plus time? Demand plus time plus personal trust accounts? Demand plus time plus personal trust accounts plus bank-administered pension funds? Which of these classes of assets belong to banks? If you choose your definition and your time period, you can get virtually any answer you want about the relative rate of growth of banks versus nonbanks.

The share of total bank assets, including trust accounts, held pretty steady from 1900 to 1929. In other words, during the period of very rapid expansion of savings intermediaries, commercial banks held their share. But since 1929 the share of total bank assets has declined, both relative to the economy and to other financial intermediaries.

However, all of the decline in the relative position of commercial banks is due to a decline in their trust department sector and their time and savings deposit accounts. Taking demand deposits alone — I think this is the important thing here — the banking sector increased faster than GNP between 1929 and 1955, much faster than total savings assets excluding demand deposits and almost as fast as nonbank intermediaries.

One must remember in this connection that nonbank intermediaries include mutual investment companies and pension funds, both of which hold substantial amounts of common stocks in their portfolios. These sectors have been rising very fast, partly on this account.

In any case, demand deposits since 1929 certainly have not been shrinking in any broad sense, relative to other financial assets. However, the important issue is not the factual one but rather what it means if the relative growth of money supply falls short of or exceeds the relative growth of financial assets.

The principal function of demand deposits is as a means of payment, and over the long run one would expect money to grow about as fast as the total flow of payments or gross national product. The volume of financial assets other than demand deposits measures accumulated savings. This may grow faster or slower than GNP, depending on the interplay of many different factors. If these factors, taken together, cause them to grow slower than GNP, they will also be growing slower than the money supply. This is what has happened since 1929. Fixed-value savings assets have been growing a little more slowly than demand deposits proper.

DEMAND DEPOSITS VERSUS NONMONEY LIABILITIES

This brings me to the important point of the Gurley-Shaw argument: Should we make this distinction between demand deposits on the one hand and nonmoney liabilities of financial intermediaries on the other? To keep things fairly straightforward, I shall assume that currency does not exist and that the only form of money is demand deposits held in commercial banks. I am also going to assume that there is always just one institution in the system — a single bank or a single savings and loan association.

John maintains that we give money much more attention than it deserves, that it is not that different and that we should not stand in awe of it either in theory or in control policy.

This contention really consists of two statements: The first is the broad one that all financial assets are simply liabilities of financial institutions and that each of them has a different characteristic. To be sure, money is a means of payment, but insurance policy reserves are a means of safety, common stocks provide a means of ownership, and so on. The second statement is: Why all the fuss about *one* of these things, namely, money?

If you examine these two statements carefully, you will find that the first is made from the Olympian point of view, from which all financial assets look alike. The second statement — why all the fuss about money — is made from the point of view of a person either trained in monetary economics or very close to the field.

Now, if you are going to be Olympian, you have to be Olympian all the way through. While more words have probably been written about money than about insurance or common stocks, I doubt if the excess is obvious — at least to the person on Olympus. The special attention money gets exists only when we deal with spending; and here, obviously, money has a special attribute which deserves the fuss. It is the only asset used as a means of payment.

It is not at all surprising that we have singled out the means of spending as an important variable when dealing with expenditures or inflation, which is caused by high levels of expenditures and things of that sort. It also is not surprising that the fact that money can be created has been treated as an important point in this kind of analysis. This brings me to another point in the Gurley-Shaw thesis.

MULTIPLE CREATION OF MONEY

The Gurley-Shaw thesis (John's particular way of looking at the creation process) comes up with the conclusion that the process of money creation is no different from the process by which other financial assets are created. But I think this depends on John's definitions of creation and multiple creation.

His first definition, or his first way of looking at creation, he calls "general multiple creation," and he points out that this exists whenever the ratio of output to input is larger than unity. For John, this is multiple

creation. Defined this way, everything indulges in multiple creation —
earthworms, people, and children making mud pies.

I think this particular definition of multiple creation, while it might
be "scientific," is not particularly useful. The question it leads to is not
merely: Why distinguish money from financial assets? It also asks: Why
distinguish money from mud pies?

The second process of creation which John examines is creation in the
legal-reserve sense. This, too, is given a rather unusual definition, again
referring to the ratio between a particular input which is controlled (bank
reserves) and an output (the liabilities of the banking system). The
conclusion here is that money is different only because the banking
system is controlled, and not the other way around.

I believe the whole history of money, particularly outside the United
States, shows that this conclusion is wrong. The British banking system
was uncontrolled until very recently. A great deal of money creation
went on through the 19th century and the first forty years of the 20th
century. A great deal of monetary destruction also went on. And there
was instability without any legal reserve requirement.

It is not the legal requirement, as such, which is important. The
difference between John's point of view and the reasoning we were all
brought up on and believe in is that John insists on looking at the whole
process from the point of view of the depositor. Certainly, if you look at
it from the depositor's point of view — the act of someone taking money
to a bank or the act of someone taking money to a savings and loan
association — banks look like any other institution. You give them money
and they give you a claim. The only difference is that it is a noninterest-
bearing claim. Any institution or person can acquire cash with an
I O U.

But this way of looking at things misses the point. When any person
or institution acquires cash with an I O U — whether it be an intermediary or not — there is no net increase in the purchasing power of
society because of that act. All that is done is to swap assets. If an
individual deposits a check in a bank, there is no net increase in purchasing power as of that time. The same is true if he deposits money in
a savings and loan association.

But if we look at it from another point of view, we do find that banks
are very different, indeed, because only a bank can acquire earning
assets with its I O U. Anybody can acquire cash with an I O U, but only
banks can acquire earning assets with an I O U. This is where creation
comes into the picture, because there is a net increase in purchasing power
when this takes place. The purchasing power of society as a whole goes
up when a bank acquires an earning asset with its I O U. This is no
mere swap of one asset for another. A net creation of new money takes
place.

SPENDABLE FUNDS CREATION

Since John has reserved the term "loanable funds" for a particular definition, I shall not use that term but shall say instead that banks create spendable funds. And banks are the only institutions that can create spendable funds in this sense. No amount of juggling with words can change this fact. It is a very important fact, because bank-created spendable funds have equal access to goods and services with income funds or with what John has defined as loanable funds. The bank-created funds can be used to buy things on the market and, as a consequence, exert potential inflationary pressures.

Oddly enough, John concedes this when he makes his next point, that banks and only banks can create spendable funds. But he goes on to say: "So what? When banks create money, this is potentially inflationary. But the other intermediaries can exert equally important upward pressure on spending by reducing the demand for money. Why not control them as well?"

In other words, inflationary pressures can come from an increase in the supply of spendable funds or from a decrease in the demand for money or spendable funds.

LIQUID ASSETS AND MONETARY VELOCITY

This is, of course, the old velocity argument. Personally, I think one of the big things left unsettled in the 1930s was the usefulness of treating velocity as if it had a life of its own rather than as the result of two other variables in society. My own feeling is that the idea that a given amount of money moves faster or slower can be a deceptive tool of analysis. I am not sure, however, that you will agree with me on this.

In any case, the whole velocity argument here in the sense that the Gurley-Shaw thesis uses it is worth following closely. In discussing it, I shall confine myself to situations in which unwanted inflationary pressures exist which the Fed is trying to restrain.

The usual definition is that inflationary pressure exists when the aggregate demand for goods and services exceeds the aggregate supply of goods and services at current prices, taxes, and interest rates. One can reword this definition as follows: Inflationary pressure exists when the aggregate demand for money falls short of the aggregate supply of money. This simply transposes the equation. Instead of demand for goods and services, one says "supply of money"; instead of supply of goods and services, one says "demand for money." This formulation is a little awkward, but there is nothing literally wrong with such a statement. But note that the demand for money is simply the counterpart of the supply of goods and services.

Now, anything that reduces the supply of goods is as inflationary as anything that increases the demand for goods. One can translate this as follows: Anything that reduces the demand for money is as inflationary as anything that increases the supply of money. So far, nothing new has been added — simply a transposition of the basic terms in the equation.

THE SHIFT FROM MONEY TO OTHER ASSETS

But now we move to the next stage and say: Financial intermediaries can persuade people to shift from money to near-money or other claims. This reduces the demand for money. Hence, it is inflationary. Hence, financial intermediaries should be controlled.

What puzzles me about this approach is why we should pick on financial intermediaries. All sorts of institutions can persuade people to shift from money. They can shift to goods or services, to direct securities or to financial intermediaries — and during a boom they generally do, especially from money to goods and services. This is what keeps the boom going in spite of monetary restraint. It shows up as an increase in velocity. Does it follow that we should control retail stores because they reduce people's demand for money? Or food stores, doctors, bond markets or pension plans? All these things persuade people to reduce their demand for money in this sense. Certainly, there is no justification for blaming upward changes in velocity, or even for attributing upward changes in velocity to a shift from demand deposits to other financial intermediaries. In fact, as far as the cyclical shifts are concerned, there seems to be very little evidence that upward shifts in velocity result from an attempted shift from demand deposits to financial intermediaries.

An increase in velocity results from the fact that people and business get into a spending mood and go ahead and spend the money they have. Corporations do this and individuals do so as well. It is interesting in this respect to examine not only the velocity of total demand deposits as we usually do, but also the individual velocities of business demand deposits and personal demand deposits. Unfortunately, the Fed discontinued its deposit ownership surveys in 1956, and the new survey started in 1957 is not comparable to the old series, so that the most recent boom cannot be examined too well.

However, we do have evidence for the 1953–54 situation. Clearly the expansion of output and income was fast enough in 1953 and money restraint was powerful enough to bring about a fall in the ratio of individual demand deposits to personal income in 1953. John's thesis suggests that this fall is due to the shift from demand deposits to financial intermediaries. But actually, in 1953, the individual demand for near-money assets at financial intermediaries also fell! All we had was an attempted movement into goods and services.

But even if there is a shift from demand deposits to financial intermediaries during a boom, is this any different from a shift from demand deposits to any interest-yielding asset? Again, why pick on intermediaries?

The whole phenomenon of monetary velocity behaves just about the way Wicksell explained it years ago. When there is such a shift out of money to securities, money interest rates do not rise as fast as they would have risen if there had not been such a shift. Hence, investment spending is not so inhibited as it otherwise might have been. But the answer to this lies in mopping up idle money balances held at banks in the first place, and not in controlling every possible avenue into which such balances might be persuaded to flow.

There is an associated argument with respect to the influence of financial assets or liquid assets which is not made directly in the Gurley-Shaw arguments. This is the indirect effect these assets might have on the general level of consumer spending. When people own liquid wealth which is easily reversible without money loss, they might be tempted to spend a higher portion of their income than if they held their wealth in the form of securities, or land, or something less liquid. I don't know the magnitude of this liquid-wealth effect. The very long-run savings to income ratio seems to reveal no marked shift in the propensity to save, and this suggests that the liquid-wealth effect is probably fairly small. However, these are fairly bad numbers in many ways and exhibit marked fluctuations over the 60-year period.

Intermediaries and Federal Reserve's Impact

Let me turn now to the implications of financial intermediaries for Federal Reserve control. I am looking, not at the indirect velocity effect which we have been discussing, but directly at the power which financial intermediaries might have to offset restrictive monetary policy through their lending practices. Again, I shall speak in terms of an inflationary situation which the Fed is trying to restrain.

Obviously, financial intermediaries that possess idle cash balances have a certain amount of leeway in their lending policies. During a boom they can dip into this pool of surplus cash, just as a corporation or an individual can. Everybody does a little better job of cash-budgeting because the reward for budgeting closely rises during a boom.

This sort of action on the part either of a savings and loan association or of a life insurance company that previously had more cash than it needed can add to inflationary pressures. However, it is subject to restraint through open-market operations. In fact, it is more likely that Fed open-market sales will mop up idle cash held by intermediaries than that directly held by individuals. When the Fed sells securities on the open market, banks are clearly affected. There is no question about it.

It does not matter who buys the securities or whether they are bought here or abroad. Savings and loan associations are affected only insofar as the Fed succeeds in selling these securities either to the associations directly, which they might do at low enough prices, or to customers of the association who then withdraw their funds from the association in order to buy the securities. This, of course, mops up idle cash of the association. The individual seems to be affected least by Federal open-market operations. So the fact that idle cash balances are transferred by the individual to nonbank institutions reduces the total cash leeway held by the economy as a whole.

A second way in which savings institutions can offset monetary restrictiveness is through exercising their potential borrowing power from the Federal Home Loan Bank (for savings and loan associations), and the Savings Banks Trust Company (for mutual savings banks in New York). Thus there is a second little pool of cash to which they have access; but this, too, will be extinguished in time if the Fed pursues its goals.

All of this provides a slight hindrance to the operations of restricted monetary policy, but nothing that did not exist before intermediaries entered the picture. In other words, there is a little monetary slack in the economy, and perhaps this is a good thing. The fact that we can adapt to Federal Reserve restrictiveness by increasing velocity is probably a desirable feature of our system. All the Fed has to do to achieve its purpose is to keep tightening the screws.

INTERMEDIARIES ASSIST FEDERAL RESERVE CONTROL

I have been suggesting that intermediaries can temporarily delay the impact of Federal Reserve policy. I want to suggest also that intermediaries have a second effect which assists the Fed in its process of monetary control. An important method through which monetary policy works is by making interest rates higher and bond prices lower. If individuals are directly involved as lenders, they are likely to be much less sensitive to this sort of thing than is the manager, say, of a savings and loan association who is watching these things very carefully. The professional management of intermediaries is much more sensitive to minor changes in interest rates than individuals are. This means that rising interest rates have a much more powerful effect now than they had in the past.

I see that my time is up, so let me summarize. (1) I feel that there is no need whatever for quantitative controls to be extended beyond the banking system. (2) If anything, the time-deposit sector of the banking system should be segregated from demand deposits and then removed completely from quantitative control; that is, time depositories should be treated as a financial intermediary. These conclusions are exactly the opposite of John's, and in all fairness I should say that I had a chance to read his speech, whereas he did not have the faintest idea what I was going to say. I suggest that we give him five or ten minutes for rebuttal.

Discussion*

WALTER MORTON: I should first like to ask a question of Mr. Solomon. When you state you do not favor a reserve requirement for savings deposits of commercial banks, are we to gather that you do not favor any other means of limiting the amount of savings deposits of commercial banks?

MR. SOLOMON: Yes. I think they ought to be as free as life insurance companies or savings and loan associations to seek out or compete for savings.

MR. MORTON: If that is true, may I ask another question? Would you want savings deposits to be as freely convertible into demand deposits as they are today under this condition?

MR. SOLOMON: I don't know. I have not thought of it as a specific piece of legislation. I simply feel there is no reason for controlling the rates payable on savings at banks. I presume they ought to be as freely convertible as any other kind of asset. In effect, I think they all are pretty convertible. For example, savings and loan shares are convertible now for all practical purposes.

MR. MORTON: I was thinking of the practice. That is, if there were no limitation whatsoever on the volume of savings deposits, and these deposits were to continue as freely convertible into demand deposits, I was wondering what the effect would be on the volume of demand deposits and the ability to control the speculative movements in the economy.

MR. SOLOMON: I confess I was not really making a positive suggestion, but simply suggesting that maybe the remedy lies not in more control over financial intermediaries but in less control over the time depositories.

JOHN GURLEY: I think that is perfectly consistent with the position that sharply distinguishes money from other types of claims on intermediaries. If you think that there should be no quantitative controls over savings and loan associations and mutual savings banks, it is perfectly consistent to advocate taking off controls over time deposit creation of commercial banks.

MR. MORTON: And control over the conversion of time deposits into demand deposits?

MR. GURLEY: Yes.

MR. MORTON: Therefore, no control over demand deposits?

* Proceedings of the Second Annual Conference, 1959, Excerpts from the Discussion, pp. 41–55.

MR. GURLEY: No. All you do is adjust the system through demand deposits. If there is an increase of time deposits, you have to determine to what extent the demand for money has fallen as a result of the increase in demand for time deposits. If you think it is on a one-to-one basis, the trick is simply to decrease through quantitative controls the supply of demand deposits in order to balance that out.

Now, in that particular case, the commercial banks would be no larger than before. They would have the same amount of total assets and total liabilities. In other cases, it would be necessary, to achieve policy goals, to permit them to increase somewhat in size, because you calculate the reduction in demand for demand deposits at less than the increase in demand for time deposits.

MR. MORTON: Mr. Solomon, isn't the distinction you have in mind that the bank's I O U continues to circulate and is held by the community without paying out assets to be converted into cash or any other earning asset? That is really the point.

MR. SOLOMON: Yes. Net new spendable funds are created.

MR. GURLEY: In other words, what we are saying is that banks can create money and savings and loan associations cannot.

But isn't the question really whether banks and savings and loan associations can both create an *excess* supply of money? The monetary authorities don't look at the absolute amount of money alone, but at the absolute amount of money in relation to the demand for money. If the demand for money can be reduced by expansion of other intermediaries, they are on the same footing as commercial banks in being able to create an excess supply of money.

MR. SOLOMON: Every institution or individual has that power to create an excess supply of money. Does it follow that all of them ought to be controlled?

MR. GURLEY: This is aside from control. Let us put it on an analytical basis first. I would almost be willing to argue that if historically it had developed that nonmonetary intermediaries had been subject to quantitative controls and commercial banks had not, there would be good reason for maintaining that status quo. Either way, I think you can really control the situation so far as excess supplies of money are concerned. I see no justification for singling out commercial banks from other financial intermediaries on this analytical plane, aside from whether we think we should extend controls.

MR. SOLOMON: You are reasoning by analogy; and although I hate to use one, I shall. When a murder takes place, both parties are responsible — murderer and murderee. We could control murderees, too, but the price is rather high.

MR. GURLEY: If we had started out controlling murderees, perhaps that would have taken care of the situation. Without any controls there are murderers. But are they on the same plane?

MR. SOLOMON: Yes, they are. I think banks create money, and this is used to buy goods and services and instruments. This is inflationary. Like an overt act of murder, the innocent murderees are all the people of society who reduce their demands for money, put their money into a savings and loan, and so on.

MR. GURLEY: So you are just extending it. Then we agree. Financial intermediaries and economic units are on the same plane as banks in the ability to create excess supplies of money.

MR. SOLOMON: But do we want to control everybody who has that power? Advertising agencies? They are primarily responsible for creating the excess supply of money, you know, by reducing the demand for it. This is a roundabout way of looking at things. If we have complete control over murderers, why bother with murderees in a free society?

MR. GURLEY: If we are willing to agree that A is like B; if we now have controls only over A; if we feel these are working well and that there are special difficulties connected with extending the controls to B — then there is reason for advocating the status quo. There may be special difficulties in extending the controls. But I also feel that if we had controls over B without any controls over A, much the same arguments could be used for maintaining that status quo.

MR. SOLOMON: What you are saying, in effect, John, is that Federal Reserve control is ineffective, that it cannot control murderers. I say the Fed *can* control murderers and has the power to stop all murder if it wanted to.

MR. GURLEY: I should hate to say you are dead wrong.

MR. SOLOMON: We can go just as far in stopping inflationary pressure as the Fed wants to go.

MR. GURLEY: Right. However, if there were controls only over non-monetary intermediaries, I think there is no question that a central association could achieve the same policy aims.

WARREN NUTTER: I should like to suggest that I think both of you are right about different things and for different reasons, if I may raise a question by way of a comment. Dr. Gurley is quite right if he is talking about long-run situations — long-run theory — and Dr. Solomon is right in talking about short-run theory.

There is a great difference, it seems to me, if I may be old-fashioned, about the nature of creation of money through financial intermediaries and other assets. The difference is that the commercial banking system, in effect, makes people think that certain loans they make are more liquid than the loans really are.

This will work all right in some cases, but not in other cases. In direct loans, people know that the loans are just as liquid as *they* are. This is fine, so long as there is nothing to upset this deception. But as soon as something does upset it, people realize that their loans are not as liquid as they believed. Then you get the volatile movements.

Now, I raise the question as to whether this is correct. If so, there is a primary distinction to be made, at least in terms of short-run fluctuations in those problems between intermediaries creating money and those creating other assets.

MR. SOLOMON: I agree completely. I think that secularly the presence of financial intermediaries could have, on the average, a huge long-run effect on money, if you want to put it that way. But this does not involve the problem of control at all, which presumably has caught up with the situation as it emerges over the long pull.

3

Should Commercial Banks
Accept Savings Deposits?–I*

Leland J. Pritchard is professor of finance and chairman of the Department of Economics at the University of Kansas. He is the author of *Money and Banking*, and has written widely for professional journals. Among his more notable articles are "Bank Capital and Lending Ability of Commercial Banks," *American Economic Review*, June 1953; "Toward a More Meaningful Statistical Concept of the Money Supply," *Journal of Finance*, March 1955; and "Commercial Banks and Financial Intermediaries: Fallacies and Policy Implications," *Journal of Political Economy*, October 1960. Mr. Pritchard earned his bachelor's degree at Cornell College, his master's at Syracuse University, and his doctorate at the University of Illinois.

THE TITLE "SHOULD COMMERCIAL BANKS ACCEPT SAVINGS DEPOSITS?" is both inaccurate and misleading, but I hasten to add that I accept responsibility. I felt that a title that reflected the "conventional wisdom" would provide a better expository "launching pad."

The title is inaccurate for the reason that commercial bankers, so long as they keep their banks open for business, have, to a certain extent, no choice in the matter of accepting or not accepting savings. This is as true for individual banks as for the system, for savings can be, and are, held in the commercial banks in the form of idle demand deposits as well as in

* Proceedings of the Fourth Annual Conference, 1961, pp. 12–27.

the form of time and savings deposits. I use the term "time deposits" in an all-inclusive sense to include all types of savings deposits, although there is a technical and legal difference. Technically, time deposits refer to time certificates of deposits held by corporations and others, whereas savings deposits refer to the passbook type of account.

The title is misleading because it suggests that the banks are accepting something which is brought to them; that they are acting as intermediaries between savers and borrowers. Our title asks the question: Should commercial banks accept savings deposits? A more appropriate query would be: Should commercial banks incur interest, advertising, and other expenses in order to induce their customers to transfer their demand deposits into time deposits?

A few years ago the Savings and Mortgage Division of the American Bankers Association sponsored a study to determine the profit or loss on savings accounts in commercial banks.[1] After collecting detailed, and no doubt accurate, cost and income data for 2,208 banks, and after matching the net return per $814.70 of loans with the interest and administrative cost associated with $1,000 of time deposits (on the assumption that 81.47% of savings deposits are invested on the average), the conclusion was reached that time deposit banking was profitable.

Had the ABA study covered all 13,000-plus commercial banks in the country, the rate data probably would not have been materially different, and the conclusion concerning the profitability of time deposit banking probably no different and just as open to question.

In effect, the ABA study asked this question: Was the net interest income on loans derived from time deposits greater than the interest paid on these deposits plus other direct and indirect operating expenses chargeable to time deposits? The implicit, and false, premise in this question is that time deposits are a *source* of loan funds to the banking *system.*

I submit that the question the ABA should have asked and based its study on was this: Does a shift from demand to time deposits result in a sufficient modification of monetary policy toward greater ease or less restraint as to allow the banks to acquire earning assets of a volume sufficient to offset the increased costs associated with this shift?

This paper is concerned not only with the profitability of time deposit banking, but also with the effects of time deposit banking on the size and earnings of savings and loan associations and other financial intermediaries; on interest rates and the supply of loan funds; and on production, employment and prices.

You will not be surprised to learn that I shall not supply you with

[1] *Plan for the Determination of Profit or Loss of Savings Accounts in Commercial Banks* (New York, 1951).

definitive answers to all these questions. Take, for example, the question: What is the relationship of the monetary savings practices of the public to the lending ability of the commercial banks? In effect we are asking what monetary policy would have been had the public held more, or less, savings in the form of currency hoards, time deposits, and idle demand deposits. Obviously, such a question precludes a definitive answer; but this does not bar us from seeking more generalized, but nonetheless valid, conclusions.

The Economics of Time Deposit Banking

We shall now proceed to seek these more generalized answers to the questions raised concerning the economics of time deposit banking.

From the beginning of the World War II period down to the present, there has been a vast growth in the volume of time deposits in the commercial banks, and in the last decade there has been a marked increase in the proportion that time deposits are of demand deposits. Time deposits increased from $15.9 billion as of the end of 1941 to $71.3 billion as of the end of 1960. The proportion time deposits are of demand deposits rose to 62.3% by the end of 1960 after remaining at approximately 40% from 1941 to 1952.

Accompanying this absolute and relative growth in time deposits there has been a fairly steady increase in interest rates paid on time deposits. Average rates paid by member banks increased from approximately 1.5% in 1956 to 2.0% in 1957, to 2.2% in 1958, to 2.36% in 1959 and to 2.58% in 1960. Similar increases have occurred among the insured nonmember banks.[2]

The higher rates, combined with the larger volume of time deposits, have not only increased the absolute amount of interest expense, but this item now constitutes a much larger proportion of total bank expenses. Thus, for member banks, interest expense on time deposits as a percentage of total operating expenses (before taxes on net income) increased from about 17% in 1955 to approximately 25% in 1959 and 1960.

The policies for both higher rates and a larger volume of time deposits have been fostered by bankers and their organizations, and have been abetted by the national and state monetary authorities. The continuation of the uptrend in interest rates on time deposits paid by member and nonmember insured banks was made possible in part through action of

[2] The volume of time deposits and the interest rates paid on time deposits has continued (and is continuing) upward. Average interest rates paid on time deposits by member banks averaged 3.23 per cent in 1962 and will probably reach a figure of around 3.5 per cent in 1963. As of the end of 1963, total time deposits held by all commercial banks amounted to $111.0 billions.

the Board of Governors and the Federal Deposit Insurance Corporation, acting under pressure from some banks, in raising the maximum permissible rates from 2½% to 3% effective January 1, 1957.[3]

The basic premise on which this support for bigger and more costly time deposits rests is apparently the mistaken belief that the commercial banks, at least insofar as their time deposit business is concerned, act as intermediaries between savers and borrowers; that every dollar of savings placed with a savings and loan association, mutual savings bank or other thrift institutions deprives the commercial banks of a corresponding amount of loanable funds.

It is the position of this paper that the time (or savings) deposit function of commercial bank operation: (1) tends, from a system standpoint, to reduce bank profits; (2) arrests the flow of monetary savings into investment; (3) retards the growth of savings and loan associations and other financial intermediaries; and (4) acts as a depressant, slowing down economic activity and retarding economic growth.

Bank profits are reduced because the banks, by paying interest on time deposits, are paying for something they already have. The net source of time deposits is demand deposits, and demand deposits are largely derived from the credit-creating activities of the commercial banks. In other words, the earning assets which are erroneously regarded as being derived from time deposits actually were in existence before the time deposits came into being.

Time deposit banking arrests the flow of monetary savings into investment because in their time deposit function the commercial banks are neither intermediaries nor creators of loan funds; they are simply custodians of stagnant money. The commercial banks do not loan out time deposits, nor the "proceeds" of time deposits; they do not even loan out excess legal reserves, although their lending capacity is determined by their excess legal reserve position. When the banks acquire earning assets, that is, when they make loans to, or buy securities from, the non-bank public, they pay for these earning assets with newly created money. This newly created money initially takes the form of demand deposits.

Because the payment velocity of funds shifted into time deposits becomes zero, these funds obviously are not being made available for either direct or indirect investment. The stoppage of the flow of monetary savings into investment channels not only has adverse effects on the size of savings and loan associations and other financial intermediaries; but, as would a stoppage of the flow of funds in any sector of the economy, adverse effects are exerted on the economy. The net effect of the

---

[3] The maximum rate which may be paid by insured banks was raised to 4 per cent effective January 1, 1962. See *Federal Reserve Bulletin,* December 1956, p. 1301; and 1956 Annual Report, Federal Deposit Insurance Corporation, pp. 83–84.

growth of time deposit banking, therefore, is to depress the economy, to retard economic growth and to accentuate unemployment.

THE EVIDENCE OF UNPROFITABILITY

What is the evidence to support these broad across-the-board generalizations? Are time deposits really a drag on the economy and an unprofitable phase of commercial bank operation? Time deposits have been given legislative status in virtually all the states, Congress provided for time deposit banking in the original Federal Reserve Act, and time deposit banking obviously has the support of nearly all bankers. Have all of these people been confused in their thinking and laboring under misapprehensions concerning the true economic character of time deposits?

Rather than indulge in any more sweeping generalizations, let us examine the facts. A good place to begin is with the facts concerning the profitability of the time deposit function to the commercial banks, a function which bankers and nonbankers alike generally assume to be profitable.

All the data which I have examined seem to substantiate the *a priori* deduction stated above that the banks are losing money on their time deposit business. The universal conclusion has been that the higher the ratio of time deposits to total deposits, the lower the profit ratios.[4]

The adverse effects of time deposit banking on bank earnings is apparently not a recent phenomenon. From a detailed compilation of member bank statistics, Horace Secrist in 1930 drew these conclusions: "(1) . . . where ratios of time deposits to total deposits are high, ratios of net earnings are low. (2) The higher the ratios of time deposits to total deposits, the higher the ratios of total expense to gross earnings; and . . . the lower are ratios of net earnings to gross earnings."[5]

And at least one attempt has been made to estimate the actual losses incurred by the banks on their time deposit business. Alhadeff and Alhadeff estimate the absolute loss of the increased volume of time deposits acquired by the banking system during the 1956–57 period at $140,893,000[6]

If time deposit banking is a losing proposition for the commercial banks, it would seem that bankers should look with favor on the growth of

---

[4] Joseph Aschheim, "Commercial Banks and Financial Intermediaries; Fallacies and Policy Implications," *The Journal of Political Economy*, February 1959, pp. 59–71; Deane Carson, "Bank Earnings and the Competition for Savings Deposits," *The Journal of Political Economy*, December 1959, pp. 580–588.

[5] Horace Secrist, *Banking Ratios* (Stanford, Calif.: Stanford University Press, 1930), pp. 154–155.

[6] David A. Alhadeff and Charlotte P. Alhadeff, "A Note on Bank Earnings and Savings Deposit Rate Policy," *The Journal of Finance*, September 1959, p. 408.

"competing" savings institutions. Carson suggests that they should: "In general, a shift of savings deposits from commercial banks to SLA (savings and loan associations) will improve the net earnings of the former. . . ."[7] His recommendations are confirmed by a recent monograph published by the New York State Banking Department. This study reveals that the presence of mutual savings banks and savings and loan associations in the same community with commercial banks enhances the earnings of the latter.[8]

The above findings raise two obvious questions. If commercial banks are losing money on their time deposit business, how is it possible for the mutual savings banks and the savings and loan associations, which pay higher rates on their savings accounts, to make a profit? And if the banks are losing money on this phase of their operations, why do they seek higher rate ceilings on time deposits and go to such effort and expense in order to expand their time deposit accounts?

The seeming paradox raised by the first question is resolved if the differences in the savings-investment process of the commercial banks as compared with the savings-investment process of the financial intermediaries (savings and loan associations, mutual savings banks, and so on) are understood. These differences are apparently not understood by bankers (or nonbankers), and this lack of understanding is at the root of the irrational behavior inferred by the second question. The notion that commercial banks loan out savings, that they act as intermediaries between savers and borrowers and that savings held by the commercial banks originate outside the system seems to have almost universal acceptance both in and out of the banking fraternity. The evidence to support this statement is too numerous to warrant citation.

COMMERCIAL BANKS VERSUS INTERMEDIARIES

For the sake of clarity and brevity I shall set forth in outline form the salient differences in the savings-investment process of the commercial banks *vis-à-vis* the financial intermediaries:

1. The commercial banks create new money (in the form of demand deposits) when making loans to, or buying securities from, the nonbank public, whereas lending by the intermediaries simply activates existing money.

2. Bank lending expands the volume of money and directly affects the velocity of money, while intermediary lending directly affects only the velocity of money.

3. The lending capacity of the commercial banks, singly and collectively, is related exclusively to their excess legal reserve position, and the components of

[7] Carson, *op. cit.*, p. 583.
[8] *Postwar Banking Developments in New York State* (1958), Chap. 3, "Impact of Savings Institutions on Commercial Banks."

the excess legal reserve position of the banks is a prime concern of, and is determined by, monetary policy.

4. The lending capacity of the intermediaries is almost exclusively dependent on the volume of monetary savings placed at their disposal; the continued existence of the intermediaries is in fact dependent upon the ability and willingness of the public to save and to place savings at their disposal.

5. The commercial banks, on the other hand, could continue to lend if the public should cease to save altogether. The lending ability of the commercial banks is dependent on monetary policy, not on the savings practices of the public. If monetary policy is "neutral," changes in monetary savings practices of the public, for example, the hoarding or dishoarding of currency, the shifting from demand to time deposits or *vice versa*, will of course affect the excess reserve position of the banks.

6. The intermediaries lend existing money which has been saved, and all of these savings originate outside the intermediaries, whereas the commercial banks lend no existing deposits or savings; they always, as noted, create new money in the lending process.

7. Whereas monetary savings held in the intermediaries originate outside the intermediaries, monetary savings held in the commercial banks (time deposits and the saved portion of demand deposits) originate, with minor exceptions, within the commercial banking system.

8. Monetary savings are never transferred from the commercial banks to the intermediaries; rather are monetary savings always transferred through the intermediaries, except to the extent that the intermediaries hold currency reserves.

9. The intermediaries can lend no more (and in practice they lend less) than the volume of savings placed at their disposal, whereas the commercial banks as a system can make loans (if monetary policy is "neutral" and the opportunity is present) which amount to several times the initial excess reserve held. In practice, due to the cash-drain factor, this coefficient of expansion is in the neighborhood of 3 rather than 6 or 7 as is commonly reported.

These are the principal criteria which distinguish the savings-investment process of the commercial banks from the savings-investment process of the intermediaries. Of these factors the principal one accounting for the unprofitability of time deposit banking is that savings held by the nonbank public in the commercial banks have their origin within the system itself.

Even though commercial banks never loan out the monetary savings of the public, the monetary savings practices of the nonbank public will — if monetary policy permits — alter the excess legal reserve position and therefore the lending capacity of the banks.

MONETARY SAVINGS AND LENDING ABILITY

It seems advisable at this juncture to set out in some detail the relationships which monetary savings practices, and time deposit practices in particular, have to the excess reserve position of the banks. Throughout the entire list given below we are assuming other things equal, including a so-called "neutral" monetary policy, and we are relating the changes in time deposits and other monetary savings practices to the excess reserve position of the banks as a system.

1. An increase in the ratio of time to demand deposits, brought about by a shift from demand to time deposits, will under prevailing reserve ratios (except for nonmember banks in a few states) cause an increase in bank excess reserves. This is almost the exclusive net source of time deposits.

2. A growth in time deposits, if as a consequence of a return flow of currency to the banking system (dishoarding of currency), will cause an increase in total, and excess, reserves in the banks. This is not a net primary source of time deposits; and since demand deposits constitute the sole source of currency in our managed currency system, it would be incorrect to say that demand deposits were not the basic source of time deposits, irrespective of changes in the public's holdings of currency.

3. A growth of time deposits consequent to net additions to our monetary gold and silver stocks from domestic sources will increase total, and excess, reserves of the banks. It is here assumed that the Treasury follows up its acquisitions by the issuance of gold and silver certificates (or silver coin) to replenish its Reserve bank balances, rather than replenishing them by a transfer of balances from the commercial banks. Otherwise the growth in time deposits would be at the expense of demand deposits.

4. A growth of time deposits consequent to expenditures of Reserve bank balances acquired by foreign holders through gold sales to the Treasury will cause an increase in total, and excess, reserves of the banks.

5. A growth of time deposits consequent to expenditures by the Reserve banks, where the recipients of the drafts are members of the nonbank public, will cause an increase in total, and excess, reserves of the banks.

6. A growth of time deposits consequent to the deposit of drafts to cover expenses drawn by the commercial banks in favor of the nonbank public will cause a decrease in excess reserves.

Although, as I have indicated, there are a number of possible sources of time deposits, in actual practice the growth of time deposits is almost exclusively at the expense of demand deposits. The other sources of time deposits enumerated are inconsequential. Virtually all recipients of checks drawn by the Treasury, the Reserve banks and the commercial banks (items 3, 4, 5 and 6 above) initially have these funds credited to their demand deposit account, either because the funds are not savings or, where a part of savings, because the recipients choose to hold their savings in a form other than time deposits.

7. An increase in the ratio of time to demand deposits, brought about by a shift from demand to time deposits, will induce a return flow of currency to the banking system, and this will increase the total, and excess, reserves of the commercial banks.

The so-called cash-drain factor simply expresses the observed relationship that the public tends to hold a fairly constant proportion of their means-of-payment money in the form of currency. In recent years the ratio of currency to deposits has approximated .25. That is, if demand deposits increase by a given amount the public will tend to draw down its deposit balances by about 20%, so that its currency holdings average about 25% of the remaining deposits.

In addition to changes in the public's holdings of time deposit balances, other monetary savings practices of the nonbank public could — if the monetary authorities allow the excess reserves created to remain intact — add to bank lending capacity. The most important of these are: (1) dishoarding of currency, involving a shift out of currency hoards into demand deposits; (2) using monetary savings to buy new issues of bank stock; and (3) transferring monetary savings held in the form of demand deposits from banks having higher reserve ratios to banks having lower reserve ratios.

Having outlined the basic differences in the savings-investment process of the commercial banks compared with the financial intermediaries, and having set forth the institutional relationships which exist between the monetary savings practices of the public and the lending capacity of the commercial banks, we are now ready to proceed to an examination of specific estimates of losses sustained (or profits obtained) by the banks from their time deposit operations.

TIME DEPOSITS AND FEDERAL RESERVE POLICY

Heretofore in this paper it has been categorically stated that the banks are losing money on their time deposit business. But conclusive proof of this proposition is not possible, since the conclusion one reaches revolves around the indeterminate question: What would Reserve policy have been had their been no growth in time deposits? In other words, do the Reserve authorities allow excess reserves brought into being by a shift from demand to time deposits to remain intact so that bank earning assets may expand approximately *pari passu* with the expansion of time deposits? Or does the growth of time deposits leave Reserve policy substantially unchanged? The techniques and criteria of monetary management would seem to affirm the latter.

1. Monetary policy has as its primary objective the creation of a desired condition of "ease" or "tightness" in the money markets. This condition is reflected, not in the size of the money supply, but rather in the size and proportions of the components of the excess reserves of the banks, and in the volume of loan funds offered by the nonbank public.[9]

[9] Robert V. Roosa, *Federal Reserve Operations in the Money and Government Securities Markets* (Federal Reserve Bank of New York, 1956), especially pp. 64 ff.

2. In their efforts to control the availability and cost of loan funds the monetary authorities must exert their initial impact almost entirely on the availability and cost of bank credit. The latter is a function of the size and components of the excess reserves of the banks, not of the money supply.

3. Monetary policy reacts to the totality of all factors which alter the excess reserve position of the banks. It does not sort out these forces and neutralize some and leave others unaffected.

4. The monetary authorities take cognizance of the money supply and many other significant data, but they do not seek to maintain the money supply at any given level. That is to say, a shift from demand to time deposits will not induce a monetary policy designed to replace the lost demand deposits, any more than a shift from time to demand deposits will induce a monetary policy designed to force bank credit contraction equal to the reduced volume of time deposits.

But it is foolish to contend that a growth in time deposits has no effect on monetary policy. We have noted that time deposit banking arrests the flow of savings into investment, and as a consequence deleterious effects are exerted on the economy. If the magnitude of these effects is pronounced, the Reserve authorities undoubtedly will be influenced to follow a somewhat less restrictive (or easier) monetary policy as a consequence of the growth in time deposits. But that this alteration in policy, if it does take place, will permit the banks to acquire sufficient excess reserves so that they are able to expand their earning assets by more than a small fraction of the expansion in time deposits is highly problematical.

It would seem that the burden of proof is upon those who would contend that a shift from demand to time deposits will induce the Reserve authorities to follow a sufficiently easier (or less restrictive) monetary policy as to enable the banks to acquire sufficient earning assets to offset the increased costs associated with such a shift.

Specific Estimates of Gain or Loss

I shall now examine specific estimates of gain or loss derived from the time deposit function under various limiting assumptions.

In the first model for the banking system it is assumed: (1) that there has been a shift of $1,000 from demand to time deposits; (2) that the excess reserves created in the banking system consequent to the return flow of currency, and the lower reserve ratios applicable to time deposits, are allowed to remain intact, that is, that monetary policy is altered sufficiently so that it is "neutral" with respect to this reserve factor; and (3) that the banks have the opportunity to exploit these reserves and that they expand their earning assets to the permissible limit.

Under these assumptions the banking system is able to make L volume of loans. The equation is written thus:

$$L = \left[\frac{T \left(\frac{c}{1+c} \right) (1-d) + T (d-t)}{d+c} \right] (1+c),$$

where

     L = volume of loans made (net volume of credit created by the banking system);

     T = volume of funds transferred from demand to time deposits;

     c = cash drain expressed as a ratio of currency to demand deposits (adjusted);

     d = average reserve ratio for demand deposits; and

     t = average reserve ratio for time deposits.

Substituting the following assigned values based upon 1959 data:

$$c = .25,\ d = .14,\ \text{and}\ \ t = .05,$$

then

$$L = \$839.681$$

Proof in "T" account form:

		− DD	1000.00
		+ TD	1000.00
+ Currency	200.0	+ DD	200.0
+ Loans	839.681	+ DD	839.681
− Currency	167.936	− DD	167.936

Summarizing,

+ Currency	32.064	− DD	128.255
+ Loans	839.681	+ TD	1000.00
+	871.745	+	871.745

     Net increase in total reserves   = $32.064

     Net increase in required reserves = 1000 (.05) − 128.255 (.14)

                                     = $32.044

From these computations, we can calculate the break-even rate of return for the banking system. You are again reminded that we are assuming that the shift from demand to time deposits alters monetary policy in the direction of greater ease, or less restraint, to an extent sufficient to allow the excess reserves brought into being by this shift to remain intact.

     The break-even equation incorporating this monetary policy assumption is written thus:

$$y = \frac{(r + e_t) - \Delta D (e_d - a)}{L'},$$

where

> y = minimum net average yield (gross yield minus acquisition and ad-
> ministrative expenses) which must be earned on incremental earn-
> ing assets in order to break even;
>
> r = average rate of interest paid on time deposits, expressed as a ratio;
>
> e_t = operating expenses associated with the time deposit function ex-
> pressed in ratio form;
>
> e_d = operating expenses associated with the demand deposit function
> expressed in ratio form;
>
> a = activity charge income derived from the demand deposit function,
> expressed in ratio form; and
>
> ΔD = ratio of net decrease in demand deposits to the increase in time
> deposits.

In equation form symbols the same as defined above),

$$\Delta D = \left[\frac{\left(\frac{c}{1+c}\right)(1-d) + (d-t)}{c+d} \right] + \frac{c}{1+c} - 1.$$

> L' = ratio of the increase in earning assets to the increase in time
> deposits.

Substituting the following values:[10]

> r = .0236 (average interest rate paid by member banks, 1959, on time
> deposits),
>
> e_t = .0057,
>
> e_d = .0231,
>
> a = .00779,
>
> ΔD = −.128255 (see "T" account proof), and
>
> L' = .839681 (see "T" account proof),

then:

$$y = 3.26\%.$$

The net profit to the banking system of a transfer of $1,000 from demand
to time deposits under the above assumptions is equal to $L (n - y)$, where
n = net rate of return on the incremental earning assets.

Assigning a value of .0376 to n, the estimated annual net profit per $1,000
transferred to time deposits becomes $4.23.[11]

[10] Values for e_t, e_d and a are based upon functional cost data for 80 member banks
in the First Federal Reserve District, 1959. See *1959 Functional Cost Analysis*, Federal Reserve Bank of Boston (mimeographed).

[11] The value of .0376 obtained from the income and functional cost study made by
the Federal Reserve Bank of Boston (*op. cit.*). This value represents the average net
rate of return on both loans and investments, and was selected on the assumption
that the expanded earning assets are distributed according to the prevailing portfolio
pattern.

It is by no means certain, even if credit expansion is allowed and does take place,
consequent to a time deposit related expansion in excess reserves, that the newly

Thus we see, by incorporating a quite unrealistic assumption concerning the effect of a shift from demand to time deposits on monetary policy, that it is possible to construct a model which yields a profit for the time deposit function. If we go to the other extreme and assume that a shift from demand to time deposits has no effect on monetary policy, then the banking system undoubtedly is incurring substantial losses on its time deposit business.

The absolute amount of loss (E) may be computed from the following equation:

$$E = \left[T\left(\frac{c}{1+c}\right)(1-d) + T(d-t) \right] g + T\left(1 - \frac{c}{1+c}\right)(e_d - a) - T(r + e_t)$$

where

g = average rate of return obtained by member banks on United States obligations in 1959; on the valid assumption that the Reserve authorities "mop up" time deposit induced excess reserves by the sale of governments to the banks through the open market. They do this by selling $T(d-t)$ volume of securities to the banks. In order to counteract the effect on excess reserves of a return flow of currency due to a shift from demand to time deposits, they sell an additional volume, $T\left(\frac{c}{1+c}\right)$ $(1-d)$, of governments to the banks.

All other symbols used in the above equation have been previously defined.

Substituting previously assigned values for the various symbols and a value of 2.79 per cent for g we obtain a figure of \$6.7422, the estimated loss per annum per \$1000 where the shift from demand to time deposits is assumed to have caused no alteration in monetary policy.

Neither of these examples provides an accurate measure of profits or losses attributable to the time deposit function. It is as unrealistic to assume that the Reserve authorities are unaffected in their monetary policy decisions by a shift from demand to time deposits, or vice versa, as to assume that they are induced by these shifts to take offsetting actions which completely nullify the effects of these shifts on the excess reserve position of the banks.

The actual situation lies somewhere between these two extremes. It is therefore as unrealistic to assume that the banks incurred a loss of \$6.74

created funds will only, or even preponderantly, be invested in the highest yielding types of earning assets. While legal sanctions tend to encourage such offsets, e.g., relating the maximum permissible volume of mortgage lending to the volume of time deposits, it does not follow that such portfolio adaptations will take place. *See* Alhadeff and Alhadeff, *op. cit.*, p. 407, footnote.

per $1,000 of time deposits in 1959 as to assume they reaped a profit of
$4.23. But it is probable that they did incur some loss on their time
deposit business in 1959. All the quantitative studies cited above point
in that direction.

Developments since 1959 suggest that these losses have increased.

THE CASE FOR INDIVIDUAL BANKS

Heretofore we have been discussing the unprofitability of the time
deposit function from the standpoint of the banking system. What of
the individual bank? May it not be to the interest of any given bank to
incur advertising, interest and other expenses in order to expand its time
deposit operations? The answer depends on the assumption made concerning the source of the new time deposits. If these deposits originate
within the bank, the bank is undoubtedly suffering a loss on this phase
of its operations. If they originate outside the bank, we can be almost
as certain that the operation is profitable. This is evident from the
following examples.

In the first example, I shall calculate the profit (or loss) for a given
bank where the time deposits are assumed to have originated in the
same bank. The various assumptions on which the model is based are as
follows:

1. Demand deposits decreased by the same amount that time deposits increased. Since we are dealing with a single bank, the cash-drain factor can be
ignored.

2. The bank was subject to a reserve ratio against demand deposits (d) of
.12 and a reserve ratio against time deposits (t) of .05.

3. The interest rate (r) paid on time deposits corresponded to the average
(.0236) paid by all member banks in 1959.

4. The operating expense ratio associated with the time deposit function
(e_t), and the activity charge ratio for demand deposit accounts (a), corresponded to the average for sample member banks in the first Federal Reserve
District. (*1959 Functional Cost Analysis, Federal Reserve Bank of Boston.*)

5. The activity charges varied directly with the operating expenses associated
with the demand deposit account function.

6. The bank had the opportunity to make bankable loans and fully exploited
these opportunities to the extent permitted by the release of excess reserves
consequent to the shift from demand to time deposits, and all such newly
created deposits flowed to other banks in the system.

These assumptions are incorporated in the following equation:

$$E = T\,(d - t)\left[n - \frac{(r + e_t) - (e_d - a)}{(d - t)}\right]$$

Substituting values indicated above and those previously assigned for the system models we obtain a figure of $ - 11.36$ (approx.), the estimated loss per annum per $1,000 of time deposits where these deposits originate in the given bank.

In the second example, I shall calculate both the profit (or loss) and the break-even rate for a given bank where the time deposits are assumed to originate outside the bank. It is further assumed that the bank had the opportunity to make bankable loans; that it fully exploited these opportunities to the extent permitted by the expansion of excess reserves; and that all deposits created as a consequence of these loans were checked out and flowed to other banks in the system.

The following equation incorporates these assumptions:

$$E = T (1 - t) \left[n - \left(\frac{r + e_t}{1 - t} \right) \right]$$

Substituting values previously used we obtain a figure of $6.42, the estimated profit per annum per $1,000 of time deposits where these deposits are assumed to originate outside the given bank.

These assumptions both overstate and understate the extent to which the bank was able to acquire additional earning assets as a consequence of a given primary time deposit. Ordinarily banks expand their excess reserves by about 3% of incoming deposits, making the effective reserve ratio for member banks around 8% rather than 5% against time deposits. Furthermore, all newly created deposits are not checked out; and of the deposits checked out, usually a small fraction "return" to the same bank.

The following equation, therefore, provides only an approximation of the real break-even rate (symbols defined as above):

$$y = \frac{r + e_t}{1 - t}.$$

Substituting (values the same as previously used):

$$y = \frac{.0236 + .0057}{1 - .05} = \frac{.0293}{.95} = .0308, \text{ or } 3.08\%.$$

This break-even rate is sufficiently low to warrant the assumption that time deposit banking can, under the conditions assumed, be profitable from the standpoint of the individual bank. This rate is substantially below the net yield rates computed by the Federal Reserve Bank of Boston in 1959. Net yields on various classes of earning assets as reported in this study are as follows: loans and investments, 3.76%; loans, 4.49%; mortgage loans, 4.27%.

Since bankers seem to view the savings-investment process from the standpoint of their individual bank operations, believing that savings originate outside their banks and that their institutions are simply intermediaries between savers and borrowers, it is quite logical for them to assume that their time deposit business is profitable. But irrespective of the viewpoint of the individual banker, he generally finds it necessary to compete with other banks for the saver's dollar. It may, therefore, actually be to the interest of any given bank to incur advertising, interest and other expenses in order to attract funds (time deposits, demand deposits and currency) because any inflow adds to the bank's lending capacity. Or the promotion of time deposits is necessary if a bank is to avoid an adverse balance of payments, and the consequent loss of reserves, earning assets and income.

Break-even Rates: Banks and Intermediaries

It is instructive at this point to compare the methods of calculating break-even rates for the commercial banks with the methods applicable to the financial intermediaries. When analyzing break-even rates on time deposits for the commercial banks, we found it necessary not only to distinguish the operation of a single bank from that of the system; it was also necessary to identify the source of the time deposits. No such distinctions need be made for the financial intermediaries, since all monetary savings originate outside the intermediaries. The break-even analysis for the intermediaries is, in fact, the same as for a single commercial bank where the savings originate outside the bank.

This is evident from the following break-even equation. For illustrative purposes the definitions and data used are based upon the savings and loan business.

The break-even equation for a single savings and loan association, or all associations collectively, may be written thus:

$$y = \frac{r + e}{1 - s},$$

where

$y =$ minimum net average yield (gross yield on earning assets minus acquisition and administrative expenses) which must be earned on incremental earning assets attributable to the expansion of share accounts in order to break even;

$r =$ average dividend rate paid on share accounts;

e = net increase in operating expenses chargeable to the expansion of share accounts, expressed in ratio form; and

s = ratio of vault cash and bank balances to the volume of share accounts.

Approximate values for the savings and loan business in 1959 were:[12]

$$r = .037, \; e = .015, \text{ and } s = .034.$$

Substituting,

$$y = \frac{.037 + .015}{1 - .034} = .054 \text{ or } 5.4\%.$$

Even with this higher break-even rate the savings and loan business was able to add to its reserves. After meeting all expenses and paying dividends at an average rate of 3.7%, savings associations in 1959 were able to allocate 17.8% of their gross income to reserves.[13]

CONCLUSIONS AND POLICY IMPLICATIONS

For time deposit banking to be profitable, it is necessary to assume that a shift from demand to time deposits induces a pronounced change in monetary policy, evidenced by a willingness on the part of the monetary authorities to supply a larger volume of legal reserves to the banking system. This increase in reserves must be of a magnitude sufficient to enable the banks to acquire enough earning assets to more than offset the increased costs associated with the growth in time deposits and the growth in demand deposits resulting from the expansion of bank credit.

But to assume this is to assume that the growth of time deposits has a markedly adverse effect on the level of economic activity. Otherwise what justification is there for postulating the shift in monetary policy toward greater ease?

Thus, even were it granted that time deposit banking is profitable, it is questionable, as a matter of public policy, that an institutional arrangement which hampers economic growth and which requires large doses of new money (and accompanying inflation) to counteract should be allowed to persist.

From the above analysis, it is evident that the more the commercial banks have succeeded through their savings campaigns in stemming the flow of funds through the savings and loan associations, the mutual savings banks, and similar institutions, the more Pyrrhic has been their victory both to themselves and to the intermediaries.

[12] *Savings and Loan Fact Book* (Chicago: United States Savings and Loan League, 1960), pp. 21, 22, 79, 80, 88, 90.
[13] *Op. cit.*, p. 90.

Not so evident is the fact that the growth of time deposits has been costly to the community at large. This growth has been, and will continue to be, costly to the community, for savings held in the commercial banks (time deposits and the saved portion of demand deposits) are lost to investment as long as they are so held.

Savings held in the commercial banks are just as much a form of stagnant money as are currency hoards; and in a pecuniary economy such as ours, stagnant money breeds economic stagnation. Therefore any net outlay of funds by the banks for the purpose of maintaining or expanding their time deposit business needlessly increases the expense of the banks; adds to the volume of stagnant money (if the expenditures are successful in inducing people to hold a larger volume of time deposits); injures the financial intermediaries; adds little or nothing to the lending ability or the earning assets of the commercial banks; and tends to create inadequate demand, unemployment and reduced bank profits.

This is not to say that the damping effect on the economy of this vast and growing body of time deposits cannot be offset. But it is much more desirable to promote prosperity by inducing a smooth and continuous flow of monetary savings into real investment than to rely, as we have done over most of the past twenty years, on a vast expansion of bank credit (with accompanying inflation) to stimulate production.

This is one of those rare instances in which public policy could simultaneously serve the welfare interests of the community and the profit interests of the specific groups immediately affected. Rather than encourage time deposit banking by reducing reserve requirements and raising interest ceilings on time deposits as the bankers and their associations are advocating, Congress and the state legislatures should — in the interest of the commercial banks, the financial intermediaries and, above all, in the interest of the community — completely eliminate the anachronism of time deposit banking from the structure of our commercial banking system.

4

Should Commercial Banks
Accept Savings Deposits?–II*

Edward E. Edwards is professor of finance in
the School of Business at Indiana University and senior vice
president of Business and Real Estate Trends, Inc. He is the
author of *Some Thoughts on Liquidity and Other Essays;* "Improvement of Federal Home Loan Bank Programs," in *Study of
Mortgage Credit; Bank Taxation in Indiana; and Indiana Consumer Credit Agencies.* He is the co-author of *Report of the
Special Committee to Study the FHLB System* and *The Next
Decade and Its Opportunities for the Savings and Loan Business.*
Mr. Edwards earned his bachelor's and master's degrees at Indiana University. He is a past president of the American Finance
Association.

I AM HERE TO SUPPORT THE PROPOSITION that commercial banks should
accept savings deposits. If I succeed in this assignment — and I certainly
intend to try — our host and my part-time employer, the United States
Savings and Loan League, may wish that Professor Pritchard had been
the only speaker on this subject. I doubt it, however, because the U. S.
League is a trade association that really has no fear of discussion or, I
should say, no fear of the truth.

Now, Professor Pritchard, while I am reading my paper, I shall give
you your questions, as you were kind enough to give me mine in advance.

* Proceedings of the Fourth Annual Conference, 1961, pp. 29–38.

I want you to be able to tell us at 11 o'clock how big you think the banking system would have been in 1960 if it had not had time deposits. Would it have been $114 billion, $185 billion, or something in between? The next question is this: How can you argue, on the one hand, that an increase in time deposits will lead to economic depression and, on the other hand, that the increase will not have any effect on monetary policy?

Now, to get back to the question: Should commercial banks accept savings deposits? I have broken this up into what seemed to me to be two logical parts: First, should banks as a matter of their own management policy accept savings deposits? Second, should banks as a matter of public policy be encouraged to accept savings deposits? This approach seemed to offer the best means of identifying and clarifying any issue of conflict between the self-interest of individual banks and the public interest.

In looking into the reasons why banks, as a matter of management policy, should accept — and promote — savings deposits, the most overpowering reason seems to be that this is absolutely necessary for most banks if they expect to maintain their relative position as financial institutions in the communities they serve. With the possible exception of a few large money centers, no community can provide demand deposits in adequate volume to serve as the sole source of funds for an ambitious bank, much less two or more competing banks. While demand deposit banking might still be profitable, not many bankers are going to be satisfied in a situation in which one after another savings and loan association or other specialized financial institution passes the banks in size.

In many cities, the largest financial institution today is a savings and loan association that a decade or so ago was "dwarfed" by the leading bank. In other cities, the emergence of an association as the leading institution has been delayed by one or more mergers of competing banks, but quite obviously there is a limit to this means of preventing the inevitable. Thus, ambitious bankers must aggressively build deposits; and, as we shall see, savings deposits offer the best opportunity for deposit building.

Banks Need More Funds to Meet Loan Demands

Ambition is not the only reason that banks need to expand their savings deposits. Banks need more funds to meet loan demands. For many years loans have been increasing more rapidly than demand deposits. For example, bank loans increased $56 billion between 1947 and 1957, a decade in which demand deposits increased by only $30 billion. Between 1957 and 1960, loans increased by $24 billion and demand deposits by only $5 billion. Banks have made up these differences in various ways, including selling governments, reducing their primary reserves, investing new capital, retaining earnings, and increasing time and savings deposits.

Bank loans for all banks combined at the end of 1960 exceeded 90% of demand deposits, as compared with less than 60% in 1950 and approximately 30% at the end of World War II. For many individual banks, loans have long since exceeded demand deposits. This situation has not come about from any lack of competitive effort in deposit building. It has resulted from the following simple, basic fact: The combined borrowing (or credit) needs of a bank's customers exceed their combined ability, or willingness, to hold cash.

Actually, this disparity is far greater than the banking statistics suggest. Despite the great increase in bank loans, borrowing needs that might have been filled by banks have been met to a large extent outside the banking system, with funds provided by the banks' own customers who preferred to hold commercial or finance paper, share accounts, or other financial assets or near monies rather than demand deposits.

Bankers have become all too familiar with corporate treasurers who want to earn something on their "idle" cash balances and with individual depositors who have the ability to carry large deposit balances but want to earn something on their liquid funds. Money, whether in currency or demand deposits, is no longer such a desirable asset that the demand for it is unlimited. Except for a necessary minimum balance, almost any other asset seems to be more desirable than cash.

The individual bank cannot concern itself with concepts such as the idea that banks create the money they loan. The individual bank can only loan (or invest) what it has received from its depositors. Thus, when loan demand increases and investment portfolios have been shrunk to minimum liquidity needs, the only hope is increased deposits.

How can a bank increase its deposits? By getting more depositors and by getting present depositors to keep larger balances. Neither is easy if the bank can offer only demand deposit service. People already have all the checking accounts they want, and all the money they want in them. Thus, a bank that grows only through demand deposits seems doomed to a rate of growth no greater, probably less, than the over-all economic growth of its community. And even to achieve this, it must compete aggressively with other banks.

If banks could pay interest on demand deposits, perhaps they could induce their depositors to carry larger balances. That is another argument, however, as is also the desirability of competing more aggressively for time deposits of corporations.

In this paper I have rather arbitrarily assumed that the term "savings deposits" means the interest-bearing deposits of individuals, thus leaving for the term "time deposits" the interest-bearing deposits of corporations.

Most of the arguments for promoting savings deposits also apply to time deposits. The prospects for building up corporate holdings of time deposits do not seem very bright for most banks, however, even including the large, money-market banks that serve large corporations. To compete with commercial paper, Treasury bills, short-term paper in foreign markets and the like, banks certainly would need more freedom than they now have in adjusting interest rates and maturities to changing conditions in the money markets.

Of course, banks could raise additional capital funds, but any substantial increase in capital would quickly drive down earnings per share to a level that would prohibit further sale of stock. Capital funds can never be more than a cushion to protect deposits; and unless capital can be matched by many times its amount in deposits, it will not be forthcoming.

THE ALTERNATIVE TO SAVINGS DEPOSIT GROWTH

With dim prospects for growth from other sources — demand deposits, time deposits of corporations, capital — it would seem rather obvious that promotion of personal savings is absolutely necessary for the ambitious bank. This conclusion becomes even more obvious when we consider what happens when banks fail to promote savings aggressively.

When banks fail to expand their savings deposits to meet growing loan demand, they encourage the growth of the nonbanking intermediaries. The willing but unsatisfied borrowers offer the opportunity, and the willing but unrewarded and unsolicited savers offer the means, for savings and loan associations and other nonbanking intermediaries to flourish. While this might not be too bitter a pill for the bankers to swallow if nothing else happened, the bankers sooner or later begin to realize that the growth of the nonbanking intermediaries makes it unnecessary for the banking system to expand and that the monetary authorities, with an eye on credit needs, are refusing to make additional reserves available to the banks. Under such conditions, competition of banks for additional demand deposits cannot possibly increase their total size. Meanwhile, competition among nonbanking intermediaries further accelerates their growth; and the greater their success, apparently, the more doomed the banks are to remain at existing levels.

Even this might not be too bad, since there will always be wars and depressions during which easy money policies will again give the banks a chance to grow. The trouble here is that, unless the banks can convert the newly created money into something people want (for example, savings deposits), depositors will, when the war or depression is over, transfer their funds into the near monies, since these serve liquidity needs and also pay interest. Then the rapid growth of the nonbanking intermediaries and the resulting credit expansion will again bring back restrictive monetary policies, and the banks will cease to grow.

Somewhere along the way the nonbanking intermediaries, which originally had only limited powers, will begin seeking broader investment powers, insurance of their obligations, expansion of their markets and other favors, no doubt including the right to offer checking account services. They may succeed, too, since they can show how necessary their continued growth is in terms of meeting credit needs.

What a colossal blow it will be to the banker who refused to promote savings deposits in order to be a commercial banker to find that the "upstairs building and loan association" or the "Friday night credit union" or the "fly-by-night finance company" is now the biggest commercial bank!

Yes, ambition alone is sufficient reason why banks should promote savings deposits. But there is at least one other reason. Savings deposits can be profitable.

Time Deposits *Can* Be Profitable

Professor Pritchard has referred to studies of the profitability of savings deposits, all of which suggested to him that such deposits are not profitable. I have seen these studies, too, but do not reach the same conclusion. What the studies show, primarily, is that savings deposits are not as profitable as demand deposits or, rather, that banks with a high percentage of demand to total deposits are generally more profitable than banks with a high percentage of savings to total deposits. This should have been rather obvious without any studies, but this conclusion does not answer the question: Are savings deposits profitable?

To digress for a moment and take a look at the statistical evidence, what we see is that banks that have no trouble reaching a satisfactory size with demand deposits do not need to promote savings. They are like married men whose incomes are so large their wives do not have to work. On the average, their single income probably exceeds the combined income of husbands and wives who both work and who both have to work because the husband's income is so small. If so, would this prove that it is not profitable for wives to work?

The same data that show that the most profitable banks have the highest percentage of demand deposits will also show that the most profitable banks paid the most taxes. Should we conclude that the road to profit is to pay more tax? The most profitable banks may contribute most to local colleges and universities, too; but I, for one, would not tell an unprofitable bank that the way to make a profit would be to endow a chair in banking.

To return to the argument, the banker's question should be this: Are savings deposits sufficiently profitable to justify the promotion of savings business?

Since each bank must answer this question for itself, we might first classify all banks into three broad groups. The first group includes those banks that have more than adequate deposits to meet loan demand. Until recently many, perhaps most, banks were in this group, and had been for many years. Quite obviously the promotion of savings deposits might not seem to be profitable to them in the short run. But not too many banks remain in this group.

More banks are in a second group, which may be described as those that are fully loaned up in terms of deposits but not in terms of capital structure. Quite obviously it would be profitable for these banks to promote savings deposits if this did not reduce demand deposits and if the net earnings on the new money exceeded its cost.

Will promotion of savings deposits by banks in this group decrease their demand deposits? Probably so; but if so, the banks are eventually going to lose this part of their demand deposits anyway, through competition from nonbanking intermediaries. Will the net earnings on the new money exceed its cost? Yes, as we shall see.

Finally, there is a third group of banks, those that are fully loaned up in terms of both capital structure and deposits. Is it profitable for them to promote savings when, if they succeed, they must raise additional capital?

Let us assume that such banks will be required by supervisory authorities to raise $1.00 in capital for each $10 increase in savings. If they use the capital funds for necessary cash reserves and highly liquid assets, with a net return on the total of only 1%, and invest the deposit funds in an equal mixture of home mortgage loans and consumer credit paper, what will be the result?

Judging from the gross earnings, the expenses and the allowances for bad debts on this kind of portfolio in banks, and from the experience of nonbanking intermediaries, savings thus invested should earn a minimum of 4%, and more likely 4½%. This would permit a 3% to 3½% rate on savings, and earnings before taxes of from 11% to 16% on capital, or after tax earnings from 5½% to 8% on capital. If from 20% to 30% of the savings were invested in municipal bonds, the before-tax earnings on capital would be cut somewhat, but there would be little tax to pay, and net profit after taxes might run to 10% or better.

REGULATORY CHANGES NEEDED

While these rates of return are not fabulous, they would seem to be more than adequate to justify additional investment of capital, whether through retention of earnings or sale of additional stock. However, savings deposits would be even more profitable if certain unnecessary and undesirable legal restrictions could be removed from our laws and regulatory codes or could be modified.

The first of these is the 5% non-income-producing legal reserve. There is no longer any need for such a requirement. I should be glad to argue the point if necessary, but at the moment I wish merely to point out that the cost of maintaining this reserve falls heavily on bank stockholders. If we assume a 10-to-1 deposit-capital ratio, the reserve requirement in effect requires one-half of the capital investment to be tied up in non-earning assets. My estimate would be that elimination of the reserve requirement would, without any deterioration in liquidity, increase the return on capital (that is, that part of a bank's capital supporting its savings) by a full 2% before taxes, 1% or more after tax. This would be an increase in rate of return of as much as one-fifth, or more than enough to justify aggressive promotion of savings by quite a few bankers who now believe that savings are unprofitable.

A second restriction that makes the savings business less profitable than it might be, and which should be liberalized or removed, is the legal language that keeps banks from competing effectively in the home mortgage markets. I refer to the limitations on amount of loan as percentage of appraised value, limits on maturities, rigid requirements as to amortization, and finally limits on total size of portfolio. Why is it that banks are free to use their own judgment when they finance cars, boats, trailers, college educations, vacations, funerals and other personal needs, but must abide by some unproved, probably false, standards when financing people's homes? What sense does it make for the federal government to permit mutual savings and loan associations, without any capital base, but whose savings the government is insuring, to make loans under terms which the government forbids to commercial banks, whose savings are also insured, and which have a capital base over and above their reserves for losses? Rather, what sense does it make to prohibit the banks, which have risk capital to fall back on, from making loans under terms that the government approves for insured savings associations, which have no risk capital?

Of course, banks do not have to invest savings deposits in home mortgages, and this is one of the important advantages they have over most of the nonbanking intermediaries. Home mortgages probably never were as profitable as consumer paper, and frequently are less profitable than corporate bonds. In periods of tight money, business loans, with their compensatory balances, probably have a better yield than mortgages. However, for most communities a bank that wants to build savings probably will have to compete aggressively in the home mortgage market.

Two other restrictions on savings growth are closely related but greatly misunderstood. I refer to the traditional capital requirements enforced on banks and the difference in provisions for tax-free loss reserves for banks and for mutual savings institutions. Of the two, the capital requirement is by far the more serious, although quite a few bankers mistakenly believe the tax difference is more important.

Let us assume, first, that there is no such thing as federal income tax but that we do have federal insurance of savings. Can commercial banks and mutual savings institutions compete fairly? Unless the commercial banks have substantially better investment opportunities or lower cost, they cannot possibly pay as high a return on savings as the mutuals. Since bank capital cannot on its own earn a return adequate to attract equity funds, the commercial banks must take out something from the return on savings to add to the return on capital funds in order to pay stockholders a satisfactory return. Thus, if savings earn 4% for both banks and mutuals, and the mutuals pay 4%, a bank may not be able to pay more than 3½%.

Now let us assume a federal income tax on corporations, but with identical provisions for tax-free reserves for all types of financial institutions. With a 50% tax on corporate earnings, and a 1-to-10 capital requirement, commercial banks would be squeezed down to a 3% rate of interest to depositors even though their savings earned 4%. This would place them at a distinct disadvantage, even though they had the same formula as the mutuals for tax-free loss reserves.

When we allow mutual institutions to accumulate relatively larger tax-free loss reserves, they have an additional slight advantage; but the really important competitive disadvantage of the banks is their capital requirement. In other words, banks are expected to have a substantial net sound capital over and above loss reserves, and mutual institutions are not. Since both are insured, it would seem that what is adequate for the one would be adequate for the other.

What banks should seek, rather than changes in the way mutuals are taxed, would, in my opinion, be one or both of the following:

1. A change in bank capital requirement formulas which in effect would eliminate or greatly reduce the need for capital behind savings deposits. Counting loss reserves as a part of capital in the formula, and permitting larger tax-free reserves, would be a logical step forward.

2. Legislation or regulatory changes that would limit interest or dividends by mutual institutions whose reserves for losses do not come up to minimum standards. Stiffer requirements for allocation of earnings to reserves would serve this purpose.

While neither of these proposals may be politically feasible, they would, if strongly advocated, contribute to clearer thinking about the two types of savings institutions we have in our economy. With a better understanding of the two, we should be able to develop a public policy that would provide for the growth of both types, in an environment in which competition will occur between savings institutions in the market place, where it belongs, rather than between trade associations in the political arena, where it does not belong.

Public Policy and Time Deposits

Now for the second part of our main question: Should banks as a matter of public policy be encouraged to accept savings deposits? My answer to this part of the question also is "yes." The reason is simple. Unless banks do grow, and grow steadily and substantially, credit needs will not be met as fully or as efficiently as required for economic growth. Unless bank growth comes largely in savings deposits, it will not occur.

Although I am prepared to argue that commercial banks are efficient allocators of financial resources, in the interest of time, I merely call attention to their widespread distribution, their broad lending and investment powers, and their competent although frequently conservative management. With adequate time, I would present the case for a system of financial institutions in which the specialized intermediaries supplement and perhaps stimulate the more generalized and more adequately financed banks. A financial system in which the banks play a minor role among specialized giants would, in my opinion, be less efficient, less responsive to public needs, more unstable in the short run and less conducive to economic growth. I hope you agree.

As to the impossibility of banks growing very rapidly if they depend solely on demand deposits, I hope I have made that point in dealing with banks as individual firms. I do want to add, however, that the ability of banks to grow in demand deposits depends on monetary policy, and that an easy money policy such as would permit substantial growth in demand deposits would quickly become inflationary and unsustainable except in time of war — or perhaps severe depression. Why? Because we do not want — and our economy does not need — a rapidly growing money supply. But the economy does need a rapidly growing volume of savings.

Professor Pritchard showed very clearly that current savings transferred to nonbanking intermediaries do become invested and that no expansion in the banking system is necessary to accommodate this saving. He also demonstrated that without expansion of the banking system, current saving cannot be accommodated if savers choose bank savings deposits as their savings medium. He then concluded that the bank system will not expand or cannot expand, hence that savings deposits are lost to investment; and he stated that "the burden of proof is upon those who would contend that a shift from demand to time deposits will induce the Reserve authorities to follow an easier (or less restrictive) monetary policy." I accept this burden.

Let us see what would happen if people chose to let their "money" savings accumulate in savings deposits in the banks. Would the deposits become stagnant, as Professor Pritchard suggests? Or would they be "activated" by a monetary policy that permitted banks to expand, hence to "accommodate" the savings generated by their depositors? There is no question in my mind. I cannot conceive of a monetary authority that paid no attention to whether savings are accumulating in banks or in nonbanking intermediaries.

This point can best be answered, perhaps, by asking ourselves what we would do if we were the monetary authority and were faced with a return — or attempted return — of savings from nonbanking intermediaries back to the banks. For example, suppose for some reason people decided they would rather have their savings in banks than in savings associations. As associations began losing their cash balances, stopped making new loans, and increased their borrowings from the Federal Home Loan Banks, would we not begin to make reserves available to the banking system so that banks could buy some Home Loan Bank obligations, make some mortgage loans, or buy some bonds so that insurance companies could make some mortgage loans? And would the doing of these things not increase deposits so that the banking system could accommodate the attempted transfer of funds from associations to banks? The answers would have to be "yes" unless we were blind to the financial needs of our economy.

Savings deposits in banks are not stagnant, nor are they lost to investment. Our banking system can invest any amount of savings its depositors wish to accumulate, and monetary policy will make certain that this is so.

But monetary policy will also see to it that in prosperity the banking system does not grow beyond its depositors' desire to hold bank deposits. If banks are to grow, they must increase the demand for their special types of financial assets and decrease the demand for the types offered by nonbank intermediaries. At the moment, savings deposits are the only type banks have to offer for which the demand seems subject to very much increase. Therefore, banks should promote savings as a matter of self-interest, and banks should be encouraged to promote savings as a matter of public policy.

5

Should Commercial Banks
Accept Savings Deposits?–III*

Lester V. Chandler is professor of economics at
Princeton University. He is the author of *An Introduction to
Monetary Theory; The Economics of Money and Banking; In-
flation in the United States, 1940–48;* and *Benjamin Strong,
Central Banker.* Mr. Chandler earned his bachelor's and master's
degrees at the University of Missouri and his doctorate at Yale
University. He was formerly a faculty member of Dartmouth
College and Amherst College; price executive, Office of Price
Administration; associate director, Manufacturing and Industrial
Materials Division, OPA; and economist to the Subcommittee on
Monetary, Credit, and Fiscal Policy of the Joint Committee on
the Economic Report (1949–50). He is a past president of the
American Finance Association.

BOTH SPEAKERS HAVE RAISED THREE principal questions: First, are savings
deposits profitable for the banking system as a whole? Second, are
savings deposits profitable for the individual bank? And third, is it in
the public interest for commercial banks to accept savings deposits? We
have had something less than unanimous agreement here. I shall not
pretend that I know the truth, but I can perhaps spotlight some of the
reasons for the differences in judgment that you have heard.

I shall spend most of my time on the first question, namely: Are savings
deposits profitable for the commercial banking system as a whole? I am

* Proceedings of the Fourth Annual Conference, 1961, pp. 40–48.

going to take a fairly long view, allowing enough time for changes in institutional structure, changes in attitudes, advertising and that sort of thing, which seems to me appropriate in view of the nature of the debate.

Professor Pritchard's argument, as I understand it, is that the commercial banking system is not enabled to increase its earning assets at all when the public decreases its holdings of demand deposits and holds savings deposits instead. He believes that if all the banks refused to accept savings deposits, the public would merely shift its holdings to demand deposits, that the banking system in the final outcome would not suffer a decrease in its total earning assets and that banks would be more profitable because they would escape the payment of interest on savings accounts.

The Case with a Neutral Monetary Policy

I shall analyze this argument in several easy stages. To do so I shall use a highly simplified model in order to reduce the number of variables to be considered. Specifically, I shall assume that there is no net currency drain from the banking system and no net inflow of currency to the banking system, that legal reserve requirements against demand deposits average 15% and that reserve requirements against savings deposits are 5%.

Suppose, now, that the public shifts $1,000 from demand deposits to savings deposits. The immediate results will of course be to increase excess reserves by $100. Required reserves against demand deposits are reduced by $150 and required reserves against savings deposits are increased by $50. This can be stated as follows:

$$E = \$1,000 \ (r_d - r_s),$$

where E is the change in excess reserves, r_d is the required ratio against demand deposits, and r_s the required ratio against savings deposits. Endowed with $100 of new excess reserves, the banking system can proceed to expand its loans. If all the proceeds of the loans give rise to demand deposits, the amount of expansion will be $100/0.15 or $666.67. Summarizing the effects of all these operations, we find that the balance sheet of the banking system has been changed as follows:

Figure 1

Assets	Liabilities
	D − $1,000
	T + $ 666.67
Loans + $666.67	D + $ 666.67

Thus, the net change in bank liabilities will be an increase of $1,000 in savings deposits and net decrease of $333.33 in demand deposits. On the asset side there will be a net loan increase of $666.67.

I am sure that Professor Pritchard and Professor Edwards would agree that this would be the outcome if the central bank followed a "neutral" policy, that is, if it did not mop up the excess reserves. But Professor Pritchard contends that the central bank is unlikely to follow such a "neutral" policy. Instead, it will note the rise of net free reserves of the banking system and the easing of money market conditions, owing to the new loans that flow into it, and will mop up the newly created excess reserves to prevent a change in the credit situation. In this case, the banking system will not be permitted to expand its loans at all and the net outcome will be merely a $1,000 decrease in demand deposits and a $1,000 increase in savings deposits, on which the banks will now have to pay interest.

Long-Run Objective of Federal Reserve Policy

I approach the matter in a somewhat different way. I agree that in the short run the Federal Reserve often looks to such things as the status of excess reserves, member bank borrowings, and the degree of tightness or ease in the money markets. But surely a more basic and, over a longer run, a far more important objective is to secure some desired behavior of the level of spending for output — to achieve a certain level of GNP, or to cause the level of GNP to increase at some desired date. Let us suppose the Fed's objective is to achieve a certain level of spending for GNP which I shall designate as y_o.

Figure 2

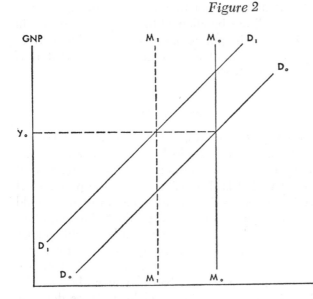

Quantity of money

I measure the quantity of money on the horizontal axis and the level
of GNP on the vertical axis. The amount of money that will be needed
for this purpose will depend, of course, on the public's demand for
money balances. This is illustrated on the chart by the line D_oD_o. Let
us assume that this is a demand for money balances on the part of the
community. Now, if we are to maintain this level of GNP measured
vertically, then the required money supply would of course be the line
M_oM_o. Any larger amount of money would give us an unwanted expansionary force and a smaller amount would prevent us from achieving
the desired level.

Suppose, now, that the $1,000 shift from demand to savings deposits
reflects an equal decrease in the public's demand for money balances.
This is shown on the chart as a $1,000 leftward shift of the demand func-
tion. Assume that we simply shift this demand function to the left by
$1,000, the new line being indicated by D_1D_1. It is perfectly obvious
that with the decrease in demand for money balances, there will be
created an excess supply of money at the y_o level of GNP, which will
exert an upward pressure on the rate of spending for output. If an
increase in spending is not to occur, then the money supply will have to
be reduced by an amount equal to the decrease in the demand function
for money. This means that the Federal Reserve will have to mop up all
the excess reserve created by the shift from demand to savings deposits
so that the banks cannot expand their earning assets at all.

Thus, it appears that whether you accept Professor Pritchard's assumptions that the Federal Reserve will act to prevent an easing of the money
market, or my assumption that it will act to prevent an unwanted rise
of GNP, the banking system will not be allowed to enjoy any increase in
its earning assets simply because the public has shifted its holdings from
demand to savings deposits. It would appear at this stage that it is
Pritchard, and not Edwards, who is right.

ALTERNATIVES TO TIME DEPOSIT BANKING

But the game is not over yet. Pritchard can claim to have established
his conclusion that the banking system would be better off if it did not
accept savings deposits at all only if he can get favorable answers to at
least two other questions. The first is this: What would the public elect
to hold in place of the savings deposits that are no longer available; would
it simply hold more demand deposits, or would it shift to holding other
liquid claims, such as accounts at mutual savings banks, credit unions,
or savings and loan associations? The second question is this: Are
accounts at other financial intermediaries as good a substitute for money
balances as savings deposits at commercial banks; will a shift by the
public from demand deposits to, say, savings and loan shares decrease

the demand for money balances as much as would an equal shift from demand deposits to savings deposits?

We can go along with Pritchard's conclusions only if we find at least one of these propositions to be true: (1) that the public, if deprived of savings deposits at banks, would shift most of these holdings to demand deposits; or (2) that accounts at other financial intermediaries are not nearly as good a substitute for money balances as are savings deposits at banks. If we grant Pritchard either of these propositions, we have probably granted him his case. We do not, of course, know what would happen, but I gravely doubt that Pritchard is right on either count. My guess is that if savings deposits at banks were not available, the public would hold instead, not more demand deposits, but more liquid assets of other kinds. In this they would not be exactly discouraged by credit unions, savings banks, savings and loan associations, and others. Beguiling advertising, free pencils and pressure cookers, and perhaps new services would all play their part in the process. Moreover, I suspect that these other liquid assets are as good, or almost as good, a substitute for money balances as are savings deposits. I believe that the public can and does reduce its demand for money balances by shifting to holdings of, say, savings and loan shares just as it does by shifting to savings deposits.

SHIFT TO SAVINGS AND LOAN ACCOUNTS

Let us see what would happen if the banks refused to make savings deposits available and if the public decided to shift $1,000 from demand deposits to savings and loan shares. The immediate effects on the balance sheets of the banks and the savings and loan associations would be as follows:

Figure 3

COMMERCIAL BANKS		SAVINGS AND LOAN ASSOCIATIONS	
ASSETS	LIABILITIES	ASSETS	LIABILITIES
	Deposits due public − $1,000 Deposits due savings and loans + $1,000	Deposits + $1,000	Shares + $1,000

At the banks, the only thing that would happen in the first instance would be that demand deposits owed to the public would go down by $1,000 and those owed to savings and loan associations would go up by $1,000. Then, the savings and loan associations would have plus $1,000 holdings of deposits and plus $1,000 liabilities in the form of shares. Thus far we see that the banks have experienced no change in their total deposits, their total reserves or their net reserve position, so their lending power remains unchanged. But the savings and loan associations have a $1,000 increase in their cash holdings. They can therefore increase their loans by that amount minus any amount they elect to retain as a reserve against the increase in their outstanding shares. Suppose they retain $50, or 5% of the increase in their shares, and lend $950 to the public. When this is all over, the change in their balance sheets from their initial position will be as follows:

Figure 4

COMMERCIAL BANKS		SAVINGS AND LOAN ASSOCIATIONS	
ASSETS	LIABILITIES	ASSETS	LIABILITIES
	Deposits due public − $50	Deposits + $50	Shares + $1,000
	Deposits due savings and loans + $50	Loans + $950	

For the commercial banks, deposits due to the public are down $50, deposits due to savings and loans are up $50 and, of course, the savings and loan associations will have increased their deposit holdings $50 and their loans $950. So at this stage we find that after the savings and loan associations have used the new funds, $50 has been used to increase their cash holdings and $950 to increase their loans. Still, the total deposits of the banking system remain unchanged.

But we are not yet through. The $950 increase of loans by the savings and loan associations is in addition to the supply of loanable funds and will presumably tend to lower interest rates and stimulate spending. If the Federal Reserve wishes to maintain the pre-existing degree of ease or tightness in credit markets, it will have to force the banks to reduce their deposits and their loans. In effect, the Federal Reserve will say to the banks, "Because the public has shifted its funds from you to the savings and loan associations, we are forcing you to reduce your loans."

Let me use here the same approach that I used earlier in connection with the public shift from demand deposits to savings deposits at banks. You will remember that I assumed that the $1,000 shift from demand to savings deposits reflected an equal decrease, a leftward shift, of the public's demand for money balances. Professor Pritchard did not, I believe, object to this assumption. I shall now assume that the $1,000 shift from demand deposits to savings and loan shares reflects an equal decrease in the public's demand for money balances. This creates an excess supply of money at the y_o level of GNP and generates an upward pressure on the rate of spending. To prevent any rise of spending, the Federal Reserve will have to reduce the money supply by an amount equal to the decrease in the public's demand for money balances, that is, by $1,000. The banks will be forced to decrease both their deposits and their loans by $1,000.

Let us now compare the two cases. In the first case, where the public shifted from demand deposits to savings deposits at commercial banks, the final outcome was that the banks were not permitted to increase their earning assets at all. The banks now had to pay interest on the $1,000 of new savings deposits but were permitted no increase in their lending power. In the second case, where the public shifted from demand deposits to savings and loan accounts, the final outcome was that the commercial banks had to reduce their loans by $1,000. Thus the moral would seem to be that if banks accept savings deposits they may not increase their total lending power, but if they do not accept savings deposits they will have to reduce their loans.

In short, I contend that it may indeed have been an unhappy day for the commercial banks when highly liquid assets were invented to compete with demand deposits. These other forms of liquid holdings tend to decrease the public's demand for demand deposits, or at least to slow their rate of secular increase, and thus to hold down the amount of earning assets that commercial banks can acquire by issuing this form of liability. Professor Pritchard is quite right, of course, in pointing out that commercial banks tend to compete with themselves when they issue savings deposits. I contend that highly liquid earning assets will be made available to the public anyway, and will be demanded by the public whether or not banks accept savings deposits. I have noticed no marked reluctance on the part of savings and loan associations, savings banks, credit unions and others to manufacture these liquid claims. My guess is that over a period of time — and I want to emphasize that this may not happen immediately — a refusal by commercial banks to accept savings deposits would bring about, not an increase in the public's demand for money balances, but a shift of funds from savings deposits to claims against these other institutions. Thus, the existence of other liquid claims may indeed reduce the profitability of commercial banking, but my point is that the profits of banking may be less adversely affected if banks continue to accept savings deposits, so that they, and not other types of institutions, hold the earning assets back of the various types of savings accounts.

THE CASE FOR INDIVIDUAL BANKS

This brings us to one of the other major questions: Is it profitable for the individual commercial bank to accept savings deposits?

Here again the answer is greatly affected by one's assumptions concern-

ing the source of savings deposits at the individual bank. One possibility
is that savings deposits at the banks represent merely a shift from demand
deposits at that bank, and that the demand deposits would have continued to be held at that bank even if it refused to accept savings deposits.
In such cases a bank would almost certainly reduce its profits by allowing
its own customers to shift from demand to savings accounts. But I doubt
the quantitative importance of such cases over a longer period. My guess
is that most savings deposits represent funds that would be shifted to
other institutions or other liquid earning assets if the individual bank
refused to pay interest on them. The individual bank would not have
the funds for free; it would not have them at all. In other words, in
determining its revenues and costs from savings accounts, a bank is in
much the same situation as a savings and loan association.

But even assuming that a bank would otherwise lose the funds represented by its savings deposits, is it profitable for the bank to accept
savings deposits? I must confess that I have little to contribute on this
subject except to deplore our lack of relevant information. I find it
impossible to interpret the various statistics that show lower percentage
profits on net worth for banks as the percentage of their savings deposits
to total deposits rises. These may indeed reflect faithfully the rates of
profits actually enjoyed on the over-all business of the banks. But they
cannot, of course, get directly to the crucial question: Would the bank's
profits be higher or lower if the bank divorced itself completely from all
savings deposit business? To answer this crucial question we need some
sort of accounting on the basis of marginal revenues and marginal costs.
I find it hard to believe that many banks, already equipped to do a
demand deposit business with all that it entails, would find that adding
on savings deposits would increase their costs more than it would increase
their revenues.

I do not see why a commercial bank should decrease its profits by
adding savings deposits to its demand deposit business, while mutual
savings banks operate profitably on the basis of savings accounts alone.
If this is the case, there must be something wrong about the portfolio
composition of commercial banks, or savings banks, or both. And the
appropriate remedy would be, not to take commercial banks out of the
savings business, but to review both government regulation and managerial policies relative to portfolios.

TIME DEPOSITS AND THE PUBLIC INTEREST

I turn now to the third question: Is it in the public interest for the
commercial banks to accept savings deposits? This involves several
issues. I confess that I cannot accept Professor Pritchard's argument

that the existence of savings deposits arrests the flow of savings into investment. I do agree that savings deposits are "stagnant" in the sense that they are not used as a medium of payment and have a velocity of zero. But exactly the same thing is true of savings deposits at mutual savings banks, accounts at credit unions, and shares of savings associations. They also have a velocity of zero. What Pritchard should add is that the existence of these near-money substitutes decreases the demand for money balances proper and frees money for spending. In effect, it increases the income velocity of money.

Professor Pritchard emphasizes his belief that if the banks refuse to accept savings deposits, the demand function for money balances would be larger; that is, the public would demand larger balances of demand deposits and other money relative to the level of GNP. I have already expressed my doubts about this. But suppose he is right; suppose that the public would indeed hold much larger money balances relative to GNP. I fail to see that this would be in the public interest. It might be profitable for the banks, which the monetary authorities would have to allow to create a larger volume of checking deposits and to acquire a larger volume of earning assets. But why be so solicitous about the banks rather than other financial institutions? Why try to deprive the public of attractive liquid assets that yield an income and try to force them to hold liquid assets that yield no income? I see no resulting public benefit that would justify depriving the public of such an attractive alternative.

In fact, such a policy, if it were successful, might well accentuate economic fluctuations by permitting an increase in the amplitude of fluctuations in the income velocity of money. The greater the holdings of money itself, in excess of the minimum amounts needed for current transactions, the greater the volume of so-called "idle balances" and the greater the scope for activating these "idle balances" under boom conditions.

Let me make one final point. I believe that it is in the public interest for banks to accept savings deposits in order to increase the mobility of loan funds among their various possible uses, especially in local markets. Some of the banks' closest competitors for savings tend to restrict their loans to a narrow range of purposes; funds gathered by savings and loan associations, for example, are channeled principally into home mortgages. But banks lend for a much wider range of purposes; their loans range all the way from consumer credit and short-term and medium-term business loans to mortgages. I believe, therefore, that a larger volume of lending power in the hands of the banks would increase the fluidity of credit within local markets. Perhaps this situation will be remedied in the future by a broader diversification of the types of loans made by savings and loan associations and mutual savings banks. But, at least until that time comes, it will be useful to maintain a large lending power by commercial banks in the interest of the fluidity of credit among uses.

Discussion*

MR. EDWARDS: Les Chandler stabbed me in the back in his presentation. This bothered me a little until a moment later he stabbed Lee in the back also, so we are both wounded. With reference to Professor Chandler's diagram, it seems to me quite obvious that over time the demand for money cannot continue to shift to the left as people build up their savings deposits; if it did, the time would come when there would be no demand for money at all. After a recession or after a war, when easy money really piles up, excess balances do shift from demand to time deposits and might produce this; but over a long time the demand for money balances is relatively independent of the quantity of savings people have, whether those savings are in the banks or elsewhere, and except for the economical use of cash the demand is more likely to shift to the right. My conclusion would be that if banks do not promote savings they will not shrink in size, they will just stay where they are; and if they do promote savings they will not retain their size, they will grow. Am I wrong in that?

MR. CHANDLER: I think your statement is factually true, but I do not agree with the conclusions. In other words, I would certainly expect that in a growing economy the demand for money balances will continually increase. But I think that with savings accounts available to people as a means of holding liquidity, the demand for money balances proper will not increase as much with these other things available as it would if these other things were not available. In other words, I think it is part of Leland's argument that if the banks refused to allow people to hold savings accounts, then people would hold, instead, largely more demand deposits.

MR. EDWARDS: No.[1]

MR. CHANDLER: Then I do not think your argument follows if this is not true.

MR. EDWARDS: That leads me right to my question, Lee. How big do you think the banking system would be today if it had no time deposits?

* Proceedings of the Fourth Annual Conference, 1961; Excerpts from the Discussion, pp. 49–62.

[1] Professor Edwards asks that his answer of "no" be explained as follows: "If people do not place their savings in bank savings accounts, they are much more likely to buy more savings bonds or to increase their savings and loan accounts or other income-producing near-monies than they are to add to their checking accounts. Whatever effect savings account balances have on the demand for money, that effect is likely to be the same no matter whether the savings accounts are in or out of banks."

MR. PRITCHARD: First, I should like to make a comment on this matter of the demand for money. In the first place, I do not think that the public is able to realize its demand for money. I am not saying that there may not be a shift, a change in its demand for money. I am not saying that a change in liquid asset holdings in the form of share accounts, and what not, will not change the public's demand for money. But I do believe that the changes in the demand for money cannot be realized. In other words, if the public increases its demand for money, that will be reflected in a decrease in the velocity of money. By the same token, a decrease in the demand for money is reflected in an increase in the velocity of money. Now, what happens if there is a decrease in the public's demand for money? If the public wants to hold less money, there is a stepup in velocity, a stepup in the tempo of business activity, and the banks will expand credit if the monetary authorities allow. In other words, the public will end up with more money than they had before, because they want less.

MR. EDWARDS: That just proves the point. The monetary authorities will not allow this to happen.

MR. CHANDLER: If the monetary authorities are that pliant, you are quite right; that is exactly what would happen. But I was assuming, with you, that they would not let it happen. Rather, they would say that they are aiming for — in your terms — a given degree of ease or tightness in the market, or — in my terms — a certain level of GNP, and if they see it running away they will step in and crack down.

EUGENE LERNER: I should like to cast the first stone. I think that Dr. Pritchard has practiced some slippery footwork here. The rise in velocity associated with inflation has to be analyzed in terms of both real and money balances; and unless it is specified just which one a person is referring to, some paradoxes can arise.

In his prepared talk, Dr. Pritchard begins with the assumption that the banking system always has all the money. It then seems clear that if demand deposits are costless and time deposits cost the bank 3%, the promotion of time deposits is foolhardy. This conclusion is not unfamiliar to the regulatory authority. It assumes the over-all view; like monopolists, it sees the industry schedules. How else can you rationalize its efforts to stop financial intermediaries from paying higher rates to their customers?

Once the perspective is changed to that of the individual firm — and Dr. Edwards does that — it becomes a new ball game. The conclusion that raising interest rates will not stimulate deposit expansion because others will retaliate is equivalent to saying growth industries should not raise wage rates to attract new workers because other firms will only raise their wage rates. I think the perspective of the firm, rather than that of the industry, suggests a different set of answers from the ones you give.

MR. PRITCHARD: In the first place, you are saying that the regulatory authorities are aware of this, and maybe some of them are. I have had personal correspondence which indicates that even the chairman of the Board of Governors thinks that banks actually pick up savings and pass them out the window, that they are intermediaries in the true sense of the word.

MR. EDWARDS: Oh, let me rise to his defense! You are the one who does not understand these things. I think a stronger case can be made that the monetary authorities in this country take a look at the change in quantities of currency in circulation and adjust the bank reserves so that this has no effect on the banking system. I think they take a look at the changes in time and savings deposits and provide reserves for these independently. So in terms of the kind of monetary policy we have in this country, reserves are made available to the banks to cover their increases in savings before the Board ever takes a look at the reserve positions on the demand side. In other words, the monetary policy assumes that the savings function is outside the banking system and that the banks to this extent are intermediaries.

MR. CHANDLER: Now, wait a minute, Eddie. Are you implying that their criteria are in the monetary system? Is it that somehow or other they want to achieve a certain quantity of money proper and therefore they supply the reserves for the quantity of money proper? Or do they have some other guides that are more basic?

MR. EDWARDS: I think they have some other guides which probably are more basic, the most important of which is the credit needs. Obviously, the people are trying to save money, and this needs to be loaned to somebody and invested; otherwise you get a classical downward spiral. And if savings accumulate outside the banking system in the intermediaries, they quickly become invested. The only way that they can become invested in a banking system (and I agree with Lee on this), assuming the banks are loaned up already, is for the monetary authorities to make additional reserves available to provide for this form of savings, and this I think they do. In other words, to get back to the question, if banks had no savings deposits the size of the banks would, in my opinion, be a whole lot nearer $114 billion than $185 billion. They would have been held to the lower amount by the monetary authority.

MR. PRITCHARD: I am inclined to agree that the banks are larger in the aggregate because of time deposit banking. But how much larger, no one can say. I think that the growth of time deposits does have an effect on monetary policy toward greater ease in the banking system. If you admit that, however, you admit that time deposits have a dampening effect on the economy, and that is a sufficient argument in itself to foster public policy to abolish time deposits.

MR. CHANDLER: Lee, this is the one part of your argument that I just do not understand. Let us take your pure case of a shift from demand deposits to time deposits. Immediately you say, "These are stagnant; they are dry." And yet, if we take your case of neutral money, it comes out quite clearly that the banking system can increase the volume of its loans. You must be assuming that if the public continued holding demand deposits, those would be turning over somehow, but that if it shifts to time deposits they will not turn over. I submit that there is at least a good chance that if the public simply held the demand deposits, those would have a velocity of zero, too.

MR. PRITCHARD: Exactly. But the reason that the public shifts into time deposits is that they obtain earnings; and if this opportunity were not provided, then they would shift into other types of earning assets, and the saving would then have an income velocity.

JOHN CLENDENIN: I should like to take the discussion back to a point Mr. Chandler tried to make and I think was enticed away from. This is something of a rhetorical question. On a purely practical public interest basis, may we not assume that the monetary authorities will control bank reserves with an eye to business activity, prices and gross national product? Hence, need we worry at all about the impact of savings account growth on money velocity?

MR. CHANDLER: At least in principle, monetary authorities should be able to so adjust the money supply as to compensate for changes in velocity. Particularly would this be true if you take a long-run view. They ought to be able to look at the rate of spendings, see whether that is behaving satisfactorily, and then adjust the money supply in whatever way it proved to be necessary, in view of velocity.

MR. CLENDENIN: And will this not be their major objective?

MR. CHANDLER: I would assume that over a longer period of time, it would be. I think it is very difficult to say precisely what they look at in the short run. They talk net free reserves and all the rest of it in the short run, but surely this is merely a sort of money market guide or a guidepost and they are looking at the more basic time. But it is of course very relevant, this question of which institutions grow how much.

MR. CLENDENIN: Quite true. But if my interest is in the social point of view, you have given me the answer I wanted and hurdled my real question. Is not the major issue before us here a free market allocation of resources within a country, and should we not therefore encourage or discourage commercial bank savings accounts with an eye to asking: Will this strengthen the free-market allocation of resources and make loan funds available more broadly on a competitive basis?

MR. PRITCHARD: Thank you, Mr. Clendenin.

MR. EDWARDS: Let me thank him, too, because I think the one thing that we need is for thousands of these unit banks to get off their duffs and do a better job of growth in their communities, or we need some extension of branch banking or something, so that more aggressive management will do so. Whichever way you go, there must be active solicitation of savings by the banks in local communities. Incidentally, if they succeed, if out in the hinterland all the banks grow on savings deposits and the Federal Reserve does not make any reserves available, the New York banks are going to holler loud enough for easy money that they are going to be taken care of, in my opinion.

Mr. Pritchard: I should like to say a word about growth. I have some figures for the last twenty years, from the end of 1939 to the end of 1959. During that period mutual savings banks grew by $27.1 billion; savings and loan associations, by $57.9 billion; life insurance companies, by $84.4 billion. Those are the three largest financial intermediaries, and their combined growth was $169.4 billion, or $10 billion less than the commercial banks alone grew in that twenty-year period.

6

Criteria of a Well-functioning Financial System*

B. Haggott Beckhart was in 1962, professor of banking at Columbia University. He is the author of *The Discount Policy of the Federal Reserve System;* co-author of *Foreign Banking Systems;* and co-author and editor of *The New York Money Market* and *Business Loans of Commercial Banks.* Mr. Beckhart earned his bachelor's degree at Princeton University, and his master's and doctoral degrees at Columbia University. He was formerly on the faculty of Princeton University and on the visiting faculty of the Universities of Melbourne and Sydney; director of research and consultant, The Chase Manhattan Bank; economic consultant, Equitable Life Assurance Society of the United States; and president, American Finance Association.

A FINANCIAL SYSTEM IS THE WHOLE congeries of institutions and of institutional arrangements which have been established to serve the needs of modern economies: to meet the borrowing requirements of business firms, individuals and government; to gather and to invest savings funds; and to provide a payments mechanism. The institutions may be publicly or privately owned, may be partnerships or corporations, may be specialized or nonspecialized in character. Whatever their legal or economic

* Proceedings of the Fifth Annual Conference, 1962, pp. 61–85.

character, either they have evolved over time in response to developing needs or they were established to meet specific credit requirements.

In their origins and growth, financial institutions have paralleled the rise of modern capitalism, both private and state. They could not develop until the barter economy of the Dark Ages gave way to the money economy of the Middle Ages and until that, in turn, was superseded by the credit economy of the modern age. The invention of double-entry bookkeeping; the evolution of the concept of negotiability and of negotiable instruments; the growth of the law of contracts, of real property, of partnerships and of corporations; the evolution of bonds, stocks, capital markets and stock exchanges; the growth of trade and commerce — all contributed to the rise of financial institutions. Their growth assisted in the accumulation of large aggregates of savings funds, which are a prerequisite to the establishment of huge capitalistic enterprises, turning out products in great quantity for an ever-widening market.

Capitalist and Communist Systems Compared

The functions rendered by the financial institutions of the private capitalistic economies of the Western world may be better understood if they are contrasted with those in communist nations. The Union of Soviet Socialist Republics and its satellites are money-using economies, as are the nations of the Western world. Money serves as a medium of exchange, as a unit of account, and as a storehouse of value. The structural organization of financial institutions, however, is relatively simple. It consists of one huge bank serving as both a central and commercial bank (the Gosbank in Russia), a network of savings banks catering to the needs of individuals, and a group of specialized institutions.

Financial institutions in the Soviet world are, on the whole, passive. Their function is simply that of financing and implementing the production plan. They do not initiate the establishment of enterprises; they do not engage in "creative capitalism." The production plan is first set forth in real terms, in terms of labor and raw materials, and is then translated into money terms. Once this is done, the currency and credit plans follow.

In implementing the credit plan, the manager of a branch of the Gosbank has no discretionary authority. He cannot select the entities to which the funds are loaned; he merely disburses funds according to plan. He must, it is true, see to it that loans are repaid on schedule, and in this way he acts as one of the control organs of the state and has responsibility for the fulfillment of the plan. His control is termed "control by the ruble."

In communist countries, the criterion of a well-functioning financial system is simply one which helps to implement the production plan. The financial structure of a competitive capitalistic society is much more complicated than that of a communist nation and the role of financial institutions is both more difficult and more important. Goods and services are produced not according to an all-embracing plan but mainly in response to price changes, which reflect varying intensity of demand on the part of consumers, business enterprise and government. Market competition is the principal factor determining the allocation of the factors of production — labor, raw materials, and capital. Financial institutions stand ready to finance those enterprises which, on the basis of market demand, are deemed most eligible. In financing these enterprises, financial institutions must be prepared to evaluate the credit standing of business firms, to pass judgment upon management, and to forecast the demand for products and services. Financial institutions in the Western world finance the evolving needs of the marketplace and they often stimulate those needs. They are active participants in the market plan.

To have funds to disburse, Western financial institutions must either create credit (as indeed does the Gosbank) or collect savings funds. The product mix must be such as to stimulate growth but not to induce inflation. In this process of disbursing and collecting funds, the rate of interest plays a highly significant role. It serves to ration the loan demand, it serves to cover the credit risk, and it serves to reward the thrifty. In the Soviet world the rate of interest has no economic significance, serving rather as a service fee to cover the bookkeeping costs of lending institutions. There is, however, a growing disposition in Russia to give more importance to the rate of interest as a cost factor in the allocation of resources.

The tasks of financial institutions in the free world are highlighted by this brief comparison with their counterparts in Soviet economics. They are not mere disbursers of funds. They assist in meeting the objectives of modern economies: the stimulation of growth within the framework of a stable price level; the promotion of full employment (in whatever way this may be defined); the strengthening of competitive forces; and the reduction of the amplitude of cyclical fluctuations. They may play their role well, they may play it badly, but they cannot play a neutral role. Their very existence affects the functioning of the economy.

RECENT SURVEYS OF FINANCIAL SYSTEMS

Financial systems should be reviewed and surveyed frequently in order to make certain they are meeting all productive credit needs at lowest cost and that there are no credit gaps. Two surveys have been made recently and a third is taking place. The two that have been completed are those by the British Radcliffe Committee[1] and by the American

---

[1] Report of the Committee on the Working of the Monetary System (London: Her Majesty's Stationery Office, August 1959).

Commission on Money and Credit.[2] The first was appointed and financed by the British government and the second, by private interests.

The Radcliffe Commission concluded that there were certain credit gaps in the British economy; these included the need for term loans on the part of farmers and small businessmen and the need for more liberal export credit guarantees. The Commission on Money and Credit proposed a number of structural changes in the American banking system. A third group, a royal commission, is at work now, studying and evaluating the Canadian financial system.

Periodic reviews of financial systems by groups of disinterested experts have great merit, and the proposals which emanate from such studies are often highly beneficial and constructive. The Radcliffe Committee was composed of disinterested experts, whereas the Commission on Money and Credit was a heterogeneous group of widely varying experience and background. In consequence, it made a smaller contribution than did its British counterpart.

FINANCIAL INSTITUTIONS IN WESTERN ECONOMIES

Financial institutions in the communist world are all state-owned and state-controlled. This is necessarily the case in economic systems in which private ownership is virtually nonexistent and in which financial institutions constitute an important part of the control apparatus of the state. Financial institutions in the Western world, on the other hand, are usually privately owned and managed, and thus subject to the continuous tests imposed by a competitive economy.

Private ownership and operation of the financial institutions in the Western economies are by no means universal. State intervention is very important and has taken the form either of the ownership of credit institutions or of the guarantee of loans. State ownership was very common in our own country prior to the Civil War and in recent years has been exemplified by a host of federal credit institutions. State guarantee of loans also has been very important, particularly in such areas as defense loans, rural credits, urban mortgage credits, small business loans and export credits.

State intervention has occurred for a number of reasons: economic, political, and social. Central banks are usually state-owned and, where they were not established as state banks, have been nationalized over the past generation. The purpose of state intervention in this field is to ensure direction of monetary policy towards a nation's economic goals. Nationalization, however, is not necessary to make certain that central

[2] *Money and Credit: Their Influence on Jobs, Prices, and Growth*, Report of the Commission on Money and Credit (Englewood Cliffs, N. J.: Prentice-Hall, Inc., 1961).

banks will not deviate from established economic policy. Even in those few cases, including the Federal Reserve banks, in which vestiges of private ownership still remain, central banks are what Lord Keynes termed mutualized institutions. Their activities and policies are state-oriented.

Western nations have intervened in the credit sectors of their economies for reasons other than ensuring full cooperation on the part of the central bank. These reasons include the desire to promote competition, to provide banking accommodations to remote areas, to provide savings facilities, to fill credit gaps and to facilitate international lending. A few cases will suffice to illustrate these points.

The Commonwealth of Australia established the Commonwealth Bank, now divided into a central and a commercial bank, to compete actively with the commercial banks. The State Bank of India, the successor of the Presidency banks, was nationalized in order to carry banking facilities to the remote areas of that country. Many nations have endeavored to stimulate and to gather savings through a postal savings system or through the establishment of special savings institutions. And Western nations frequently have intervened in credit markets to fill credit gaps in such fields as urban mortgage credit, agricultural credit, development credits and foreign lending. In the field of foreign credits, nations have embarked on joint ventures, illustrated in the case of the International Monetary Fund and the International Bank for Reconstruction and Development.

State intervention may occur, too, by reason of strong psychological undercurrents. Thus France in the early postwar period embarked on extensive programs of socialization which engulfed the four large deposit banks. They have, however, interestingly enough, maintained their own individuality and compete much as before. The wave of socialization which spread over postwar Europe barely missed the British joint stock banks. It was a period of rapid change, of upheaval, and of acute disturbances.

The upshot is that the Western credit structures are mixed in character. The trend, certainly since the Great Depression, has been in the direction of increased state intervention. In appraising this movement, one needs to keep in mind that a publicly owned credit institution may be quite as efficient or inefficient as one which is privately owned. It may be well managed or poorly managed. It is not, however, subjected to the rigorous tests of a competitive, profit-and-loss economy. It may be tempted to extend credits to state-owned enterprises on easier terms than to private enterprise. Whether publicly or privately owned, financial institutions must meet certain criteria if they are to serve well the needs of the growing economy.

STRUCTURAL CRITERIA

To function well, financial institutions must meet certain structural criteria. They must be able to provide facilities which are adequate to the growing needs and the changing requirements of an economy. They must be able to withstand shock and to sustain losses. They must be able to make provision for an efficient and competent management.

Adequacy usually is judged by the number of commercial banking or savings banking offices in relation to population, and was so measured years ago in studies by the League of Nations. By these standards, the American banking system is deficient. There are about 8,000 persons per commercial banking office in the United States as contrasted with 4,300 in the United Kingdom and 3,500 in Switzerland. There are about 25,000 persons per savings and loan office and 73,000 per mutual savings bank office in those states in which they operate. The evidence seems to indicate that the United States is underbanked. This conclusion is underscored by the fact that in some nations, such as Switzerland, the post offices render services offered here only by commercial banks, such as the furnishing of checking facilities.

ADVANTAGES OF BRANCH BANKING

The remedy for America's underbanked condition is a drastic liberalization of the laws respecting branch banking. Here I agree with the recommendation of the Commission on Money and Credit that commercial banks be given the right to establish branches over large areas — preferably over Federal Reserve Districts; that savings and loan associations have the same right; and that mutual savings banks, if incorporated under federal law, have like privileges. Lifting the restrictions now prevailing on branch banking would not only provide the country with more banking offices, but would also promote the mobility of funds from one part of the country to another and thus help reduce geographical differences in rates of interest.

Branch banking would not only provide more facilities but would also furnish better facilities. The branches of a large commercial bank are able to operate at lower cost than unit banks, are able to extend larger loans and are able to furnish specialized services such as trust services, investment advice and information respecting the credit standing of firms at home and abroad. Branches bring to each hamlet the specialized services of a large organization.

The United States in its early history fostered branch banking; the first and second Banks of the United States and the Bank of the State of Indiana are examples. The nation quite inadvertently, I believe, got shunted off on the road to unit banking when the 1864 revision of the National Bank Act, possibly through clerical error, changed the plural of the word "offices," where a national bank was to conduct its operations, to the singular. Various devices have been introduced in the effort to give our unit banking system some of the advantages of branch banking such as holding companies and correspondent relations, but no device can make a unit system comparable in efficiency to a branch system.

Branch banking on the part of all financial institutions, both commercial banks and financial intermediaries, has further advantages. It can provide for management succession in a way not possible for the unit institutions. It can shift staff from one branch to another, from positions of lesser to positions of greater responsibility. It can train future bank officers. It has the funds to send promising talent to banking schools. It can develop men of broad background, vision, and experience.

Unit banking would not survive in the United States were it not entrenched by law. In Illinois, branch banking is prohibited by the state constitution. Opposition to branch banking comes not only from the management of the unit banks, but also from many who sincerely fear the growth of financial monopoly. Often those who fear monopoly fail to realize that the small unit bank, facing no competition in a small locality, is frequently the true monopolist. Where branch banking is permitted by law, as in the state of California, it quickly demonstrates its competitive superiority over unit banking. There is a strong undercurrent in this nation working in the direction of branch banking. The increase in banking offices since the end of the war has taken the form principally of branches.

Branch banking systems are able to withstand shock and to suffer losses in a manner denied to unit banks. They can not only employ competent management but can diversify risk. One has only to recall that there was not a single bank failure in Canada or in the United Kingdom during the Great Depression, whereas 50% of our banks by number suspended operations. To be sure, the country now has the Federal Deposit Insurance Corporation, but we should strive for a banking system which, by reason of its own superior management and the quality of its assets, will endure. Branch systems have demonstrated their superiority in this respect.

A good financial system must be able to adapt itself readily to changing needs and requirements. On the whole, the American banking system has been able to adapt itself to the credit needs of the consumer and the capital needs of business enterprise. It has introduced the overdraft for consumer financing and the term loan for business finance. It has shown adaptability; it may indeed have shown too much zeal and initiative in that the innovations may have promoted instability.

The American financial system stands in need of structural changes. We have concentrated largely on the need for a liberalization of the laws respecting branch banking. Later on we will speak of the need for other structural changes, the need for specialization in lending function, the need for more savings institutions and the need for a cheaper payments mechanism. We have emphasized, too, the desirability of periodic reviews and appraisals of our financial system.

CRITERIA MEASURING CONTRIBUTION TO GROWTH

The basic test of a well-functioning financial system, whether in this or in any other nation, is its ability to finance credit needs, which contribute to economic growth, and to finance those needs in such fashion that inflation and economic instability are not engendered. The goal of credit policy is economic growth within the framework of a stable price level.

A financial system can, of course, in various ways finance the borrowing needs which are associated with growth. It can do so through the instrumentality of commercial banks and their credit-creating powers. It can do so through the instrumentality of financial intermediaries and their utilization of financial savings. And, finally, it can do so through the services of the capital markets in selling securities not only to financial intermediaries but also to individuals.

Industrial enterprises may finance their need for funds through the retention of earnings, and have done so in all nations since the end of the war. The importance of internal funds as a source of earnings reflects in part the sellers' markets which have prevailed through much of the postwar period, causing prices to be above "competitive levels." Self-financing is a form of forced saving and, as a form of forced saving, often stimulated by tax laws, may not be without disadvantage in periods, such as the years following the war, when individual savings are frequently deficient relative to demand. Self-financing, however, may not be as important in the decade of the '60s when competitive relationships are more fully established. Industry may have to rely more heavily on the financial system as a source of funds.

SPECIALIZATION IN LENDING FUNCTION DESIRABLE

My basic point of view is that growth needs must be financed and should be financed in such fashion that economic instability and inflation do not result. Many questions naturally arise: What borrowing needs should and what should not be financed? What borrowing needs should be financed by commercial banks and what by financial intermediaries? What debt instruments should be monetized? What controls, if any, should be exercised over qualitative standards in credit extension? Should financial institutions specialize in lending function?

To discuss the last question first, a financial system in which institutions specialize in lending function would seem to have the best opportunity of financing the credit needs of growth without causing instability or inflation. Specialized institutions become experts in various lending fields — in such areas as consumer credit, urban mortgage and agricultural credit — where lending procedures and techniques are vastly different.

Specialized institutions also are able to exercise independent judgment in evaluating credit risks. Judgment often becomes blurred in an institution which renders many functions. Thus the existence of the security affiliates in the 1920s caused commercial banks having such affiliates to give a preferred status in their loan portfolios to the securities underwritten and sold by the affiliates and to give a preferred position in their trust accounts to such securities.

An institutional separation of lending function is important, too, in preventing the monetization by commercial banks of those types of debt which are related to cyclical swings in business activity and which induce those swings. This debt comprises consumer installment debt, urban and rural mortgage debt, government debt and long-term corporate debt. The financing of debt of this character should be related to savings and, in being related to savings, should be extended by financial intermediaries.

It is quite true that if the funds at the disposal of the financial intermediaries are increased by the transfer of "idle" demand balances, deposit velocity will rise. This is tantamount to an increase in the money supply at former rates of turnover and will itself aggravate cyclical swings. Even so, the extent to which velocity can rise, if the money supply is held constant, is limited by the liquidity needs of the economy. Sooner or later, individuals and business enterprise will find that they cannot transfer additional amounts of demand deposits to the savings category. Depositors must have a certain volume of cash and demand deposits to fulfill liquidity requirements.

Specialization in lending functions is necessary to relate certain credit requirements to the credit-creating powers of commercial banks, and others to the money-using powers of the financial intermediaries. Specialization is needed to assure an expert and independent appraisal of credit risks. And, finally, specialization is needed to ensure the maturity of the assets of financial institutions being related to the maturity of their liabilities; in other words, to make certain that short-term funds are not used to finance long-term requirements. The use of short-term funds to finance long-term requirements aggravates the liquidity needs of certain financial institutions and may cause, and indeed often has caused, economic instability.

A fairly recent example is afforded by developments respecting the

German banking system following the First World War. In the decade of the '20s, the German banks financed the long-term credit needs of German industry, as was their practice prior to 1914. The lending banks, however, lacked the capital funds they possessed prior to World War I, which, in effect, had been used to finance the long-term requirements of German industry. Lacking long-term funds and making use of short-term funds to finance industrial requirements, the German banks found, once the Great Depression set in, that their assets became frozen and were not available to meet depositors' withdrawals. To be sure, such assets under these conditions might be transferred to a central bank. Such a transfer means simply that losses are socialized. And if the assets so transferred are large in amount, as was the case in Austria, the currency itself may be jeopardized and may have to be devalued. We cannot comfort ourselves by repeating in parrot fashion that central banks, as lenders of last resort, should take care of such situations when they arise. The central bank has no magic wellspring of funds. It can, to be sure, issue paper money; but the converting of all types of assets into paper money will, through inflationary consequences, serve as a very unjust and inequitable tax on the populace.

"Department Store" Financial Institutions

In the United States, commercial banks over the past fifty years have developed into department-store institutions. First came the establishment of the security affiliates prior to World War I. Then the Federal Reserve Act legalized the acceptance of savings deposits by national banks, permitted them to establish trust departments, and allowed them to extend loans secured by mortgages on farm land (the first time that mortgage loans had been authorized) and to establish overseas branches. As time went on, these powers were greatly liberalized. The only reversal occurred in the case of the security affiliates, which were outlawed by the Banking Act of 1933.

The great liquidity flood of the '30s caused national and state banks to enter vigorously into the field of consumer and mortgage credit and to begin to grant term loans. Through the war the banking system rapidly built up its portfolio of government obligations, which it liquidated in part in the postwar period in order to resume the prewar lending trends. The upshot is that loan-deposit ratios are high and capital-loan ratios are low. This in itself would not constitute a serious situation if the assets of banks were not long relative to their liabilities and if a large proportion of bank assets were not dependent for their repayment upon the receipt of income by individuals and corporations. Loan liquidation is related to future income — on occasion far into the future. Hence, a decline in income will have an adverse effect upon the banks and in turn upon income itself. In consequence, the banks look to Washington to maintain income. Washington, in its zeal to maintain and increase money income will, over the long run, take measures which will aggravate inflationary pressures. The creeping inflation which some economists excuse and justify may become the running or galloping inflation of tomorrow.

CLASSIFICATION OF CREDIT NEEDS

This brings me to the next section in my paper, which endeavors to classify credit needs with respect to their bearing on economic growth and stability. I suggest the following threefold classification:
1. Loans which make little or no contribution to economic growth and yet provoke economic instability and inflation.
2. Loans which may contribute to growth and yet at the same time may cause economic instability and inflation.
3. Loans which contribute to growth without inducing economic instability and inflation.

Admittedly, our classification of bank loans into these three categories represents, in part at least, a subjective evaluation. It is a classification, however, which is buttressed, I believe, by credit experience in this and other nations. Evaluations of the desirability or undesirability of certain types of loans underlie all legislation, attempting to regulate the assets which commercial banks and financial intermediaries may or may not hold. They also form the basis of the classifications of loans into those of an essential and those of a nonessential character which were set forth, for example, in this country during the time of the Korean war and which recently were established by the United Kingdom in its effort to correct the imbalance in its balance of payments.

CREDIT FOR SECURITY TRADING AND SPECULATION

In the first category — loans which make little or no contribution to economic growth and yet which induce economic instability and inflation — I would, for example, put loans to finance security trading and speculation. Stock market credit, the term used by the Federal Reserve officials, has made no or very little contribution to economic growth, has proved insensitive to interest rate change, has provoked cyclical fluctuations, and on occasion has played havoc with our balance of payments. These loans should be subject to strict control, and of course can be subject to such control under the terms of Regulations T and U. Certain loopholes in these regulations need to be plugged. Over-the-counter securities, which

have no loan value in brokers' portfolios, should fall subject to Regulation
U, governing the security loans of the commercial banks and other
lenders. Government obligations, too, save for those in dealers' inventories, should fall subject to special margin requirements.

A small amount of stock market credit is necessary for an efficiently
functioning securities market. The amount need not be large and is not
large in foreign financial centers. The current total of customers' credit
balances is probably ample to finance essential stock market credit needs.
Stock market credit should continue to be subject to high margin and
retention requirements — not less than the present requirements of 70%
and 50%, respectively.

What I have said respecting the control of stock market credit does
not apply to loans to finance the distribution of securities passing rapidly
into the hands of investors, or to loans to finance seasonal shifts in the
inventories of security dealers. Both types respond quickly to interest rate
change, and a well-functioning financial system will finance these credit
needs without, at the same time, financing speculative borrowings on
securities.

This brings us to the second type of loan, that which may, whether it
stimulates growth or not, induce cyclical instability and inflation. This
type of loan includes cyclical working capital loans, related largely to
business inventory fluctuations; consumer credits, related primarily to
consumer demand for durable goods; urban mortgage loans, related
principally to home construction; and plant and equipment loans. All
these loans are concerned with the kind of activity which, although it may
in varying degrees be related to growth, is nevertheless characterized by
cyclical change. Eliminate the cycle in these areas and the cycle itself
will largely vanish.

Working Capital Loans

Working capital loans, in between the seasonal and the term loans
of commercial banks, make up a large proportion of the business loans
of commercial banks. They were given impetus in England by the
substitution of the overdraft for the inland bill, a development which
divorced loans from specific transactions. They were promoted in Canada
by Section 88 and correlative sections in the Bank Act, which confer
certain legal safeguards on banks extending this type of loan. They are
abetted in American bank portfolios by frequent renewals of promissory
notes and by the practice of revolving credits.

Working capital loans are difficult to control; indeed the Commission
on Money and Credit had no remedy for this particular problem. Their
heterogeneous character does not lend itself to selective credit control.

They are, theoretically at least, subject to more control in the United Kingdom where the businessman borrows from only one bank. They can have a very unstabilizing effect upon the economy, as the developments of 1919–1920 demonstrated. They are not self-liquidating.

In view of the nature of working capital loans, it is questionable whether commercial banks in a well-functioning financial system should grant such credits unless the lending bank possesses long-term offsetting liabilities in the form of capital funds, savings accounts, or debentures. In the absence of such long-term liabilities, working capital loans can best be financed from the equity funds of business enterprise, from the capital market, or from loans extended by financial intermediaries.

The individual commercial banker, because of his own special interests, has a responsibility for the control of these loans through continuous review of the financial statements of borrowing firms. Bank examiners, too, have a responsibility to seeing to it that banks with a large volume of such loans have an adequate cushion of capital funds (not less than 25% of such loans) and sufficient earning power to care for possible losses. Some nations attempt to exercise a certain measure of control by requiring commercial banks to maintain large liquid (financially liquid) reserves.

Consumer or Installment Credit

The other types of loans in this particular category, you will recall, are consumer credit, mortgage loans and loans to finance plant and equipment expenditures. Consumer credit — or, more particularly, installment credit — is deeply embedded in modern social usage, is related principally to the purchase of durable goods, and is to be found in varying degrees in all industrially advanced nations. Installment credit is more important relatively in the United States than in the United Kingdom and more important there than, for example, in Switzerland. Its use is spreading and, as we all know, the volume of installment credit has increased greatly since the end of the war, being related to such factors as the increase in the quantity and price of durable goods; the reductions occurring in down payments and the lengthening of maturity terms; the introduction into this field of various new techniques such as the overdraft; the rapid increase in family formation; the spreading use of installment credit to such items of consumer expenditure as travel, consumer soft goods, etc.; and perhaps, finally, to a decline in the quality of such credit. Among all these factors there has been action and reaction, and all have combined to increase the total volume of such credit.

Probably only a relatively small amount of installment credit contributes to growth. The part that does includes, for example, loans extended to a family that formerly sent its laundry out, to purchase a washing machine; loans extended to a workman to purchase a car which he needs in his employment; loans extended to a student to go to college. Many installment loans simply enable families to purchase status symbols. Better for them and for the economy if they were to save their funds to purchase goods of the kind that do not contribute to economic growth.

The consumer demand for durable goods, however little or much it may be related to growth, does have cyclical attributes which, for the good of the economy, need to be repressed. This can be done through the control of terms, in particular through control of the maturity of such credits. General credit control is ineffective. Installment credits are relatively insensitive to interest rate change. Selective control is required and has been introduced in all nations in which consumer credit has become important. Denmark has found an easy way to enforce controls simply by stipulating that all contracts made in violation of the regulations are null and void.

It is important, then, to set a ceiling on maturity terms; to make the buyer fully aware of the interest rate and of other charges which he is incurring; and to channel such loans through financial intermediaries such as co-operative banks and mutual savings banks. The commercial banks would extend such loans only as they possessed offsetting savings funds compartmentalized in separate savings departments. Consumer credit is a leading and amplifying force in cyclical fluctuations, generating economic instability and calling for selective credit controls.

URBAN MORTGAGE LOANS

What I have said with respect to installment credits applies with the same force to urban mortgage credits. The net flow of funds into mortgages in the postwar period has resulted not only from increased construction but from a rapid rise in loan-to-value ratios and from an increase in loan maturities. These developments, related directly to federal insurance and guarantees, have reduced the rate at which mortgage loans are repaid, have caused a sharp increase in borrowing, and have been responsible in no small measure for the inflation which has plagued the real estate markets. The inflation, in turn, has stimulated further borrowing. Government intervention in the real estate markets since World War II has inflated costs and diminished the rate of mortgage repayment. Government intervention has introduced great instability by reason of rigid interest rate ceilings.

A well-functioning financial system will try to see to it that the mortgage credit demand is met in such fashion that inflation and instability are not engendered. To achieve these goals the government should abandon its insurance and guarantee programs and should also eliminate all interest rate ceilings.

By reason of legal problems, of intricacies of appraisal and of maturity terms, the urban mortgage loan is one which should be extended by specialized savings institutions. Such institutions have developed in this and other nations, and include the mutual savings banks, savings and loan associations, the Crédit Foncier of France, and the Hypotheken banks of Germany. Mortgage lending institutions need to be linked together by central mortgage institutions which can extend loans to member institutions in case of need and which can grant member institutions access to the capital markets.

Residential construction has in the past exhibited wide cyclical swings. These swings are intensified if mortgage credits are the result of credit creation. The cyclical swings in the mortgage loans granted by commercial banks exceed those extended by other financial institutions.

The prerequisite for a mortgage market intent upon making its contribution to growth and stability is the withdrawal of government intervention. Intervention was prompted by the Great Depression and the desire to revive the construction industry. The terms then established for insured loans were conservative. But over the years they have been greatly liberalized, with the consequence that the building boom following World War II has been marked by a sharp inflationary trend which was absent from the building boom following World War I. The prerequisite for a well-functioning mortgage market is not only one devoid of government intervention but one which relies upon the funds of savings institutions, linked together by central mortgage banks. Economic rather than sociopolitical considerations should govern lending policies.

FINANCING PLANT AND EQUIPMENT

The fourth type of loan which promotes growth but which, in stimulating growth, may cause economic instability is that to finance plant and equipment expenditures. These loans, like the other loans which we have discussed in this section, should be extended by financial intermediaries or should emanate from the capital markets. The experience of commercial banks with loans to finance capital expenditures, save in those cases in which their capital funds and offsetting long-term liabilities were large, has not been a particularly happy one. The reason is that the lending banks become victims of the buoyant psychology marking the upward phase of the business cycle and lend freely to companies to expand their plant and equipment, which in turn adds a further stimulus to the upward sweep of the cycle.

American commercial banks in the middle '30s began to grant term loans, subject to amortization, extending over a period as long as ten years. Initially, these loans were extended by large banks to those industries deemed relatively immune from cyclical change; now they are granted by all banks to all industries. In being subject to periodic repayment, term loans are superior to the capital loans of indefinite tenure which were granted so frequently in the past. They have won favor abroad, and their use is commended to British bankers in the Radcliffe report.

Despite the current popularity of term loans, we raise the point whether, in a well-functioning financial system directed toward the goals of economic stability and growth, such loans should be extended by commercial banks unless they possess a sizable buffer of capital funds or of debentures. Otherwise funds for capital expansion should be obtained from the internal earnings of business enterprise, from the sale of stocks and bonds, and from financial intermediaries. Specialized institutions such as the Banques d'Affaires of France seem admirably fitted to make capital loans to industry. They are equipped to judge long-term credits; and in the days of their greatest activity prior to World War I, they extended investment credits from savings funds. Development banks, too, can play an important role in financing the equity needs of new and small business; in reality, they can supply risk capital requirements.

What I have said relative to loans extended to finance plant and equipment expenditures applies with equal force to issues of state and local governments. They are floated principally to finance the construction of highways and schools and thus may contribute to growth; but if these issues are sold to commercial banks, they may well stimulate economic instability. And the amount purchased by commercial banks in the postwar period has been extremely large by reason of the tax-exempt features pertaining to these securities.

Financing Marketing of Seasonal Goods

Finally we come to the loans which contribute to growth without causing economic instability. These are the loans extended to finance seasonal expansions in production as well as the marketing of goods. It is peculiarly fitting that commercial banks finance these particular credit needs. Loans associated with these requirements are self-liquidating and thus constitute an ideal basis of the money supply.

These particular credit needs — seasonalities in production and the marketing of goods — have been financed in many ways by the commercial banks by the use of the overdraft, the promissory note, and the banker's and trade acceptance. The form of financing is not so important as the nature of the underlying transaction. It should be noted, however, that the use of the promissory note, accompanied by the requirement of compensating balances, raises the cost of financing to the borrower in the United States as contrasted with the use of the overdraft in the United Kingdom. It also should be noted that branch banking systems are better able to finance varying seasonal requirements in production than are unit systems. Branch systems may, in effect, shift funds about through the banking system, financing requirements as they arise in this or that area of the country.

The inland bill of exchange, i.e., the trade acceptance, seems admirably fitted to finance the marketing of goods within a nation. Although its use in the United Kingdom has been superseded by the overdraft and in the United States by the promissory note, it still is employed in other nations such as Brazil, Finland, France, Russia and Sweden, to mention a few. Indeed, it is the principal type of short-term credit instrument in the USSR.

FINANCING NEEDS OF CENTRAL GOVERNMENTS

There is a credit sector of which we have not spoken — perhaps the most important of all — that having to do with the borrowing requirements of central governments. In the face of large increases in the public debt such as those which occurred in World Wars I and II, a financial system is hard put to prevent inflation. A large portion of the debt is placed with commercial and central banks, causing rapid increases in the money supply at the very time that the supply of goods available for consumers is dwindling. The inflationary consequences of more money chasing fewer consumer goods may be suppressed during the period of hostilities by price and rationing controls. Eventually the excess liquidity engendered by monetary expansion breaks out of bonds to provoke a sharp though delayed reaction. The reaction may cause a marked depreciation in the currency and at times even its repudiation.

During World War I, the increase in commercial and central bank credit in the United States took the form of loans secured by government obligations. During World War II, the increase took the form of purchases of the public debt. The inflationary consequences of the particular method used to finance World War II were aggravated by the decision to continue pegging the interest rate curve.

Public obligations have become one of the most important debt instruments of the modern age. They constitute the principal, and in some cases the only, asset of central banks; they constitute an important part of the assets of commercial banks and of financial intermediaries; and they constitute the main investment for short-term foreign funds in the New York and London money markets. The fact that they have greatly increased over the past fifty years and the fact that the increase was financed to a large extent on the basis of central and commercial bank credit expansion have caused the present era to be termed the age of inflation.

CANONS OF DEBT MANAGEMENT

Financial institutions must function within a credit environment established by modern states. Their ability to function well, *i.e.*, to promote growth and not to stimulate instability or inflation, is contingent in part upon the policies of the Treasury in the management of the public debt. At the risk of seeming pretentious, I have taken the liberty of listing certain canons of public debt management:

1. The central bank, in fulfilling its responsibilities of credit control, should have the primary obligation of influencing rates of interest in the short- and long-term money markets.
2. The Treasury should adjust its own debt operations to the rates of interest prevailing in the short- and long-term money markets as conditioned by the supply of and demand for loanable funds and as influenced by central bank action.
3. The Treasury should, in the financing and refinancing of the debt, place its obligations largely with investment and not with liquidity holders, and no ceiling should exist on the coupon rate which the Treasury may pay on government securities.
4. The Treasury should maintain a balanced maturity distribution of the debt. (In the United States, massive advance refunding operations comparable to the Canadian refunding of 1958 are necessary to restore the type of maturity distribution which prevailed before World War II.)
5. Any increase in the federal debt in recession should be matched rigorously by a decrease in the succeeding upturn in business activity.
6. The long-run policy of the federal government should be to reduce the debt.

Problems of debt management were eased after the Civil War and World War I by the substantial reduction taking place in total federal debt. Instead of declining, the debt since the end of World War II has increased. The increase taking place has passed into the hands of liquidity holders, state and local governments, and foreign commercial and central banks. Holdings by state and local governments anticipate expenditures on roads and schools, and holdings by foreign commercial and central banks reflect our adverse balance of payments. The fact that such a large proportion of the federal debt is held by those interested primarily in liquidity — fair-weather holders — renders our commercial and central banking systems vulnerable in case these holders wish to reduce their portfolios. They can do so in rapid fashion only as commercial bank credit expands.

The Treasury must not be given a privileged position in the market; it must be willing to compete for savings funds. The rise of debt in recession should, as I have indicated, be matched by a decline in prosperity. If this were the case, the cyclical swings in federal debt would tend to offset cyclical swings in bank loans arising from the inventory cycle. In the long run, let us say through the decade of the '60s, the federal government should budget for a surplus to reduce debt. Debt reduction will help to augment the savings funds which will be urgently needed. A financial system subject to the importunities of a Treasury cannot function well.

CRITERIA DIFFERENTIATING CREDIT DEMANDS

To recapitulate some of the points which I have tried to make in this section:

1. Certain types of credit demand, such as that arising from security speculation, make no or very little contribution to economic growth and yet provoke cyclical disturbances. This type of credit demand should be subject to strict control through the imposition of high margin and retention requirements.

2. Certain types of credit demand, such as those arising from cyclical fluctuations in inventories, from consumer demand for durable goods and housing, and from plant and equipment expenditures, while contributing to growth, do provoke cyclical fluctuations. Credit demands of this type should be met by financial intermediaries.

3. Finally, the credit needs arising from seasonalities in production and from the marketing of goods are appropriate for commercial bank financing.

These statements are based upon several premises. First, credit institutions best serve the goals of economic policy (growth in the absence of cyclical fluctuations) if they specialize in lending function. Second, the present trend in the United States toward department-store banking or one-stop banking will aggravate cyclical fluctuations and inflationary trends. Third, the impact of the monetization of certain types of debt by commercial banks, such as consumer and mortgage credit, upon the economy is different from that of the monetization of self-liquidating bills. Fourth, the maturity of the liabilities of a financial institution should govern the maturity of its assets; borrowing short and lending long have caused the breakdown of many commercial banking systems. Fifth, commercial banks should play a passive role in economic development; the financial intermediaries, including the development banks, should play the dynamic role in stimulating growth.

Our task was to discuss the criteria of a well-functioning financial system. On the basis of our criteria, perhaps we should conclude that our own system is not well-functioning. American commercial banks have monetized all types of debt since the end of World War II and doubtless will continue to do so. In my opinion, this means that we will experience continuous inflationary pressures and, in time, possibly may have to resort to the devaluation of the dollar.

Trends in commercial bank portfolios mean that the Reserve Banks will have to give continuous attention to changes in the financial statements of the commercial banks. They will need to note changes in the ratio of equity funds to risk assets, of liquid assets (financially liquid assets) to deposit liabilities, and of long-term assets to long-term liabilities. They must be given power to apply selective credit control not only to security loans but also to such areas as consumer credit, mortgage credit, and term loans. They must stand ready to change reserve requirements and to operate vigorously in the open market. Changes in the character of commercial bank portfolios which we are now experiencing demand constant supervision and intervention by the central bank. This would not be required save in minor degree if the portfolios of commercial banks consisted of self-liquidating bills.

STIMULATION AND COLLECTION OF SAVINGS

A growing economy needs a large volume of savings in order that expanding capital needs may be met in noninflationary fashion. In communist economies, savings are forced, taking the form principally of taxes levied on the consumer and embodied in the price of the commodities which the consumer buys. In capitalist economies, savings used to finance social capital needs are largely forced and those used to finance gross private domestic investment are largely induced.

A well-functioning financial system may itself play an important role in the stimulation of individual savings: (1) through establishing savings institutions adequate in number and convenient in location, and (2) through offering saving plans and programs with widespread appeal.

Specialized savings institutions take many forms: credit unions, mutual savings banks, postal savings banks, savings and loan associations, insurance companies and investment trusts. Such institutions are interested in promoting thrift. They have a singleness of purpose absent in the case of the department-store commercial bank. The time departments of commercial banks are a side line to other and, from the point of view of bank management, often more significant activities. As a side line, the time departments of commercial banks are given support when interest rates are rising and high, and are not promoted when interest rates are falling and low. Specialized savings institutions are directed toward the saver; the commercial bank, toward the borrower. The psychological attitude of the one is vastly different from that of the other.

Specialized savings institutions can play a more important role than they do in the stimulation of savings in the United States. Mutual savings banks exist in only seventeen states and are often limited in their ability to establish branches. The postal savings system could itself be used to stimulate savings and to use those savings in the purchase of the public debt.

Again, a well-functioning financial system can stimulate savings by offering savings plans and programs of wide appeal. An example is the packaged savings plan offered by some mutual savings banks, combining a deposit account with the purchase of a life insurance policy and federal redemption obligations. Insurance companies concerned over inflation have begun to issue variable annuities. Various governments, too, have tried to tailor their obligations to individual preferences by offering purchasing-power bonds to the thrifty and lottery bonds to the speculatively minded.

Although there are many motives for thrift on the part of individuals, a well-functioning financial system may itself help to stimulate savings through the establishment of specialized savings institutions and through offering savings plans and programs of wide appeal.

EFFICIENT PAYMENTS MECHANISM

A well-functioning financial system must be able to transfer funds cheaply and efficiently. This is a mechanical but highly important function. In English-speaking nations, transfer is accomplished by the use of checks, and, on the continent of Europe, mainly by what is termed the giro system. The transfer of funds by check takes place quickly but at higher cost to the depositor than equally quick transfers under the giro system.

With the advent of automation, the giro system, if operated by post offices, could become an instantaneous means of transferring funds from one depositor to another wherever located in the country. If a financial system were being established *de novo*, as is the situation with many developing nations, the giro system might well be introduced as superior to the check system. Individuals would maintain their household ac-

LEWIS AND CLARK COLLEGE LIBRARY
PORTLAND, OREGON   97219

counts with post offices, which upon request would effect a quick and cheap transfer.

The giro system has intrigued various banking committees of inquiry in the British Commonwealth, including a committee in New Zealand and also the Radcliffe Committee. The interest of the Radcliffe Committee in this system stemmed from its conviction that the joint stock banks did not cater to the needs of the wage-earning classes, who, like other groups, stood in need of a cheap and efficient transfer system. To forestall the introduction of the continental system, the joint stock banks rushed to introduce special checking accounts and also a credit clearing. The credit clearing permits anyone in the United Kingdom, whether depositor or not, to place cash with a bank for transfer, at a small fee, to anyone else in the country. The nationalized industries of Britain, as well as other concerns, are beginning to attach credit transfer forms to their bills, facilitating the payment of the amounts owed.

The transfer of funds, a mechanical function, in a well-functioning financial system could best be undertaken by post offices, which reach into every hamlet. If the post offices were to have this responsibility, the giro system would necessarily be adopted.

ROLE OF THE CENTRAL BANK

In our hypothetical model of a well-functioning financial system, the role of the central bank would be a modest one in contrast to the responsibilities which it shoulders in the actual world. The central bank would probably issue bank notes, although this function could be performed equally well by commercial banks. It would doubtless hold the reserve balances of commercial banks, primarily, to expedite the clearance of checks and, secondarily, to influence the volume of bank credit. It would hold the gold and foreign exchange reserves of the nation. It would make loans to commercial banks by rediscounting their paper to finance seasonal credit needs and to enable funds to be shifted from one part of the country to another.

The gold and foreign exchange reserves held by the central bank would not need to be large. Our hypothetical model assumed that trade barriers would be minimal and that goods would clear against goods. International liquidity would rest upon goods and services moving swiftly across frontiers. The picture which we paint bears marked resemblance to the Victorian period.

We are far removed from a world of this character. The present-day responsibilities of central banks result from economic and political developments of the past 50 years. These developments date from the large government deficits of World War I and the effect of these deficits upon the portfolios of commercial and central banks. They had their origins, too, in the attempts of nations in the interwar period to try to "protect" their economic position by tariffs, import quotas, foreign exchange controls and like impediments to trade and capital movements.

BANKS AS INSTRUMENTS OF NATIONAL POLICY

The two world wars and the Great Depression caused commercial banking systems to become instrumentalities of national policy. They were drafted, as in Germany, into the task of financing rearmament. They were expected to coin government securities into bank credit and to maintain prices on the bond market. The change occurring in the portfolios of the commercial banks brought about a close relationship between short- and long-term rates of interest, between the money and the capital markets. The change occurring in the portfolios of commercial banks also caused bank practitioners and theorists to begin to define liquidity in terms of shiftability. Central banking statutes were changed so that assets of every description could be shifted to the central bank. It became, indeed, the bank of last resort in the sense that it stood ready to monetize all debt instruments.

Defining liquidity in terms of shiftability prompted commercial banks to add further to their long-term assets. In this they were stimulated by the fact that long-term rates of interest have stood above short-term rates over much of the past thirty years. The distinction between credit and savings tended to disappear in the monetary literature. Indeed, Lord Keynes affirmed that there was no distinction. Bank credit was used not only as a substitute for savings but also as a substitute for the adoption of constructive economic policies. Thus, in the '20s, the loans extended to German industry by American commercial banks enabled that country to discharge in a financial sense its reparations which should have been discharged by exports of goods and would have been so discharged if American tariff rates had been lowered instead of raised.

As commercial banking systems to an increasing extent became servants of the state, the doctrine arose, paradoxically enough, that monetary policy could not be employed to influence fluctuations in prices and business activity and that fiscal policy must necessarily take its place. Those who held to this point of view reasoned that if monetary policy were restrictive enough to influence the economy, it would plunge the nation into deep depression. A rise in long-term interest rates would, so it was alleged, cause the bond market to sink into a bottomless pit.

Low interest rates had, therefore, to be continued in order to prevent the economy from collapsing and to stimulate growth. Through the war and early postwar period, many reasoned that economic stagnation lay ahead: the future would be marked by lower, not higher, rates of interest. This doctrine reached its apogee when Sir Hugh Dalton issued the 2½%

consols shortly after the end of the war. Moreover, this school of thought argued that, should perchance inflation and not deflation be our fate, fiscal policy represented the only effective remedy. Those who advocated reliance upon monetary policy received hoots of derision until its efficacy was demonstrated in such countries as Belgium, Italy, and Western Germany.

Role of Financial Intermediaries

In our well-functioning financial system, the commercial banking system will, as we have remarked, play a role of lesser importance than it does at the present time. Financial intermediaries, including the development banks, will be the active dynamic institutions. Financial savings will be differentiated from bank credit. Interest rates, short- and long-term, will not be as closely related as they are in the real world in which we live. Cyclical fluctuations will be less, the danger of inflation more remote, gains in productivity more likely to be passed on to the consumer.

Even in this ideal world, the central bank will have to exercise some measure of credit control. I am not so unrealistic as to suppose that all the bills drawn will be true bills. The central bank must therefore, as did the Bank of England prior to World War I, closely follow developments in the bill market, warning against deviations from good practice and raising its bank rates in case of need. The increase in the bank rate will evoke responsiveness on the part of commercial banks and their borrowers.

Of course we do not have this type of world, nor are we likely to achieve it. In consequence, the central bank must ever be ready to intervene in the market, making use of all its monetary instruments, the bank rate, selective credit control, changes in reserve requirements and moral suasion. Even such measures cannot be used to their full effectiveness in an economy wedded to doctrines of full employment and growth.

Many years ago, Irving Fisher used to refer to the veil which monetary institutions caused to be drawn over real phenomena. My plea, if I have one, is that we tear aside this veil, that we give emphasis to the real phenomena in our society and that we regard the commercial bank credit system simply as a refined type of barter.

Model Financial System

The time has arrived to summarize the attributes which I believe a well-functioning financial system should possess:

1. It should be able to perform well certain mechanical functions such

as the clearance and collection of checks. This function could be rendered more efficient, perhaps, by a post office giro system than by the use of checking accounts.

2. Financial institutions — commercial banks and financial intermediaries — must be adequate in number and location to serve efficiently the needs of a community. Branch banking serves the requirements of a nation better than does unit banking.
3. A modern state should, through a diversity of institutions and debt instruments, endeavor to stimulate thrift.
4. A well-functioning financial system will possess a host of institutions which will specialize in lending function.
5. A well-functioning financial system is one in which there is a minimum of state intervention in the form of loan guarantees and insurance, of attempts to control interest rate levels, etc.

Such a system would, in my opinion, serve well the interests of a people. In serving their interests, it would promote economic growth. I am not sanguine, however, that we will establish such a system in this or other nations. In consequence, we must reconcile ourselves to continuous inflationary pressures. These pressures will be interrupted from time to time by increases in the price of gold, which will be blamed not upon the policies which we have adopted but upon speculators, who are always the scapegoats of erroneous action.

Discussion *

THEODORE ECK: I wonder whether we can actually achieve the goal here of balancing the maturities that borrowers prefer with the maturities that the lender is willing to extend. We have had an obvious preference of lenders for deposit-type savings, that is, at least implied liquidity; could we reasonably expect these intermediaries to be able to attract sufficient lines of long-term money to support long-term lending?

MR. BECKHART: I think we have to be governed by past experience. The life insurance companies during the Great Depression encountered no particular liquidity problems; that is, their inflow of funds right through the depression exceeded the outflow of funds. Mutual savings banks also, in the main, experienced no liquidity problems; there were only a few failures among mutual savings banks in New York state.

I think our past experience points to the desirability of offsetting assets and liabilities of closely similar maturities. It also points to the desirability of financial intermediaries building up a portfolio of long-term securities, as do the insurance companies and, to a lesser extent, the

* Proceedings of the Fifth Annual Conference, 1962, Excerpts from the Discussion, pp. 85–94.

mutual savings banks. Deposit turnover in a mutual savings bank is much less than that in a commercial bank, even in the case of the time deposits of commercial banks. This smaller rate of deposit turnover, as well as the nature of the deposits, warrants the acquisition of long-term assets.

I believe it would be perfectly feasible for financial institutions to bring about this matching, and may I again refer to experience in Europe. If one will look at the financial statement of the Swiss banks, he will find on the liability side the item "debentures" which are sold in the market; the holder may in turn sell them at any time, and the price he gets will depend upon the coupon rates as measured against the market rate of interest. On the asset side are the time loans of the Swiss banks. Thus, they do match one against the other. The Belgian banks and the Dutch banks are beginning to issue debentures, too. So I think there is a certain merit in trying to match the longevity of assets by liabilities. And I believe that financial intermediaries, by offering attractive terms, may acquire sufficient funds to meet the demand for long-term funds.

ELI SHAPIRO: Do you think the RFC and the HOLC had anything to do with this very pleasant experience which insurance companies and mutual savings banks enjoyed?

MR. BECKHART: Quite right, Eli. The RFC and the HOLC — the RFC with respect to American railroads and the HOLC with respect to mortgages — helped the commercial banks as well as the financial intermediaries. Those were institutions which we had to set up during the Great Depression. Other countries followed a similar course; Italy set up several institutions to help bail out the commercial banks, and as a consequence the large Italian banks now are controlled by the Italian government. I think Eli's point is very well taken — that the establishment of these special credit institutions was then of great benefit to the insurance companies and to the mutual savings banks. The severity of the Great Depression was itself caused in part by the fact that commercial banks in this and other countries offset demand deposits with long-term assets. It was this action that required state intervention.

HOWARD GORDMAN: Regarding your concluding comment, if achieving domestic stability and preserving the international value of the dollar are both possible, which should have priority?

MR. BECKHART: The Commission on Money and Credit assumed, if I interpret its conclusions correctly, that the various national goals were compatible. The goals were low unemployment falling to 4%, steady growth and price stability; and finally, in a separate chapter, the Commission referred to the international position of the dollar.

The Radcliffe report suggested that there might be inconsistency between such goals, and I agree with the Radcliffe report that inconsistencies might develop. No particular goal has permanency. What particular goal is important at the moment? If you think that the promotion of full employment is important in the short run — and here we have to differentiate between the short and the long run — then you would follow the suggestion of the Joint Committee on the Economic Report, namely, that the Federal Reserve Banks have been making money too tight and that they should make it easier. Discount rates should be lowered and net reserves should be increased.

If we do all that, we are not going to defend the dollar. You may conclude that it is not important to defend the dollar. You may be convinced that it is better to achieve short-term domestic recovery and let the dollar go. You may feel that short-run growth will help us compete abroad.

Growth over the short run, may I point out, will worsen the position of the dollar. Growth over the short run — I am not speaking of the long run — will lead to an increase in imports. According to some who have looked into the problem, imports will increase $40 million for every $1 billion increase in gross national product. Thus, if we get gross national product up to $600 billion, our imports will increase by $2 billion or some such figure. So growth over the short run may worsen our balance of payments; over the long run it will help our balance of payments.

Now, will the stability of the dollar help growth over the long run? I think it will, because I think it will preserve the Atlantic Community, the Common Market, and the economic unity of the free world. However, if you disagree with me, then you would follow the other policy, which would mean, first, that foreign exchange controls may have to be imposed to protect the dollar. This could be done very quickly under the Trading with the Enemy Act of 1917. Then eventually the dollar would have to be devalued and the price of gold raised. So, you see, these different goals may not be consistent, one with the other. We have to select our goals, do we not?

MARSHALL KAPLAN: You do not seem to like fair-weather operators in the credit field, and you took some cracks at the department-store operations of banks. This perplexes me, because one of the goals in the financial area that we stress a great deal is mobility of funds, the ability of funds to shift as the demands for certain types of funds change. How do you reconcile your dislike of the fair-weather operators with this very interesting and important criterion of mobility?

MR. BECKHART: To illustrate my point, one can perhaps refer to the experience of France in this regard. Prior to World War I and, to a certain extent, prior to World War II, France had a specialized set of credit institutions. There were the commercial banks operating in the financing of the short-term credit needs of French industry, and there were the investment banks operating in the longer-term field. The investment bankers were able to accumulate the savings funds of France through the sale of debentures and shares throughout the French economy. The commercial banks financed mainly short-term credit needs. There was a separation of functions, and the French economy experienced a very rapid growth.

In Germany, the large banks operated in both the long-term and the short-term sectors of the economy, and you will probably conclude that by operating in these two sectors they were able to bring the funds together quickly from the money and capital markets. In operating in these two sectors, they operated as two institutions. In other words, the German banks had a very large volume of capital funds, and they used their own capital to finance the long-term credit needs of German industry. They sold their own stock and used the money received to finance long-term credit needs, so that they really were operating as investment trusts.

Thus, on the one hand, the situation in Germany was one of successful operation of the banks as compartmentalized units and, on the other, the situation in France was one of specialized institutions catering to different sectors of the economy. In both instances the money and capital markets were separated more than is the case today. In my opinion, the current ease in the mobility of funds from the money to the capital markets promotes instability.

Mr. Kaplan: I am a little disturbed by the lag this might introduce in causing funds to go into new channels when it is desirable.

Mr. Beckhart: I am concerned, perhaps, by the opposite. I am concerned about the use of short-term credit to finance long-term needs. In other words, you are concerned about the lag and I am concerned about the lead.

Economic Growth

Financial institutions, as is true of all other institutional arrange-ments, can make the maximum contribution to our economy and can thrive only under conditions of acceptable economic growth and stability. The first series of lectures in this part sets forth two views on economic growth in the United States, emphasizing the conditions that are determining in the rate of growth and how these conditions are likely to react upon growth in the decades to come. An important facet of the problem is the rate of growth in European countries compared to that in the United States. Edward Denison believes that we in the United States need not "feel our economy is failing because we have a growth rate of productive potential below that in western Europe or elsewhere." Gerhard Colm presents a decision model with a target rate of 4.1 per cent annual growth rate. He is uneasy about the fact that 1962 and 1963 were below the assumed growth trend line, but, on the other hand, he appears more sanguine than Denison that the 4.1 per cent trend line can be reached, and he believes that this achievement does not require the "heroic measures" that Denison has assumed.

In the second paper in Part Two, Robert Solow considers the problem of economic growth and residential housing, or, as he described what he was going to talk about, "The Present State of Growthmanship in the World." With respect to specific projections of the prospects for United States economic growth, he classifies most economists in one of two groups, the three-percenters and the four-percenters. He places Edward Denison, whose paper at the 1963 Conference is included in this part, in the three-percenter group. He classifies as a four-percenter the National Planning Association whose chief economist, Gerhard Colm, appeared with Denison at the 1963 Conference. Solow places himself in the four-percenter group.

Part Two concludes with a paper by Robert Turner on "The Role of Government in Residential Financing." He believes that we must be willing to experiment with new techniques for effectuating public policies in housing if this industry is to contribute significantly to economic growth; and in the final pages of his paper, he makes a number of definite suggestions for changes in techniques.

7

Long-run Growth:

Prospects and Problems–I*

Edward F. Denison is senior staff member of the Brookings Institution. He is the author of *The Sources of Economic Growth in the United States and the Alternatives before Us* and of numerous articles in professional journals on economic growth. Mr. Denison earned his bachelor's degree at Oberlin College and his master's and doctoral degrees at Brown University. He was formerly associate director of research, Office of Business Economics, U. S. Department of Commerce; unit chief, U. S. Strategic Bombing Survey, Germany; and a part-time member of the faculties of Brown and American universities.

DISSATISFACTION WITH OUR ECONOMIC GROWTH stems largely from three comparisons. First, in the past half-dozen years or so, our growth rate has fallen slightly below that we have ourselves enjoyed in the past. Second, to use popular terminology, we have not grown fast enough to use our resources fully. Third, our growth rate has been exceeded in a number of other countries during the postwar period.

The first two of these are really the same thing. Higher unemployment caused the growth rate of actual national product since 1956 or 1957 to be below our average past record. This provides ample reason for dissatisfaction. It indicates a real failure of our economic policy. But we should be clear that it is failure of United States employment policy, not of policies affecting the growth of our productive potential.

The cure is sufficient aggregate demand to eliminate excessive unem-

* Proceedings of the Sixth Annual Conference, 1963, pp. 12–26.

111

ployment. If we can get back to high employment, this in itself will place our growth record since 1956 a bit above its historic rate. There also will be some indirect benefits to further long-term growth. Attainment of high employment is our immediate economic problem. A large tax reduction right now appears to be the most promising action available.

But we ought to be clear that our recent record in raising our productive potential is not unfavorable by the criterion of past performance. Since 1956 or 1957, our ability to produce has increased at least as fast as it did, on the average, in the past, and in all probability faster.

The growth of our productive potential has, however, been less than that experienced in a number of other countries, notably those in western Europe, and restoration of high employment will not change this fact. Ought this to be grounds for dissatisfaction, a sense of failure, or even shame? Given that the level of output per man or per capita in the United States is far above that in any of the rapidly growing countries, the answer is not obvious. Perhaps Europe is getting rapid growth because relevant conditions are fundamentally different and the comparison is not pertinent. To judge whether our performance ought to be considered unsatisfactory because our growth is slower than Europe's, we surely need to know a great deal about the sources of growth in the two areas. We need to estimate what we would have to do to raise our growth rate and to know whether Europe is getting its rapid growth from sources not available to us. We might also want to consider whether growth is as important to us, although that question is outside the scope of this paper.

In my study of United States growth for the Committee for Economic Development, I tried to allocate our past growth rate among the sources of growth and also to estimate what we would have to do to change our future growth rate. The methods and assumptions are fully described there.

What Were the Sources of Past U. S. Growth?

Let me, however, review quickly my estimates of the main sources of our past growth in productive potential. I focus here upon the period from 1929 to 1957. In that period the real national income, or net national product at factor cost, increased at an average annual rate of 2.93%. I have tried to break this rate down among its sources. The results are given in Table 1. My estimates are rough and their derivation required some strong assumptions, but I think they place the matter in correct perspective.

1. The changes that occurred in employment and working hours accounted for 0.80 of the total growth rate. The increase in employment would have contributed an amount equal to 1.00 point had hours not been shortened. The shortening of hours provided an offset equal to 0.20

in the total growth rate. This offset would have been much larger if the shortening of hours had not led directly to an increase in the amount of work done in an hour. But my estimates imply that such an increase did occur and was sufficient to reduce greatly the adverse effect of shorter hours, especially in the early part of the period. This results from the usual assumption that greater efficiency largely offsets hours shortening when normal hours are long, but is progressively less as hours are shortened.

2. The quality of the labor force was greatly improved by additional education. In fact, the average person in the labor force in 1957 had spent four-fifths more days in school than his 1929 counterpart. It is not always realized that if the 1960 labor force had been only as well educated as that of 1930, there would have been only 47% as many college graduates as there actually were and only 43% as many high school graduates who had not finished college. One-third of the labor force would not have finished the eighth grade.

Table 1

Contribution of Sources of Growth to Growth Rate of
Total Real National Income
Estimated, 1929–57, and Projected, 1960–80

ITEM	ESTIMATED, 1929–57		PROJECTED, 1960–80 (HIGH-EMPLOYMENT RATE)	
	PERCENTAGE POINTS	PERCENT OF GROWTH RATE	PERCENTAGE POINTS	PERCENT OF GROWTH RATE
Total growth rate	2.93	100%	3.33	100%
Increase in employment	1.00	34	1.33	40
Shortening of hours	−0.20	− 7	−0.35	− 11
Increased education	0.67	23	0.64	19
Increased experience and better utilization of women workers	0.11	4	0.09	3
Changes in age-sex composition of labor force	−0.01	0	−0.01	0
Quantity of capital	0.43	15	0.49	15
Advance of knowledge	0.58	20	0.75	23
Change in lag in application of knowledge	0.01	0	0.03	1
Reduced waste of labor in agriculture	0.02	1	0.02	1
Economies of scale due to automobile and concentration of population	0.07	2	0.05	2
Industry shift from agriculture	0.05	2	0.01	0
Increased restrictions against optimum use of resources	−0.07	− 2	0.00	0
Economies of scale due to growth of the economy	0.27	9	0.28	8

I estimate that the four-fifths increase in education from 1929 to 1957 raised the average ability of employed persons to contribute to production by three-tenths and that increased education contributed 0.67 point to the total growth rate of national product. This improvement in the quality of the labor force reflected changes that had been made in education of the young before the period began more than it did improvements made after 1929, although the latter also were important.

3. By 1957, women were remaining in the labor force far longer than in 1929 and in consequence were, on the average, more experienced and effective workers. In addition, discrimination against the employment of women on jobs utilizing their maximum capacities had diminished, so that their skills were more effectively utilized. These developments were responsible for 0.11 of the growth rate from 1929 to 1957.

Altogether, combining the changes discussed so far, I find that changes in the quantity and quality of labor were responsible for 54% of economic growth in this period.

4. The capital stock did not increase very fast from 1929 to 1957 in comparison with earlier periods in our history. I estimate that the increase in the capital stock that did occur contributed 0.43 point to total growth. Of this amount, the increase in nonfarm residences contributed 0.05 point and the increase in our net international investments, 0.02 point. The remaining 0.36 point was the contribution of the increase in business capital.

5. Advances in all kinds of knowledge relevant to production, by permitting more to be produced with a given quantity of resources, contributed 0.58 point to total growth. This includes both advances in technology and advances in techniques of business management and industrial organization. Let me note that this source is the residual in my calculations.

6. Three developments that increased the efficiency with which the economy operates together contributed 0.10 point to the growth rate. New knowledge was incorporated into the productive process a little faster. The excess of labor used in agriculture over the amount actually required for production was reduced. Adaptation by business to the widespread ownership of automobiles and to the increasing concentration of the population in urban areas broadened local markets (quite apart from the growth of the national economy), permitting increased efficiency.

AGRICULTURE'S ROLE

7. Agricultural output had a lower value on the market than other output requiring the same use of resources in the base year (1954) of the real national product series. Consequently, a reduction in agriculture's

share of resources actually utilized had the effect of raising the real national product. This development contributed 0.05 point to measured economic growth.

8. A number of institutional changes that led to increased misallocation of resources or prevented their most efficient use subtracted 0.07 point from the growth rate. The introduction of resale price maintenance laws, which did not exist in 1929, was among the most important. Tariffs, monopoly pricing, differential excise taxes, and union obstacles to the introduction of new processes are other examples of such obstacles to efficient production.

9. Economies of scale made possible by the increase in the size of the national economy (including the associated increase in the size of local and regional markets) contributed 0.27 point to economic growth from 1929 to 1957. This is, of course, a passive element in growth made possible by the other developments. Consequently, its contribution could, if desired, be reallocated among the active ingredients in proportion to their contributions to growth.

In summary, from 1929 to 1957 five sources contributed an amount equal to 101% of the growth rate, out of a total of 109% contributed by all sources making a positive contribution. These were increased employment (34%), increased education (23%), increased capital input (15%), the advance of knowledge (20%), and economies of scale associated with the growth of the national market (9%). The reduction of working hours accounted for −7% of the total negative "contribution" of −9% to the growth rate provided by sources adverse to growth, and increased restrictions against the optimum use of resources for the remainder.

This breakdown, of course, refers only to a particular time and place, the United States from 1929 to 1957. There is every reason to expect the relative contributions of various sources to differ greatly among periods and places. For example, from 1909 to 1929 the increase in capital contributed twice as much to the United States growth rate as did improvement in the quality of the labor force through education, but much less after 1929.

WHAT WOULD CONTRIBUTE TO FUTURE GROWTH?

Let us now consider what choices are open to us if we wish to raise the growth rate of productive potential over the next 20 years above what it otherwise would be — whether that is the 3⅓% I have projected or some other rate, such as Dr. Colm's. To give quantitative dimensions, I shall indicate what I conclude would be necessary to raise the growth rate by one-tenth of a percentage point, as from 3.3% to 3.4%. Such a change would yield a national product in 1980 higher than otherwise by about 2%, or $20 billion. Put the other way round, to change the growth rate over the next 20 years by one-tenth of a percentage point would require some action that would make the 1980 national product 2%, or $20 billion, larger than it would be in the absence of that action.

Such an action would have to either increase the quantity or quality of the total input of labor, land, and capital into the productive system or increase their productivity.

To raise the national product by 2% by increasing inputs would, because of the existence of economies of scale, require slightly less than a 2% increase in total inputs. I estimate that total input in 1980 would have to be increased about 1.83%. One way to do this would be to increase all inputs by 1.83%; the other would be to increase only one kind of input by a larger percentage. I estimate from national income data that labor represents about 77% of total inputs, land and natural resources 3%, and capital 20%; this is what they earn. It follows that we could raise *total* input by 1.83% in 1980 if we could raise labor input alone by 2.4% over what it would otherwise be or capital input alone by 9%, or land input alone by 61%.

Suppose we wish to add 0.1 to the growth rate by increasing the quantity or the average quality of labor input in 1980 by 2.4% over and above what it would otherwise be. This could be done if we wished, and could find ways, to achieve changes such as the following:

Draw into the labor force one-tenth of all able-bodied persons over 20 years of age who would not otherwise be working in 1980; or

Double the rate of net immigration over the next twenty years; or

Prevent half the deaths that will otherwise occur from 1960 to 1980 among individuals less than sixty-five years of age; or

Operate with a workweek one hour longer than otherwise; or

Add one and one-half years to the average time that would otherwise be spent in school by everyone completing school between now and 1980, or make an equivalent improvement in the quality of education.

To increase land input offers no significant possibilities.

To raise the growth rate one-tenth of a percentage point by raising 1980 capital input by 9% would require devoting an additional 1% of the national income to net saving and investment in nonresidential capital throughout the next twenty years. This would be an increase of about one-sixth in what has been the nation's net saving rate in good years.

WAYS TO INCREASE PRODUCTIVITY

The alternative to increasing the quantity or quality of inputs is to increase productivity by accelerating the advance of knowledge or the efficiency with which the economy works. One important source of increase in productivity, the economies of scale that occur when the economy grows for other reasons, cannot be affected directly. I have taken it into account in estimating the yield from increasing inputs and shall do so also in examining other ways of increasing productivity. Let us consider the others.

I estimated that advances in knowledge of all types relevant to production, a somewhat broader notion than technological progress, contributed 0.6 to the growth rate in 1929–57 and will contribute 0.8 in the future. Thus, we could add an extra 0.1 to the growth rate if we could raise by one-eighth the rate at which knowledge relevant to production advances. But many discoveries and inventions originate abroad, and many are not the result of deliberate research. On possible assumptions, we would have to increase by one-half the annual increment to knowledge that both originates in the United States and is subject to being affected by deliberate action.

We could also add 0.1 to the growth rate over the next twenty years if we could reduce the lag of average production practices behind the best known by two and two-thirds years, in addition to any reduction that would otherwise take place. A high rate of gross capital formation would help to make this possible, but it should be recognized that two and two-thirds years would be a huge reduction.

There are a number of smaller possibilities which we could combine to add 0.1 to the growth rate over twenty years.

Thus, I estimate that the misallocation and wasteful use of resources resulting from barriers to international trade costs us around 1½% of our national income, and misallocation resulting from private monopoly in markets for products costs another ½%. Eliminating both by 1980 could raise the national product 2% and contribute 0.1 to the growth rate. Or we might eliminate state resale price maintenance laws and racial discrimination in hiring.

The discussion so far suggests that it would take some doing to add a point or two to the growth rate of productive potential in the United States. The more important possibilities for stimulating growth involve important costs, and large results impose large costs. Decisions on whether or not to try to affect the growth rate by any of the means I have suggested cannot sensibly be made without full consideration of their costs and of their other consequences, desirable or undesirable.

EUROPEAN VS. U. S. GROWTH SOURCES

One question that inevitably emerges from such a discussion is: How has northwest Europe[1] achieved such a high postwar growth rate? I should like to use my remaining time to take a quick and most tentative

[1] I shall use northwest Europe to include Belgium, Denmark, France, West Germany, Netherlands, Norway and the United Kingdom.

look at northwest European experience during the decade of the '50s. I am not now in a position to attempt to quantify the contribution of most of the sources of European growth, as I have tried to do for the United States, but qualitative statements seem possible as to whether the major possibilities are likely to be important. As before, I am not looking at the demand side of the picture, nor at government policies and other influences that affect the behavior of the sources of growth, but at growth sources themselves in the same sense as I use the term for the United States.

During the '50s, GNP in northwest Europe grew at an average rate of 4.3%. In West Germany the rate was as high as 7.5 for the decade as a whole, although down to 6.0 from 1955 to 1960. Elsewhere the 1950–60 rate ranged down from 4.9 in the Netherlands and 4.3 in France to 2.9 in Belgium and 2.6 in the United Kingdom. Let us quickly run through some of the more important sources and compare growth in western Europe in the decade of the '50s with that in the United States from 1929 to 1957.

First, employment in the United States increased at an average rate of 1.3% from 1929 to 1957 and 1.2% in the '50's. In northwest Europe the 1950–60 annual increase in employment was larger than this in the Netherlands and, especially, in Germany, where it increased 2.3%. Elsewhere, annual employment increases were rather small. In northwest Europe as a whole, employment increased at a slightly lower rate than in the United States. We cannot explain more rapid growth in the area as a whole by employment changes.

Second, in the majority of the European countries there was only a moderate reduction in normal hours of work. In addition, European hours were so long, generally around 46 or 47 a week, that application of the curve relating hours to output that I used for the United States would yield little cost of shorter hours to output even if there had been an appreciable hours reduction. In my United States study, I estimated that shorter hours cost us one-fifth of a point in the 1929–57 growth rate. Other studies imply a much greater cost — over half a point. This is a drag on growth which postwar Europe has not had to offset.

Third, it appears that much less of European than of American growth can be ascribed to improvement in the quality of the labor force through additional education. In the United Kingdom the average number of years of education held by the labor force increased by 4½% from 1951 to 1961 and in Norway by 5½%. The change in the United States was about 7½% in the same period and about 9% per decade from 1929 to 1957. Moreover, the number of days of schooling embodied in a year's education probably was increasing much more rapidly in the United States. If the change in education of the labor force in the United Kingdom and Norway is reasonably typical of northwest Europe, and I suspect it is, perhaps 0.2 or 0.3 of the European growth rate in the '50s should be allocated to additional education, as compared to my estimate of almost 0.7 in the United States from 1929 to 1957.

The fourth factor to examine is capital. I shall consider residential construction and other fixed investment separately. Substantial inventory investment also occurred, but I shall not discuss it here.

RESIDENTIAL CONSTRUCTION

About one-fourth of gross fixed investment in northwest Europe has gone into residential construction, so the residential construction boom is important in explaining the high ratio of gross investment to GNP in most European countries. Investment in residential construction contributes directly to the national product through the services subsequently provided by housing. We can compute the contribution of residential investment to growth of GNP rather easily by examining the increase over the decade in real GNP originating in the "ownership of dwellings" industry. From these data, it appears that the increase in the stock of housing contributed 0.3 percentage point to the growth rate of GNP in Germany and the United Kingdom, 0.2 in Denmark and 0.1 in Belgium, France, the Netherlands, and Norway. For the area as a whole it is about 0.2. Much of this increase is offset in real national income, or net product, by depreciation. Thus, the contribution of the increased housing stock to the 1950–60 growth rate of real national income in northwest Europe may have been around 0.1, or one-twentieth of a percentage point more than my estimate of 0.05 for the United States from 1929 to 1957. Both residential construction costs and rents are cheaper, relative to the general price level, in Europe than in America, and if European output were valued in United States prices, both the fraction of GNP devoted to residential construction and the contribution of additional housing to growth would be somewhat larger.

OTHER FIXED CAPITAL

The contribution of other fixed capital — producers' durables and non-residential construction — is far harder to estimate, especially since I lack satisfactory time series for the capital stock. I shall try only to bring out a few facts that suggest to me that investment has contributed greatly to European growth. This was not because investment was larger than ours, but because capital was far scarcer.

The well-known study of comparative national products and prices by Milton Gilbert and associates for OEEC shows that the price of producers' durables is much higher, relative to average prices, in Europe than in the United States. Thus, the fact that gross investment in these assets has been a higher fraction of GNP than in the United States when each country's own prices are used in the calculation does not mean that the Europeans have been getting more capital goods relative to their GNPs when the same prices are used for all countries. In fact, they have not.

One calculation seems to me particularly interesting. For each country I cumulated gross investment in producers' durables and nonresidential construction, valued in United States prices of 1955, over the period from 1948 through 1960. I then divided the results by the labor force in each country. It turns out that investment per man in producers' durables and nonresidential construction in northwest Europe as a whole from 1948 through 1960 was only 42% as large as comparable investment per man in the United States. Although some of this capital has already been discarded, this suggests that northwest European workers in 1961 had roughly 42% as much fixed capital (other than housing) less than fourteen years old to work with as did American workers. European labor appears to be of only moderately lower quality than American labor. Hence, this suggests that the ratio of new nonresidential capital to labor input, even after adjustment for labor quality, can hardly be even half as high in Europe as in America. The ratio for older capital must be even lower.

The ratio of 42% for capital less than fourteen years old available per worker compares with a ratio of European to American GNP per man, also expressed in United States prices of 1955, of about 57%. The ratio for national income cannot be very different from that for GNP.

The ratio of European to United States new capital was substantially below the corresponding GNP ratio in all the northwest European countries except Norway and Denmark. In Germany, gross capital formation per person in the labor force during the thirteen-year period was only 36% as large as in the United States, whereas GNP per man in 1960 was about 55% as large (when both comparisons are based on United States prices). Even in the 1955–60 period, German nonresidential capital formation per man was only 41% of ours.

If the increase in nonresidential capital has made a major contribution to rapid postwar European growth, and I suspect that it has, it certainly is not because capital formation was extraordinarily large by United States standards, nor because Europe has become exceptionally well endowed with capital or with new capital, but simply because even a moderate rate of capital formation provided enormous improvement in a capital-scarce situation.

Of course Europe came out of the war with a capital stock in abysmal shape — small, old, and unbalanced. As one looks at the data, he may doubt that Europe has yet regained a capital position even as favorable relative to ours as it held before the war. The yield of additional investment in capital-hungry postwar Europe would have been extraordinarily high even if the postwar stock had been small but balanced. When we consider that, because of wartime destruction, it was in fact quite unbalanced, so that additional investment also brought existing facilities back into effective use, it is reasonable to suppose the yield from much of the new investment was very large indeed. But the low ratio of capital to labor, by United States standards, is not just a temporary phenomenon but one that should result in a much greater contribution to growth from a dollar invested in Europe than in America for a long time to come.

ROLE OF ECONOMIES OF SCALE IN EUROPEAN GROWTH

The fifth source, or really group of sources, to which I shall refer is economies of scale. I mean to include here both economies of scale internal and external to the firm, including the gains from greater specialization possible in a larger economy. I shall also consider the gains from international trade in this context. Economies of scale, in this broad sense, enter the picture in several ways in Europe and seem likely to be of major importance in explaining European growth.

In my United States study I assumed, and it was only an assumption, that in the 1929–57 period economies of scale raised the contribution of any other source of growth by one-tenth. Whatever the true figure for an economy as large as ours, it is generally accepted that additional economies of scale are larger, percentagewise, in a smaller economy. All the European national economies are far smaller than the American economy, and some of them very small indeed. Since they normally engage much more in international trade, it would be wrong to judge the likely importance of economies of scale solely by the size of their individual national products. Even so, it is probable that the impact of any other source of growth is re-enforced very much more by economies of scale in European countries than in America.

Another aspect of economies of scale may be of great significance. The Paige-Bombach comparisons of output and productivity in the United States and the United Kingdom show that, among industries, the international ratios of output per man are closely related to the total output ratios. The higher the ratio of British to American output, the smaller is the international productivity gap, and the slope of the line of relationship is steep. There is every reason, on the evidence of relative price relationships from the Gilbert study, to suppose this would also hold in comparisons of other European countries with the United States. It is reasonable to suppose this relationship stems in large part, though not entirely, from economies of scale. The relationship is important in a study of growth because the increase in European output is not distributed proportionately among products. It is especially large in income-elastic products that Europe produces and consumes in particularly small quantities as compared to the United States. It is just here that economies of scale are especially large as output grows. Let me try to illustrate the possible significance of this in the following way.

When national products per person employed in 1960 are compared by use of United States price weights, the American figure is only about 72% above the northwest European. But it is 122% higher if European price weights are used for the comparison. The reason for the difference, of course, is that the composition of national product differs and commodities used in small quantities tend to have high relative prices, and conversely. Gilbert and associates concluded that consumption patterns differ mainly because of differences in income level and relative prices, not because of differences in tastes. But systematic differences in relative prices result largely from differences in consumption patterns that themselves result from differences in income level. To overstate the case, if income levels were the same, consumption patterns would be the same and relative prices would then also be the same. Hence, aside from future differential rates of technological and managerial progress in different activities, we can expect that when European income levels reach the present United States level, European relative prices will resemble those now prevailing in the United States. A comparison of the national products of the two areas would then yield about the same result, whether based on future European prices or present American prices.

MEASURING GROWTH THROUGH RELATIVE PRICE WEIGHTS TRICKY

Based on 1960 United States or future European relative price weights, 1960 European output per man must increase 72% to reach the 1960 American level. However, based on recent European price weights, it must increase 122%. A 122% increase based on recent European price weights, the weights underlying the European growth rates, would then be equivalent to a 72% increase based on recent United States or future European prices, or only three-fifths as much. This calculation certainly overstates the real difference; European price relationships will actually not be identical with those now prevailing in the United States, nor are the assumptions necessarily even generally valid outside the area of private consumption. Neither can we identify all differences in relative prices with economies of scale. But even if the calculation is discounted by half or more, it suggests that as European incomes rise, the economies of scale in increasing output where it is especially low may be a large factor in accounting for high European growth rates.

It would be helpful to quantify the effect of substituting United States for European price weights on European growth rates during the '50s. Unfortunately, Gilbert and associates made detailed comparisons only for 1950, and whatever is subsequently available is so rough and summary that it probably greatly understates the effect of using alternative weights. However, even on the basis of Gilbert's rough extrapolations from 1950 to 1955, the difference is in the expected direction in all the northwestern European countries.[2] In the case of Germany, it amounts to as much as 0.6 in the 1950–55 growth rate, but less for other countries.

The discussion of scale economies thus far has supposed no change in access to international trade, so that gains depend on the growth of the domestic economy and the composition of growth. But markets also can be broadened by extending their geographic area. In 1950, as a response to the European balance-of-payments problem, Europe was a nightmare of exchange controls, quotas and other special restrictions on international transactions, most of them far more hampering to efficiency than tariffs. These were viewed at the time as very costly, and rightly so. During the decade the special nontariff barriers to the flow of trade and capital were largely, though by no means completely, dismantled. Late in the decade the Common Market gave the integration movement a new impetus, which continues. During the '50s, trade liberalization probably contributed most to growth of productivity in Germany, where the ratio of imports of goods and services to GNP rose from a strikingly small 12% in 1950 to 26% in 1960. The ratio rose much less, but still appreciably, in Belgium and Denmark. Elsewhere, changes were not striking, and in both France and the United Kingdom the ratio of imports to GNP actually declined slightly in current prices. In the conditions prevailing in Europe in the '50s, however, even a stable or slightly declining ratio is consistent with significant gains deriving from relaxation of international economic barriers.

Taking all these factors together, it seems likely that scale economies, including increased specialization, are of major importance in European growth.

ADVANCE OF KNOWLEDGE AS A GROWTH SOURCE

A sixth growth source is the advance of knowledge, which I credited with a contribution of about 0.6 to the United States growth rate from 1929 to 1957. The best estimate of the contribution of the advance of

---

[2] In the case of Italy, however, it is in the expected direction only for consumption, not for total GNP, because of an offsetting shift in the importance of defense expenditures.

world knowledge to European growth is probably that it was the same as in the United States.

It seems to me impossible to deduce anything at all about the contribution to growth of advances in society's stock of knowledge from European experience. Knowledge is a world possession, available to all who seek it and not confined by national boundaries. Output per man in Europe is far below that in the United States. While part of the gap is due to differences in the quantity of natural resources and of capital, the quality of labor, the size of markets and so on, I suspect that if these influences could be measured, much would remain to be explained by differences in production and distribution practices. It seems probable that in postwar Europe large gains in productivity have been possible by adopting practices already prevalent in the United States (or elsewhere). Certainly a major organized effort was undertaken to bring this about. If there is a larger "residual" in European growth rates that is left after accounting for inputs and scale economies than in prewar Europe or in America, this cannot be used as evidence of an acceleration in the world community's acquisition of knowledge relevant to production. It is merely an indication of a narrowing gap between European and American practice.

It is likely that what I called in my United States study the "change in the lag in the application of knowledge" has been a major growth source in Europe. I suspect that the spread of knowledge about best technology and business practice, from America and among European countries, has itself been an important source of postwar European growth. In addition, persistent labor shortage in most countries has surely contributed strongly to the diminution of wasteful use of labor by the employment of unneeded workers or such inefficient practices as finishing automobile surfaces beyond the point where improvement is worth the cost, practices that do not really arise from lack of knowledge but from inertia and resistance to change.

FURTHER STUDY NECESSARY

I shall not attempt now to tie up these brief and tentative comments on some of the sources of European growth into a quantitative or fully integrated picture of European growth. In fact, I do not believe it is possible to get an adequate explanation of the sources of European growth, at least in a way that might help us to understand our own growth better, until we can simultaneously explain the large gap between Europe and America in the level of output per person employed.

I plan, in a study in which I am now engaged, to look at both the sources of postwar European growth and the sources of the difference in level of output per man, and particularly at the relationship between the two. I have no illusions that I am likely to arrive at anything like definitive results, but there is no harm in trying.

Is U. S. Growth Rate Unsatisfactory?

In the meantime, the preliminary, almost cursory look just attempted at the probable importance of various major sources to European growth does not seem to suggest that the Europeans are obtaining rapid growth primarily by exploiting sources that we could also exploit to obtain a much higher growth rate of productive potential. It seems more likely that the high postwar growth rate in western Europe is associated with the removal of limitations on output per man imposed by extreme shortage of capital, small markets, failure to economize in the use of labor, and relatively backward business practice and even technology. These are limitations we do not share in at all similar degree. In addition, long European hours can be shortened at much less cost. Let me stress that this is a very tentative judgment, that further research may well suggest different conclusions and that I am fully prepared to change my mind about the importance of some of the growth sources I have mentioned.

But at the moment I am not persuaded that we need apologize or feel our economy is failing because we have a growth rate of productive potential below that in western Europe or elsewhere. Our obvious failure, as I said at the beginning, is represented by an unemployment rate persistently above our own standards of what is necessary and attainable, let alone the standards now acceptable in Europe.

8

Long-run Growth:
Prospects and Problems–II*

Gerhard Colm is chief economist, National Planning Association. He is the co-author of *The Economy of the
American People, Targets for United States Economic Growth
in the Early '60's* and *Long-Range Projections for Economic
Growth: The American Economy in 1970.* Mr. Colm earned his
doctorate (Dr. Rer. Pol.) at the University of Freiburg. He was
formerly economist, Federal Statistical Bureau, Berlin; faculty
member, University of Kiel and The New School for Social Research; fiscal adviser, U. S. Department of Commerce; chief,
fiscal division, U. S. Bureau of the Budget; economist, President's
Council of Economic Advisers; member, special mission, American Military Government to Germany; and member, UNKRA
mission to Korea.

WHEN I TOLD A FRIEND I WAS GOING to be in Chicago, where the question
of long-term growth was to be discussed, his comment was, "Is that not
a bit early for the 1964 election?" Some people think of growth merely
as a political issue. I am very glad that Dr. Ketchum apparently does
not share that view and that he thinks that prospects of growth are
useful for the discussion of problems of business management and, in
this case, of financial management, savings problems, real estate
problems, etc.

I should like to talk about three related problems. First, I want to say
something about the use of estimates of economic growth for business

* Proceedings of the Sixth Annual Conference, 1963, pp. 28–38.

decisions; I should say "use and misuse." Second, I want to take a look back at how good or bad estimates have been in trying to forecast economic growth, a kind of autopsy of what we have done in the past. And third, I want to venture some opinions about the future, the probable rate of growth for the decade ahead.

First, the use and misuse of projections as a tool for evaluating the prospects of growth and market development.

If we want to analyze developments in a particular market, we need some general bench marks. We can go from the top down, from the total GNP to specific products and then to the specific market and firm in which we are interested; or we can go from the bottom up, from the detail to the aggregates. Usually we are using both methods in trying to reconcile forecasts which go from the top down and from the bottom up. These projections are then used by many, if not most, of the larger companies for their own investment and management planning. They are not used, or at least should not be used, in a mechanical fashion. Projections are no substitute for guidance by the signals of the market, such as price and profit expectations. They are to be interrelated and are to supplement each other. They are good for getting a long-term perspective, but then one must watch the signals of the market to see to what extent one's anticipations are confirmed and, if necessary, revise the plans.

WHAT IF THE PROJECTION IS WRONG?

Even the best projections, whether made in a more or less sophisticated manner, or more or less intuitively by a business manager, never remove uncertainty; so a very important aspect in the use of projections is to evaluate the probability of error. Never should a projection be used without considering what will happen if the projection is wrong. There probably will be different biases, intentional biases, by various corporations. Let us consider a corporation in a strong financial position; it may evaluate its market in a somewhat optimistic fashion because it wants to be sure it is not missing any opportunity. A weak firm, however, would be on the cautious side and would use somewhat more pessimistic forecasts in order not to overextend its resources. Both firms will consider what to do if the projections they have been using turn out to be wrong. They will ask: How can we curtail an investment program in one case or add to it in the other, and what are the costs of such changes? So planning has to consider the "rule of minimum harm in case of error."

Now, let us say we agree that projections can be useful, that it is useful to look ahead at the rate of growth in specific markets in which we are interested. The skeptic may still say: "Yes, it would be useful if we could do it, but we really can't. These are exercises in arithmetic, but the probability of error is such that it has no value."

Let us look at the record. We made one projection in the year 1952 for the year 1960. That is in Table 1. We had good luck and came out within a fraction of 1% for the annual rate of growth in GNP; the estimate of productivity increase was good, too. So we can be quite satisfied with that projection.

However, to be honest, I shall give a second example. Each year we make a projection for five to ten years. In 1959 we made a projection for 1970 and then asked: Where should we be in 1963 if we were right on the path toward our 1970 goal? In the first column of the right-hand part of Table 1, you find an interpolated 1963 figure — where we should be if we were right on the path toward our 1970 estimate. You see that the population was estimated correctly, but that the employed labor force and GNP were overestimated. In Table 2 you will find the percentage analysis of the discrepancy between the interpolated figure and what we call "actual" for 1963. Actual for 1963 was estimated as what it is likely to be.

Table 1

Two NPA Projections in Retrospect
(All Value Data in 1962 Prices)

INDICATOR	1960 PROJECTED IN 1952[1]	1960 ACTUAL	1963 PROJECTED IN 1959[2]	1963 ACTUAL (ESTIMATED IN 1962 PRICES)
Population (millions)	175	181	189.8	189.8
Total labor force "	72.5	72.8	76.7	75.7
Civilian labor force "	69.0	70.3	74.3	72.9
Civilian employment "	66.2	66.4	71.7	68.8
Unemployment "	2.8	3.9	2.6	4.1
Unemployment rate (%)	4.0	5.6	3.5	5.6
GNP (billions of dollars)	519	516	611	575
Distribution of GNP				
Consumption (%)	68	65	65	64
Residential construc-				
tion "	3	4	5	4
Business investment				
(including interna-				
tional) "	11	11	11	10
Government "	18	20	20	22
Federal "	11	10	10	12
State-local "	7	10	10	10
Annual growth rate				
between years shown	1951–1960		1956–1963	
GNP (%)	2.9	2.9	3.8	2.9
GNP per man-hour "	2.5	2.5	3.2	2.5

[1] *The American Economy in 1960.*
[2] National Economic Projection Series.
Source: National Planning Association.

Table 2

Analysis of Difference between Projected and Actual GNP Growth Rates, 1956–1963

ANALYSIS	PROJECTED	ACTUAL	DIFFERENCE (PROJECTED MINUS ACTUAL)
Average annual % growth rate in GNP	3.8	2.9	+0.9
Percentage-point contribution by change in:			
Population	1.7	1.7	0
+Labor participation rate	−0.5	−0.7	+0.2
=Labor force	1.2	1.0	+0.2
+Employment rate[1]	0.1	−0.2	+0.3
=Employment	1.3	0.8	+0.5
+Average weekly hours	−0.7	−0.4	−0.3
=Man-hours	0.6	0.4	+0.2
+GNP per man-hour	3.2	2.5	+0.7
=GNP	3.8	2.9	+0.9

[1] Employment rate defined as 100% minus unemployment rate; unemployment rate was 4.2% in 1956, projected to 3.5% in 1963, estimated at 5.6% for 1963.
Source: National Planning Association.

Here I should like to make a correction. The table gives a GNP estimated actual of $575 billion for 1963. We are now estimating that we shall come out with at least $580 billion for 1963 as a whole. This is within a $5 billion margin, which I think is not too bad. However, our 1963 performance will still remain about 5% below where we ought to be if the 1959 to 1970 projection should be correct. This interpolation assumes that we always stay just on the trend line, since our whole projection disregards the cycle. We are not trying to forecast the cycle, although we do assume that there will be some cycle. In the estimate for 1970, we assume that there will be some temporary interruption of growth in the period; otherwise we would come out somewhat higher.

Here, I want to ask: Why are we 5% below where we should be, and what can we learn from this experience for the making of projections, particularly for use by business management? This brings me to my second part, which I call the autopsy of projections of the past. Let us look at the beautiful corpse.

Table 3

Selected 10-Year Projections, 1962–1972
(All Value Data in 1962 Prices)

INDICATOR		1962		1972	
Population	(millions)	186.6		222.5	
Households	"	54.7		63.6	
Labor participation	(%)	40.0		40.0	
Total labor force	(millions)	74.7		89.0	
Civilian labor force	"	71.9		86.6	
Civilian employment	"	67.8		83.1	
Unemployment	"	4.0		3.5	
Unemployment rate	(%)	5.6		4.0	
Average workweek	(hours)	40.5		37.6	

	BILLIONS OF DOLLARS	% OF GNP	BILLIONS OF DOLLARS	% OF GNP
Consumption expenditures	357	64	530	61
Durables	48	9	79	9
Nondurables	162	29	226	26
Services	147	27	225	26
Residential construction	24	4	36	4
Business investment (including international)	56	10	103	12
Federal goods and services	62	11	98	11
State-local goods and services	55	10	103	12
GNP	554	100	870	100
Total government expenditures	161	29	261	30
Corporate profits	51	9	82	9
Disposable personal income	385	69	593	67

Source: National Planning Association.

AUTOPSY OF METHODOLOGY PROJECTIONS

First, let me say that each projection has three logical steps. I am not talking about the statistical method we are using. I might say, as a footnote, that we are not using methods of simultaneous equations but successive approximations.

The first logical step in making projections is what I call "current policy projection." Here we are assuming that major governmental policies and major attitudes of business, consumers, and labor remain the same. We do assume an increase in government expenditures in this model only to the extent that decisions have already been made which imply such an increase, but we are not assuming the adoption of entirely new programs of government or new extensions of programs. In this particular case we also assumed that there would not be a tax reduction in 1963. This current policy projection basically gave us an extrapolation of the past trend. We have no reason to assume, according to our statistical experiments, that we would get a higher rate of growth than that of the recent past, say 3% or 2.9%, with a productivity increase of perhaps 2.5% a year. I use "productivity" as an inaccurate short term for GNP per man-hour.

The second logical step is what I call a "decision model." I use this term in a somewhat different sense from that used by Tinbergen and others. In the decision model we do not say that we should have a target, a rate of growth, let us say, of 5%, as the study of the Rockefeller brothers said. And we do not estimate what policies are needed in order to achieve such a predetermined target. What we have been doing is trying our different targets, such as 4%, 5% and 6%, and then finding out what policies are needed in order to reach these different targets, partly using the methods that Ed Denison has suggested, even though we do not agree with all his estimates in detail. Then we ask: What target appears reasonable in the light of policies needed to achieve it within given economic and social institutions? For instance, we could (and I am sure Denison would agree) have a rate of growth of 5% or 6%; but it would require material and manpower controls for breaking down bottlenecks, it would require wage and price controls and it probably would require quite heroic measures for cutting down consumption. However, in case of a national emergency it could be done. Now, we rule out such a rate of growth under the conditions we assume in our projections with respect to the international situation.

By this trial and error method of relating targets to policies, we have come to a target of between 4% and 4½% per year. We made this estimate about five years ago, and we still think it is a reasonable target and is feasible with policies which are short of being heroic. Even this modest target requires changes in existing policies which some people may characterize as bold. Nevertheless, the required policies would be compatible with our country's economic and social institutions.

This is how we got a decision model of around 4% annual growth. You will find our decision model reflected in Table 4. There, however, you see a rate of 4.6%. The reason it is higher than the 4.1% target rate is that it is measured from the low employment level of 1962. Of course, we get a higher rate of growth if we use a low point as the initial year. It would come to 4.1% or 4.2% if the base year had been on the trend line. Actually, 1962 was below the trend line and 1963 will still be below the trend line. To approximate the full-employment line by the end of 1964 would require a rate of growth of more than 6%.

This model is useful in itself because we think it is a good tool for the kind of consideration Denison engaged us in. What kind of policies are needed for a 4.1% growth rate? Actually, we think less heroic

Table 4

Average Annual % Rates of Growth, 1948–1962,
and Alternative Projections, 1962–1972

| | | | | 1962-72[1] | | | | | |
| | | | | FULL-EMPLOYMENT PROJECTIONS[2] | | | | | CHRONIC UNEM- |
INDICATOR	1948-56	1956-62	1948-62	DECI-SION MODEL	SLOW GROWTH	FAST GROWTH	LOW DE-FENSE	HIGH DE-FENSE	PLOYMENT PROJEC-TIONS[3]
GNP	4.0	2.7	3.5	4.6	3.9	5.0	4.6	5.1	3.1
GNP per man-hour	3.2	2.6	2.9	3.3	2.9	3.4	3.3	3.4	2.4

[1] In the projections, the base year relates to the *actual* figures for 1962. When adjusted for the higher 1962 *potentials* available at full utilization of manpower and other resources, the projected decision-model rates of increase would show 4.1% for GNP and 3.2% for GNP per man-hour.
[2] Implying a 4% unemployment rate in 1972.
[3] Implying a 5½% unemployment rate in 1972.
Source: National Planning Association.

measures are needed than Denison has assumed. For instance, he paid considerable attention to the problem of knowledge. We think that the tremendous research and expenditure developments in the space field provide us with a reservoir of knowledge which will have a spillover effect into the general economy. With some deliberate policy, this could give us a very great push in technology. We think that this fact alone could have a considerable effect on the productivity factor and add to future investment opportunities and to the potential rate of growth.

BUSINESS NEEDS FORECASTS, NOT DECISION MODELS

But for business managers, the decision model is not what is wanted. The decision model is useful for government policy planning and for people in business or labor or citizens in general who participate in appraising and determining government policies. Business, for its own planning, needs forecasts, not decision models. So we have to go from policy projections to the decision model as the third logical step to forecasts.

The problem here is that we have to forecast, not only economic relationships in which we as economists are supposed to be experts, but also what kind of policies are likely to be adopted. In making these projections, we do not feel able to make forecasts of all relevant political events, which include what Khrushchev is up to, how the next election will go, and many other factors. So our way out, from the beginning, was to use alternative forecasts and tell businessmen to take their own pick, depending on what policies they think will be adopted and what will happen in the international situation.

We did not get away with that, however. Businessmen said, "That's well and good; we want to have that, but we also want your judgment of what is best to use for our purposes." So we were somewhat forced into presenting the judgment model, which we do in all humility. We say, "Okay, if you want us to, we will make the best guess we can." But we spell out in the material that is available to business exactly what assumptions we have made with reference to future defense expenditures and other policies. Defense policy is, of course, one of the crucial problems. So you have in Table 1 a judgment model which assumes no fundamental change in international relations. It is in this model that we have the discrepancy between the current level of activity and the level of activity implied in our 1970 target.

Now, what was wrong with our judgment? You will find in Tables 1 to 3 some details of our judgment model. We estimated what the 1963 actual would be, although, as I said, it looks now as if we may come out somewhat above our previous estimate. But economic relationships, in general, were correctly estimated, I think, with one exception. Productivity, which means GNP per man-hour, was projected to increase at a rate of 3.2%, and it actually shows 2.5%. Here is one economic relationship where our estimate appears to be wrong. I believe that this is a result of the fact that we are running below the potential of activity. Output per man-hour is to a large extent a function of the level of activity relative to the potential. If we are below the potential, if we have between 5% and 6% unemployed, there is, for example, less migration from the farms to the cities. Such a migration from low-to high-productivity occupations increases the average production per man-hour. In periods of high activity, we have an upgrading of the economy and a general increase in productivity.

Also, in periods of high unemployment there is much labor resistance to managerial and technological advances. In recent collective bargaining agreements, there was a shift from pressing for substantial increases in wages to a desire for greater job security. This means a lower rate of advancement in management and technology, which, in turn, means less increase in productivity than we could have under conditions of ample employment opportunities.

PRODUCTIVITY INFLUENCED BY MANY FACTORS

There are quite a number of factors which I think influence this ratio. I have no reason to doubt, on the basis of our study, that with a sustained high level of economic activity we could have a 3.2% increase in GNP per man-hour, that is, in the rate of productivity. When I refer to productivity as production per man-hour, you realize that this is a statistical measure which includes increases in capital productivity as well as increases in labor productivity in a narrower definition.

We erred, I think, less in the estimate of economic relationships than in a political judgment. We had assumed that once unemployment stayed for a considerable time above 5%, there would be political pressure for a bolder, more effective program in support of economic growth. Actually, in addition to the people recorded as unemployed in the official statistics, there are about 800,000 people who gave up looking for a job and withdrew from the labor force, even though they probably would have preferred to work if there had been opportunities. Also we should consider those involuntarily working short hours, with loss in wage income as a result.

There are several reasons why there is more tolerance with respect to continuing high unemployment or underemployment than we had expected. There is the particular character of unemployment, heavily concentrated on youth, with lesser unemployment among breadwinners for a family. There is the relatively heavy unemployment among minority groups. And, finally, there is the focus of public attention on international political affairs, compared with which our specific domestic problems appear to be of less urgency, so long as economic conditions in general are satisfactory.

However, we cannot take it for granted that the high rate of unemployment can be continued for long without political repercussions, even if it is concentrated in specific groups. Therefore I cannot easily accept Ed Denison's projected 3.3% rate of growth, which would not, in my opinion, permit us to reduce substantially the rate of chronic unemployment. In short, the fact that we have for the recent past erred in the assumption that high unemployment would be tolerated without prompting adoption of effective policy measures in support of growth should not lead to the conclusion that the same attitude will continue in the future.

This brings me to the concluding part, the outlook for the future. Proceeding with some trepidation, I still use an annual growth rate of better than 4% as a sustainable, desirable target for the formation of policies. Any target closer to 3% than to 4% would make no dent on unemployment, as the 3.1% growth projection in Table 4 indicates.

It is more difficult to defend the 4% rate in connection with the forecast model. However, I believe that there is a good chance for a step-up in the rate of growth and, associated with that, in the related rate of productivity.

Factors Hindering Economic Growth

I shall list a few of the factors which I think have held back the rate of growth in the recent past, and we shall see to what extent these factors are likely to continue:

1. One of the main and most serious factors is the real or alleged conflict between a policy of promoting accelerated economic growth and a policy designed to reduce the balance-of-payments deficit. For example, an increase in the rate of interest designed to discourage the outflow of capital is not, despite some "twisting," a policy conducive to the promotion of domestic economic growth.

2. The fear of generating excessive demand and inflation has prevented us from adopting a more expansionary fiscal and credit policy. The same effect has resulted also from price increases which were less the result of excess demand than of "cost push" and the exercise of "market power."

3. The high tax structure has absorbed a substantial part of rising incomes and profits into the Treasury and thereby has blunted the force of expansion and contributed to abortive recoveries.

4. By mutual causation, inadequate rates of growth and high chronic unemployment have increased the resistance of labor to managerial and technological advance and thereby have slowed down gains in productivity and economic growth.

5. Increased foreign competition has resulted in raising imports and slowing down exports, thereby having an unfavorable impact on domestic production.

6. Scarcity in key personnel with specialized training and experience has caused bottlenecks in production.

Factors Favoring More Rapid Growth

I have no doubt that these unfavorable factors will continue in various degrees to influence the rate of growth during the next decade. There are, on the other hand, also factors which will work in the direction of more rapid economic growth:

1. Beginning with the supply side, the resources for a higher rate of growth certainly do exist. Besides those at present unemployed or having temporarily withdrawn from the labor force because of lack of opportunities, and those involuntarily working short hours, there will be a rising annual net influx into the labor market during the next few years. That is a factor Denison mentioned.

2. The training program that has been initiated will contribute increasingly to better matching of available and required skills, and should increase the employable labor force and productivity.

3. The tremendous accumulation of know-how in the military-space sector of production is bound to result in an increasing spillover into general production. This spillover, which is already under way, will be promoted and accelerated by deliberate policies of the government. This, again, will lead to managerial and technological improvement and rising productivity. It also will lead to the development of new or improved products for the foreign and domestic markets.

4. Advances in technology and the need for modernization also will stimulate new investments in plant and equipment, thereby adding to the expansionary force of the economy. The recent McGraw-Hill survey confirms the opinion that this will be a strong factor in the economic outlook.

5. The expected rise in household formation will support the demand for new housing and community facilities.

6. The likelihood is for a more deliberately expansionist fiscal policy on the part of the government. I think it is likely that Congress will take some action on the President's proposal for tax reduction. If it happens, it may be regarded as a breakthrough in fiscal policy in support of economic growth.

7. The fact that formulation and adoption of policies designed to reduce chronic unemployment and to support economic growth have taken so long — certainly longer than we anticipated — should not lead to the conclusion that the country and the political parties are reconciled to continuing high chronic unemployment of 5% to 6%.

8. There is a theoretical possibility of reducing unemployment by a drastic curtailment in the workweek and by a slowing down of managerial and technological advances. I believe that the pressure of international competition for cost reduction virtually excludes these solutions of the unemployment problem. This will leave no other solution than the creation of additional job opportunities in private and public investment programs and through the generation of adequate demand. All this adds up to accelerated economic growth.

ACCELERATED GROWTH NOT A FOREGONE CONCLUSION

Considering the factors which hinder and those which favor increased economic growth, it becomes clear that a forecast of the net result of these in part contradictory forces is very difficult indeed. In the light of these contradictory forces, it cannot be accepted as a foregone conclusion that the predicted acceleration will take place.

It is perhaps the most difficult task for policy to develop methods for dealing with the balance-of-payments and inflation problems by other measures than those which would restrict a reasonable rate of growth.

The judgment you will form on the economic outlook for the coming decade will, I believe, to a large extent hinge on your conviction or lack of conviction that these twin problems can be solved without undue resort to restrictive fiscal and monetary policies.

My personal conviction that we shall be forced to adopt adequate policies in support of economic growth is based in part on the analysis of what would happen if we failed to do so. Continuing high unemployment will make demands for shorter hours and for controls of managerial and technological advances irresistible, thereby increasing costs of production and slowing down increases in productivity. This would, in the longer run, have a much more unfavorable effect on the competitive situation of American industry and on the balance of payments than might result from an expansionary credit and fiscal policy. Therefore I believe that, in the last analysis, the objectives of accelerated growth, reasonable price stability and the straightening out of international economic relations need not remain in conflict.

My reasoning for believing that an increased rate of growth is a probability for the next decade may be criticized for following the logic that an event is likely to take place because it should take place. Perhaps I am influenced by my conviction that a democracy sometimes moves a bit slowly but that it moves in the right direction.

Discussion*

ARTHUR MEYERS: One of the things that concerns me is that you start with a 1950 position for both Europe and the United States and ask yourself in 1963 if the rates of growth have been different over the period. You do this by taking only the two points and finding what rate will get you from one to the other, instead of going through a step-by-step, year-by-year comparison. It appears to me that we had our growth through the war, when we increased our productivity and Europe did not. Now we are leveling off, whereas Europe experienced a much slower rate for a while. It looks like a parallelogram, pulled a little crooked. We went through our great growth and now are leveling; Europe had at first a gradual growth and now a steeper growth. Maybe we are being alarmist. Do you have some comment on this?

MR. DENISON: First of all, let me say there is a great deal in this. There is an interesting chart which shows output per man-hour in industry, running back to about 1922 in the United States, Sweden, and other countries. The index is on a 1929 base. The chart goes something like this: Sweden goes happily along almost at a constant rate. The United

* Proceedings of the Sixth Annual Conference, 1963, Excerpts from the Discussion, pp. 39–53.

States has the Great Depression, flops around and ends up just a shade below Sweden. The United Kingdom has less fluctuation and ends up still lower. But all three countries are in one band, as it were. The countries which were heavily involved in the war other than the United Kingdom come along fairly evenly before the war and then go way down, with Italy and Germany going up again but still, as of about three years ago, far below Sweden. This kind of chart makes your point very effectively.

On the other hand, let me tell you why I do not consider this quite good enough from my standpoint. Wherever we are at any given time, something has to happen to get us from here to there. I do not think there is any point in starting at 1945 in Europe, but by 1950 the craziest distortions created by the war had been left behind. Still, something actually had to happen to get from where we were in 1950 to where we were in 1960, and it is interesting to find out what it was.

SHERMAN SHAPIRO: I should like to ask Gerhard Colm a question. I am concerned about a 5% to 6% possible rate of growth, especially in light of the fact that you suggest that a large dose of direct controls will really assist in achieving it as a long-run possibility. You suggest price controls, wage controls and the allocation of materials as aids in achieving a much higher rate of economic growth. I am not sure how these would help.

MR. COLM: I might answer this in the following way, and at the same time comment on some relevant points in the previous discussion. Much of the discussion has focused on what is the potential rate of growth, looking at the supply side, at the production side — manpower, hours of work, knowledge which is incorporated in new technology and all that — and we find differences. Let me assert something I cannot prove by statistics; it is my impression that all these factors have a great deal of leeway.

Take the first long-term OEEC projection for Europe. You might also take the Twentieth Century Fund projection for Europe, which predicted for 1960 a very considerable decline in the rate of growth and underestimated it by a wide margin. As a matter of fact, when the Twentieth Century Fund projection was published (printing took a long time), two-thirds of the ten-year projection had already been achieved. Now, why was that? What happened was a very strong demand and great flexibility in the supply of the factors of production. These estimates were based on a demographic extrapolation, but they underestimated the flexibility in the labor supply.

We went wrong in the other direction. In one year we lost 800,000 people who simply disappeared from the labor force. In Europe, an addition to the labor force came out of nowhere; workers came out of southern Italy, and women who were not supposed to work, according to the statistics, went to work. A great increase in the labor force happened which was not anticipated by the experts.

So I do believe that, with a very strong demand factor, we shall be surprised at the growth rate we can achieve. We experienced it to some extent during the war. We could get a forced rate of growth under conditions of excess demand, but we would need controls in order not to get into a runaway wage and price spiral which would undermine our results, our efficiency, through inflation. That was in the back of my mind when I said that we could have a rate of growth of 5% or 6%, but that it would require such an expansion of fiscal and monetary policy as would be compatible with a reasonable degree of stabilization only in case of rigid price and wage controls, which we are not likely to adopt except in conditions of a national emergency.

Secondly, such a rate of growth also would create bottlenecks, and we would need some drastic measures in order to break them. That is why I mentioned materials controls. We also would have to do something to break manpower bottlenecks.

But looking only at the human and material resources and possible technological advance, I should say that a 5% or 6% rate of growth is not impossible. I do not recommend it except if there is an emergency, because I think the gain in additional production would not be worth the costs in regulation, which, by the way, I think would not work under conditions short of emergency.

MR. SHAPIRO: It seems to me that reasoning by analogy from World War II is quite tenuous. It was only two or two and a half years after the war started for us that we achieved full employment, and I thought you suggested that we could not in fact have a rate of growth of 5% to 6% for a long-sustained period. Experiences under both OPA and OPS and the wage controls suggest that after a short period of time we develop some severe rigidities, and this probably also applies to the allocation of materials. Is it your presumption that the administration of these controls would necessarily be much more efficient than a market system?

MR. COLM: Let it be understood that I am not recommending anything like that. It is an intellectual exercise. Under any conditions which did not create the national discipline which we would have in an extreme emergency, I should say that controls would not be as efficient as the market system. Under such an expansion as would be necessary to produce such a high rate of growth, the market system would give us inflation.

PAUL DARLING: I should like to put my question in the context of planning. Since Dr. Colm is with the National Planning Association, I hope this is an appropriate question for him. On the basis of a considerable amount of inexpert knowledge of European economies, I have the impression that there is considerable economic planning, for example, in the French economy; and I would guess that there is considerably more planning in the German economy than perhaps is immediately apparent. I wonder whether a high rate of growth in some European countries may not be the result of achieving a more balanced growth, let us say a better meshing of fixed investment, both privately owned capital and what might be called the social-overhead capital, including transportation, education, health, recreation, and all other inputs necessary for a productive economy. Is not some part of the faster growth rate in these countries due to this?

MR. COLM: The Europeans have made a much greater advance in a planning effort in which France, Japan, the Netherlands, and Sweden are probably pioneers. That is indicative planning, where the government sets some goals which become bench marks for the specific plans for government programs and business investment planning. As a matter of fact, our government, too, is obligated under the Employment Act, as far as it is feasible, to set some goals. But in the United States this is to a large extent discarded as politics. When the President says, "I think we can do better than 4%," or Rockefeller counters that we should grow 5%, it is not taken seriously as a guidepost for evaluating future markets for business. In Japan and France, such a statement is taken seriously. Businessmen say, "If that is the policy of the government, we don't want to be behind. We know certain markets will develop and we don't want to lose our share of the market." They have confidence in the goals because they participate in the process of evolving them. In France there are 1,500 people involved with advisory committees, and in Japan there are about the same number. Virtually every important businessman is on one or another of the so-called deliberating committees. They take part in the formulation of the goals, they believe in them and they use them as bench marks for their own investment policy.

Now, I think that the essence of a dynamic economy is that every major sector of the economy goes ahead without waiting for the other. If the government only evolves expenditure plans based on this year's revenue, and says, "If we embark on these plans we get into a big deficit," rather than saying, "This will create expenditures two or three years from now, when revenue, because of the growth of the country, will also go up," or if business sits back and waits for the orders to come in rather than anticipating the future markets, then the economy will not go ahead.

The essence of a dynamic economy is that it works on the basis of anticipation: If everybody anticipates approximately correctly, then everybody moves ahead in accord; if everybody waits for the other, we get stagnation. The essence of planning in a free-enterprise economy,

I think, is the creation of an atmosphere in which anticipation influences decision-making. If there is some consensus, it makes very little difference whether it is 4% or 4½%; if business knows that the government means business in playing its role, and if the government knows that there is certain response in business to its own policy, then we are assured that the development will be closer to the potential than it otherwise would be. I think this is essential for planning in a free-enterprise economy.

9

Economic Growth and

Residential Housing*

Robert M. Solow is professor of economics at the Massachusetts Institute of Technology; consultant, President's Council of Economic Advisers; consultant, Rand Corporation; and John Bates Clark Medal award winner. He is the co-author of *Linear Programing and Economic Analysis* and the author of "On the Structure of Linear Models," *Econometrica*, January 1952; "The Production Function and the Theory of Capital," *Review of Economic Studies*, April 1956; "Contribution to the Theory of Economic Growth," *Quarterly Journal of Economics*, February 1956; "Investment and Technical Progress," *Mathematical Methods in the Social Sciences*, 1959; "Note on a Two-Sector Model of Economic Growth," *Review of Economics and Statistics*, October 1961; and other articles. Mr. Solow earned his bachelor's, master's and doctoral degrees at Harvard University.

I SUPPOSE THE BEST DESCRIPTION of what I have to say is "The Present State of Growthmanship in the World."

You may remember the subtitle of Stephen Potter's original treatise on gamesmanship: "How to Win at Games without Actually Cheating." When Vice-President Nixon (or was it really Allen Wallis?) invented the label "growthmanship," I suppose he meant to suggest a subtitle for what the opposition was doing — something like "How to Talk about

* Proceedings of the Fifth Annual Conference, 1962, pp. 120–39.

Economics without Actually Saying Anything." There may have been the least little bit of truth in that description of the kind of discussion that went on then and occasionally still goes on now. But history will record that Mr. Kennedy accepted the challenge, and economic growth was, for the first time that I can recall, actually an explicit object of political debate. Growthmanship won, by about 50.1 to 49.9.

I speak on the subject as a "growthman" myself. I believe economic growth is important, so naturally I have spent a lot of time working on it; or else I have spent a lot of time working on the subject of economic growth, so naturally I think it is important.

It is fair to say, I suppose, that the acceleration of economic growth is a declared goal of the Kennedy Administration's economic policy. I should explain at the very beginning that in my vocabulary, economic growth means the expansion of the economy's potential output, its capacity to produce. What is produced in a particular quarter or year or decade cannot for long exceed the economy's normal potential or capacity. But it may well fall short, if the level of demand is insufficient to buy what the economy is capable of producing.

Growthmanship: Domestic Status

The President, the chairman of the Council of Economic Advisers, and the Secretary of the Treasury have all, on occasion after occasion, said that the administration believes recent rates of growth to be unsatisfactorily low and that it sets itself the task of raising them. Sometimes, to be sure, a little confusion creeps in (though never in the remarks of Walter Heller). One sometimes hears it said, for instance, that we need rapid economic growth in order to provide employment for our swiftly expanding labor force during the next few years. But what we need to create employment is an expansion of demand, not an expansion of capacity. The logical connection is the other way round: a rapidly expanding labor force permits a rapid rate of growth of output. But most of the time we get the story straight. For reasons we can go into in the discussion, the administration would like to see potential output rise faster than it has been doing.

One could not say that the Kennedy Administration now has a systematic, coherent policy for economic growth, as it does for short-run economic stabilization. It has justified some of its legislative and administrative proposals (notably the investment tax credit still before the Senate, and the Bulletin F revision promised for this summer), mainly in terms of their favorable effects on economic growth, and it probably could justify some others among its proposals, at least partially, on that ground. But we could not point to any tightly knit bundle of legislative

proposals and describe it as a growth-oriented program. Indeed, one
sometimes gets the feeling that economic growth is being used as a way
of changing the subject when the conversation turns to such embarrassing
questions as whether full employment is likely to be achieved before the
next downturn.

There is something a little premature in going all out for growth of
capacity when we have not, during the last five years, succeeded in
using all the capacity we have. In principle, there is nothing inconsistent
in this; if the economy were going to steer a fairly steady course for full
employment sometime in 1963, say, it would not be a moment too soon
to be planning a policy for future growth. But if one does not have full
confidence in a safe passage to full employment in 1963, then some talk
about growth does indeed sound like growthmanship, like pie in the sky.

Nevertheless, it probably would not be excessively sympathetic to say
that the administration takes the goal of accelerated economic growth
seriously and is prepared to adopt policies to achieve it. Growthmanship
has become respectable, to the extent that a Democratic administration
can confer respectability on anything.

GROWTHMANSHIP: INTERNATIONAL STATUS

In Europe and in Japan, economic growth is an even more immediate
and urgent goal. In most of those countries, capacity has been increasing
at unprecedented rates since the war and demand has been pressing on
capacity and asking for more. It is only natural that Europeans should
care more intensely about economic growth than we do. Appetite comes
with eating, and European standards of living are still well below American. If we are in a position to wonder whether current sacrifice on behalf
of future income is a matter of very high priority, apparently Europeans
are not.

In any case, having apparently solved the problem of making their
economies operate under a full head of steam and having in many,
though not all, cases a strong balance of payments position from which
to operate, the major economies of western Europe are throwing themselves seriously into the search for economic growth. In this we have
joined them.

In November of last year, the Council of Ministers of the twenty-nation
Organization for Economic Cooperation and Development launched the
new organization on a program explicitly designed to generate a 50%
increase in the combined gross national product of the member countries
between 1960 and 1970. The initiative for this step came primarily from
the United States and Belgium. The warmth with which the other countries supported the resolution varied considerably, and some originally

believed the 50% growth target to be unrealistically stiff. I think it is fair to say that, as the national capitals have looked into the problem individually and jointly, apprehensions over the feasibility of this joint venture into growthmanship have evaporated, and nowadays the target is thought to be entirely achievable provided the United States can get back on the full-employment track again.

The European essay in growthmanship has one especially interesting aspect that deserves mention. Among the spectacular success stories of the postwar period is France. Between 1950 and 1961, real GNP in France increased at an average annual rate of some 4.3 or 4.4%, of which 3.9 or 4.0% represents an increase in GNP per person employed. This is one of the best records in Europe.

Now, the French themselves believe that the secret of their success is the particular style of "indicative planning" they have adopted. Outsiders are less clear about the extent to which French planning has teeth — if it has teeth, presumably they bite mainly because of official influence and control over capital markets — and the extent to which it is all some kind of Gallic jolly-up. But the French are in no doubt. And some of the slower-growing countries have caught the fever and are starting similar ventures of their own. Belgium and the United Kingdom are the main examples; Sweden has been doing its own brand of "indicative planning" for a while. So far as Germany is concerned, we in the United States have the impression that since the war the Federal Republic has become the adopted country of Adam Schmidt. I am less certain of that. Careful official analyses of postwar German growth seem to be saying something like this: "Our success is simply a result of our devotion to the pure principles of unfettered competition and laissez faire. In support of this policy we have done the following twenty things, each of which would be classified in the United States as open socialism." In any case, our allies in Europe are now growthmen.

GROWTHMANSHIP AND THE ECONOMISTS

I should perhaps say a word about the fact that so many of the world's leading growthmen are either academic economists or so close to being academic economists as to make the distinction hardly worth having. There are at least three reasons why the economics of long-run growth is such a popular subject in universities and learned journals these days.

One reason is the way in which the problem of the economic development of preindustrial areas has captured the attention and the imagination of the postwar world and become a matter of some international political importance.

A second reason is purely intellectual. The dominant Keynesian approach to macroeconomics left a yawning gap through its concentration on short-run flow equilibrium with the stock of capital held constant. Harrod and Domar leaped in and we are still going.

My final reason would seem less strange anywhere but in Chicago. I think that most economists feel that short-run macroeconomic theory is pretty well in hand along exactly the line that Lerner described yesterday. The basic outlines of the dominant theory have not changed in years. All that is left is the trivial job of filling in the empty boxes, and that will not take more than fifty years of concentrated effort at a maximum. This has the implication that most economists think that knowledge is adequate for at least a crudely rational full employment policy — only the rest of the population does not realize it yet. So, given that feeling, it is natural to look for new and slightly different problems.

Remember that by economic growth I mean fundamentally the growth of capacity to produce rather than the growth of demand, although that is an important but separate problem. So the foundation of any broad view of economic growth has to be an evaluation of the major determinants of potential output and productivity in an economy, the chances of influencing them and the effectiveness of changes in the determinants on capacity output itself.

DETERMINANTS OF POTENTIAL OUTPUT

Everyone is in broad agreement about the nature of the major determinants of potential output, but there is some disagreement about their relative influence, and recent research has led to some revision of earlier opinions. The main sources of potential output we can name pretty clearly:

1. The first determinant is the number of people available for employment; the number of hours they wish to work; and the level and distribution of skills, education, health, and attitudes toward work. I suppose one ought to include managerial and entrepreneurial knowledge and ability as a special kind of labor, or perhaps it deserves a heading to itself.

2. The second broad and important determinant is the size of the existing stock of capital goods and its distribution by age, by industry, and by location.

3. The third important determinant is the level of technology. Here one must distinguish between the extent of technological knowledge and the degree to which it can be made effective, because that may depend in large part on the age distribution of the existing capital stock. There is a sense in which the whole civilized world shares the discoveries of modern science and engineering on an equal basis, but an economy saddled with

an antiquated stock of capital may be unable to use what in principle it knows.

4. The fourth determinant, I would say, is the terms on which the economy has access to natural resources, whether through domestic production or through imports.

5. The fifth determinant is the efficiency with which resources are allocated to different economic ends; the extent of monopolistic or other barriers to the movement of capital and labor from low productivity to high productivity uses; and the degree of resistance to the introduction of new technology.

If these are the basic determinants of potential output, then the growth of productive capacity is largely limited by the rate at which the basic determinants can be expanded and improved. That, in turn, depends upon the ease with which these determinants themselves can be influenced by conscious policy or fortuitous events, and upon the sensitivity of potential output to changes in the determinants themselves.

Opinions about this have changed drastically over the last century, and even over the last dozen years. The classical economists believed that the ultimate limit to economic growth was given by the finite availability of natural resources. It has always been a source of wonder to me how such intelligent and perceptive men, writing at a time when the industrial revolution had clearly taken secure hold on England, could so underestimate the power of technological progress in offsetting the effects of diminishing returns. Maybe this is a high standard to apply. We still occasionally read dire predictions that we are about to run out of natural resources.

TECHNOLOGY AND RESOURCE SCARCITY

The truth is, of course, that as certain raw materials become physically scarce, it becomes more expensive to extract them from nature; but this tendency is offset partly by technical progress, partly by investment in improved methods and management, partly by increased reliance on imports, and partly by the substitution of cheap raw materials for expensive ones. Even these "partly's" may not add up to the whole. If the offsets are not fully effective, resources can be obtained at somewhat higher cost by digging deeper, using leaner ores, conserving wastes, and using heavier equipment. The necessity of devoting more labor and capital to extractive industry is indeed equivalent to a net decline in the productivity of the economy as a whole; but it certainly does not set, as far as we can see, an absolute limit to the growth of the economy.

One way of measuring the effects of resource scarcity is by looking at the long-term trend of raw materials prices relative to finished product

prices in general. When one does so, one finds that all raw materials are
now about 25% more expensive relative to finished products than they
were at the turn of the century, but only 5% more expensive than they
were in 1925–1959. More interesting than this very gentle tendency
toward increased real cost of raw materials is the wide variety of behavior
exhibited by different classes of raw materials. Lumber products have
indeed increased rapidly in relative price, almost doubling since 1925–
1929, and almost tripling since the turn of the century. This is the way
Ricardo presumably expected all raw materials to behave. But there
actually may have been some tendency for this trend to moderate in
recent years. Mineral construction materials, on the other hand, are
cheaper relative to finished goods in general than they were at the turn
of the century, though not quite as cheap as they were just before 1914.
In any case, the only sound conclusion is that there is much less to
natural resource scarcity than meets the eye.

We are a long way from having reliable quantitative answers to the
kind of question I am now discussing, but about some gross facts I think
we can be fairly confident. I believe, for instance, that it would now be
generally accepted that earlier thinking on this subject substantially
underestimated the influence of improving the quality of human resources
on the economy's capacity to produce.

EDUCATIONAL LEVEL AND INCOME

This is a particularly tricky area in which to make quantitative
inferences, mainly because of the difficulty of imputing observed differences in income at different educational levels in part to differences in
native ability and in part to education itself. But if one takes Edward
Denison's recent estimates as a fair example, he attributes some 40% of
the average annual growth between 1929 and 1957 in national income
per person employed to the effects of education in improving the quality
of the average man-hour of work. Between 1909 and 1929, he estimates
the contribution of education to have been only about a quarter of the
annual growth rate in productivity. Notice that this estimate excludes
the contribution of education to the advance of knowledge itself.

In other words, had the educational level of the labor force remained
stationary where it was in 1929, national income per person employed
would have risen not at an average annual rate of 1.6%, as it did between
1929 and 1957, but at something less than 1.0% per year. That is a big
difference. I do not know the exact present state of knowledge in this
area; it is changing rapidly as new research is completed, much of it
here in Chicago.

The other big revaluation that has taken place in recent years has to do with the relative importance of capital investment and technical change. The older economists seemed to think of increases in output per man-hour (of constant quality, though they did not often mention that) as being primarily or exclusively a matter of the deepening of capital, of increased capital per worker. Within the last 10 years, research done by Schmookler, Abramovitz, Kendrick and others, including myself, seemed to show that this was not the case. An explanation of the macro-economic facts appeared to require the conclusion that observed increases in output per man-hour over a 50-year period had only little to do with the increase in capital per worker. The bulk of the explanation, between 85% and 90%, had to come from other sources such as labor quality, technological progress and the like.

CAPITAL INVESTMENT AND ECONOMIC GROWTH

This downgrading of fixed investment as a source of growth had genuine policy implications. Calculations based on these ideas suggested that substantial rates of growth were obtainable with little or no net investment, and that any visible acceleration of growth through the stimulation of capital formation would require fantastic amounts of investment — although people sometimes forget that with net investment only about half of gross, a 10% increase in the rate of gross investment means in the short run a 20% increase in the rate of net investment.

I finally came to think that this undervaluation, or downgrading, of the importance of capital investment was really a little implausible and that all reasoning like that, including my own, overlooked the fact that at least some technological progress requires being embodied in newly designed types of fixed capital before it becomes effective in production. Investment thus serves the purpose not only of adding to the stock of capital per worker, but also of improving its quality, of carrying new technology into operation.

You could easily devise numerical examples that would convince you that this could make a real difference in the story. When account is taken of "embodied" inventions, the kind of inventions that need new kinds of capital to become effective, then a surge in the rate of capital formation will have bigger effects on potential output than the simple notion of "residual" productivity increase would lead one to expect.

Some rough econometric estimates I once made seem to me to give a plausible figure for the size of the investment effort needed to support a somewhat higher growth rate over the next ten years. For example, a growth rate of 4% annually in potential GNP between 1960 and 1970, which means a growth rate of some 4½% in realized GNP if 1970, unlike 1960, is a year of full utilization, would require investment in plant and equipment of roughly 11% of GNP as compared with about 9% in the last few years and slightly higher than we had in 1955–1957. This is on the assumption that all technical changes need to be embodied in new fixed capital.

One of the troubles with this whole line of thought is that it is just about impossible to make aggregate data tell anything about the extent to which innovations are of the embodied kind and the extent to which they are disembodied. Denison simply assumes it is half and half, and comes to the conclusion that between 1929 and 1957 less than 10% of the annual growth rate of national income per person employed can be imputed to the increase in reproducible capital per employee, while over a third of the annual growth rate of productivity in the same period can be attributed to the advance of knowledge. My casual guess would be that more than half of technical progress is the embodied kind, but I do not know how to find out.

CAPITAL STOCK: SIZE, AGE DISTRIBUTION

The extra "oomph" one gets from investment in this new view comes from the fact that a burst of investment changes not only the size of the capital stock, but also its age distribution. Lowering the average age of the capital stock gives a productivity bonus. But it is not easy to change the average age of a long-lived stock. An increase in plant and equipment investment relative to GNP will eventually move the age distribution of capital as far as it is ever going to move it, and then it will not move it any further. Then the average age remains stationary and the higher growth rate lapses back to what it was when the investment quota was lower, relative to GNP. Output will be forever at a higher level, but the very long-run growth rate will not change. But over a ten- or twenty-year period, the change in the investment quota might make a substantial difference.

I might conclude this section by remarking that we probably know least about the contribution to economic growth that could be made by more efficient allocation of resources, the costs of monopoly, restriction, and immobility. In some areas — agriculture, perhaps — the costs may be great, and therefore the growth advantage, temporary of course, from removing the restriction may be correspondingly great. But not much is known about the economic costs of monopoly and similar sources or malallocation.

I have been dealing at a fairly general level with the trends in ideas about economic growth. When one comes to specific projections of the prospects for economic growth in the United States over the next decade, it turns out that there are at least two schools of thought. They might be described, following my friend Arthur Okun, as the three-percenters and the four-percenters. The five-percenter is a dying race.

THREE-PERCENTERS VS. FOUR-PERCENTERS

The most important three-percenter is Denison, whose monumental work I have already cited. Denison estimates that in the absence of a massive policy effort to raise the rate of growth — and the elements of that effort need only be mentioned to scare the pants off you — potential output will grow at something like 3.3% a year over the next decade. Note that this growth rate refers to potential output, not realized output. If, as the evidence seems to suggest, real GNP in 1960 fell 5% or 6% below potential, then the path from 1960 to full employment in 1970 would rise at about 3.8% or 3.9% a year on the average.

The four-percenters are represented by the National Planning Association, the Council of Economic Advisers and, apparently, John F. Kennedy. They estimate that a moderate policy program favoring economic growth could make potential output rise at something like 4% a year between 1960 and 1970 — perhaps even a little faster. And if the path to 1970 winds up at full employment, the actual annual growth rate could exceed 4½%.

No one has yet tried to trace back the difference between the two schools of thought to critical hypotheses or evaluations, and I think it is worth doing. Maybe we ought to begin by laying out the assumptions the two schools hold in common. One would suppose that both schools of thought would at least begin from one piece of common ground: the rate of growth in the past. But even there one finds a vague but important difference in view.

The long-term rate of growth of potential GNP in the United States from 1929 to 1960, or even from 1909 to 1960, is about 3% a year. The three-percenters tend to start from that figure and ask where one might find grounds to hope for an acceleration. But the fifteen years since the end of the Second World War have already seen a substantial acceleration beyond 3%. Between 1947 and 1960, actual GNP rose at an average rate of 3½%, and rough allowance for the slack existing in 1960 can raise the postwar rate of growth of potential output to 4%. Some of that extraordinarily rapid growth was undoubtedly a consequence of unrepeatable factors: the war itself, and the long depression that preceded it. Even so, the Council of Economic Advisers has estimated that since 1954 or 1955, by which time the legacy of war and depression had probably run its course, potential GNP has been increasing at some 3½% a year.

The four-percenters tend to start from the more recent record, and this explains in part their more optimistic conclusions. But one cannot decide the issue on such grounds. There is no general law of economics or nature which tells you whether the last 50 years or the last 15 years provide a better guide to the next 10 years. No analogies about tails wagging dogs or dogs wagging tails have any explanatory power, because the economy, whatever it is, is probably not a dog. You have to look closer.

LABOR FORCE AND HOURS WORKED

The least controversial element in projections of economic growth for the 1960s is the labor force and the trend of annual hours worked. The three-percenters and the four-percenters are in rough agreement that the labor force will grow at an annual rate of about 1¾% between 1960 and 1970, substantially faster than the 1.3% annual rate recorded between 1947 and 1960. As usual, part of this growth in potential employment will be offset by a continuation of the trend toward shorter hours. The fairly universal conclusion is that annual man-hours at full employment will rise at about 1¼% a year to 1970, compared with ¾ of 1% from 1947 to 1960. This already gives us a leg up toward faster growth of aggregate output during the coming decade. But what actually happens depends, of course, on the path of output per man-hour, and that is the nub of the difference between the two schools of thought.

Between 1947 and 1960, potential GNP per man-hour rose at an annual rate of 3.2% a year — 3.8% between 1947 and 1954, and 2.6% between 1954 and 1960. If productivity rises between 1960 and 1970 at the same rate as it did from 1954 to 1960, potential GNP will grow at an annual rate of 3.8% a year in the coming decade. If productivity rises somewhat faster than it did between 1954 and 1960, but slightly less fast than between 1947 and 1960, and considerably slower than between 1947 and 1954 — say, at 3% a year or thereabouts — then potential GNP can rise at 4% a year between now and 1970. To bring about this acceleration will cost something, perhaps an increase in the plant and equipment share in GNP from the 9.5% of 1954–1960 (even with 1955–1957) toward the 11.2% of 1947–1954. Indeed, the four-percenters project for 1960 to 1970 a growth in the stock of capital of about 3½% a year, about the rate achieved from 1947 to 1960, and a bit faster than 1954–1960.

The three-percenters, on the other hand, project a rise in output per man-hour at only about 2% a year, roughly the rate observed in the 1929–1960 period, and considerably slower than the postwar, or even the 1954–1960, rate. Correspondingly, Denison, for example, projects capital stock growth at 2.5% a year rather than 3.5%, faster than 1929–1957 (1.9% a year including the Great Depression) but slower than anything observed in the postwar period.

SOURCES OF DIFFERENCES OF OPINION

To sum up the gross difference of opinion: Starting from the same projection for employment and hours, the four-percenters estimate productivity to rise at a rate of about 0.7% or 0.8% a year faster than the three-percenters do, and this makes the difference between 3.3% and 4.0% in the annual rate of growth of GNP.

Can we track down this difference to more specific hypotheses? We can. The seven-tenths of a point in the growth rate can be accounted for in this way:

1. The one percentage point difference in the estimated rate of growth of capital accounts for about 0.20 to 0.25 point in the rate of growth of GNP.

2. Denison estimates pure technological change to proceed at an annual rate about 0.2 point below that of the postwar period, and this accounts for about the same difference in the rate of growth of GNP. Optimists expect no such deceleration, and some even hope for a slight increase.

3. The pessimistic projections have investment in education contributing 0.1 point less to productivity growth than in the recent past.

4. By a complicated bit of guesswork, Denison estimates that a much smaller part of the expected decline in hours worked will be offset by automatic improvement in productivity resulting from lessened fatigue and the like; this is enough to account for 0.2 percentage point in the growth of productivity and of output.

I have time for only a few cursory comments on these ultimate components of the difference between a 3% and a 4% growth of potential.

1. There can be no doubt that some part of the postwar spurt of fixed investment was a "make-up" phenomenon, and the rate of growth of the capital stock has slowed visibly in recent years. But the weakness of fixed investment is both cause and effect of the slack that has developed in the economy since 1956, and that slack is remediable by policy.

Even so, the problem should not be blinked. If there is anything to the law of diminishing returns, then extra growth of output through the deepening of capital can be bought only at the expense of a lower profit rate on capital. It is the combined job of fiscal and monetary policy to sweeten that profit rate a little at the margin and to make a somewhat lower profit rate more acceptable by lowering the return on assets alternative to real capital. There might then be difficulties on the side of saving, and this might call for additional policy measures or be taken as a sign that economic growth is not a highly valued social goal.

2. On the rate of pure technological progress, nobody is in a position to speak with authority. There has certainly been an immense increase

in research and development expenditure in the postwar period, much
of it financed by the federal government and concentrated on industries
connected with defense. Whether those outlays have already borne fruit
or whether there is more to come, it is difficult to say. But there is
perhaps a case for believing that federal policy could contribute to the
acceleration of economic growth by an effort to spread into purely
civilian industries the kind of technological pressure that seems to have
had major results in electronics and space technology.

3. It may be that as time goes on, given the finite number of days in
the year, the all but universal diffusion of primary and secondary education, and human impatience, there is an inevitable retardation in the
rate at which the quality of the labor force can be improved through
education. The unevenness of educational quality from state to state
suggests that perhaps something can be done there to pick up the 0.1
point on the growth rate that Denison loses. I am not competent to judge.

4. On this point I think Denison is not so much vulnerable as un-
convincing. His assumption is that as late as 1929, when the average
employee worked about 2,500 hours a year (between 48 and 49 hours a
week), any small reduction in the hours of work was fully compensated
by a corresponding increase in productivity because of diminished fatigue,
better attentiveness and the like. By 1957, on the other hand, when the
average employee worked about 2,050 hours a year, or just about 40
hours a week, he assumes that a further slight reduction in hours was
offset to the extent of 40% by the same forces. Extrapolation leads to the
conclusion that further reduction in hours will be only about 20% offset
and, therefore, more damaging to output.

That some such process is at work is surely true, but Denison himself
emphasizes how little is known about the exact relationship. I cannot
bring myself to believe that as recently as 1929 the marginal product of
an additional hour worked was negative, and I suspect that those
European countries which still have a workweek close to 48 hours would
be surprised to learn that they could add to output by working less.

Moreover, the reduction in average hours since 1929 has been much
sharper in the diminishing agricultural work force than in industry. The
average workweek in manufacturing was 44 hours in 1929. It does not
matter so much exactly what the degree of offset was in 1929. If the
change in the offset was more gradual than Denison suggests, his conclusion would not be so pessimistic.

I conclude that when it is tracked down to its origin, the difference
between the three-percenters and the four-percenters is not solidly based.
That does not say who is right, but it does suggest the possibility that
economic policy need not turn our society on its ear to elicit a growth
of potential output near to 4% a year.

FULL EMPLOYMENT AND ECONOMIC GROWTH

I had intended to spend some time considering the full range of possible economic policy measures to stimulate growth. But since I have already touched on some of them, and have gone on far too long about other things, I will have to skip over that, with one exception. I would like to say something about the relation between full employment and economic growth as goals of policy. Does an aggressive full employment policy also stimulate economic growth or retard it?

There are a number of subquestions here which need to be disentangled. The view has recently been expressed in the United Kingdom by Paish, and recently again by Phillips, that some decrease in the average pressure of demand on resources, accompanied by a small increase in the unemployment rate, would be desirable for several reasons and could be engineered without any deterioration in the growth rate and perhaps with some improvement.

I am not sufficiently well acquainted with conditions in the United Kingdom to hold a strong opinion on this subject, but I do not find this view wholly implausible. For one thing, continuous full employment may tend to generate inflationary pressure on prices (whether originating in labor markets or product markets) and recurrent balance-of-payments crises, which require that the upward march of demand be halted frequently.

In turn, the necessary restriction of demand, either through credit tightness or tax policy, may for one reason or another fall heavily on fixed investment. I can easily image that this chain of events could make it true that a little extra slack could be engineered without ultimately reducing the growth rate, and perhaps even help it over a decent interval of time.

Secondly, it is often said that a perpetually tight economy builds up immobilities, barriers to the adoption of new technology, and resistance to competition. This may be so. It has been so long since the American economy operated with that degree of tightness that I have no fresh observations to report. What I have observed in the United States is the reverse phenomenon. Too much slack in an economy can build up the same kinds of pressures against innovation, against technological advance, against the mobility of labor and capital from declining to advancing sectors of the economy. In the United States, at least, one even observes an ebb and flow of sentiment for a shortening of the workweek with the business cycle, which relates not to any real preferences for leisure as against income, but to a feeling that there is simply not enough employment to go around without a decrease in weekly hours.

Other examples are not hard to find. The movement of labor out of agriculture, for instance, is clearly intimately related to labor market conditions in industry. When urban unemployment is low, the rate of migration out of agriculture is high, and vice versa. Of course the rate of migration is also sensitive to the market for agricultural products. When farmers are doing well, as during the Korean war, even a tight demand for labor in industry will not pull up the migration rate. But that does not contradict my observations.

To take another example, the recent report of a presidentially appointed commission to study work rules on the railroads showed a majority, including all the public members, agreeing that there is altogether too much featherbedding, too much stultification of technical progress by clinging to antiquated work rules. Such commissions usually try hard, too hard, to be neutral, so the finding is almost certainly true. Now, even in a full-employment economy, an elite occupational group would probably cling to its quasi-rents, but I do not believe the resistance to change would be so great if the demand for labor in the economy at large were considerably higher.

GROWTH AND ECONOMIC EFFICIENCY

Even if I am right and the American economy loses some efficiency because the level of demand is too low, it might still be true that other economies lose some efficiency because the pressure of demand is too high. There might indeed, from this point of view, be an optimal degree of tightness. I am only concerned to say that the United States is clearly on the slack side of that. There exists no conflict on these grounds between the goals of full, or at least fuller, employment and rapid growth.

This position that — to quote the recent Report of the Council of Economic Advisers — "a full employment economy can achieve more rapid growth than an economy alternating between boom and recession; for that reason effective stabilization policy is the first step toward a policy of economic growth" has been attacked as theoretically weak and even anti-Schumpeterian. I suppose it is the latter, but not the former.

Schumpeter, who was a teacher of mine, argued that the business cycle is the way in which a capitalistic economy makes progress. Eliminate or damp the business cycle, and you slow down the rate of progress. More specifically, of course, Schumpeter had a theory of the bunching of technical innovations. The depression is a way of shaking the unsuccessful or obsolete ones out of the system. Anyone who believes this doctrine believes in strong medicine. The business cycle Schumpeter was thinking of, which is supposed to be necessary for capitalist progress, was not the minor postwar business cycle, but the deeper ten-year major cycle of the 19th century and the prewar years. If that is necessary for economic growth, then the almost world-wide acceleration of growth during the last fifteen years becomes very difficult to explain.

SHORT BUSINESS CYCLE AND ECONOMIC GROWTH

Indeed, even the belief that the short business cycle is an indispensable midwife for economic growth is hard to maintain in the face of the postwar history of western European countries. Most of them have experienced faster productivity growth than we have; most of them have shown a sharper acceleration of their prewar trends; and all of them have maintained a consistently tighter pressure of demand and a consistently lower unemployment rate than we have, even allowing for differences in definition and statistical practice.

I have been arguing that steady full employment need not prejudice the growth of potential output. It is a more difficult question whether steady full employment might itself increase the rate of growth. This is once again largely a question of the rate of investment. Despite the fact that plant and equipment spending falls off in recession and rises in recovery, it is logically possible that wiping out the business cycle might not increase the average rate of investment relative to aggregate output. It might be that over a complete business cycle we get all the investment we would get even if the business cycle were not there, only we get it concentrated in periods of high employment, filling in the holes left by periods of low employment.

If, for example, investment were governed simply by the acceleration principle, this would be the case. Nobody can say for sure what the true state of affairs is. I am inclined to believe that the main effect of high-level stability on the volume of investment would be a reduction in the riskiness of investment. It seems plausible that one of the reasons businesses seem to demand a high expected rate of return on new projects is to compensate for the risk of inadequate markets.

The confident expectation of full employment by reducing that risk would probably make for a somewhat lower acceptable average rate of return. In my neoclassical view, that is an important part of the battle to generate higher capacity through the deepening of capital, for, apart from the effects of technical progress, each successive increment to productivity bought in this way involves diminished profitability. If I am right on this, an aggressive full-employment policy would elicit more investment averaged over a cycle than we now have, and this would contribute to economic growth. This argument also suggests than an important part of a fiscal policy designed to add to growth through investment might be an extension of income averaging for tax purposes, more complete loss offsets for corporations and, in this way, some socialization of risk.

Housing as a Form of Capital

So far I have not talked about housing at all. When I have mentioned capital formation I have pretty clearly had plant and equipment in mind, not houses. Why is this? After all, housing services are as important an item of consumption as nearly anything else, and houses are the unique kind of capital which produces housing services. How do houses as capital goods differ from plant and equipment?

One difference, of course, is that the services of houses are directly consumed, while nearly all other capital goods are used to produce other goods, which may be directly consumed or may be used to produce still other goods. I do not lay much stress on the mere fact that houses produce services while machines produce goods. The distinction between goods and services is much overdone in economics. But I suspect it does matter that houses are so directly involved in consumption. The decision to buy a particular house is more like the decision to buy a particular dress than it is like the decision to buy a machine.

That says something about why we might want to distinguish between houses and other forms of capital, but not about why we do not readily think of building houses as the kind of investment that promotes economic growth. The special character of the end product is probably at the root of this question, too. Houses are a highly specific form of capital. They produce shelter and nothing else. I suppose one could find equally specific kinds of plant and equipment, tools or dies which are capable of producing only one single product. But when we speak of investment, not as a source of demand but as a generator of supply, we usually have in mind the picture of capital goods capable of ultimately producing a wide variety of end products. Then sensible creation of generalized capacity does not presuppose any clear initial idea of what form the final demand will actually take. Building houses does presuppose that.

Of course, housing is a superior good. It is a safe bet that as incomes rise, people buy more housing or better housing. So in the process of economic growth, the market will see to it that approximately the right number of houses will be built to accommodate population growth and normal upgrading.

As I mentioned earlier, one of the reasons capital formation is so important in economic growth is that new capital goods may be an indispensable carrier of technological progress. One normally does not think of houses in that way. No doubt houses are more efficient producers of housing services than they used to be. Since it is so hard to measure the output of housing services in physical terms, I do not suppose we will ever know how fast efficiency does increase. In any case, the specificity of houses as a kind of capital means that technical improvements in houses have their full, direct impact on only one narrow sector of the economy, though there are market effects which certainly diffuse widely through the economy.

RESIDENTIAL CONSTRUCTION AND GNP

Capital formation in the form of houses as a fraction of GNP has fluctuated quite widely through that part of our history which is covered by statistics. In part this is a consequence of changes in the rate of growth and the rate of internal migration of the population. In part it is a consequence of the complicated interaction between the level of new construction and the general level of business activity. And in part, of course, it is the consequence of wartime restrictions.

It is tricky to say anything about the long-term trend in residential construction as a share of GNP, because of the tendency for construction-cost indexes and home prices to rise through time more rapidly than the general price level, whether this is a true indication of relative prices or simply a fault of the indexes. In constant prices, there is some tendency for residential construction to decline slowly as a share of real GNP over long periods of time; but in current prices, this looks more like a fairly horizontal trend with fluctuations.

Just to take an example: In 1929 prices, nonfarm residential construction was 5.2% of GNP in 1869–1873 and, after rising to the great height of 8.7% in 1887–1891, it fell to 3.6% in 1927–1931. But in current dollars, nonfarm residential construction was only 3.3% of GNP in 1869–1873, rose more sharply to 6.6% in 1887–1891, and was 3.6% in 1927–1931 — higher, not lower, than it had been 60 years before.

During the postwar period by itself, the movements of the current-price and constant-price series have been fairly similar, partly because the period is short, and partly because, especially after 1950, the deflators have not diverged very much. What is noteworthy about the postwar period is both the absence of a trend and the mildness of the fluctuations in the residential construction share of GNP. The figure never got above 5% of GNP in 1950, and never fell below the Korean war figure of 3.7% in 1952.

European postwar figures have been very similar in their behavior. Taking the eighteen OEEC countries as a whole, residential construction as a share of GNP (1954 prices) started at 3% in 1949; it rose gradually to 4.3% in 1954, as the reconstruction of the industrial machinery was completed, and has hardly budged since then. The greater stability of residential construction relative to GNP in Europe is not surprising. It is probably related both to the greater freedom of economic activity from cyclical fluctuations and to the fact that the volume of house construction is much more definitely an object of public policy with European countries than it is with us.

I have dwelt on this rather odd number, the share of residential construction in GNP, for two reasons: first, because its behavior does seem to suggest, as one would expect, that periods of above-average increase in productivity do not seem in general to be periods of above-average investment in houses, although they are generally periods of above-average investment in plant and equipment; and, second, as a preparation for some crude remarks about prospects for the future.

Some Housing Projections

I am not a housing analyst, and there are people here far better equipped than I to make projections of the demand for new housing over the next ten years. But I can mention the following kind of calculation, made by HHFA. I think Mr. Schechter, who is sitting back there, knows about the calculations and probably did them.

Start with the housing inventory of 1960, corrected for vacant and seasonal units probably missed by the Census enumerators. Estimate losses from the 1950–1956 experience, with additional allowance for losses due to urban renewal and highway programs. Then add an allowance to bring the number of housing units classified by the Census as "dilapidated" down to half their 1960 level by 1965 and to zero in 1970. Then estimate the required additions to the housing inventory to house the estimated number of households in 1965 and 1970 (Census Series II) with a vacancy rate equal to what it was in 1960, with a slow rise in owner-occupancy, plausible changes in tenure, shifts from farm to nonfarm, income distribution, value-to-income ratios and the like. Make straight trend projections of outlays in additions and alterations and nonhousekeeping units.

The result is an estimate of the number and construction cost, in 1961 prices, of new housing units required during the 1960s to house all American families in nondilapidated structures. With considerable smoothing, the result is a series of annual housing starts rising from 1,350,000 in 1961 to 1,825,000 in 1965 and 2,050,000 in 1970. The corresponding construction cost, in 1961 prices, rises from $23.1 billion in 1961 to $26.5 billion in 1965 and $33.5 billion in 1970. I hardly need to repeat that this is not a prediction, but a kind of combination of projection and target.

If GNP rises between now and 1970 about as the four-percenters think it can and might, and if Lorenz curves do not change much, then some fraction of the nonfarm units required to meet this target will need public assistance of some kind. How big that fraction would be depends on yet further assumptions. If owners who can afford units valued up to only $6,000 and renters who can afford gross rents up to only $49 will need assistance, then something like 15% of the units constructed in 1965 and 12% of those for 1970 will need assistance. If owners who can afford units valued up to only $7,500 and renters who can pay gross rents up to only $59 require assistance, then the fractions requiring assistance would be 20% in 1965 and 17% in 1970. I am not the man to say whether this is plausible.

But if the four-percenters are right, and real GNP rises from $511 billion in 1960 to a round $800 billion in 1970 (4% yearly growth of potential plus a 5% closing of the gap to full employment), then even this fairly ambitious target, involving a 50% increase in housing starts, would require residential construction at only the standard postwar 4.1% to 4.3% of GNP in constant 1961 prices. It sounds reasonable but, unfortunately, what is reasonable is not always true.

Discussion*

ABBA LERNER: I am particularly allergic to growthmanship — I have been trying to avoid it for many years — but I think some of it creeps in, in using the very notion of GNP as a measure of growth. We get credit for increasing population, which seems to me is not at all what is being acknowledged. What is being acknowledged, it seems to me, is the increase in the degree to which we are able to raise the standard of living. I am not at all concerned with what creeps in, in the same kind of way, in supposing that future standards of living are more important than present standards of living. I think that this has no particular basis. In the future, or for a long time, if we remain alive, the standard of living is going to go up anyway, so we need more income now than we need in the future.

MR. SOLOW: I think I am in full agreement with this. If you go around grading the economy as the professor does (B, B+ or B−) then output per head, the standard of living, is the true measure.

MR. LERNER: I want to go a step further and say I would take output per man-hour.

MR. SOLOW: You would take output per man-hour? That is not a measure of consumption standards.

MR. LERNER: I think it is. The reduction in man-hours means that people are taking more leisure. I do not see any reason for not considering leisure as just as good a product as housing or anything else.

MR. SOLOW: That is quite right. I accept that. But I am not certain it

* Proceedings of the Fifth Annual Conference, 1962, Excerpts from the Discussion, pp. 139–47.

means that output per man-hour is the correct measure of performance.

MR. LERNER: On the one hand, I think that if we have full employment, then growth is easier, or rather investment is easier. It is easier for people to give up some of their consumption if they have more to begin with. But one point where I disagree with you is that it makes sense to talk about growth in your much more useful sense of capacity rather than output, even if we do not have full employment, and you suggested that it does not make any sense at all.

I would say that if we have some mechanism like the one I was alluding to yesterday, in which we maintain a fairly stable percentage of our capacity operating, then we can work the rest of it as if we had full employment. Instead of having 100% we have 90%, but everything we could do in the case of full employment applies if a stable level of activity is somehow maintained.

MR. SOLOW: Yes, I think that is so, Abba, but I was not thinking of the problem you raised yesterday about the possible inability of the economy to increase its rate of utilization above what we would consider a satisfactory level without running into the problem of inflation. Certainly it is a much cheaper way of getting extra output to use existing underutilized capacity than to create new capacity. But if, in effect, for one institutional reason or another, we find it is impossible to increase the rate of utilization, then I would agree with what you just said.

CLIFTON KREPS: If our capacity to produce GNP in 1970 at 1961 prices would be $800 billion at full-employment levels, which I think is the figure you suggested, could you hazard any guess as to what that magnitude would be in 1970 prices?

MR. SOLOW: No. Will you say something about that?

MR. KREPS: I am apparently a member of a dying race, but I like to attach considerable significance to price stability. I am also concerned about the possible effect on that of emphasizing growthmanship, full employment, and so on. I hate to see it left out altogether.

MR. SOLOW: Let me say something about that. I think it is rather odd to find people (I find myself doing it sometimes) thinking of price stability as an ultimate economic goal in the same sense as full employment or improved standards of living as an ultimate economic goal. Price stability, I think, is something instrumental.

The main problems that inflation raises for an economy are two. One is the redistribution of income that inflation brings about. Any change in the price level redistributes income from one group of people in a society to another group of people in a society in a kind of haphazard way or, if in a systematic way, not necessarily in a way that we as citizens would consider desirable. So what we object to in inflation is the redistributive effect rather than the mere fact of the recorded increase in the price level. One could imagine the possibility of society finding ways of compensating for the damage that is done by inflation by redistribution through one method or another.

The second objection to inflation, from the social point of view, is the balance-of-payments problem. Of the two, the balance-of-payments problem seems to me to be the major disadvantage of inflation.

MR. KREPS: I certainly agree with that. I do not mean to assert that this is the thing we should seek above all else; but if we can achieve these higher-order goals without inflation, I think it would be the preferable way of doing it.

MR. SOLOW: Yes.

DUANE SAUNDERS: You are really talking about a third effect, a third objection to inflation, which is the effect it has on future growth. It can dampen down future growth if it gets out of kilter. Price stability in and of itself does not produce goods for us. It has to have an objective, too.

MR. SOLOW: That is right, and I think Duane would agree that this is a strong argument against hyperinflation. If the price level rises at 50% or 100% a year, it undoubtedly is going to have bad effects on future capacity and on the organization of the economy. But exactly what the effect of a price increase of the order of magnitude of 1%, 1½%, or 2% per year would be is very difficult to measure.

EDWARD EDWARDS: I do not want to be associated with the idea that a house is not capital, but I do have the suspicion that different kinds of capital make different degrees of contribution to productivity. For example, I think it was a good idea for Robinson Crusoe to make the spear first and not the house.

Now, my question is this: Do we need as much effort on the part of the federal government to stimulate capital investment in housing as we have had, and is it good public policy to insure savings that go into housing and to insure mortgages that insure savings associations and so on?

MR. SOLOW: I think that is a kind of value-judgment question. If one feels or thinks or believes that the present allocation of resources to the production of different kinds of capital and different kinds of consumer goods, durable or nondurable, is just right, then there is no need for any further change. But if one comes to the conclusion that it would be a good thing if resources were allocated in such a way that more was spent on providing services to consumers of the kind houses provide, and if the only apparent way of doing this is through insurance programs or something like that, then they are a good idea; otherwise they are not. But I do not see how one can answer a question like that in principle.

MARSHALL KETCHUM: You indicated some of the research that has been done by three-percenters and four-percenters in arriving at their conclusions, and you presented some of your analysis of their research. I suppose this question involves some element of subjectivity on your part, but would you be willing to stick your neck out and say which is more nearly right, the three-percenters or the four-percenters?

MR. SOLOW: I am a four-percenter. I am inclined to feel that the analysis of the three-percenters is excessively pessimistic. It attaches more weight to the distant past than ought to be done.

LEON KENDALL: Based on the success or enchantment with indicative planning on the part of the French, are we or should we in this country entertain or consider indicative planning?

MR. SOLOW: As I say, the great mystery to me is exactly what it is that the French are doing.

As I understand the process, it is not something which is capable of being carried over to an economy whose structure is like the American economy. In France, it is possible to get 95% of the representatives of heavy industry into one room and talk with them, jolly them up a bit and induce them to do this or do that. It is not something you can do in an economy as extensive and as decentralized as is the American economy. I think it is not something you can do easily in an economy which has the prejudice against cartels and monopolies that our economy has and that the French do not at all share. So I cannot see anything really like the French system of indicative planning as a prospect for the United States.

On the other hand, I can easily see some value to the American economy of rather more extensive public projections two or three or four years ahead made both by responsible private agencies and by responsible government agencies, so that all of industry can have before it in its own planning what informed people in and out of government think to be the prospect for the next few years. These I hope we will have.

MR. KENDALL: You did not see the 1962 steel experience or the labor conversations as in any sense equivalent to an American version of indicative planning?

MR. SOLOW: Not in any sense.

ELI SHAPIRO: It is just indicative.

MR. SOLOW: Grammatically speaking, it was more like imperative.

10

The Role of Government
in Residential Financing*

Robert C. Turner was, in 1959, professor of business administration at Indiana University. He has written monographs and articles in the field of business cycles and forecasting, as well as on business-government relations. Mr. Turner received his A.B. from Hiram College, his M.B.A. from Northwestern University and his Ph.D. from Ohio State University. He was formerly a faculty member of Wayne University and the University of Notre Dame; director, Warren Branch, Hiram College; director, Foreign Division, War Production Board; adviser on international operations, Office of War Mobilization and Reconversion; economic adviser to the Assistant to the President; and member, Council of Economic Advisers.

IT IS WITH A GOOD DEAL OF TREPIDATION that I appear before this group, because I am not an expert in real estate financing. Rather, somewhat by accident, I have become one of those generalists who is supposed to know a little bit about everything and you know what. Furthermore, as anchor man on your excellent program, some of what I have to say has already been said. Fortunately, there are no serious discrepancies between what has been said and what I plan to say, but in some cases it has been said better.

There is probably no object of consumer expenditure that has more political appeal than housing. The main reason for this, I suppose, is

* Proceedings of the Second Annual Conference, 1959, pp. 135–52.

that so many normal human emotions are intimately associated with a home. Marital love, love of children, sex, avocational pleasures, rest and relaxation, social intercourse, love of nature, religion, and other emotional aspects of life are focused in the home.

For many men, the instinct for creativity and the desire for recognition both find their expression in a house — a man's monument to himself. Innumerable sentimental songs, from "Home, Sweet Home" to "Goin' Home," have been written about the virtues of one's place of residence. People become much more emotionally attached to a house than to any other object of ownership. They will make investments of time and money in a house that are uneconomic by any purely rational test. They will pass up opportunities for professional advancement rather than leave home, that is, change houses. Whole communities will suffer chronic unemployment for a generation, largely because people are unwilling to leave their homes and move to new communities where jobs are available.

Even with today's well advertised mobility of population, a great many people buy only one house during the course of a lifetime, and an even larger number plan to buy only one when the first purchase is made. It is therefore an economic act of great importance. Moreover, it is an act in which the great majority of us are thwarted; income limitations prevent us from achieving our felt desires fully or even approximately.

In the case of almost any other tangible object of expenditure, for most families in the United States, a person can get what he wants — even a Cadillac — if he wants it badly enough to make a tolerable sacrifice of other forms of consumption. Not so with a house. We all want a house; and if we already have a house, we want a better one. Any Congressman knows that, whereas advocacy of more and better automobiles or clothing or vacations is of rather limited campaign value, uncompromising support for more and better houses for their constituents has never lost a vote.

Incidentally, I suppose that one of the reasons for farm programs getting so much political support from nonfarm groups is that in the case of farming, the home is a part of the place of business. To change jobs, a farmer must usually give up his home. This is too much to ask.

The highly emotional content of home ownership and occupancy is one reason for political activity in this area, but there is another that is perhaps more immediately relevant. This is the widespread conviction that unregulated private activity somehow does not or would not serve our needs well in this area. In part, this attitude is a product of the disenchantment with unregulated capitalism that emerged during the Great Depression. Housing, even if it were not of the special kind of consumption that it is, could hardly have escaped the ideological wreckage of the 1930s.

But housing *is* a special kind of consumption. It is special not only by reason of the unusual emotional connotations involved in home purchase and ownership, but also by reason of some very hard economic facts of life. It is expensive — so expensive that the vast majority of home purchases are partially, if not largely, financed with funds supplied by someone other than the buyer. For a variety of reasons the outside funds almost always take the form of debt rather than equity capital. What a difference it might have made in the 1930s if house building had been financed entirely by equity capital. The fact that so much trading on the equity is involved magnifies the risk of gain or loss. Housing is also unusual in that funds have traditionally been supplied largely by lending institutions that also trade on the equity; that is, their sources of funds are largely fixed dollar obligations. Moreover, these obligations are payable, by law or by practice, on demand or on relatively short notice. Thus we have trading on the equity compounded. This is a vulnerable kind of business, with the home owner sitting on the end of a very long limb. So long as everything proceeded smoothly, little trouble could occur. But when the economic system faltered and values and incomes declined, the home owner was likely to fall off his limb, and the financial institutions in turn were in trouble. This condition of extraordinary vulnerability provided a special reason for government intervention in housing.

REASONS FOR CHANGE IN GOVERNMENT'S ROLE

These, as I see it, are the three main reasons for the major change in the role of government in housing that has occurred in the past quarter century: the highly emotional content of home ownership and occupancy; the general ideological revolution growing out of the Great Depression; and the extraordinary financial circumstances involved in housing.

To these should be added another supplementary reason: in this country and elsewhere, there has been a long tradition of government interference in many aspects of residential property. Because home ownership inevitably involves title to land, government has long been a party to every real estate transaction, if only to the extent of recording and processing the legal evidence of ownership. But government's activities have extended far beyond into such matters as land grants, exercise of the power of eminent domain, zoning, enforcement of building regulations, subdivision planning, and so on. Also, governments have long been in the business of regulating certain types of financial institutions because of the character of their liabilities.

So government interference in housing did not involve as much of a break with the past as it did in, say, regulation of labor relations. So far as I know, the constitutionality of none of the New Deal housing laws was ever challenged; if there was such a challenge, it did not make enough progress to reach the level of the Supreme Court. Indeed, the New Deal housing programs ran into about as little vocal opposition as any of the reform programs of that day. And the laws have stayed on the books, modified to be sure in many important details to accommodate to the changing circumstances of depression, war, reconversion and prosperity, but unaltered in their basic philosophy.

PHILOSOPHICAL PREMISES

It is difficult to appraise this basic philosophy or the manner in which it has been translated into action without allowing the appraisal to be colored with one's own philosophical predilections. Before proceeding further, therefore, it is appropriate that I state explicitly some of the relevant philosophical premises on which my subsequent comments are based. This exercise will assist you in applying the appropriate discount to my conclusions.

These premises may be summarized as an intelligent and rational pragmatism. I am unwilling to commit myself in advance and regardless of circumstances to any ideological system or method of achieving objectives. The more one studies the pattern of human objectives in life, the more one is impressed with its fantastic complexity. For any individual, the list of personal goals is long and capable of almost unlimited subdivision. Conflicts among these goals arise at every turn, and we are constantly faced with the necessity of choosing among competing goals or compromising between them. When one adds the inevitable conflicts among objectives of different persons in a large and highly interdependent society, the web of action and interaction almost defies understanding.

It is, in my mind, an act of fanaticism to assert that any one ideological system will, automatically and without any exception, provide the optimum compromise among all of these competing objectives, interpersonal and intrapersonal. Rather, I would propose that we start with the system as it is and then, assisted by such intelligent and rational thought as we can bring to bear, devise ways and means to change the "as is" system to make it a better instrument for achieving our collective objectives. The essence of the social process is not achievement of utopia, but maximum progress toward our aspirations as the level of our aspiration rises before us.

CONSUMER SOVEREIGNTY A PIVOTAL ISSUE

One of the pivotal issues in relation to housing, to get down to cases, has to do with the choice between individual and collective decision-making — consumer sovereignty. Should we leave decisions about the quantity and kind of housing entirely to the individual consumer, or should we use the instrumentality of government to make collective decisions that are, in greater or lesser degree, binding upon us as individuals?

In a wide range of circumstances, studies of consumer behavior lead us to conclude that individual consumers are in the best position to know what they want and to make their own personal decisions. But these studies of consumer behavior also show that there are many circumstances where individual consumers, through ignorance, weakness of will, over-susceptibility to persuasion by the avaricious, or temporary lapses into sheer emotional irrationality, are not in the best position to make their own decisions. Collective decision-making via government usually, but not always, has the advantage of being deliberate, slow, argumentative, and open to public inspection — an environment which is generally conducive to rational action. Collective decision-making also has the advantage of providing a device whereby we, as individuals, can voluntarily subject ourselves to an external discipline that will force behavior which, in our more rational moments, we know to be in our own best interests.

A college or university, for example, is a form of government. The student subjects himself to its discipline. He does so presumably because he has a genuine desire to be educated, to learn. But it may be that on any given afternoon he would much prefer playing tennis or dating his girl to participating in the learning process, that is, studying. So at the beginning of the semester, he "hires" a group of professors to undertake the job not only of imparting knowledge but also, through tests, quizzes, term papers, required performances in class, and so on, of forcing him to forego the tennis and involve himself in the learning process. So it is with government per se. In our more rational moments, via the democratic process, we hire organized agencies of government to compel us to do what, at any particular moment, we might not like to do but what we know, in the abstract, is in our own best interest. A simple example of this is traffic regulations.

Thus, I do not think that we can conclude that individual decision-making is always better or worse than collective decision-making. It depends on the type of decision and the circumstances in which it must be or is normally made. We need to weigh and test and then decide on the basis of experience which is preferable in a given combination of circumstances. It follows, of course, that this weighing and testing should be a continuous process; that is, that these decisions should be subject to constant review.

In the recent hearings of the Subcommittee on Housing of the Senate Committee on Banking and Currency, several of the witnesses complained that the FHA acts under temporary grants of authority and that the Congress is constantly changing the rules of the game by passing a new housing act every year or two. There is much merit in this complaint, but at least the automatic reopening of the issues provides an opportunity for renewed weighing and testing. We would be better off, in my judgment, if the Federal Reserve Act were subject to automatic periodic review.

THE CONCEPT OF GOVERNMENT SUBSIDIES

Closely related to the issues of consumer sovereignty is that of government subsidies. The dictionary definition of "subsidy" — "a government grant to assist a private enterprise deemed advantageous to the public" — incidentally, is no longer adequate. A subsidy is any governmental action which has the effect of shifting wealth or income from one economic group to another. Five per cent loans by the Small Business Administration to marginal businesses involve an element of subsidy, even though no "grant" is involved. Price supports of agricultural products are a subsidy. The Wagner Act is a subsidy to labor. So defined, subsidies have become so ubiquitous that it is difficult to find an unsubsidized business — or consumer, either, for that matter. Most of us are, or have been, the beneficiaries of either veterans' benefits, a state-financed education, or a holiday in the public parks.

I would argue that one cannot say, in the abstract, that these or any of a thousand similar subsidies are either good or bad per se. Subsidies are enacted when, again via the democratic process, we collectively decide that we would prefer an economic result different from what the presubsidy market is giving us. Notice, incidentally, that I said, not "unregulated" market, but "presubsidy" market. A variety of previous regulatory acts, almost always involving some element of subsidy, have already conditioned the results of the market. Indeed, probably the most legitimate objection to subsidies is the fact that subsidies tend to beget subsidies, ultimately to the point where detecting the consequences of another subsidy becomes a terribly complicated business.

But aside from this unfortunate tendency, each individual subsidy needs to be looked at on its merits in order to decide, as best we can decide on the basis of experience and rational analysis, wherein the social advantage lies.

We could go on and on, but these two examples are enough to illustrate what I mean by intelligent and rational pragmatism. I do not mean to imply, by the way, that there is anything new or startling in this concept. Quite the contrary. Indeed, I think it is the philosophical concept to which the vast majority of the American people, implicitly or explicitly, are committed. Our actual behavior in the past quarter-century has been pretty generally consistent with it. Personally, I like it and, in the main, I like the hodgepodge, mixed-up, no-name economic system that it has generated.

OBJECTIVES OF FEDERAL HOUSING POLICY

The origins of contemporary public policies in housing can be traced back many decades, but probably the first major governmental effort to formulate policies was the Conference on Home Finance and Home Ownership, called by President Hoover in 1931, which led to the establishment of the Federal Home Loan Bank System a year later. This conference, it should be noted, was not uniquely related to the depression; indeed, there are some people who think that President Hoover was not aware of the depression in 1931. Its purpose was simply to improve the functioning of the mortgage market and to encourage the growth of savings institutions.

For reasons of time, I propose to give only passing attention to the Home Loan Banks. With regard to this, I suggest that you see Edward E. Edwards' "Improvement of Federal Home Loan Bank Programs,"[1] for a current and penetrating analysis of the role of the Federal Home Loan Bank System. I wish to concentrate instead on the housing programs launched in 1934. By this I do not mean to deprecate the importance of the Home Loan Banks, which are very important institutions, but their role has been overshadowed by the later insurance and guarantee systems. For similar reasons I shall not give much attention to public housing programs; they also have been overshadowed by the insurance and guarantee programs.

The New Deal objectives of public policy in relation to housing were mainly two. The first related to economic activity generally, and the second to housing in particular. The federal housing programs were a product of the depression; they were among the measures taken to dredge us out of the slump. The first objective was to stimulate a recovery in the levels of income and employment via an expansion in residential construction. The New Dealers recognized well that there was no single, simple answer to the problem of revival of business activity — that we had to proceed on all fronts at once and that success on one front would reinforce efforts on other fronts. Housing was one of these fronts.

Although in 1934 people were thinking only in terms of emergence from the depression, today I think we would redefine this goal in terms of the Employment Act of 1946, that is, the maintenance of a high level of employment, production and purchasing power, and — it is implicit in the Act — of a reasonably stable price level. In other words, residential construction should make its contribution to reasonably steady growth in economic activity, commensurate with our capacities for growth, at reasonably stable price levels. It follows, in terms of this objective, that

[1] *Study of Mortgage Credit*, Committee on Banking and Currency, Subcommittee on Housing, United States Senate (Washington, D. C.: United States Government Printing Office, 1958).

changes in the level of housing construction should not be a one-way street. On occasion it may be desirable to accelerate residential construction, on other occasions to apply the brakes. Moreover performance in other sectors of the economy will be relevant criteria for determining proper public policy with respect to housing. When the rest of the economy is booming, a decline in housing can be accepted with greater equanimity than when the rest of the economy is declining.

The second objective grew out of the widespread conviction that a large proportion of the population was poorly housed, that the economic system of the day was not meeting our housing needs as well as they should be met. President Roosevelt referred to "a third of the nation," but I think that our concern was with a much larger fraction. The objective was simply and obviously to raise the quantity and quality of housing to a level substantially above that which would otherwise occur.

Now, here we run into trouble. Economic stability can be approximately defined, within limits imposed by the relative priorities that we attach to high employment and avoidance of inflation. But there is no absolute standard of performance with respect to the quantity and quality of housing. There will never be enough housing of good enough quality. Even if we limited our objective to the elimination of so-called substandard housing, we would have at least a 100% margin of error resulting from varying definitions of the term "substandard." About all we could agree upon is that we need more and better, but how much more and how much better is a wide-open question.

HOUSING OBJECTIVES IN CONFLICT

It is obvious that these two objectives of public policy in respect to housing can, in certain circumstances, be in conflict as they were in 1946–48 when general inflationary pressures were compounded by programs instituted to meet an urgent need for veterans' housing.

They were in conflict in 1950–51 when the need for more housing collided with rising prices growing out of the Korean conflict and booming business conditions. The stepped-up housing program of 1954 continued into 1955 when it ran into the "consumer boom" of that year and the resumption of inflationary pressures late in the year. In November 1955, I testified at a congressional hearing called chiefly to provide those giving high priority to the second objective — more and better housing — an opportunity to voice their criticism of the restrictive policies of the Federal Reserve. At that hearing I disappointed my senatorial hosts by pointing up this conflict of objectives and defending the Federal Reserve. It was my conclusion that the combination of a heavy postwar volume of home building, a decline in the rate of net family formation, and a reduction in the doubled-up ratio had altered the underlying situation. We could now afford to increase the relative priority given to economic stability.

There are also conflicts within each of these objectives. The "more and better housing" objective has both quantitative and qualitative aspects. Should we seek a maximum number of units, or fewer units of better and more lasting quality? Public policy has compromised, but generally in the direction of quantity rather than quality, especially in the immediate postwar years. Some of the early postwar housing developments are already residential slums. Even so, there are many who criticized the housing program for failing to meet the needs of the lowest income group. Abrams and Schussheim in their article in the *Study of Mortgage Credit,* say: "The main point we wish to emphasize is that current federally aided financing and mortgage insurance programs do not meet the needs of families most in need of housing. A large portion of these families are provided for neither in the home ownership nor in the rental housing programs of the Federal Government." They then proceed to advocate very low or zero interest-rate government loans to enable families in the very low income group to obtain new housing.

The criticism of Abrams and Schussheim, by the way, is not consistent with my philosophy of rational pragmatism. It fails on two counts. First, it ignores the fact that provision of new housing for the lowest income groups would almost inevitably require, as they propose, direct loans at zero interest rates. This, I contend, involves too big a break with traditional concepts of property rights and duties. But more important, it ignores the fact that when any new house comes on the market, regardless of size or price, the supply of houses available to persons in lower income groups tends to be increased. "Trading up" of housing is a normal process, going on all the time. When a family decides that it can afford a new, bigger and better house, and acquires one, it releases its old house to some lower-income family. This, in turn, may be acquired by another family living in a still less expensive house, and so on down the line. There is no reason why those at the bottom end of the income scale should necessarily have newly built houses. Newness is only one of the attributes which determines the amount of utility and psychic satisfaction that can be obtained from a house. I have yet to hear a serious proposal for zero interest rate loans to enable those who now buy and drive old cars to buy new ones.

Before concluding this discussion of public policy objectives regarding housing, I should note the obvious fact that our housing objectives frequently also run into conflict with other high priority objectives. We need more and better schools, hospitals, highways and recreational areas. We need adequate preparations for national defense and to give support to the peoples of underdeveloped countries. We need better income for farmers and more security for the aged, the ill, and the unemployed. We want more research in both the physical and social sciences. We need more adequate development of the nation's natural resources. All the while we want lower taxes and less governmental interference with private economic behavior. Housing policy is only one stone in the mosaic of total public policy. It has been a prominent stone in the past twenty-five years, indeed a conspicuously prominent one during the early days of the veterans' housing program. Rational pragmatism requires that we consider simultaneously all of our objectives, juxtapose them against all of our capacities, and strike an optimum balance.

TECHNIQUES FOR EFFECTUATING FEDERAL HOUSING POLICY

The federal government's mortgage insurance and guarantee programs are an example of the way in which partial socialization can be knitted into the fabric of capitalism with relatively little alteration in nominal institutional relationships.

In 1934, both of the objectives of federal housing policy called for more houses. The direct approach would have been a massive public housing program. But public housing, even in the 1930s, played a relatively minor role. (Incidentally, I was rather surprised, in looking back over the figures, to find how consistently minor public housing has been.) Instead, we adhered in the main to private financing, and attempted to increase the effective demand for housing by reducing the financing costs and to increase the flow of funds into mortgage lending by reducing the risks.

The risks involved in mortgage lending are of two types: (1) those which relate to the individual transaction, that is, the credit worthiness of the borrower, the value of the property, the character of the neighborhood and so on; and (2) those attributable to general swings in the level of business activity, employment, prices and so on. Risks of the first type are within the competence of the lending institution to appraise, minimize and control. Indeed, in the case of institutional lenders, their principal economic function, if they are to be more than mere brokers in funds, is to invest those funds wisely, that is, to apply critical judgment to each loan application. Risks of the second type, however, are social in origin. The lending institution has no control over them. If it is to do business at all, it must operate on a reasonably optimistic forecast of business activity. And if, in spite of this forecast, business activity and prices swing sharply downward, as they did in 1929–33, any attempt by lending institutions generally to limit their losses by calling loans or selling securities will only add to the collapse.

In 1934 this experience was fresh in the minds of the Congress. It was clearly their intent that this second type of risk should be collectivized. Incidentally, it is entirely conceivable that the Federal Home Loan Banks could have been used to assume the social risks; that they were not so used reflects, I suppose, the determination of the President and the Congress to achieve results by more direct action. It is not so clear that the Congress intended to collectivize the first type of risk, that is, the individual risk. It did so partly for reasons of practicality: it was easier not to make the distinction. But also it seemed that collectivization of all risks was the only practical way to make mortgages in deficit areas attractive to the distant lender of funds.

So all risks were collectivized. One of the issues of the day was whether or not the risks should be nationalized, that is, assumed by all the people, or whether partial collectivization via the private insurance company model should be followed. The result was a compromise: insured mortgagors assume the first stage of risk by contributing annually a ½ of 1% premium; but (after the first three years) if this proves to be inadequate to cover losses, the entire credit of the U. S. government is behind the insurance policy. In the case of VA mortgage guarantees, the risks have been nationalized from the beginning; the veteran pays no insurance premium. On the other hand, in contrast to FHA insurance, which covers the full amount of the mortgage loan, the VA guarantee covers only a top portion of the loan, the exact amount depending on the size of the loan.

COLLECTIVIZATION IN CONFLICT WITH CAPITALISM

In return for this reduction in risk, the lender was expected to take, and the market to reflect, a lower rate of interest than he would otherwise have obtained. It is at this point that collectivization runs into conflict with the practicalities of capitalism. We might have relied entirely on market forces to determine the value of the insurance, that is, the proper differential in interest yield between an insured and an uninsured mortgage contract. But by so doing, the federal government would have abandoned any direct control over one strategic term of the contract it was insuring. Many advocates of the housing program were (and are) convinced that mortgage rates are, in some absolute sense, too high. There was a suspicion of exploitation, captured by the cartoonists in a moustached and steely-eyed character symbolizing mortgage lenders, and by the "westerns," in which the mortgagee is invariably the villain. To the extent that mortgage insurance and guarantee programs involve a subsidy, Congress wanted to be sure that the subsidy was passed on to the house buyer and not absorbed by the mortgage lender.

In the early years of the program, interest ceilings were high enough, relative to other market rates of interest, not to interfere with the flow of funds into mortgages. But in more recent years, in spite of repeated increases, they have created a recurrent problem, recently complicated by the statutory proviso that the VA rate shall be at least one-half percentage point below the comparable FHA rate. This proviso reflects a stubborn determination by the Congress to give veterans an advantage over other borrowers, plus an impression that the VA guarantee is worth more than the FHA insurance. The fact seems to be that lenders of funds see no significant difference between the two techniques for collectivizing risks. The consequence of fixed interest rates is disequilibrium in the mortgage market, reflected in the issuance and sale of mortgages at varying and sometimes heavy discounts below par.

This recurrent fact of disequilibrium in the mortgage market is one reason why, on several occasions, the Congress has resorted to the Federal National Mortgage Association to add to the supply of funds in the mortgage market.

Now there is nothing wrong per se, by my value test, in pumping public funds into the mortgage market. Whether the transaction is consummated via a sale of FNMA issues to the Treasury and increased Treasury borrowing from the public, or via a sale of FNMA debentures to the public, the net effect is a siphoning of private funds, via government, into the mortgage market. The lender obtains a government bond or government agency obligations rather than a mortgage loan, but the funds wind up in the same place — in residential financing.

The point is that the entire process is cumbersome, roundabout and likely to be overdone or underdone at particular times because congressional action, which takes time, is required periodically. And the government is likely to get loaded down with mortgages of dubious quality on which the lender has assumed no risk. The whole process would be sounder and work much more smoothly if the disequilibrium did not exist in the first place.

TECHNIQUES VERSUS OBJECTIVES

It follows that one of the chief shortcomings of the techniques for effectuating public policy in residential construction is that their contribution toward the objective of economic stability has been sporadic, undependable and, as often as not, perverse. In drawing such a conclusion, however, we should be careful to differentiate between destabilizing influences that are the consequence of inherent defects in the techniques and those that are the result of conscious policy choice. In 1946–47, for example, government programs in home financing resulted in more money flowing into residential construction than the industry was prepared to absorb. The result was rapid inflation in real estate prices. This may have been, however, a matter of deliberate choice. The need for veterans' housing was acute. Perhaps the price we had to pay for a quick expansion of the capacity of the industry was a considerable rise in real estate prices, relative to other prices, and in contractor profits. At least the program did have the effect of increasing in the short space of a few years the annual capacity of the industry, which had withered away to almost nothing during World War II, to nearly a million and a half houses. This was no mean achievement.

But this argument cannot be used to explain away the inflationary consequences in 1950 and 1955, when capacity to produce was not in obvious need of further stimulus. And the decline in residential construction in 1956-58 was much more than could be justified on stabilization grounds. It was the effect, unintended at least in degree, of the peculiar character of the mortgage insurance and guarantee techniques.

Let me digress a bit at this point to challenge a criticism of the FHA-VA programs, somewhat similar to the one I have just been making. The fact is observed that the number of housing starts under conventional financing in recent years has been remarkably stable, varying between 600,000 and 700,000 units, whereas the number of starts under FHA and VA financing has fluctuated widely, ranging from 670,000 in 1955 down to less than 300,000 in 1957 and 1958. Thus, my good and able friend, Miles Colean, concludes: "The range of these fluctuations makes that part of house building that depends on FHA and VA financing one of the most volatile elements in the entire economy." This statement is from Miles Colean, "A More Effective Mortgage Insurance System," in the *Study of Mortgage Credit*. The statement is obviously correct, but I think it overstates the case to conclude, as Colean seems to conclude, that the destabilizing influence of the FHA-VA programs should be measured by starts under FHA and VA financing alone. What happens is that when interest rates rise so that FHA and VA loans become unattractive to lenders, some funds that would otherwise have flowed into FHA or VA mortgages find their way into conventional mortgages. This is particularly true of savings and loan associations, which have a strong preference for conventional mortgages. The point is that a portion of the decline in FHA and VA mortgage funds shows up in conventional mortgages. The volume of conventional mortgages made does not decline as much as it otherwise would, and may even rise. The stabilizing or destabilizing effect of the FHA-VA instruments should be measured by total housing starts, not by FHA and VA starts alone.

Furthermore, the fact that the fixed interest rates on FHA and VA mortgage loans have caused instability in housing construction does not necessarily lead to the conclusion that the over-all economic effect is unstabilizing. Fixed interest rates begin to bite when business activity is high and rising and when the demand for funds generally is strong. Or perhaps we should say they begin to bite when, in the judgment of the Federal Reserve, demand is rising too briskly and inflationary dangers are appearing. In either case, this *may* be the time for some downward pressure on housing starts in the interest of overall economic stability.

Conversely, I would argue that the automatic fluctuation in FHA and VA starts that results from fixed interest rates is not necessarily, or even likely, the appropriate degree of variation from the viewpoint of over-all economic stability. Too much of the burden of restraint is imposed on housing. In terms of the objective of economic stability alone, the alternating dampening and stimulating effect of fixed interest rates usually, but not necessarily, is in the right direction, but it tends to be exaggerated in degree.

Looking at the techniques of effectuating public policy in terms of the objective of improving the quantity and quality of housing for the American people, I think that, on the whole, the record has been good. In some instances, as I noted earlier, the effect has been too low-cost housing. In other instances, houses have been built in the wrong neighborhoods, of the wrong style, by people who should not be home owners, because the lender is not under the normal compulsion to scrutinize the transaction closely. After all, if the deal meets the FHA or VA specifications, he has little to lose except foreclosure costs. Why should he be the villain of the piece? This is a proper criticism, but one that can easily be overemphasized. Probably the most trouble in this direction has come not from the FHA-VA insurance and guarantee programs per se, but from the fact that these programs have served as a convenient vehicle for a variety of other programs not uniquely related to housing, such as help for the aged, subsidies for veterans, urban renewal, winning the war and so on.

Also — and this, in my mind, is a more important criticism — the requirements for meeting FHA and VA specifications have interfered with the introduction of new technological developments in housing that would have improved quality and perhaps lowered cost. In those industries which are the most typically American and of which we are proudest, we have moved to satisfy our wants, not just by producing more of a minimum acceptable quality, but by vastly improving the product via rapid technological change, both in the product itself and in its method of manufacture. Not so with housing. It must be admitted that these same requirements have prevented the construction of some definitely substandard dwellings.

Another related criticism that can be leveled at the insurance and guarantee features is that, because of the uncertainties as to the availability of FHA and VA financing introduced by the interest rate problem, builders have often found it extremely difficult to engage in any long-range planning in their building programs. This has interfered with land acquisition and development, with the introduction of mass production techniques in house construction and with the recruitment of a permanent labor force. It has tended to keep a technologically backward industry backward.

My principal criticism of these techniques, however, takes me beyond my assigned topic. This is that they have been directed at lowering only one cost of housing: financing costs. Little or nothing has been done, as a consequence of public policy action, to lower costs of building materials, of actual construction, or of land development.

BUILDING CONSTRUCTION PROBLEMS IN THE 1960s

Fisher and Boorstein, in their article in the *Study of Mortgage Credit,* show three projections of construction of dwelling units in the 1960s — low, medium, and high. They are a little different, but generally consistent with Gordon McKinley's projections. The medium projection, which they believe is the best indication of what is likely, given a high level of economic activity, increases from 1.6 million units in 1960 to 2.1 million in 1970. This compares with 1.56 million units in 1950 and with about 1.47 million in 1955. If these estimates are even approximately correct, we have a problem in the decade of the 1960s of expanding considerably the size of the industry. The main difference between their figures and Gordon's is that they go to 1970. The wave starts gradually in '60, '61 and '62, picks up steam as it gets to '64, and by '65 and '66 assumes sizable proportions.

Fisher and Boorstein go on to say that this volume of construction is likely to impose some rather substantial strains on our supply of certain building materials. Even severer difficulties are likely to arise in obtaining an adequate supply of developed land. Here the accent is not on the land itself, although even raw land prices have been skyrocketing, but on streets, water supply, and sewers.

Much, perhaps most, of this residential growth is going to take place, not in the regularly organized municipality, but in the strip city, a mixed industrial, commercial and residential band following the main highways, often without organized municipal government. In these strip cities, the problem of community facilities, notably sewers, will be acute.

We had a crisis in housing immediately after World War II. In the past ten years, the pressure has eased considerably. But another crisis is coming in the 1960s, especially in the years beginning around 1965. The one redeeming feature is that rising productivity in industry generally should bring about a substantial increase in real incomes of American families. We will be able to afford better housing.

Needed Revisions in Objectives

The basic objectives of housing policy in the 1960s will be the same as in the 1950s. But some changes in emphasis are indicated.

First, in contrast to the 1950s, the time has arrived, or soon will arrive, to quit thinking of residential construction as an industry that can be freely manipulated for general economic stabilization reasons. In the past five to eight years, no serious harm has been done in letting the brunt of anti-inflation policy fall on housing. Family formation was down; our acute postwar needs were largely met; most of the postwar babies were not yet old enough to be rapacious users of housing. But that day is passing. This tide has turned in the past year or so. From here on out, if there is a conflict of objectives, stabilization should take second priority to more and better housing.

And much as we will need more housing, I think the time has come to put much more emphasis on quality of housing. Particularly, we need a major wave of technological innovation in construction that will greatly improve the livability of houses. And some of these technological improvements should actually decrease costs.

Needed Changes in Techniques

Specifically, I would propose that the following changes be made in our techniques of effectuating housing policy:

1. Abandon fixed interest rates for government-insured and guaranteed loans. What borrowers on federally underwritten mortgages want is a low down payment and long maturity, not a subsidized rate that may end up by forcing the borrower to pay a big chunk of interest in addition to his down payment. Or, if it is politically inexpedient to take maximums out of the law, as was suggested yesterday, the same result could be achieved by setting the statutory ceiling high enough to be inoperative and charging the administrative agencies with the duty and responsibility to determine administratively a ceiling that will avoid any serious interference with the flow of funds into FHA and VA mortgages. In either case, let the market determine the value of the insurance or guarantee. It is competitive enough to do the job. Freeing interest rates will add greatly to the fluidity and stability of residential construction and thus facilitate long-range planning and large-scale operation. It will eliminate or at least minimize discounts which actually interfere with home buying.

2. Change the character of the insurance or guarantee to require the mortgage lender to assume a greater measure of responsibility for testing and screening loan applications. This could be done, for example, by

collectivizing only 90%, say, of the risk. Let the lender bear any losses incurred on the top 10% of the particular loan. This, I think, is a necessary counteraction to the freeing of interest rates.

3. Significantly relax FHA and VA construction standards as they relate to the use of new materials and products. Open the door for experimentation and technological change.

4. Inaugurate a major government-subsidized program of research in building materials, methods and products. What an enormous contribution to the housing problem would be made, for example, by the development of a self-contained household sewage disposal unit. For some reason, research scientists in the past have not found the disposal of human sewage to be a particularly romantic area for research. It is high time we did something about it.

We spend hundreds of millions of dollars each year in research directed toward increasing the supply of agricultural products, of which we already have a plethora. The housing industry qualifies for government-subsidized research on the same grounds that agriculture qualifies: it comprises a large number of small entrepreneurs, few of whom are large enough to engage in research; and the product of the industry is a basic necessity of life, used by all citizens. If a research agency had 2% of the Department of Defense research budget, what enormous technological and consequent social progress might ensue.

5. Subsidize programs for community planning and development, not only in organized cities, but, even more importantly, in unorganized areas in strip cities. Conversely, I would soft-pedal, though probably not eliminate, public housing programs, largely for the reason that they often become slums — even though they are slums with a certain elegance about them. I think government's greatest contribution can be made in assisting communities in planning residential and community development, not in subsidizing housing directly. There are circumstances, however, where public housing is the only practical answer to acute problems.

6. Revise the housing statutes to make the construction of rental housing relatively more attractive. With all due respect to the institutional bias of our hosts, I believe that we are putting a bit too much stress on home ownership. A mobile population requires an adequate supply of both rental housing and owner-occupied housing.

7. Launch a major program to reduce building code and labor union restrictions on technological developments in housing. This is a tall order, I realize, but it is a necessary prerequisite to real technological progress in housing.

8. Encourage large-scale production and prefabrication of housing and housing components. One way to do this, incidentally, would be to use

the antitrust laws to crack down on manufacturers of building materials who conspire to eliminate quantity discounts to large builders. We need some countervailing power in the building industry.

9. Inaugurate a program of government-financed development of residential land, using powers of eminent domain if necessary. Land development is a classic example of a business in which the economies of scale are large. It is a business which must obtain a great deal of cooperation from local governmental authorities. It is also a business requiring large sums of capital and in which the risks are substantial and largely social in origin. It is natural for direct governmental intervention or for some combination of government and private action.

As a next best bet, change the laws so as to permit banks and savings and loan associations to finance land development. Actually, the higher level of risks assumed might be more than compensated for by the greater control which these lending institutions would thereby have over the types of neighborhoods and properties in which they would subsequently be sinking their funds. For further development of this point, I suggest that you see Edward E. Edwards' "Improvement of Federal Home Loan Bank Programs" in the *Study of Mortgage Credit*.

These — some of them — are radical proposals. But we will meet our housing needs of the 1960s adequately and at reasonable cost only if we are willing to experiment with some new techniques for effectuating public policies in housing.

Discussion*

LEO GREBLER: Bob has pointed up one question: Housing is a priority area in our scheme of things. It conflicts, however, with many other high-priority things — foreign aid, agriculture, and whatnot. Now, in your pragmatic scheme of things, how can we develop criteria for determining the relative importance of these social priority areas? It is easy to be cynical about it and say it is a politician's job, and indeed it is a political decision, but the politician can turn around and say, "What do you economists have to offer along that line?"

MR. TURNER: I do not have any answer to that. There are no simple criteria, and the criteria extend far beyond economic considerations. It is a political decision that has to be made. My concern is with the fact that too often people who spend their lives working in the housing area or who have spent time in a housing agency get so imbued with the housing-objective point of view that they forget these other objectives. We need to see housing as a high-priority objective, but as only one of many.

* Proceedings of the Second Annual Conference, 1959, Excerpts from the Discussion, pp. 153–58.

MR. GREBLER: There is no disagreement between the two of us, but the housing economist is often asked, "Now, how can you help a Congressman to determine relative priorities, housing and foreign assistance, relative to other programs involving federal insurance and so on?" Somehow I feel we have not been of great help.

LESTER MCALLISTER: On a small scale, you have already partly anticipated Dr. Grebler's question, I think, by suggesting that you would abandon the FHA-VA ceiling. I think you also said you would let the market determine the value of the insurance guarantee feature, which is a partial answer, I suppose.

MR. TURNER: I would give a larger play to consumer sovereignty than we have been giving. But I still think housing is one area in which collective decision-making is sometimes and to some degree appropriate, for reasons stated earlier.

SAUL KLAMAN: Bob, let's go a step further in Leo's reasoning to make it easy for you to answer "yes" or "no." This is a radical question, but not posed by a radical. As you pointed out very well, the origination and purpose behind the federal insurance program were to stimulate economic activity, employment, and manufacture of building materials, and to entice funds into this particular area which was so depressed.

The changes that have ensued since then are obvious. This whole innovation was basic in pointing the way to showing relatively how riskless mortgages are, compared to other investments in terms of the amortization feature, long maturity, and so forth. Now that this has been accomplished, what is the basic justification remaining for the continuation of a federal mortgage insurance program?

MR. TURNER: I do not agree that it has been accomplished.

MR. KLAMAN: We already have conventional lenders with the authority to make 80% and 90% loans, a concept which would have been considered an extreme even five or ten years ago. Such loans are now permitted in New York State by savings and loan associations and savings banks, without any federal guarantee.

I am simply asking whether the mortgage instrument is basically so risky that the private institutions can no longer stay in this area without aid. Is it inherently so much riskier than consumer credit, which has been liberalized? Is it so much riskier than any other capital market instrument, that forevermore we need government aid to keep this field alive? This, I think, is a very basic part of the question.

MR. TURNER: Yes, it is certainly a less risky type of instrument now, but I would argue that the improvement in the quality of mortgages has resulted not so much from anything that has been done to the mortgages as from the fact that prices have risen. Mortgages are good risks only if price levels stay up.

WALTER MORTON: I should like to hear the philosophy as to how far you carry the collectivization of risk. There is a feeling in small business that there is too much risk and that we ought to have government guarantees there. Now, we can carry that further. Many people feel that if we have more government enterprise, the government assumes the risk. What I should like to know is this: Is there anybody who defends the thesis that special circumstances require this collectivization of risk and guarantee by the government today, or is it merely that institutions see this as an easy way to get a good yield on a riskless security?

That is the way I look at it, and that is what I think is back of this thing. Let the institutions that buy mortgages take the risk just the same as they take it for every corporate security and every municipal security and every other type of security they buy.

CHAIRMAN EDWARDS: I take it this is not a question.

MR. MORTON: It is a view almost everywhere you go that people in a business merely want more and more government subsidy. That is the interesting thing.

RICHARD LINDHOLM: Regarding this risk involved in government securities and investment in mortgage companies, I wonder if really what Dr. Turner is saying is that because of continuous inflation the mortgage is not a risky investment, while the bond is a risky investment.

Is this part of the background here, so that a claimant can say, "We will go into mortgages continuously; we don't need a guarantee here" and so that the man who talks for the insurance people can say that the government bond is a riskier investment than his investment in mortgages?

MR. TURNER: The government bond is a risky investment only because monetary policy has made it so. We have concentrated our instability on interest rates. This is a different kind of risk from that involved in residential mortgages.

GEORGE MITCHELL: It is especially risky when you buy it on a shoestring — 1% equity, or even less. Your equity disappears pretty fast.

JOHN PFAHL: Dr. Turner, you made the point that this fixed interest rate in effect attempts to control the cost of housing and that there is no control on other costs. Do you have some data on the importance of the financing cost relative to other costs in these kinds of projects?

MR. TURNER: There are a couple of articles in the *Study of Mortgage Credit* that go into that.

MR. PFAHL: Am I right in assuming that it runs somewhere around 50% of total cost?

MR. TURNER: Somewhere in that vicinity, at least in the early years of a mortgage loan.

MR. PFAHL: So, in effect, we are working probably on the most important single cost if we work on that.

GORDON McKINLEY: It is true that over the period you probably pay twice the cost of your house if you borrow the standard amount. On the other hand, it is also important to you what happens to the price of that house, because you compound the interest on that price, too. We calculated for a congressional committee a while ago the effect of an assumed rate of change in the interest rate and the actual rate that has taken place in the case of the price of homes. We showed them, I think clearly, that you pay that price not once but twice.

MR. TURNER: At best, we could hope to cut the interest cost down a percentage point or so. But from what I have seen happen to land prices in communities because of the difficulties involved in developing land, I am convinced there is an enormous possibility for savings there. Lots that a few years ago cost $2,000 are now selling for $10,000.

ROBERT FISHER: You mentioned very early in your speech that you have three objectives for monetary and fiscal policy, one of which is a stable level of home prices. What is your observation, then, as to the effect of federal programs in the postwar period toward stabilization of prices or otherwise? And what federal programs might be effective in stabilizing home prices in the event of a downturn in housing construction and activity?

MR. TURNER: My objective is a stable level of prices generally, and not just home prices. Clearly, in the postwar years, public policy has not achieved the objective of stable prices, either of houses or generally. This may have been the price we had to pay for a very rapid expansion in house construction capacity. I am not sure whether or not this was a conscious choice on the part of Congress. I think it knew, in some degree at least, what it was doing, deliberately pushing housing, knowing it would have an inflationary effect, because it wanted capacity to be stepped up in a hurry.

PART THREE

Monetary Policy

In Part One we explored the thesis of Gurley and Shaw that monetary policy cannot operate effectively solely by controlling the stock of money in the form of currency and bank deposits, and that, in the interest of achieving an acceptable rate of economic growth and stability, we must undertake more regulation of the non-bank financial intermediaries. In the first series of lectures in this part, we examine the contention that monetary policy operating through commercial banks, when placed in the hands of a discretionary monetary authority such as the Federal Reserve System, leads to an unacceptable degree of economic instability. In the first lecture, Milton Friedman traces the history which leads to his policy proposal that the rule of a steady rate of growth in the stock of money, at say 4 per cent per year, will lead to better results than follow from decisions of monetary authorities. In the second lecture in the series, Abba Lerner replies to Friedman. Lerner says, "Essentially, the difference between Friedman and me is one of temperament. I do not believe that we are quite incapable of getting intelligent and informed action." On this issue the lines are drawn.

In the other paper in Part Three, James S. Dusenberry of Harvard University discusses "the criteria for the use of monetary policy and the associated credit controls in relation to housing." He is concerned with the fact that there has been a decade or more of controversy over the ways in which monetary policy and credit controls have been used, and further controversy as to the impact of these policies and controls on the provision of residential housing. Dusenberry concludes that we should think first about monetary policy "as a part of the total set of decisions about the level of demand and allocation of resources," and secondly about monetary policy in relation to housing and housing policy.

11

A Program for
Monetary Stability–I*

Milton Friedman is professor of economics at the University of Chicago; member, research staff, National Bureau of Economic Research; fellow, American Statistical Association, Institute of Mathematical Statistics and Econometric Society; and John Bates Clark Medallist. He is the author of *Essays in Positive Economics, A Theory of the Consumption Function* and *A Program for Monetary Stability;* co-author, *Incomes from Independent Professional Practice, Taxing to Prevent Inflation* and *Sampling Inspection;* and editor, *Studies in the Quantity Theory of Money.* Mr. Friedman earned his bachelor's degree at Rutgers University, his master's at the University of Chicago, and his doctorate at Columbia University. He was formerly on the faculties of the Universities of Wisconsin and Minnesota; principal economist, U. S. Treasury Department; and associate director of research, Statistical Research Group, Division of War Research, Columbia University.

OUR SUBJECT THIS MORNING IS the arrangements in the United States for monetary stability. This topic is an ancient one in the deliberations of economists, going back many centuries. However, there was a hiatus for about twenty years, from about 1935 to about 1955, when there was very little discussion or work in this area.

* Proceedings of the Fifth Annual Conference, 1962, pp. 12–32.

As you all know, the unduly high hopes which were placed in the Reserve System in the 1920s as a means of promoting a permanent new era and a high level of stability were disappointed by the Great Depression of 1929 to 1933.

The profession of economics as a whole then shifted very radically from one course to another. From a general belief that the stock of money and the changes in it are tremendously important in controlling economic affairs, the profession shifted toward the view that money has little importance and does not matter except in rather trivial ways. It shifted toward the belief that the important things to look at are the flows of investment expenditures, on the one hand, and consumer expenditures, on the other. It was said that if these are taken into account, it really does not make much difference what happens to the stock of money.

In the last five or ten years or so, there has been something of a counterrevolution with respect to these ideas, both in this country and abroad. This has been partly a result of the experience which countries had after the war with the policies which seemed to follow from the neglect of money. Those policies called for easy money, for trying to keep interest rates low. Their adoption was very widely accompanied by problems of inflation. These problems of inflation, in turn, caused renewed attention to and emphasis upon money.

At the same time, there have been developments in the world of ideas and theories which also led to a reincorporation of monetary factors into economic thought, so that by now economists are again putting a great deal of emphasis on monetary matters. They are once again concerned about the problems of how money ought to be managed, although the reasons they now give for these concerns may be somewhat different from what they were thirty or forty years ago.

It is surprising that economists, even for so short a period as several decades, should have adopted so extreme a position as they did about the unimportance of money. This is particularly surprising in the United States, it seems to me. In looking over our own historical background, it is clear that the problems of controlling the stock of money have played a major role in both political and economic affairs ever since the founding of this nation. The problem of money probably has been of greater importance in American experience than in that of many another country.

HISTORICAL BACKGROUND

This problem goes back to the Revolutionary War when, as all governments do in time of war and in time of need, we resorted to the printing press. As you know, the phrase "not worth a Continental" arose out of the Continental currency which was issued during the Revolutionary

War and which came to be regarded as worthless. I should make clear that there is such a thing as progress in human affairs. The degree of inflation in the Revolutionary War was very modest, measured by modern standards. It was nothing like the German hyperinflation, or the hyperinflation in Hungary after World War II. It was of a much more moderate order of magnitude — prices increased only several thousand-fold — but this did start us off on the idea that there is some problem about money.

The Constitution assigns the responsibility to government to fix the value of money. It specifies also that the government may not emit bills of credit. This was intended to prevent the issuance of paper money by the federal government — like the Continental currency. One of the most interesting episodes related to this provision had to do with the issuance of greenbacks during the Civil War. Samuel P. Chase was Secretary of the Treasury at the time, and hence responsible for their issuance. Less than ten years later, when he was Chief Justice of the Supreme Court, he wrote a decision, concurred in by a majority of the Court, asserting that the notes he had issued were unconstitutional and illegal.

From the time of the Revolutionary War, the monetary issue has remained a major theme in politics and economics. You all know about the great bank war which raged in the 1830s and which brought together, as antagonists, Andrew Jackson and Nicholas Biddle. The issue was whether the charter of the Second Bank of the United States should be renewed in 1936. The Second Bank of the United States was a central bank; it was somewhat similar to what the Federal Reserve System has now become.

Many people will argue that the great mistake made was not to renew the charter of the Second Bank at that time. Personally, I think the mistake was made in 1816 in issuing the charter, but that is not a dispute of immediate interest. The bank war was a very important episode because it laid the groundwork for what was the greatest depression in American history prior to 1929–1933, namely, the one which was experienced from 1839 to 1843.

After the failure to renew the charter of the Second Bank of the United States, Biddle started a private bank as a continuation of the Second Bank in Pennsylvania and proceeded to use this private bank in many ways that, as a government official, he had never used the Second Bank. He tried to use it to support the price of cotton; as later episodes have shown, this is a tough thing to do. It did not work then, and it has not worked since. The result was a very severe and extreme depression, one which is interesting because the monetary aspects were almost identical with those of the 1929 to 1933 episode. The stock of money from 1839 to

1843 fell by a third, which is roughly the amount it fell from 1929 to 1933. The percentage of the banks that failed was almost the same at that time as nearly a century later, and in both cases there were long and deep depressions.

THE GREENBACK AND SILVER ISSUES

The Civil War greenback issue and subsequent agitation for the resumption of gold payment in 1879 is the next episode that needs mention. Again money became of the greatest importance in politics and in economics. There was a great contraction from 1873 to 1879, a six-year period, as a result of the measures and the attitudes that were involved in seeking to go back on gold.

The silver issue came next. It started with the alleged crime of 1873, which was supposedly a crime in that the provision for the coining of silver was left out of an act to reform the coinage. Whether it was a crime or not, there is no doubt that when prices in general tended to decline from 1882 to about 1890, there was a widespread movement in this country to leave gold and to coin silver freely. The movement gained strength in the early 1890s. Again, this was both a major political issue and a major economic issue.

The 1890–1896 episode is one that would bear restudying in terms of our present situation, because the economic problem was in many ways exactly the problem we now face. At that time there was a fear that the United States would go off gold and onto silver. This led foreigners who held dollars in this country to fear that the dollar would not remain fixed at its then price in terms of gold. This led to capital outflows, just as now we are faced with recurring capital outflows because of doubts that the price of $35 an ounce for gold will be maintained. These capital outflows could be kept from driving the United States off gold only by what was essentially an exceedingly tight money policy.

It is generally believed that the trouble with the silver agitation was that it produced an inflation of the money supply. That is the reverse of the truth. The trouble with the silver agitation was that it kept the money supply from growing as much as it otherwise might have grown. It did this by threatening an outflow of gold. This meant that the stock of money had to be held down in order to maintain international balance, i.e., in order to ensure the amounts we earned from abroad equaling the amounts we spent abroad.

This is exactly our situation today. The continued threat of outflow of gold is forcing on us a tight money policy, again for the same kinds of purposes: to try to hold foreign balances here, and to reassure foreigners that we are not going to change the price of gold.

The high spot of the silver agitation, in dramatic impact, was of course the great Cross of Gold speech made by William Jennings Bryan. I wonder how many of you know that it was made in Chicago, not far from the University of Chicago — at the corner of 63rd and Cottage Grove, which is now known as "Sin Corner." It is so named, not because of Bryan's presence, but because it happens to be the center of some unsavory aspects of Chicago life that people from the outside know more about than we do. But it was at "Sin Corner" in 1899 that William Jennings Bryan was nominated by the Democratic Convention, and it was there that he made the Cross of Gold speech that was the high spot of political agitation.

From that point on, the silver agitation declined, but not because of any decline in Bryan's oratory. His silver voice remained as silver. The political agitation of the Democratic Party became no less effective. Silver declined because of things that were happening in other corners of the world: the discovery of the cyanide process of extracting gold from ore, plus the discovery of new gold mines.

INCREASE IN WORLD GOLD SUPPLY

At the very same time that the great political campaign was going on here as to whether there would be a proper expansion of the money supply with gold as the base, there was a sizable increase in the rate of growth of the world's gold stock. From 1890 to 1896, the gold stock had been expanding elsewhere. The growth had not reached the United States because the fear that we would leave gold drove capital out of the country, and this prevented our sharing in the world's increase in the gold stock.

From 1896 on, gold started to increase in the United States. From 1896 to 1913, gold produced the results that Bryan and his advocates wished to have silver produce. We had a gold inflation, with prices rising over a third from 1896 to 1913. Since we got what the silver advocates were really interested in, their appeal to the public disappeared and Bryan was defeated resoundingly the next time he ran. His defeat in 1896 was by a rather small margin; and if we had not had a turn-around in the production of gold, it is very likely he would have made it the next time.

Retrospective history is interesting. I am not sure but that the United States would have been better off if we had had silver from the period of 1879 to 1893. I bring this up because it illustrates a very important point I think one needs to keep in mind. What was bad about the silver agitation was not that silver would have been bad. What was bad was the lack of certainty about what the monetary standard was going to be.

There was introduced into affairs a degree of uncertainty which caused capital outflows.

Let us say that in 1879 we had resumed on silver instead of gold and everybody had known we were on silver and were going to stay on silver. I think that would have been better than what actually happened. We might have had relatively stable prices, both in the United States and in the rest of the world, because silver would have enabled the stock of money to grow more rapidly than it was able to do from 1879 to 1896. Equally, if we had been on gold and everybody had been certain we were going to remain on it, there would have been no doubt about it. That would have been better than what we actually had. What was really disturbing was a lack of certainty about what the system was going to be, and consequently there was the possibility that we might move in one direction or the other.

The gold inflation solved the political agitation about the problem of money. But it brought to the fore another aspect of this general problem that had recurred before, namely, concern about banking and about the structure of the banking system.

THE PANIC OF 1907

The United States had developed, as you know, with a unit banking system of the kind we still have — a unit fractional reserve banking system. From time to time there had been so-called banking crises and panics; the last one before World War I was the panic of 1907. Those panics arose under circumstances in which, for one reason or another, many people questioned the ability of the banks to convert their deposits into currency.

In a fractional reserve system, if a large number of people try to convert their deposits into currency they cannot succeed in doing so. There are few words in the English language which are greater misnomers than the term "deposits" for those liabilities that are on the bank's books. People think that a deposit means "you go and leave it there." Now, we all know that the money goes in at one window and goes out at another, and that what is deposited is only a small percentage, the so-called fractional reserve. Consequently, if everybody tries to get "his" deposit, he cannot do so.

When doubts arose about banks, people would tend to try to withdraw their deposits. This would have caused widespread bank failures. Such bank failures were prevented by a concerted refusal on the part of the banks to pay currency for deposits, called a suspension of payments. That term is a misnomer, too.

Those of us who remember the banking panic of 1933 are inclined to believe that early banking panics were like the one in 1933. They were not. In the early banking panics, like 1907, the banks stayed open for business despite a suspension of payments. People continued to make payments and to do business through banks. The only thing changed was that the bank would not hand currency over the counter for deposits. It would transfer checks from one account to another, but checks had to be marked payable only through the clearinghouse. What was called suspension of payments was, in fact, a restriction of convertibility of deposits into currency. The business of the country could continue, and indeed expand, until the panicky fear of bank failures was over and payments could be resumed.

Suspension of payments of this kind was a severe step, but it was a therapeutic measure which prevented the failure of a few banks from leading to the failure of a large number of other banks. However, it was widely believed that this represented a severe and serious defect in the banking system. This led to the establishment of the National Monetary Commission in 1909, and this in turn led to a series of proposals for reform which ultimately ended in the Federal Reserve Act and the establishment of the Reserve System in 1914.

Now, a major purpose in establishing this system, it is quite clear, was to prevent any such banking panic or suspension of payments by the banks to the public.

EXPERIENCE UNDER THE RESERVE SYSTEM

The period since 1914, under the Federal Reserve System, is well known, but it is interesting nonetheless to contrast it with the prior period. The interesting thing to ask, I think, is: Comparing the period from 1914 to the present date with the preceding forty to fifty years, in which case did we have a greater degree of monetary stability?

There is no doubt about the answer. There was a greater degree of monetary stability in the period before the establishment of the Federal Reserve System than in the period after, whether measured by changes in interest rates, instability in the stock of money, instability in prices, or instability in economic activity. By any measure I know of, the period after has been more unstable than the one before.

One obvious reason is that there were two world wars after 1914. Those wars would have caused instability under any system. But omit the wars and the answer is still the same. The period since 1914 has been more unstable, in the peacetime years alone, than the period before 1914.

I hasten to add that this is an oversimplification. The great period of instability was the 20 years between the wars, 1919 to 1939. There is no other 20-year period in our history that comes anywhere close to having such great instability. That period contained three major contractions.

First there was an inflation from 1919 to 1920, then a severe contraction, then the 1929 to 1933 episode and then the 1937 to 1938 contraction. The period since the end of World War II has not been more unstable than earlier periods, but rather more stable than most.

GREATER INSTABILITY SINCE 1914

Yet, taking as a whole the period since 1914, there is no question that it has been more unstable. Moreover, that period contains the worst banking panic in our history. The 1933 banking panic with its bank holiday, when banks were closed for a week, was incomparably severer and more sweeping than any earlier panic. Whereas the earlier panics came before banks failed and prevented them from failing, the 1933 panic came after the banks had failed and indeed closed the doors of many good banks that were open the day before the panic. The number of banks that opened their doors after the banking holiday in March 1933 was decidedly less than the number that had been open before, and a large fraction of the banks that did not reopen ultimately paid out 100% to their depositors.

So here was a system, established in 1914 for the purpose of preventing banking panics and providing monetary stability, which in practice was associated with the greatest banking panic in U. S. history and a great deal of instability of money.

Is the reason simply that the problems the System had to cope with were severer after the war, so that the earlier system, too, would have had the same problems? I cannot hope to indicate here the reasons I think the answer is in the negative, but if you were to examine in detail the successive episodes in the period after 1918, I think you would agree that that is the only conclusion justified by the evidence.

Under the earlier monetary and banking system, imperfect though it was, we would have had less of an inflation in World War I. The wartime inflation would have been there anyway, but the postwar inflation from 1918 to 1920 would not have occurred, which would have eliminated a third of the total inflation. We would not have had the drastic fall in prices in 1920 and 1921, the sharpest fall within a brief period in the whole history of the United States and perhaps of any other country. Prices fell nearly 50%, and two-thirds of the decline came in the six months from August 1920 to February 1921.

THE GREAT DEPRESSION

Most important of all, under the earlier system we would not have had the Great Depression of 1929 to 1933. This depression had a traumatic effect upon the thinking of people and their attitude with respect to money and many other matters. It was this event that led to a shift from the belief that money is of the greatest importance to the belief that it is a minor matter which can be left to one side. It was the major event that led to a shift of emphasis from monetary policy to fiscal policy and that produced a widespread expansion in the role of government in the economy after 1933.

It has been widely taken for granted that 1929 to 1933 demonstrated the impotence of monetary control. It has been said that here we had a system which was established to prevent such a depression and which had the power, but which in fact did not prevent it. Therefore it was concluded that it must be that money is not very important. I myself think that the episode suggests just the opposite. It suggests that money is so powerful that it needs to be controlled more closely than it was then. If you examine the 1929 to 1933 episode, you will conclude that it was a needless episode. There is no doubt that with the powers then existing in the hands of the System, a very large part of the decline could have been prevented.

I do not mean to be casting blame or suggesting incompetence or lack of will or anything like that. It may be that the ablest, the most intelligent, the most public-spirited men would have made the mistakes that were made at that time.

Economists as a whole have no reason for feeling proud of their own record during that period. A year ago I read over the volumes of the Proceedings of the American Economic Association from 1929 to 1933. They are not something to make you feel proud of your profession. While the world was tumbling around the economists' ears on the outside, there was hardly a sign of it in the papers presented at those annual meetings. They dealt with strictly academic matters, even monetary and long-term banking matters. I remember one study, in 1932, of the failure of banks. It was concerned primarily with what had happened during the '20s and stressed the fact that country banks which failed had made poor mortgage loans, whereas in fact the important thing happening at the time was the widespread failure of city banks.

GREAT POWER IN A FEW HANDS

So I am not trying to say that the mistakes made were not understandable. What I am trying to say is that a system which could produce mistakes of that magnitude is a bad system by its very nature. It is like the cartoon in the *New Yorker* a couple of weeks ago, in which one man is sitting at a table in front of a big computer and another man is looking over his shoulder and saying, "Four thousand mathematicians in four thousand years couldn't have made a mistake like that." That is exactly the point. A mistake like that could not have been made under our earlier system or under a system which did not concentrate so much power in a few hands.

Let me spend a few minutes more in discussing the details of that episode, because it was so important in forming people's ideas. I think it is very important, in judging the episode, to distinguish the first year, from mid-1929 to the fall of 1930, from the subsequent years. We have had business recessions for several hundreds of years and we will have them for hundreds of years more. I have no doubt about that. Economic affairs move in fluctuations. The most we can hope for is that we can keep them relatively mild.

It may be that, monetary policy or no monetary policy, there would have been a recession from 1929 to 1930. There were signs of monetary tightness in that period as a result of the undue concern of the System with the stock market. In point of fact, the expansion of 1927 to 1929 is the only one I know of on record in which prices did not rise during a period of business expansion and in which the stock of money was lower at the end than it was at the beginning of the expansion. From 1929 to 1930, the stock of money fell about 3%. This was more than it had fallen in all except the severest previous depressions. Nevertheless, 1929 to 1930 can be described as an ordinary garden variety of recession — somewhat severer than most recessions, but not out of line. There were, in particular, no aspects of monetary weakness and no bank failures on any substantial scale, and no sign of any weakening of public confidence in the banking system. The ratio of deposits to currency prior to the Federal Deposit Insurance Corporation was an infallible sign of public attitude. This ratio stayed up or went up a little over that period, so that up to September or October of 1930 there was no sign of a liquidity crisis or a banking problem.

That period must be distinguished sharply from the one that followed. It is the later period, from late 1930 to 1933, for which, it seems to me, the Reserve System or the monetary authorities bear responsibility of a real kind.

In October and November of 1930, a series of bank failures started out here in the west and spread, culminating on December 11, 1930, with the failure of the Bank of the United States in New York. That was a large bank with something like $200 million of deposits. Its name made its failure more important than it otherwise would have been. Although it was an ordinary commercial bank, it was widely interpreted by people abroad, and also by immigrants in New York and throughout the United States, as being a government bank. Indeed, this may be one reason that it was permitted to fail. The banks in New York were very unhappy about having a bank with the name "Bank of the United States" in New York, as well as being unhappy about some of the irrelevant characteristics of the owners and managers of the bank. As a result, there was less sympathy for this bank than there would have been for many another bank. It was allowed to fail, and it precipitated a real liquidity crisis.

From this point on, the character of the contraction changed. The ratio of deposits to currency started to fall. Time and again, depositors sought to withdraw deposits; this caused a stream of bank failures, with one bank failure bringing on another. The crisis would taper off for a while and then start again.

FAILURE TO PROVIDE LIQUIDITY

What did the Federal Reserve System do during this period? It behaved as impassively and inactively as you can conceive of its doing. In 1931, after six months of this kind of behavior, Federal Reserve credit outstanding was less than it had been two years earlier in the middle of 1929. There is not a single sign that the Federal Reserve engaged in extensive open-market operations or in any other way tried on its own initiative to provide banks with the liquidity which would enable them to withstand a run, although this is what it had been set up to do. Every time there is a sequence of runs, discounts rise, but only as a necessity of the banks and not because of any encouragement from the Federal Reserve System.

I may say that there were voices within the System arguing for a more appropriate policy. George Harrison, the governor of the Federal Reserve Bank of New York, pleaded for the System to engage in open-market operations, but he was vetoed as a result of an administrative change that had occurred in the Open Market Committee. It had been changed from a five-man to a twelve-man committee — hardly a change likely to facilitate vigorous action. The twelve-man committee of bank presidents continuously vetoed Harrison's proposals for open-market operations, and the Reserve System did nothing and allowed banks to fail by the score.

The next important date is September 1931, when Britain went off the gold standard. This time the Reserve System reacted to the external threat as it had not to the internal threat. Within two weeks it raised discount rates more than it had before or has since, and there was a sudden increase in bank failures. There was a decline in the stock of money and, in the course of six months following this episode, something like 10% of the banks in the United States went out of business and deposits fell by something like 15%. But there is no sign at all of any autonomous easing action on the part of the Reserve System until the spring of 1932, when, faced by great congressional pressure and threats of congressional investigation, the System engaged in open-market operations to the tune of a billion dollars. It stopped two weeks after Congress adjourned.

The final episode was the last series of bank failures ending with the banking panic of 1933.

CAUSE OF DECLINE IN THE STOCK OF MONEY

The main lesson I want to drive home is that the 1929–1933 period was not one in which the economic depression forced a decline in the stock of money. The decline in the stock of money was a direct consequence of the sequence of bank failures. The banking failures were not important primarily because they involved the failures of financial institutions. They were important because they forced a decline in the stock of money. They forced a decline in the stock of money because the therapeutic device that was earlier available, the device of concerted restriction of convertibility of deposits into currency, was not available because the Reserve System had been established as a lender of last resort. However, the lender of the last resort did not perform the function of providing the liquidity in the market that would have enabled the banks to meet their obligations.

At all times the Reserve System had ample power to keep the stock of money from declining. It is literally inconceivable that if the stock of money had stayed constant instead of falling by a third, money income could have fallen by a half or that prices could have fallen by a third. I do not mean to say there would not have been a recession or contraction. It might have been a severe one, but it would have been of a wholly different order of magnitude, and not a catastrophe.

We come to the very important step that was taken: the establishment of the FDIC in 1934, which did prevent banking panics by insuring depositors, thus preventing contagion from spreading as a result of bank failures. In the latter 1930s, the Federal Reserve System was almost entirely passive. The Treasury took over the role of being the money manager.

THE FED'S POSTWAR PERFORMANCE

The Federal Reserve did not assume an active role in monetary policy again until after the Treasury-Federal Reserve accord in 1951. This postwar period is one with which you are all familiar in great detail; but nonetheless, let me comment very briefly on the last few episodes in order to suggest that the capacity to make mistakes has not been eliminated. The actual performance in the postwar period has been vastly better. This is because the performance has been within a narrower range. We have not moved very vigorously in either direction.

When we had a contraction in 1957 to 1958, the Federal Reserve

System was severely criticized for having maintained what was regarded as a tight money policy for too long, for not reversing itself until late in 1957. It was widely feared that the contraction would be sharp and that the Reserve's hesitancy in reacting to it would make it sharper still. So in early 1958 the System turned around, and in late 1958 there was a very rapid expansion in the stock of money. The increase in the rate of expansion in the stock of money coincided with economic expansion. The recession turned out to be milder than many people expected it to be. The Reserve System, in consequence, must have felt that its own position was rather supported by contrast with that of its critics. It felt that the reason it had had to be so tight from 1956 to 1957 was that it had maintained ease for a very long time before 1955.

This time it decided to have a different policy. The expansion had been underway barely six months when the Reserve System tightened up, early in 1959. The rate of change in the stock of money reached a peak during the summer of that year, and then started going down. I think this clearly was one of the major factors that produced a business cycle peak in 1960 after a very short and brief expansion. That expansion did not run its natural course; it was choked to death early. The steel strike which came at the end of 1959 made it a little difficult to see what was going on, but I think the fact of the matter was that money was tightened up unduly early and that the effect was not felt for something like a year or a year and a half. When it was felt, there was a contraction from 1960 to 1961.

Once again the Reserve System turned around and started to put on a great deal of steam, and again the contraction turned out to be relatively mild, reaching its trough in the spring of 1961. Since then we have been in an expansion, and already there are signs that exactly the same policy is being repeated. Once again we are taking monetary measures, it seems to me, that are likely to spell an early end to this expansion. In this latest episode there is more excuse because of the so-called gold problem, which if I have time I will come to for a moment at the end. Nonetheless, the main point I want to make is that we again have a series of erratic changes.

In retrospect, it seems perfectly clear that we would have been better off if we had avoided the tightening and the easing and had kept the policy of a steady, even keel instead of shoving one way and then shoving too far the other way.

The lesson I draw from this brief survey of history is that the major problem is how to avoid major mistakes, how to prevent such a concentration of power in a small number of hands that that group can make a major mistake. The great virtue of a decentralized system is that mistakes average out. If one unit does something wrong, it does not have a wide effect. If the power is centralized, there is a great deal of power to do good but, along with it, a great deal of power to do harm. The problem is how to erect a system which will have the effect of reducing the power for harm without unduly reducing the power for good, and which will provide a background of monetary stability.

THE PROBLEMS OF MONETARY REFORM

That brings me to the problems of monetary reform. These can be classified under three headings: institutional organization of the private banking system; monetary powers of the Federal Reserve and the Treasury; and criteria for controlling the stock of money.

With respect to the institutional organization of the private banking system, we have had extension of governmental control over the private banking system largely because of the intimate relation of banks to the stock of money. Banks have been controlled more closely than other financial institutions for this reason primarily. It recently has been argued extensively, as you know, that the commercial banking system has been declining relative to financial intermediaries such as savings and loan associations, mutual savings banks and so on, that in some way or other the expansion of these intermediaries limits the effectiveness of monetary management and that it would be desirable to extend control by the Federal Reserve to them.

I think this whole argument reflects a fundamental misconception of wherein the power of the Federal Reserve System lies. The detailed control of banks has almost nothing to do with the essential power of the System. The essential power of the System is the power to determine the total stock of what we call high-powered money — pieces of paper we carry around in our pockets and the reserve balances which the banks hold at the Federal Reserve Banks.

Conceive for a moment a system in which no commercial banks are members of anything called the Federal Reserve System and in which no government agency has any direct control of banks. Let there be no legal reserve requirements for banks at all. Let there be, however, an agency which has an exclusive monopoly of the printing of pieces of paper that can be used for hand-to-hand currency or for vault cash by banks to meet their obligations.

I submit to you that such a system retains all the essential power which the Federal Reserve System now has and that all the rest is trimming. Legal reserve requirements of banks, the ability of the Federal Reserve System to alter these requirements, the requirements that banks keep their reserves as deposits with the Federal Reserve System, the supervision by the Federal Reserve System over day-to-day operations of banks, the clearing of checks by the System — these are all trimmings. You could strip them away and you would not destroy the Reserve System's power.

On the other hand, set up an alternate agency that can print the green paper stuff available for hand-to-hand currency or for vault cash by banks, and the power of the System is destroyed. In consequence, I really think that there is no justification for extending control to financial intermediaries.

CONTROLLING INTEREST ON DEPOSITS

What we want to do along these lines is to reduce the degree of control which the System exercises over commercial banks. The most obvious way in which the degree of control could be reduced is in minor respects. The present ceilings on interest rates and the present law that makes it illegal to pay interest on demand deposits could and should both be abolished. Their potential for harm has been demonstrated very clearly in recent months.

The prohibition of interest on demand deposits makes for a greater degree of instability in the relationship between demand deposits and time deposits than would otherwise prevail. When interest rates in general go up, the interest rate that commercial banks pay on time deposits tends to go up also, and this tends to increase time deposits in relation to demand deposits. If interest were paid on demand deposits, it could go up, too, and offset the rise in interest on time deposits. Because of the interest ceiling on time deposits, every now and then a still greater degree of instability is introduced into the banking situation because of the arbitrary movement in the fixed price.

In December 1956, the price that banks could pay on time deposits was raised. There was a period, prior to that, of a very slow rise in commercial bank time deposits, and then a very rapid rise. In December 1961, the rate of interest that could be paid by banks was raised again. There has been an extraordinarily rapid rise in time deposits since then, which has made it very difficult to read the monetary figures and to know what they are saying and what is going on.

This instability has nothing to do with the nature of the system. It is introduced entirely by arbitrary regulations of prices; and a very minor, but not negligible, reform would be obtained by either of two devices. The Reserve System could inaugurate one of these on its own. It could set the maximum that the commercial banks could pay on time deposits at 20%; that would keep the regulation from being a source of difficulty. Or, preferably, Congress could pass a law repealing the provision that the banks may not pay interest on demand deposits and repealing any price fixing on time deposits. Either of these would be a minor reform, but worthwhile.

Banking under 100% Reserves

To go much further in reforming the institutional organization of the banking system, it would be necessary to go in the radical direction of eliminating controls over individual banks, in the direction of 100% reserve banking. This move would tend to eliminate all control over the lending and investing activities of banks and would separate out the two functions of banking. On the one hand, we would have banks as depository institutions, safe-keeping money and arranging for the services of transferring liabilities by check. They would be 100% reserve banks, pure depository institutions. Their assets would be government liabilities — either pieces of paper or deposits to the credit of the bank on the books of a reserve bank or its equivalent. I would favor the government's paying interest on those liabilities just as it now pays interest on its general government debts. Under a 100% reserve bank, it would be desirable to do this in part because it would provide such banks with an appropriate source of income to enable them to compete on the right level with other banks for funds. Even if we did not go this far, it would be desirable, under present law, to have the government pay interest on its liabilities to commercial banks, namely, on commercial bank demand deposits with the reserve system.

If 100% banking were established, our present banks would be sliced off into other branches operating like small-scale investment trusts. They would be lending and investment agencies in which private individuals would invest funds as they now do in investment trusts and other firms, and these funds would be used to make loans. Such organizations could be completely exempt from the kind of detailed control over financial activities that banks now are subject to.

So much for the institutional organization of the private banking system, which I am skipping over very hastily because I want to turn to matters that perhaps are more important, namely, the monetary powers of the Federal Reserve System and the Treasury.

Supervisory and Monetary Powers

In addition to its monetary powers, the Federal Reserve System currently has supervisory and examination responsibilities with respect to member banks. In practice, the actual examination is done by an examiner employed by the Comptroller of Currency, by the FDIC or by a state banking commission, so that each bank is not in fact examined by the three agencies that technically have supervisory responsibilities. It seems to me that it would be desirable to go further along these lines. Even if nothing more is done now in the way of extensive reform, supervisory power should be concentrated in one of the other agencies, such as the FDIC, rather than in the Reserve System; and the Reserve System should be relieved of any technical supervisory responsibility and its role legally concentrated on exercising monetary powers.

The more important problem is these monetary powers of the Reserve System. As you know, they consist primarily of three items: (1) the power to change reserve requirements of member banks; (2) the power to rediscount for member banks; and (3) the power to engage in open-market operations.

Of these three powers, the first two are, I think, inefficient and poorly designed tools of monetary management. In making this judgment, I am assuming that our present system is in all respects unchanged, that the institutional organization of the banking system is what it is and that the criteria for controlling the stock of money are whatever they now are. My purpose in doing this is to separate issues: whatever the criteria are, there remains the question whether present powers are efficient tools for achieving them.

What changes in the present powers of the System would make it more efficient? There seems to be a very strong case for streamlining these powers by eliminating the power of the System to change reserve requirements and to rediscount, and by requiring it to limit its activities to open-market operations. It really is not true that three tools are necessarily better than one, if they can go in opposite directions or if they get in one another's way. That is the case here. To change the metaphor, it is easier to juggle one ball than three.

SUGGESTED CHANGES IN PRESENT POWERS

The power to change reserve requirements is a poor tool because it is discontinuous. Changes in reserve requirements tend to be by one percentage point or half a percentage point. If they were by 1/100 of a percentage point it might not be so bad, but a change of 1% in reserves is a very large change. In order to offset the effect, the Reserve System does two things at once. If it makes a one percentage point decrease in reserve requirements with the one hand, with the other hand it pulls out the reserves released; similarly, if it increases the required reserve ratio, it provides additional reserves by open-market operations. This is what it must do if it is going to smooth the effect of reserve requirement changes and prevent them from becoming a serious source of difficulty. But because it is hard to predict the effect of a reserve requirement change, the offset is never accurate and the whole operation becomes simply an unnecessary source of disturbance. Anything that can be done with reserve requirement changes can be done with open-market operations.

Hence, the power to vary reserve requirements ought to be abolished.

So far as rediscounting is concerned, it no longer serves the function of providing a lender of last resort. It was introduced originally for the purpose of enabling banks to have an additional source of liquidity in time of need. That function is now performed indirectly by the FDIC, whose existence helps to prevent banks from getting into a position where there may be a run on them or, if there is a run on one bank, prevents that run from spreading to other banks.

As a tool of monetary management, rediscounting is unsatisfactory. It tends to lead the Reserve System to do things at times that it has no intention of doing. How tight a particular discount rate is depends on market conditions. Suppose market rates are falling, for whatever reason, as in late 1959, while the Federal Reserve rediscount rate is stable. The same rate then becomes tighter than it was before. The willingness of banks to borrow depends upon the relation between the discount rate and the market rate. If the market rate is high compared to the discount rate, banks have an incentive to borrow. If it is low, they have an incentive to get out of debt to the Reserve Banks, which is the situation now.

The fall of 1959 is a good example. The discount rate was held stable. Market rates moved from a level above the discount rate to below. I am oversimplifying, but the result was that Federal Reserve credit outstanding declined, but not because of any desire on the part of the System to make it decline. The stock of money fell, but not because of any explicit design on the part of the System to make it fall. The System did not deliberately intend to produce a decline in the stock of money from 1959 to 1960; this happened in spite of the System's behavior and, in that particular case, largely because the rediscount rate, being fixed, led to this result. I could give many other examples, but I think this one illustrates my point that the rediscount rate gets the System into trouble.

One way to prevent the discount rate from being a source of trouble would be to fix it at 20%. That would solve the problem. As an alternative, the power of the System to engage in rediscounting could be abolished by law. That would leave available only open-market operations, which are by all odds the most effective way to control the stock of money.

With respect to open-market operations, I should add, however, that there are two agencies now operating. The Federal Reserve and the Treasury both engage in open-market operations.

ROLE OF TREASURY IN OPEN MARKET

The Treasury's operations illustrate the general principle that the problem is to keep people from making mistakes. The Treasury's debt operations could promote stability, but in fact they have been highly irregular and a source of uncertainty in the market. The best thing to do would be to eliminate the effect. Technically, the best way to do it would be to put all debt management in the hands of the Federal Reserve; it does not make any sense to have two independent agencies in debt management. There would, however, be great political objections to consolidating debt management in the Federal Reserve System.

An alternative that would be just about as good would be to have the Treasury Department adopt a policy that would be stable and predictable. One component of such a policy would be for it to sell no further securities except by auction. To do so it would have to alter the present system of auctioning, which cannot be used in this way for long-term bonds because it is a system in which people pay the price they bid. It is a discriminatory pricing system. The Treasury ought to sell all securities by a method of auction under which all actual purchases are made at the same price. A second component of such a policy would be to reduce the sale of securities to only two kinds or at most a small number of securities, perhaps a very short-term bill and a long-term bond. A third component would be that it should offer them for sale at regular intervals and in stated amounts, so that the public would know six months or a year ahead of time that every week, say, there is going to be an auction for a specified amount of bills and every month for a specified amount of the longer bonds. Further manipulations of the amounts outstanding could be left to the Federal Reserve in connection with its policy for open-market operations.

These changes would provide a streamlined system in which, on the one hand, the Federal Reserve has a simple and efficient tool — open-market operations — and, on the other hand, the Treasury no longer messes up the monetary situation by its erratic debt issues — by its experiments first with one long-term bond and then another, first with advance refunding and then some other "gimmick."

CRITERIA FOR CONTROLLING THE STOCK OF MONEY

What should this streamlined machinery be used for? What should be the criteria for deciding how to change the stock of money? With an old professorial habit, I have let myself talk so long that all I can do on this subject is to make a few dogmatic remarks. I apologize for the dogmatism, but exigencies of the clock leave me no alternative.

As I see it, there are only three kinds of criteria for controlling the stock of money.

One is the kind of automatic criterion that is provided by a commodity standard, a gold standard in which we do not have discretionary management of the system but in which the amount of money in the system is determined entirely by external affairs.

I think such a system is neither desirable nor feasible in the United States today. It is not desirable because of the cost involved in getting people to dig up the gold in one part of the world in order to bury it in another part of the world. It is not feasible because we cannot do it on our own; it depends on the willingness of nations all over the world to engage in an international gold standard, and this, I believe, they are not willing to do. It also is not feasible because we are not willing at home to obey its discipline; we are not willing to subordinate domestic stability to the necessities of the external balance of payments.

I should qualify this last statement. Nobody will say he is willing to sacrifice domestic stability to the balance of payments, yet our present policy is one in which we are doing it. Precisely because we are not willing to face the issue clearly, I think we are doing in practice what nobody will say explicitly he is willing to do. Mr. Lerner will have more to say on that, I suspect, in his talk.

So I do not believe that a "real" gold standard is feasible or possible.

The second alternative is to have discretionary management of money on the part of a group of managers. I have gone at great lengths into our historical record to show the kinds of results discretionary management yields. I do not believe that we have learned so much more than our predecessors that it now is safe to trust these powerful tools in the hands of discretionary managers. The conclusion I have reached on the basis of both the past and recent records is that money is too important to be left to central bankers, if you will permit me to paraphrase Clemenceau.

I come to the conclusion that there is only one other alternative. That is to adopt some kind of rule which will guide our monetary managers, the Reserve System, or anybody that controls the stock of money. Many economists have been in favor of the rule that the System be instructed to keep a price level stable. I myself think it is not a good rule. I think the relation between the stock of money and the price level, while close, is too loose, in short intervals and over short periods, for that rule to specify precisely what the Federal Reserve System or any other governmental authorities should do. It still leaves a dispersal of responsibility and the possibility of major mistakes being made.

Steady Rate of Growth Desirable

So I am led to suggest as a rule the simple rule of a steady rate of growth in the stock of money: that the Reserve System be instructed to keep the stock of money growing at a fixed rate, $\frac{1}{3}$ of 1% per month or $1/12$ of 1% per week, or such and such a percentage per day. We instruct it that day after day and week after week it has one thing, and one thing only, to do and that is to keep the stock of money moving at a steady, predictable, defined rate in time.

This is not, under our present System, an easy thing to do. It involves a great many technical difficulties and there will be some deviations from it. If the other changes I suggested were made in the System, it would make the task easier; but even without those changes, it could be done under the present System. While this is by no means necessarily an ideal gadget, it seems, in looking at the record, that it would work pretty well. It would have worked far better, as far as I can see, over the last fifty years than what we actually had, and I think it would continue to work well in the future. I think we do not really know enough under present circumstances to do much better — and this has nothing to do with the particular people who are in control.

I do not believe anybody here, including myself, knows enough to do any better. Almost everyone is in favor of countercyclical monetary policy. However, when you ask each one what he means by that policy, you find that Mr. Jones's policy is anathema to Mr. Smith, and Mr. Smith's to Mr. Robinson. In point of fact, there is agreement only on the glittering generalities that the Reserve System should do the right thing in the right way at the right time. There is no agreement on how you know the right time and the right thing to do. The appearance of agreement dissolves, once you put it to the test.

Thank you.

12

A Program for

Monetary Stability–II*

Abba P. Lerner is professor of economics at Michigan State University. He is the author of *The Economics of Control, The Economics of Employment, Essays in Economic Analysis* and *Everybody's Business,* and the co-author of *Planning and Paying for Full Employment.* Mr. Lerner earned his bachelor of science degree and his doctorate at the University of London. He was formerly on the faculties of the London School of Economics, the University of Kansas City, the New School for Social Research, John Hopkins University, Columbia University, the University of California and Roosevelt University; consultant, Rand Corporation; adviser to the Treasury, the government of Israel and the Bank of Israel; fellow, University of London, Rockefeller Foundation and Center for Advanced Study in the Behavioral Sciences.

I FIND MYSELF 95% IN AGREEMENT with what Milton has said; in fact, I find myself 105% in agreement with some of it. Unfortunately, this does not add up to 100% agreement with everything he said. I like many of his suggestions for streamlining and improving the efficiency of the monetary control mechanism — I would even go a little further with some of them — and that is why I say I am 105% in agreement. I do not, however, agree that, having improved and strengthened the mechanism, we should decide not to use it. I think we would then be able to do many things with it much better than we have done in the past.

* Proceedings of the Fifth Annual Conference, 1962, pp. 34–47.

What Friedman has shown is that if we set up a system for providing money in the last resort and it does not provide money in the last resort, we get into a mess. The moral, to my mind, is that we should have people running the system who *will* in fact provide the money in the last resort. Essentially, the difference between Friedman and me is one of temperament. I do not believe that we are quite incapable of getting intelligent and informed action. I am quite sure, although Friedman is modest about this, that if people like him had been in charge, many of the big mistakes would not have been made. With the better mechanism which Friedman has shown us we can have, we can really go about doing what we want to do, which is not merely to minimize cycles but to obtain a satisfactory level of employment and economic activity all the time.

I would like also to put a somewhat different emphasis on the importance or unimportance of money in the Keynesian revolution and in the so-called anti-Keynesian counterrevolution in economic thought.

In discussing the way in which thought has developed in the area, I am really leading up to something which is outside this question altogether. We may have a discretionary monetary and fiscal policy for maintaining economic stability, as I think we should have, or we may depend on nondiscretionary monetary policy following rigid rules, as suggested by Friedman, but we will get into serious difficulties in either case. This is because we live in a society where the price mechanism does not work in the way in which we economists have been in the habit of assuming. In the real world, prices do not adjust themselves to supply and demand the way they do in theoretical economic systems of perfect competition.

Since the same problem remains, whether we have rules or whether we permit discretion in our policy for economic stability, much of our debate becomes somewhat beside the point. I will therefore try to go quickly through the trend in economic thought on inflation and depression.

Looking over my notes reminds me of the first lecture I gave at the London School of Economics when I first began teaching economics. I wrote my lecture out in full and then found that it lasted me the whole semester. I will try not to keep you as long as that.

THE DEVIL THEORY AND THE CRUDE THEORY

Much older than any kind of economics is the "devil theory" of inflation and depression, the theory that inflation is due to wicked profiteers and that depression is due to heartless capitalist employers. This semisocialist or sentimental approach says that to stop inflation we must pass laws against rising prices and punish the profiteers, and that to prevent depression we must get rid of the capitalists.

It was such a great advance on this, when economists connected inflation and depression with the quantity of money, that one should not be surprised at the development of an *overemphasis* on the quantity of money. I think Mr. Friedman provides the latest example of this.

The first economic theory of inflation and depression is what I call the "crude monetary theory." It attributes inflation to the creation of too much money, deflation to the creation of too little money, and depression to the rigidity of wages. This theory of depression is very natural for businessmen. Each businessman looks at his own experience and knows that if he were only able to lower his prices he would be able to sell much more and to employ many more people, and that that would cure the depression. However, he cannot reduce his prices because his costs are high. Since wages are the most important item in his costs, he declares that a cut in wages would solve the problem. If labor unions were not obstinate and the laborers were not stupid, they would agree to the wage cut and the depression would be cured!

It is the sad task of the economist to show that this argument is no good because it does not consider the economy as a whole. The economist has to point out that the businessman is forgetting that what he is proposing would also have to be done by his competitors, and that if their wages and their costs and their prices fall, too, the wage-cut cure does not work.

LESS-CRUDE AND KEYNESIAN THEORIES

When this is pointed out, what happens is not that the remedy is given up. What happens is that other reasons are dreamed up for keeping on proposing the same cure. The second or "not quite so crude monetary theory" recognizes that if everybody cuts wages and costs and prices, this changes the picture. However, it argues that the same income will still be able to buy more goods. A 5% wage cut leading to a 5% reduction in prices would enable people with the same income to purchase about 5% more goods, and this would cure a 5% depression.

Then the economist has to come along and earn his name as a practitioner of the dismal science by showing that this argument is no good either, because it cannot be assumed that incomes would remain the same. If we cut wages, costs and prices (and the profit margin between them), we also cut wage incomes (and profit incomes). Income goes down together with prices, so that we are just about where we were before.

We then get a third argument for the same remedy of cutting the wage. This argument is usually put forward as a criticism of Keynes, but a very large part of it is pure Keynesian theory. Notice that the first monetary argument proposed reducing money wages relative to prices. The second monetary argument proposed reducing money wages *and prices* relative to incomes. The third argument proposes reducing wages and prices *and incomes* relative to the money stock, as illustrated in the following Keynesian set of equations:

$$M/P = M^* \rightarrow [i^* \rightarrow I^* \rightarrow (Y^* \rightarrow C^*) \rightarrow Y^* \rightarrow L^*] \rightarrow Y^*$$

(*Indicates *real* measures; (1) and (2) are feedbacks.)

What this says is that to cure a depression we must increase M/P, the quantity of money in real terms (or money relative to prices). One way of doing that is to reduce P, or prices (by reducing wages and prices and incomes). We will then get an increase in the real quantity of money (M^*), people will find themselves more liquid, and this will result in a reduction in the rate of interest (i). The reduction in the rate of interest will result in more investment (I). Extra investment will result in people earning more income (Y), and people who earn more will spend more on consumption (C). We then get feedback (1): the expenditure on consumption (C) again creates more income (Y), this again creates more consumption and so on, and we have a multiplier effect on income (Y). By this long series of steps, the increase in the real quantity of money (M/P or M^*) results in an increase in income, in expenditures and in employment, and so cures the depression.

Now all this is Keynesian analysis. It is nothing but a summary of the monetary theory that takes up the greater part of Keynes's great book, *The General Theory of Employment Interest and Money*. This hardly fits in with the notion that Keynesian theory plays down the importance of money.

It is, however, unquestionable that there is a widespread impression that Keynes did say that money was unimportant. This impression is due to the fact that there was a depression in America at the time Keynes wrote and that American economists, while trying to listen to Keynes, were really thinking about the depression. The result was that they absorbed only the part that was immediately relevant to the severe depression going on in the United States.

Severe Depression a Special Case

A severe depression is a special case, which Keynes does discuss, when the mechanism sketched above does not work. In a severe depression the difficulty is not that people cannot get hold of money but that investment does not look profitable. An increase in the quantity of money does not make the rate of interest go down, because it is already at the lowest point it can reach. This is called the liquidity trap. If the rate of interest does go down, we still do not get more investment. People are afraid they will lose money if they invest, and they are not eager to lose money if they can borrow it at 2% instead of 4%. This is called the collapse of confidence.

In such cases monetary policy, with which the greater part of Keynesian analysis is concerned, does not work and something else is needed to cure the depression. This is where fiscal policy comes in. Fiscal policy can cure depression by increasing expenditure and incomes *directly* instead of by way of an increase in the stock of money in real terms. The government can increase its own expenditure or it can reduce taxes, leaving more money for the taxpayers to spend.

KEYNESIAN VS. CLASSICAL APPROACH

The Keynesian general approach differs from the classical approach only in the method by which the ratio of money to prices (M/P) is increased. The classical approach calls for increasing the real value of the money stock by reducing the denominator P of the fraction M/P. If prices fall, the real value of the money stock increases (unless M decreases as much as P). The Keynesian approach stresses the difficulties and delays in waiting for P to fall enough. This takes too long. But we can achieve the same increase in M/P by increasing M, the *nominal* quantity of money, instead of waiting for P to fall. The rest of the process is exactly the same.

Incidentally, I want to point out that in this connection Friedman shows himself more Keynesian than classical because, in his rule, he calls for the required increase in the real quantity of money (M/P or M^*), not by waiting for prices to fall, but by increasing the quantity of nominal money. Like Keynes, he recognizes that to wait for the required fall in prices is not practical; that we do not have a system in which the market makes prices fall rapidly as soon as we have any depression, i.e., a level of employment that is less than satisfactory.

Where the process of curing the depression by increasing the real quantity of money does not work, either because a liquidity trap prevents the reduction in the rate of interest, or because a collapse of confidence prevents an increase in investment even if the rate of interest does fall, monetary policy does not work. Only fiscal policy works. This is the Keynesian special case.

There also is the opposite special case when, instead of a very low response of the rate of interest to the quantity of money or of investment to the rate of interest, there are very high responses of interest to money and of investment to interest. This is the classical special case when fiscal policy does not work. Only monetary policy works.

The Keynesian general theory includes both of these extremes and the whole range in between when both monetary and fiscal policy work and we can make use of whichever one seems more convenient. That, of course, involves a certain amount of discretion.

THE NEOCLASSICAL THEORY

I have gone through a series of monetary theories, from the very crude through the more refined up to the Keynesian general theory which reaches from the Keynesian special case to the classical special case. I want to mention one more, which I call neoclassical, usually put forward by people who call themselves anti-Keynesian.

These people bring up a fourth argument for the same cure for depression, namely, to let wages and prices fall. They say that Keynes is "all wet." Even in the Keynesian special case with the liquidity trap and the collapse of confidence, the authorities should still hold firm and wait for falling wages to bring the automatic cure. If only the authorities will let everybody know that they will not be bullied or bluffed into undertaking dangerous increases in the quantity of money, they say, wages and prices will have to fall. If wages and prices keep on falling, ultimately this will cure the situation. Even with the liquidity trap and the collapse of confidence, if prices fall enough, people are bound to buy more goods, thus curing the depression. If prices fall enough, everybody who has a dollar will become a millionaire, and before that happens he will decide to buy a yacht, as befits his new situation. Without going to such extreme cases, one can say that as prices keep on falling, the result is a *wealth effect* which by-passes even the Keynesian special case.

The wealth effect is most closely associated with Professor Pigou of Cambridge, England, and Professor Patinkin of Jerusalem, Israel. But they developed this theory not because they were thinking of any practical policy. They just wanted to round out an ideal abstract theoretical system, and I sympathize very much with them because I am prone to this kind of aesthetics myself.

The wealth effect does complete the picture. But one must be careful, as Pigou and Patinkin were careful, to point out that it is of no practical significance as an automatic cure for depression because it calls for a degree of price flexibility which does not exist and which could not possibly exist. Its aesthetic purpose is to show that there is no internal contradiction in the classical system of economics. If we had perfect flexibility of prices, full employment *would be* automatic and none of the problems we are talking about could arise. There are some careless expressions in Keynes where he says that depression does not depend on price inflexibility, but what he means is that it does not depend on such price inflexibilities as we could hope to remove.

ADMINISTERED DEPRESSION

Let me go on to discuss what I have called administered depression. This is one place where I think Keynes "missed the boat." He spoke about the problems arising because of the *downward stickiness* of wages and prices. It is because wages and prices do not fall quickly and easily enough to cure or prevent depression that we have to increase the quantity of money instead of waiting for wages and prices to fall.

Friedman recognizes this, too. In his rule he has the quantity of money increasing only because of the downward stickiness of wages and prices. But why are wages and prices sticky downward? What does this mean? I think this is a much more serious matter than is recognized by either Keynes or Friedman. It means that the market mechanism is not working. If the market mechanism did work, anyone who was unemployed would offer to work for less and instantaneously all those who are employed would have to offer to work for still less if they did not want to lose their jobs to the unemployed. Wages and prices would fall instantaneously, thus increasing M/P, the real stock of money, setting in motion the Keynesian, and if necessary the neoclassical, process for restoring or maintaining full employment.

STICKINESS IN WAGES AND PRICES

The downward stickiness of wages and prices means that it is not *the market* which is determining wages and prices but some *people,* or organizations of people in *institutions,* who have the power to tell wages and prices to disobey the market. If there is an excess of supply, the market says that the price should fall. But monopolies, trade unions, cartels, government controls or other institutions say, "No, prices should not fall," and wages and prices obey them and do not fall.

Once it is recognized that the downward stickiness of prices is something about people and organizations who make these decisions and give these orders, and not about prices (which cannot really make decisions themselves), the greater seriousness of the situation becomes apparent. The same people who can stop prices from falling when the market says they should fall, can make the prices rise when the market says they should remain steady or should fall.

And this is exactly our situation. There is a continuing pressure for wages and prices to go up. Even at less than full employment, *i.e.,* if there is more than the 2% unemployment that is needed for the efficient operation of the economy, the upward pressure on wages and prices regularly causes inflation.

What can be done to stop this kind of inflation? One way is to introduce enough depression to cause some prices — those which are governed by the market — to go down enough to offset the increase in those prices which are being pushed up, so that the general or average price level will stay where it is. This is the nature of the administered depression which we are now enjoying.

From Keynes to Adam Smith

Our situation can be described in the following way: Keynes has been victorious. The monetary and fiscal authorities all have a copy of Keynes's *General Theory* hidden away in the closet because they are all officially anti-Keynesian. When there is a depression, they secretly go to their closets and look up their Keynes. It says there that if we have unemployment, what they must do is to increase the quantity of money or decrease taxes or increase government spending. They do this faithfully in an attempt to diminish the unemployment. Many of them do it with very bad consciences because they feel it is wicked. On the other hand, they want to be re-elected and they do not like to have a depression; so they take this action and, sure enough, it does have the effect of decreasing the unemployment.

But what happens then is that prices go up. There is no longer sufficient depression to cancel the upward pressure on prices, and there are bitter outcries of inflation. So the authorities go back to the closet, pull out Keynes again, and read that if we have rising prices, what they must do is to increase taxes, reduce government spending, and make money tighter. This will check the inflation. So they do that, and the inflation is indeed checked.

But then again there are complaints about an increase in unemployment. After several such ups and downs, the authorities lose patience with Keynes and say: "The hell with Keynes! Let's go back to Adam Smith."

I think this is part of the reason for the growing concern in the last year or two about the national debt, and for the recent ingenious attempts by several economists to appear to support the belief of the man in the street that the national debt is a burden on our grandchildren. (This is done by giving the terms "burden" and "generation" unusual meanings so that while not saying anything that is *really* incorrect, they appear to the man in the street, who misses the redefinitions, to be supporting his superstitions.)

Cost of Administered Depression

It seems to me that we need something like 6% or 7% unemployment in order to maintain price stability, and this is about what we have been getting. At the present moment we have a little less than 6% or 7%

unemployment and we are suffering from pressures to raise prices, such as the recent business about steel. This average level of unemployment — about 7% — would come about automatically if we followed a rule like Friedman's for keeping the amount of money increasing at a constant rate. If Friedman's rule kept the money stock increasing at a constant rate, and there was less than 7% unemployment (I hesitate to use the number "seven" because it looks like a very special or magic number; perhaps it is 6¾% and may vary from time to time), prices would rise and the real volume of money would not increase as much or would actually decrease. Unemployment would then increase until it reached that equilibrium level (about 7%) which keeps the price level stable. If there was more than 7% unemployment, prices would fall and the real value of the money stock would increase by more than the 3% or 4% automatic increase in nominal money supply, so that unemployment would fall to the 7% equilibrium level of unemployment which keeps the price level stable.

Exactly the same thing would happen with a discretionary monetary and fiscal policy that concentrated on stabilizing the price level. Whenever there was more than 7% unemployment, prices would fall. The authorities would then undertake expansionary policies. Whenever there was less than 7% unemployment, prices would rise. The authorities would then undertake restrictionary policies, bringing unemployment up again to the 7% price stability level.

Friedman's rule and discretionary price stabilization both would give the same average general result — administered depression on the average at the level that stabilizes prices. The difference between the two different stabilization methods becomes secondary, because that is only a question of whether one or the other would give greater fluctuations around the average 7% unemployment level — a far less important matter than the average level of depression which would automatically be established by either of these policies.

Now, what do we do about it? Here, I come to the second half of the semester.

AUTOMATIC PRICE MECHANISM UNRELIABLE

A recognition of the nature of the situation, if my analysis is sound, means that we do not and cannot depend on the automatic price mechanism as it now works to achieve both of the objectives we are interested in, namely, a satisfactory level of employment *and* price stability. The reason for this is that the market is not working in important parts of the economy. Prices do not fall whenever there is an excess of supply or of potential supply over demand. They rise unless there is a certain minimum of depression. This level of depression is what is achieved and maintained if we concentrate monetary and fiscal policy on the maintenance of price stability.

We could, instead, have a policy directed at the maintenance of full employment (i.e., with something like the 2% unemployment which is sufficient for the economy to operate efficiently and which would consist of relatively painless short rests between jobs). But this would result in rising prices in an inflation that might become cumulative if it continued for some time. Thus, as long as we limit ourselves to the automatic price mechanism as it now works, we are faced with a choice between the two objectives. We can have either price stability or full employment, but not both. We also can choose some intermediate position, with some inflation and with less than 7% unemployment, remembering that the smaller the unemployment rate below the 7%, the more rapidly will prices rise. The question, then, is what to do in such a case.

TRADING INFLATION AGAINST DEPRESSION

An economist tends to say that we should equalize the marginal disutilities. We should trade inflation against depression at the margin until we have just so much depression and just so much inflation that a little more depression would be worse than the little bit of extra inflation it would displace, and a little more inflation would be worse than the little bit of extra depression it would prevent. At that point the marginal disutilities of the two are just equal, and we will have minimized the total amount of damage from both inflation and depression.

In making a calculation of that kind, we must compare the quantities of harm done by the incremental, marginal, extra bits of inflation and depression that are the alternatives between which we can choose. If we try to make a rough calculation of this kind, it appears that inflation is much less damaging than depression, for equal per cent rates. A 5% inflation has the effect of redistributing considerably less than 5% of the national output from creditors to debtors (including in "creditors" all receivers of relatively fixed incomes and including in "debtors" all whose incomes rise more than the prices of what they buy). The redistribution would amount to 5% only if the economy were strictly divided into pure debtors and pure creditors. But this is not the case. Most people are on both sides of this account, and a large part of the redistribution cancels out. Although the redistribution is an ethically unwarranted one, some of it may even be desirable; i.e., it will be from people we do not like, to people we do like. But a significant part of the redistribution will hurt people we think ought not to be hurt.

It would be possible to compensate all the people that on balance would be hurt by a 5% inflation if we allocated not more than 2% of the national income for this purpose, and this 2% would not be an absolute loss but only a re-redistribution (by taxation and compensatory payments) from those who have gained to those who have lost by the inflation. Such a redistribution is a nuisance, but it is certainly not more so than a 1% loss of national income would be. Comparing this with the 5% absolute loss which comes from a 5% depression, a 5% inflation certainly looks like a much smaller evil. One would therefore think it rational to choose more inflation than more depression at least up to some point where inflation became cumulative and the alternative to each 1% of depression was at least five percentage points of inflation.

If my figures are good guesses, we could have either no inflation with 7% unemployment, or full employment with 5% inflation, at least to begin with. Depression begins only with more than 2% unemployment, but on the other hand each 1% of extra unemployment cuts national output by about 2%. So our choice is between 10% depression [2 × (7 − 2)] and 5% inflation. It would therefore seem rational to choose full employment (i.e., 2% unemployment) with 5% inflation or at most, say, 2% depression (i.e., 3% unemployment) with 4% inflation.

THE PRICE OF ZERO INFLATION

This is not what we are in fact doing. What we are doing is buying zero inflation by paying all the depression that is necessary for this, namely, 7% unemployment, which means a 10% depression — a loss of potential output of about 10% of national income, or about $50 billion worth of depression!

This is nicely illustrated by the President's annoyance at the recent attempt to raise the price of steel. He thought he had bought price stability at the bargain price of only 5% or 6% unemployment — i.e., only 3% or 4% of the national income, a mere $30 billion or $40 billion — and nothing annoys a politician more than someone who does not stay bought.

The choice of price stability at even this bargain price does not seem to me to be wise; but that is a matter of judgment or taste, and I cannot be dogmatic about the choice. It is probable that the actuality of depression bothers only the minority who suffer severely from it, while the thought of inflation bothers more voters, and our government recognizes and responds to this. But could we not avoid the necessity for the choice by modifying the way the automatic price mechanism now works so as to eliminate or reduce the upward pressure of prices at less than full employment?

There are those who say we are rich enough to pay the 7% unemployment or 10% depression for price stability. We are still very well off. Why bother to get involved in dangerous and new-fangled devices which involve some kind of price regulation and wage regulation? We can afford the price. We can even compensate the unemployed more generously and still come out very well.

If I were to think only of what goes on in the United States, I might agree with a proposal of this kind, like that of Galbraith. It really is not very important to raise the average standard of living in the United States. I do not think we can produce much more without people finding more ways of wasting money. As it is, we have to spend about $10 billion yearly to persuade people to buy some $100 billion worth of things they do not need. But we cannot think about the United States alone.

We have great obligations abroad, not only for defense but for the development of the rest of the world. No future can be secure, even if we should escape nuclear annihilation, with the world divided into very rich countries and very poor countries, especially if the rich countries are mostly white and the poor countries are mostly colored. The problem takes on a racial complexion, justified or not, which we cannot afford. We have to do something to cure the cruel poverty of two-thirds of the world. The remedy requires a great deal of money — but only a fraction of the $50 billion worth of stuff which we could produce but which we do not produce each year because we are feeding it to the depression that keeps inflation at bay — and its appetite is increasing more rapidly than our growing economy.

Remedy: New Type of Price and Wage Regulation

Now, I have asked several times what we can do to avoid the choice between depression and inflation without giving the answer. That is because I am a little shy. The answer is very unpalatable because it means some kind of wage and price regulation which I think the people of this country are not ready to undertake. This is largely due to a verbal confusion. There is a powerful tendency to identify wage and price regulation with price control, and price control is a terrifying term. I am myself a violent opponent of price control, and I was able to use this terror some years ago when I was an economic adviser to the government of Israel. While everybody was debating whether wages should be increased by 10% or 15%, I proposed that they be cut by 25%. I was able to survive this outrageous proposal because I pointed out to my opponents that the alternative was price control. This term made them pale. They were mostly politicians, and they knew their constituents were violently against price control. They would not even use the term in Israel. They called it "under the counter" and "queuing up" and other expressions descriptive of what happens when there is price control.

But this is a confusion which in time may be clarified, because the kind of regulation which is needed is the *direct opposite* of price control. What we need is a regulation which would prevent prices (including wages) from being raised only in situations where they could not be raised if there were competition, and which would force prices down only in situations where they would have been forced down by competitive market forces. In short, the regulation would make prices behave the way they would if they were governed by competitive markets and not by *price administrators* — by monopolies, cartels, trade unions or indeed government price controllers. "You cannot raise the price of steel," the regulation would say, "unless there is a shortage of steel, and you cannot claim that there is a shortage of steel if you are working at less than 80% of capacity; and you must reduce the price of steel if you are working at less than say 60% capacity."

How Regulation Would Work

Price control tries to keep the price of a commodity down when the price should go up because there is not enough of it to go around at the low price. It is when the price is held low so that there is not enough to go around that we naturally get black markets, "under the counter" transactions and all the evils of price control. Regulation would stop the price administrators from raising prices only when there *is* enough to go around at the lower price so that the *market* would not have told the price to rise; and it would force prices down only when there is much more than enough to go around at the current price.

In the case of wages, the regulation would be slightly different. It would have wages in general rising at a constant, regular rate, following a rule which is remarkably similar to Friedman's rule for controlling the quantity of money, namely, that wages in general must rise by ¼ of 1% per month or 3% per annum. This is necessary for price stability, given that degree of increasing productivity. But in an industry or area where labor is much scarcer than in general, wages would have to rise more; and in industries or areas where the opposite is the case, where there is an excess supply of labor much greater than in the economy as a whole, wages should not rise as fast or even should not rise at all.

Coming back to steel, many people are disturbed — I would say confused — about the President's action. They say it was probably a good thing to stop the price increase in steel. It would have led to wage increases and other price increases and inflation. But it was a bad thing for the President to have mobilized so many parts of the whole executive branch to threaten, bully and intimidate the companies into a withdrawal of the price increase. At the same time, they are violently against regulation.

That leaves them in an untenable position. They say that the end was good, that the means were bad because arbitrary, yet they are *against* the use of means that are not arbitrary because that is regulation, which they identify with the hated price control. But the only alternative to arbitrary or discretionary acts of the President and the Attorney General is to apply rules like those I have just described, which set out when prices and wages may rise and when they must fall, in those cases where this is not determined by competitive markets. If the natural market does not work, we need an artificial market which will make prices do the same thing. That is the regulation that would make it possible to have full employment without inflation.

Regulation is not going to be activated for some time. It is very unpopular. But it leads me to a suggestion for a policy which perhaps is slightly Machiavellian. As long as we do not have the regulation and must choose some combination of depression and inflation, we should lean a little toward the inflation side because it seems pretty clear that inflation arouses much more political passion than does depression. Such a policy, while very close to minimizing the combined damage from inflation and depression, might build up the political pressure necessary to establish the regulation of prices and wages that would make possible a policy for maintaining both full employment and price stability.

If this were to happen, then we ought to have the debate between Friedman and me all over again, because then the issue between discretionary monetary and fiscal policy, on the one hand, and nondiscretionary monetary policy by fixed rules, on the other hand, would not be overshadowed by the more important problem of administered depression.

Thank you.

*Discussion**

HARRY SCHWARTZ: In listening to you talk this morning, and in reading some of your articles, I come away with the impression that you feel rather strongly that money is the principal or the dominant factor in all situations. Is there not a situation in which there is a conjunction of economic parameters such as the propensity to invest in various types of capital goods — public, private, business and consumer — and the propensity to consume and so on, in which a given projection of money will give a quite different response from that under some other circumstance? And if that is true, would it not be equally logical to argue that there are circumstances in which the real parameters are significantly more important than what we might do with the supply of money?

MR. FRIEDMAN: Let us take two cases. Remember, the proposition I really asserted here is that there have been no substantial rises or falls in money income without substantial rises or falls in the stock of money.

* Proceedings of the Fifth Annual Conference, 1962, Excerpts from the Discussion, pp. 47–59.

The next case, which is the change between money income and real income, introduces a different situation. On almost all occasions, cyclical changes in money income and in real income have tended to be in the same direction. But, again, the degree of relationship, the percentage of the increase in money income which has been absorbed by prices and by real income, has varied from time to time.

Now we come to the more recent situation. I think part of the problem has been the stop-and-start business of monetary policy. We start with a sharp injection, such as in the last half of 1958. This starts things rolling and starts inflationary expectations. We then pull back tight and hold it back. A steady rate of change during this period might not, on the average, have to be any larger than it was. But the same rate of change in the stock of money over this period, if it had been relatively steady month by month, would not have been associated with the kind of pattern of wage and price movement that we have had and would, in fact, have done a good deal to cure it.

Now you ask: Can we cure it right now? That depends on what you mean. I do not have any doubt — and here Abba and I would be in agreement — that if we really wanted to pile on the stock of money very rapidly, we could eliminate unemployment in six to nine months. But we would do so at an enormous price that you and I would not want to pay, the price being what would happen *after* that six or nine months.

I would quite agree that, if we take the issue of how we can maintain a stable position for the next ten years, it would be a very short-sighted prescription and not one that you and I would want to support.

We have to work ourselves out of this problem by shifting to a steady background where we can count on what is going to happen. I think we ought not to let ourselves be tied up by any international commitments on a fixed gold price. I think we are making a mistake by allowing ourselves to be tied by that. On the other hand, I would not say we ought to go all out for very easy money policy.

I think we ought to be increasing the stock of money at an annual rate of 4% a year, and ought to announce it and stick to it. If we did, we would work ourselves out of the problem.

CHAIRMAN KETCHUM: What about that, Abba?

MR. LERNER: Yes, I was going to say I am very grateful to you for bringing this out, because this is something I want to think more about. I admit that administered prices and sticky prices are not identical. They are, I think, closely connected. I think, as Friedman said, that administered prices are often sticky. Sticky prices need not be administered, but I think they are more easily administered. If you have an annual contract, it is much easier for the people concerned to get together and decide what to do when the contract expires. I think it helps administration.

I want to think about it some more, but I do believe they are very closely connected although they are not identical.

But I do not think that stickiness would matter, for our purpose, if it were only for the fact that it is convenient to make an agreement for a long period of time. If this were the only thing, then if something happened to decrease the demand, the people who signed contracts to buy would be kicking themselves, but there would be an immediate adjustment of new contracts. The average would be sticky, but that would not be relevant for current economic performance. It reminds me of Professor Pigou, who once came out in favor of gradualness but who thought it should never by an excuse for doing nothing. The kind of stickiness that concerns us is not of prices that go down slowly, but of prices that do not go down at all.

MR. FRIEDMAN: But consider the rent case. Suppose I am a landlord and have an apartment that becomes vacant at a time when there has been a decline in demand. As it happens, I am in fact a small-scale landlord, but I do not have a vacant apartment because my prices have been sticky — they are too low. If I sign a lease for the vacant apartment, I am stuck with the contract for a year or two. I may hold my apartment off the market for some months, precisely because I do not want to enter now into a long-term contract which over a period of two years seems to me to be disadvantageous. Consequently, it is not true that sticky prices involve only past contracts or do not involve the new contracts or the problems of adjustment. That is to say, sticky prices do make the economy more resistant to either upward or downward adjustments, independently of whether they are administered prices.

MR. LERNER: I agree. Of course, you do not want to sign the contract if you think you will get a better one next month, but you are very eager to sign a contract if you do not think it will be better next month. There will be some people in both categories.

ROBERT SOLOW: It seemed to me that Abba's description of administered prices rested on asymmetry. Stickiness is not something in which there ought to be asymmetry. But if there is asymmetry, how can it be explained simply on frictional grounds?

MR. FRIEDMAN: Take the rent case again. There is stickiness both ways. That is to say, people are hesitant both when there is an expansion and when new contracts are opening up. Also, a tenant is hesitant about entering into a contract at a rental he would be willing to pay for a month or two but not for a year or two. So there is a delay. There is stickiness both ways.

MR. SOLOW: But is there administration both ways?

MR. FRIEDMAN: When we have administered prices?

MR. SOLOW: Yes.

MR. FRIEDMAN: Yes.

MR. SOLOW: That is what I think. That is where Professor Lerner ought to disagree with you.

MR. LERNER: I think administration is possible in both directions, but it happens importantly in only one direction.

MR. FRIEDMAN: But you would have difficulty with the empirical evidence. In the immediate postwar period, for example, the un-administered prices rose more rapidly than the administered; the wages of domestic servants rose by a larger percentage than the wages of steel workers.

MR. LERNER: On the question of stickiness, here again maybe I agree with Milton 105%. If there were no stickiness, if all prices quickly adjusted themselves, inflation would not matter. Nor would deflation matter. Only because there is stickiness do we have to worry about this thing altogether.

I have spoken about administered prices. What you have said reminds me of something I tend to forget, because of my bad habits as an economist. There is something I do not quite know how to describe, which I have been attributing to administered prices. I believe there is a widespread feeling that prices and wages ought to go up, and this has the same effect as administered prices. This influence is in many cases perhaps even stronger where there is no official organization. Where there is a general feeling that prices or wages ought to go up, the person who pays them feels about the same as the person who gets them. He knows that if others are paying higher wages and prices, he not only can but should do this, too. This, it seems to me, is what is going on, and I attribute it to administered wages and prices because it works the same way.

MR. FRIEDMAN: I think what you are describing is the reaction pattern that tends to arise when there is a general expectation of a movement one way or the other. If you go back in United States history, let us say to the period 1880 to 1890, when prices were generally falling, I suspect you did not have this kind of anticipation with respect to prices. On the other hand, when you come to a period like 1900 to 1913, when prices were generally rising, you did.

MR. LERNER: I think a lot of it is the feeling in the atmosphere, and a lot is based upon expectations.

This brings me to another question, rather than an answer, on the 1933 to 1937 period. You said that this was a time when prices rose for a number of reasons outside the money supply, and you said that if prices and wages had not risen for these reasons, we could have had a larger increase in employment and a better recovery from the depression low.

I wonder whether one could not argue the opposite? You are more familiar with the details than I am, but I think it is quite plausible that the expectation of rising prices and rising wages was one of the reasons for greater expenditure and investment in that period, which contributed to the recovery. You cannot assume that the money income would have grown just as much as if there had not been this expectation.

MR. FRIEDMAN: The facts happen to be different. This is another thing it has in common with the present situation. The expansion from 1933 to 1937 is almost unique among business cycle expansions in the small role which plant and equipment investment played. The expansion was primarily in consumption and government expenditures. So far as it was in investment, it was inventory investment. If you were to ask what fraction of the increase in income can be arithmetically assigned to plant and equipment expenditures, 1933 to 1937 will be about as low as anything that can be found in the record. And I think we have the same situation now, and for the same reason.

What was important with respect to the composition of the expansion was the general feeling on the part of the business community of a great lack of confidence in business-government relations produced by the Wagner Labor Act, by the labor attitude of the administration, by the undistributed profits tax and so on.

I think we are seeing exactly the same thing today. This is what you are referring to. The important influence of the steel episode is the extent to which it makes the business community feel that whatever may be the prospects for income, the prospects for profits are small and, therefore, the extent to which it is an inhibiting factor to the allocation of resources to plant and equipment investment. I believe the extraordinary investment boom that we had after 1952 reflected a reverse feeling on the part of the business community. I am not talking about whether this is good or bad, only about the actions of businessmen.

For 1933 to 1937, I do not think you can support the view you are taking.

ELI SHAPIRO: Marshall, I tend to be interested in symmetry, and it seems to me that one of the things that has been addressed to Milton is an inquiry that he explain the mystique between Delta M and something else. In the interest of symmetry, I would like to ask Abba what it is that gives rise to these feelings and whether these feelings or these forces have nothing to do with demand-supply conditions. There might be lags — I am quite prepared to concede this — but I do not quite understand why the forces behave the way they do if I ignore the market, as you suggested in your prepared talk.

MR. LERNER: You asked me how the attitudes or expectations or feelings that wages ought to go up, come about — how they come into being. I think I would agree that mostly they are started by inflationary experiences which may be due to excess demand but which continue after the excess demand has disappeared. As long as these expectations continue, the attitudes can persist and even grow stronger without any continuing excess demand.

MR. SHAPIRO: But there will be a substitution effect, presumably, which will moderate this. It has to. The growth of prestressed concrete and aluminum is not unrelated to steel prices. Steel imports are not unrelated to steel price behavior. I grant you that the adjustment may not be within a calendar year and indeed may be quite protracted, but the fact of the matter is that we do see forces operative in terms of both product substitution and substitution of factors, depending upon relative costs.

MR. LERNER: Increasing productivity permits prices to rise less than the increase in wages, and therefore many people suggest that this is where the cure is to be — in measures to increase productivity. I am all in favor of such measures, but I am not at all sure that they would help us much, because increasing productivity may increase the demands for high wages more than enough to balance the increased possibilities of granting them without raising costs. If you take the almost universal interpretation of the proposition that wages ought to rise with productivity as meaning that wages ought to rise with the productivity in the industries where productivity rises rapidly, and you get wages raised in other industries because it is not fair that they should stay behind, you get more inflation with the increase in productivity.

13

The Relation of Housing Policy
to Monetary Policy*

James S. Duesenberry is professor of economics at Harvard University and a consultant to the Committee
for Economic Development. He is the author of *Income, Saving
and the Theory of Consumer Behavior* and *Business Cycles and
Economic Growth*. Mr. Duesenberry earned his bachelor's,
master's and doctoral degrees at the University of Michigan. He
was formerly on the faculty of the Massachusetts Institute of
Technology, and formerly held a Fulbright Research Fellowship
(Cambridge University) and a Ford Foundation Research
Fellowship.

I WANT TO TALK ABOUT THE RELATION between monetary policy and residential finance. There is always a choice, with such a topic, as to whether
one should deal with practical, empirical matters and the institutional
structure of the market or whether one should attack it on a broader
theoretical plane. In a place like the Harvard Department of Economics,
where not too many people take an interest in details of money and
banking, one has a great reputation for knowing a lot about the institutional details of the market if one just knows there is a difference between
savings banks and savings and loan associations; so if I were there, I
might talk about the practical side of things. But here my stock of institutional knowledge might appear a little bit thin, so I am going to take a
more theoretical attack.

* Proceedings of the Fourth Annual Conference, 1961, pp. 110–25.

229

As everybody is aware, we have had about ten years of controversy over the ways in which monetary policy and a variety of types of credit controls have been used, and in the field of housing we have had a controversy over their impact on the housing industry. There have been wide fluctuations in the availability of residential mortgage credit, and there has been a general upward drift in mortgage interest rates over the last ten years. Of course, people who have developed the relevant policies have defended them as cyclical stabilizers or anti-inflationary devices. I think that quite naturally the use of monetary policy has been attacked by the housing industry and by a lot of people who have some concern for the rate of growth and matters of that sort.

Now, what I want to do this morning is to discuss the criteria for the use of monetary policy and the associated credit controls in relation to housing, but I want to do this in a broader context. I want to ask how our use of monetary policy and the credit controls which affect housing fit into some larger scheme, and how we decide in terms of our views on the operation of the total economy how we would like monetary policy to work.

I think the problem here is that we have to start out by making a fairly clear distinction between alleged scientific knowledge about the impact of any particular monetary policy action or credit policy action on housing or any other type of expenditure, and value judgments on some side effects of monetary and credit policy, such as effects on income distribution or the "pain in the neck" which comes from some kinds of rationing. So I shall try to make it clear which parts of the problem I am talking about as I go along.

LONG-RUN VERSUS SHORT-RUN CONSIDERATIONS

In approaching a problem, I think one has to make a rough division between long-run considerations and short-run or cyclical considerations. That is not too easy to do in practice, however, because the long run is a series of short runs, so that one cannot have a long-run policy and a short-run policy which are in conflict. On the other hand, I think it is true that we can make a distinction between the approximate level and trend of interest rates, and what should be the approximate level and trend of interest rates, on the one hand, and the way in which we would like interest rates to fluctuate around that trend in short periods, on the other hand.

In applying that kind of proposition, we have to be careful, because some types of fluctuations may turn out to give irreversibilities and things of that sort. So it is not possible to work a certain kind of short-term fluctuation and at the same time get any old trend or any old level of interest rates that you want, as you go from one cycle to the next. But with that caution in mind, I still think it is useful to start out by discussing the long-run problem.

I shall start from the point of view that we mean by credit policy the whole set of arrangements from mortgage guarantees, mortgage insurance, the regulation of terms and down payments and maturities, to all the special agencies which provide credits on noncompetitive terms to various subgroups, small business investment companies and all the rest. The operation of all those agencies I shall refer to as credit policy as distinguished from monetary policy, by which I mean the policies which are operated by the Federal Reserve in terms of changing the reserve ratios, changing the reserve base and changing the discount rate. Of course there is a third area, debt policy, which overlaps monetary policy. But I shall take the view that monetary policy, credit policy, taxation policy and expenditure policy are sets of alternative and interacting instruments for controlling the level of aggregate demand or, if not controlling, at least exercising the significant influence on the composition of aggregate demand.

Must Choose Our Target Positively

I shall take the position, first of all, that we have to have a positive attitude toward controlling the level of demand and influencing its composition; that is, that we have to make up our minds what our targets are for the level of aggregate demand and for at least variations in its composition within some range. We shall not try to shoot for some natural volume and composition of demand which will be generated by the free play of market forces.

Some people think that what we should have is some kind of a neutral fiscal policy (I am not quite sure what that means, but that is what they want to have) and a monetary policy which lets the free market reflect the supply and demand for saving. This means, of course, that you generate some natural rate of interest or something like that.

Now, I do not think that it is possible to take that view. I think we have to take the view, first of all, that taxes are necessary in a world in which we have very large government budgets, and it is impossible for the structure of taxation not to have some impact on the amount of saving and on the investment demand. We have to decide on some particular collection of taxes; we cannot just have $100 billion worth of taxes which do not have any impact. There is an enormous variety of tax structures which we can have, and it makes a great deal of difference, both to the saving and to the investment, which set of taxes we have. So, just from that point of view, we have to have a policy about the composition of demand as regards investment, saving and consumption, because we have to decide on the structure of taxes.

When we come to the interest rate, with some particular given set of taxes, there is, first of all, some trade-off, some choice, between the level of interest rates and the degree to which we use credit controls. I shall go into this further as I go on, but, roughly speaking, I think it can be argued that if you want to have a given amount of investment, you will have to have a lower interest rate if, for example, you want to have less than the most housing investment you can possibly have. If the restriction is employed through, let us say, direct regulation of down payments and maturities, you will have a lower average level of interest rates than you would have if you got the restriction entirely through competition for the interest rate.

So there is some choice as to what the level of interest rate should be and what the level of impact of credit control should be. Now, beyond that, it is also true that there is no uniquely correct level of aggregate demand which corresponds to the right level. There is a range of choice of levels of aggregate demand which could be regarded as consistent with the broad proposition that you want to have full employment. Naturally, you can have levels of demand which are greatly excessive in the sense that the demand for labor is way above the supply at current wage rates with a lot of inflationary pressure, or you can have a great deal of unemployment. Both of those would be situations which anybody would refuse. But within the range of situations which some reasonable man might call full employment, there is still considerable choice.

If we compare the United States with European countries, we generally run at higher levels of unemployment than they do. While some of this is due to differences in structure of the labor market, some of it is also due to differences in the choices which we make as to the extent to which we want to squeeze our labor force and squeeze the potential output of our economy. In the long run, this makes quite a difference, because there is some connection between the pressure you put upon the labor force through demand, and the rate at which the labor force grows, because of variations in participation rates, variations in the rates at which people move from farms, variations even in international immigration, with the degree of ease of getting a job in the labor market.

So I take the view that we cannot say that we are trying to set up a monetary and fiscal policy which will bring us out on some target which is predetermined and known and agreed upon by everybody in advance. We have to make a choice as to what the target should be. For all three of these reasons, then — the impact of taxes, the trade-off between interest rates and credit controls, and the play in the range of demand level which could be called full employment — I take the view that there is not any natural target to shoot for. There is not anything for the free market to come out with as a predetermined goal. That means that we have a range in which we can manipulate.

To summarize this part of my argument, I take the view that the choice of interest rate levels and of credit controls to be used should be regarded as a part of the process of choosing the level and composition of demand. That choice involves some value judgments, although it may involve other things.

THE STRUCTURE OF THE CHOICES

Now, I want to put down the structure of choices that we have before us very briefly. Naturally, we do not ever make a fiscal and monetary policy starting from scratch. Let us imagine that we sit down in a dark room and we do not know anything about what anybody is doing right now, that we do not concern ourselves with Congress or any matters of that sort, and that we ask ourselves just what kind of a monetary and fiscal policy we would like to have, pretending we do not know what it is now and that we do not know in practice we can move only a little bit, one step, away from where we are in any direction.

Naturally, these things overlap, and you would think, if you considered one aspect of the problem, that you could decide it without regard to the others. But you would find that you would have to come back and modify your decision after you saw its implications for the range of other decisions available to you. But if you looked at it in a crude way without being too fussy about it, I think you would begin by saying that you want to select a demand target. If you thought of it as a point decision, if you were just interested in a particular year, you would say you want to decide what level of GNP you would like to shoot for. I would suppose that you would like to shoot for a level of GNP which would be associated with a certain level of unemployment and capacity utilization. This might vary a bit with the structure of the labor market.

You must make a choice as to how much pressure you want to put on our available resources. If you are a man who wants to squeeze out every drop, you might say, "What I want to do is to find the level of GNP which will give me 2% or 3% unemployment, and have industrial capacity work at high levels." You would be saying, then, "In order to squeeze out that last drop of output, I am willing to take a good deal of inflationary pressure." On the other hand, you might say, "I am not a man who likes inflationary pressure, and I am not so worried about getting that last little bit of output, so what I would like is 5% unemployment, and I am willing to sacrifice some output in order to get rid of the inflationary pressure." I do not mean to maintain the proposition that 5% is the figure at which you get zero inflationary pressure. I just mean that you have to think about a trade-off between inflationary pressure and actual current output and probably the rate of growth in a longer-run context.

It seems to me that there is no right answer here. It is a matter of value judgments. It is also a matter of scientific judgment as to how much you have to pay in terms of inflation to get another ½% off the unemployment. But, at any rate, it seems to me that in the structure of choices the very first thing is at least a preliminary decision as to what a target level of demand would be.

Now, if you have a given aggregate target for demand, you can have consistently with that a variety of mixes of government expenditures, consumption and total investment which add up to a GNP of $540 billion or whatever you regard as a satisfactory position. And within a given total investment you can have some range of mixes as between industrial investment, agricultural investment, commercial construction, residential construction and so on. They all have to add up to the total.

If you are already at full employment, then when you think about which of these mixes you would like to have, you must recognize at the outset that if you start from full employment you naturally have some mix or output. You have to decide, then, that if you want to have more than you now have of any one of these things, you will have to have less of something else. If you are not already at full employment, it will be possible to increase everything to some degree, but you then have to think about the choice in terms of potential sacrifices. That is, if you are now at $500 billion GNP and you could get $540 billion, you have some choice as to the composition of that $40 billion. If you choose that more of it should be in government expenditures, then less of it has to be in private investment or private consumption or something else. In one case you make, so to speak, an actual sacrifice of one thing to get another. In the other case you make sacrifices of potential gain in one sphere in order to get a gain in the other sphere.

SAVINGS-INVESTMENT ORTHODOXY?

My next remark is going to take me a little bit off the track, but I think it connects up with some things that were considered yesterday. I detected a certain lack of Keynesian orthodoxy in the discussion of investment. It seemed to me that those fellows were left deviationists. In the summary of the meeting which involved oversaving and under-saving, the impression I gained was that people were saying, "Let's do a lot of things to soup up investment demand, and the saving will take care of itself." Now, it is perfectly true that saving equals investment in the national income accounts, so that if you do anything that will raise investment it must be that you will raise the saving. But that is in a context that if you raise the investment and do not do anything else, you raise the income.

Up to a point, that is fine; that is exactly what we want to do. But if you assume you have some particular full-employment target level of income and you get to that target, and then if you raise the investment without doing anything else, you will indeed raise the saving but you will also raise the income and you will overshoot your target. It seems to me that in the sense in which we want to talk about saving, we want to ask the questions: Is there enough saving, or as much saving as we would like to have with a given structure of taxation and government expenditures? Would there be enough saving at a level of income which we regard as satisfactory to provide us with as much investment as we would like to have?

Now, it seems to me that one can always usefully increase saving as long as the amount of saving at the level of income, which I shall call roughly a full-employment level of income, is greater than the greatest amount of investment that could be generated by having the easiest possible monetary policy, the credit policy which most favored investment and the least repressive business taxes which are politically feasible.

If it turned out that when you pushed everything to the limits to encourage investment as much as possible, and you added up how much investment you were going to get, and it then turned out that at a full-employment income people would be willing to save more than that, then there would be no point in encouraging saving. But unless you feel you can say that this is true, then I will not say that you always want to encourage saving. But it is sensible to ask: Is it desirable to do things which would increase saving? Is it worth the cost of doing the things which would increase saving, or is it not?

I do not think it gets you very far just to make the proposition that saving is equal to investment, so that if you do something to increase investment you automatically do something to increase saving, because as soon as you constrain yourself by saying there is some limit to the level of income which you can achieve within some inflationary constraints, or even within the physical constraints, then you get back to a more old-fashioned point of view in which you really say that the most saving you can get is what you get at a full-employment level of income; and that limits the amount of investment you can have consistently with your demand targets. Then you would have to decide whether you want to do something to get some more saving.

I would not have said that except for the fact that I thought the statement made in summary yesterday was a little bit over-Keynesian. Very seldom do I find it necessary to undersell a Keynesian analysis, but occasionally it happens.

Now, let me return to our next problem. I said, before I introduced this side point about saving, that consistently with a given demand target you can get a variety of compositions of output in terms of consumption, investment and government expenditure and the sub-components of investment. Now, the mix which you will actually get depends, of course, on the level of government expenditures, on the level and structure of taxation, on interest rates and on the way in which your credit aids and credit controls operate. It is necessary to have such a collection of these policies as to generate the target level of income. Then the problem to which I am addressing myself really is the choice of a particular composition of output within that target. That involves a particular composition or mix of these instruments of monetary or fiscal credit policy and debt management.

CHOOSING A PARTICULAR INSTRUMENT MIX

Just to give you an example, suppose you are at a full-employment level of income, and you have some particular collection of fiscal and monetary policies, and this produces some kind of output. Now, suppose you think that there ought to be more investment in housing. The question is: What do you have to do? You have to do two things. First of all, you want to increase the demand for housing, and you do that by pushing those policy instruments which encourage a demand for housing. This could be by pushing for lower interest rates through monetary policy and debt management policy, through low down payments and long maturities on insured and guaranteed mortgages, through fussing with the tax system so as to feed federal revenues to local governments in order to take some of the burden off real estate taxes, through public expenditures on housing or public expenditures on urban renewal — things of that sort. Those things all push in the direction of increasing the demand for housing.

But if by assumption you are already at a full-employment level of income, you cannot just go around doing those things and stay with your target. You have to do something else which is going to contract the demand for something else. You could contract government expenditures, or raise the kinds of taxes which bear upon general consumption — personal income taxes in the low brackets and sales taxes. You could do things which would discourage corporation investment, such as reversing the trend of depreciation allowances. It could be that you would do some things which would work against housing, and offset them with other things in order to work on a third sector. For example, some people might think there are not enough houses and that there are too many supermarkets. In that case, you might like to raise interest rates and ease credit controls on housing, so that you would be working two things in opposite directions, because the same instrument has its impact on more than one sector of the economy.

The important things here are: first, there are a number of instruments which influence the demand in any one sector of the economy; second, in employing these instruments you must recognize that once you get to full employment, anything you do to increase the demand in one sector must be offset by something which will contract the demand in another sector; and third, you ought to keep in mind that this is a rule which applies only when you have reached full employment and does not apply in that form when you are short of full employment, but only in this potential form which I mentioned earlier.

Since more than one instrument influences one sector and, even after you take into account some of the overlap, the same instrument affects more than one sector, it will turn out that there is more than one combination of instruments which will achieve a given output mix. Then a third area in the structure of choices is how to choose the instrument mix from among those instrument mixes which will achieve a given output mix.

SIDE EFFECTS OF THE INSTRUMENT MIX

I suppose that one makes this choice, insofar as it is available, by reference to what might be called the side effects of the instrument mix. For instance, recently we have been concerned about interest rates and international matters. In a situation where we did not have any international problems you might go for achieving a given stimulus to a certain kind of investment by pushing on the interest rate front; but if you are worried about the interest rate and international capital movements, you may want to try to achieve the same effect by using an instrument which does not have the international side effects.

Similarly, but in an opposite direction, many people are worried about income distribution. I myself am not so populous-minded as to get terribly concerned about the income distribution effects of interest rates, but I remember that I had some discussion with Kenneth Galbraith about the 4¼% ceiling. I said, "This income distribution problem is sort of a petty problem. Why are you worrying about it?" He gave me a 20-minute speech that would have done credit to Bryan. But some people are worried about income distribution, and I am not going to say what is the right answer or how much weight you should give to it. All I want to say is that this is one of the considerations which come into one's choice of the instruments to use in trying to achieve a given output mix.

Now, as I have mentioned, one way to lower the interest rate required to achieve a given degree of restraint on some kind of investment is to employ things which are more in the nature of direct controls, because you always lower the price of something if you ration it directly. But direct controls have their cost, too, and a good deal depends on their nature; there are costs in terms of administrative difficulties, or inefficiencies which arise out of the strange applications of any kind of direct regulation. So one gets into the problem of making a choice between the painful side effects on income distribution account, the painful side effects of using the price, and the painful side effects of not using the price and using some rationing device instead.

Now, it seems to me that there are value judgments here and there are different ranges of circumstances. I think you can imagine some situations in which you will find that perhaps very high interest rates would be required in order to achieve some objective, and you would not think there was any social function for that, so you would like to use some degree of direct controls to skim off the major part of the problem and use the interest rate only for the last bit of it. I am not trying to make a case for or against direct controls; I am just trying to lay out what seem to me to be the relevant considerations involved.

Now, as I have already mentioned, you cannot think about these choices with respect to one sector only, for example, the interest rate and housing. After all, there is a related structure of interest rates; and while I do not think the structure is so tightly knit, some people say it is true that you cannot move one rate without moving all the others to a considerable degree. That means that you cannot have high interest rates for commercial construction and low interest rates for housing, except by introducing some complicated, rather special devices into the market.

It is possible to break some of the links in the market by various special devices. Indeed, that is exactly the rationale of all kinds of special credit agencies: to find some device by which it is possible to move one interest rate without at the same time moving another interest rate by an equal amount. But, in general, whenever one thinks about moving an instrument which affects any one sector, one has to consider its impact on other sectors as well.

FUNCTION OF MONETARY AND CREDIT POLICY

We could sum up this part of the problem as follows: First of all, I think of the function of monetary policy and credit policy as being part of a set of instruments to set the level and influence the composition of demand. In doing that, one has to raise certain philosophical problems as to whether one wishes to manipulate things in such a way as to give maximum play to the market forces. We may admit that they are never going to work out perfectly, but nevertheless say, "Let us think about policy in such a way as to try to work everything out so that market forces will have the greatest run for their money that is possible." Or we may, on the other hand, take the view that we want to have a direct and conscious influence on the composition of demand.

This is partly, I think, a question of judgment as to how well the market actually works, and partly a question of judgment as to how well anybody else's judgment can work. The main thing here is not to argue about a free market versus a nonfree market, but to take an explicit view of what it is one is trying to do in manipulating a set of policies which by their very nature are bound to influence the composition of demand. Having made up one's mind that one wants a specific level of demand, one must then decide whether to try to think about criteria for the use of policy instruments within the available mix which will provide a given level of demand in such a way as to let the instruments come out in a way as to reflect the supply and demand forces to a maximum degree, whether to choose some specific targets and go for those or whether to compromise by choosing specific targets in some areas and not in others, and then try to design a consistent policy to achieve those objectives through the whole range of these policies. Particularly, one would never think about fiscal policy or tax policy or expenditure policy without thinking about monetary policy implications, and one would never think about credit policy or monetary policy without thinking about the fiscal policy implications that go with it. In general, one cannot play with one of these instruments without looking at the others at the same time.

THE ECONOMIC GROWTH PROBLEM

Now, let me make a final note to try to move this into a less static framework. I do not want to talk about the growth problem at any length, but I do want to make one comment about it.

I have talked so far about the problem of choosing a specific demand target, as though we have just one full-employment level of income and we are stuck with that. Naturally, income, the potential output, goes up all the time, so that the level of output that corresponds to 4% unemployment this year would not be the level that corresponds to 4% next year; next year's 4% level of output would be higher. Now, this means that we have an opportunity to expand somewhere.

In other words, we are unfortunately constrained within the limits of our potential output at a level of unemployment which does not produce too much inflation. We are constrained by that. We are poor in the sense that there are usually more things that we want to do than we can do. That constraint is fortunately being gradually released because our potential output gets a little larger every year, so that we have the opportunity to release some of these constraints.

All of these instruments which we speak of are in effect instruments which constrain demand to some degree. That is, unless we have everything set at the position which maximizes everybody's expenditures, then really all taxes are devices for keeping people from spending, and interest rates and credit controls are devices for preventing people from buying things. If we removed all those restraints, if we did not have any taxes or interest rates, and everybody could borrow money on the easiest possible terms, I think we would have much more demand than the potential output of the economy. So we always have to have a set of constraints to prevent the demand from being too big. Since the potential output gets a little bigger every year, we can ease those constraints a little every year. We can have a little more investment, a little more housing, a little more government expenditures and so on.

Since the scale of the economy grows, it will in general be true that if you have a given set of taxes, interest rates and so on, in a world in which there are more people every year and more income every year, even if you do not change the taxes there will be an increase in the volume of investment every year; so you do not remove all the constraints. But I think we have to be very careful about our response to this expansion. Not only do we have to recognize that there is an opportunity in general to raise some type of expenditures — government, consumption or investment expenditures — but we ought to be very sure that every year some type of expenditure does get raised.

Let me put it this way. If we do not raise the federal expenditure budget every year, then in order to keep moving along with that increased potential output we must either reduce consumption taxes or we must move in the direction of easier monetary policy or easier credit policy or easier business taxation. If we do not do that, we will find that even though expansion in income increases investment demands, with a given set of taxes and a given set of interest rates, investment demand cannot possibly keep on increasing at 4% a year while federal expenditures are fixed. I just wanted to make that one point.

Short-Run Stabilization Policy

Now I want to shift over to the question of short-run policy. Our considerations in the choice of short-run policy are very different in character from the considerations which are relevant for long-run policy, and this choice poses one of the most difficult parts of the strategy in policy making.

The problem of short-run stabilization policy is presumably to move policy variables in such a way as to offset undesired movements or tendencies generated someplace else in the economy. You want to move taxes, government expenditures, interest rates and credit controls in such a way as to expand or contract expenditures to offset the tendencies for expenditures generated from some other source to contract too much or expand too much.

You have to make your choices in the face of the fact that many policies operate only with relatively long lags. That is, you make the policy decision today and the effect comes out a year from now or two years from now. If we had very good forecasting, then you could figure out what policy you should adopt today in order to have the desired effect two years from now. It would be like gunnery; it would always lead the target. Unfortunately, forecasting is not so accurate. It is very difficult to make top policy choices on the basis that what you predict is going to happen two years from now; you would be mostly wrong if you operated on that basis.

STABILIZATION INSTRUMENTS NEED REVERSIBILITY

To some extent we cannot beat those problems; we are stuck with them. This means that we are never going to achieve perfect stabilization; we may as well face it. But that does not mean that we cannot do anything which will improve the stability of the economy. The presence of long lags in operation of policy and the difficulties of forecasting imply that the most effective stabilization instruments are going to be those which work most quickly and which not only work quickly but can be reversed, because a policy which works quickly but leaves you stuck with it after you have worked it will not necessarily be a very helpful stabilizer. It may be helpful once, but when the problem changes its character in the opposite direction it may be harmful. So the most satisfactory policies will be those which work in both directions and those which work fairly quickly.

When we say they are reversible, we want to use some care, because with respect to some policies there is no trend in the level. If, from a long-run point of view, you think you do not want the level of interest rates to rise secularly, your criterion for reversibility is an absolute criterion; if it goes up, it has to come down. On the other hand, there are some variables where the long-run policy will suggest that the variables should have a consistent upward trend. My long-run policy suggests that there should be a consistent upward trend in government expenditures — maybe not yours, but mine does. In that case, when I talk about reversibility, what I am concerned with is not absolute reversibility, but reversibility that is variable relative to its trend. That means that, if it turns out that in a slump I should speed up government expenditures and it is impossible to get them down, it does not worry me. The only question is whether I can get them down to their trend, or below their trend, at some future date.

It is the same way with taxes. You may not share my view about government expenditures, and you may think that the long-run trend of taxes should be down. I contend that you must take one of these views or the other. If you are a man who does not want government expenditures to expand, then you must be a man who wants taxes to contract. Now, if you expect taxes to contract in the long run, and if it turns out that in a slump you reduce taxes and you cannot get them back up again, that does not matter as long as you get the tax rates below the trend during the slump and get them back to the trend during the boom simply by not reducing them any further. So the meaning of reversibility has to be stated with considerable caution.

Some weapons probably work out more advantageously for slump purposes and it may be possible, because of these trend factors, to play one way in a slump and another way in a boom. In the few minutes left to me I shall run through some of the possibilities, and finally I shall connect them up with the question of interest rate ceilings.

The alternatives, as far as I can see, are to play with consumer tax changes, investment tax changes, government expenditures, general monetary policy and housing controls. By and large, if you can get away with it politically, consumer tax changes, such as frequent changes in the first-bracket rate without any changes in structure, could be worked both ways. I am not sure that it would be politically possible, but one can imagine making a percentage cut in the first bracket rate in a slump and not only return to normal after a certain point, but actually have a supernormal first bracket rate during a boom. It may be that this is a one-way street politically and that the best you can do is to get subnormal taxation in the slump and later get it back to normal. But, on the whole, this strikes me as a weapon which has a good deal of power in terms of speed or effect if you can get the decision mechanism to work fast, and it has fairly good reversibility properties.

Investment tax changes are less satisfactory in that respect because, although they can be reversed in a similar way and you can decide one as fast as you can decide the other, it turns out from a good deal of evidence that the ultimate impact on production of any change in investment decisions is spread out over a much longer time than the effect on production of any change in consumption decisions. You can get people to give out orders fairly fast, but the actual production is going to occur over a long period. This means that investment tax changes have less mileage in them from a speed and reversibility point of view than consumption tax changes.

On government expenditures, I would take the view that, if one is willing to take a rather *ad hoc* approach, it is probably true that in a slump one can push a variety of government expenditures above their trend levels and in a boom one is limited in the sense that about the most one can do is to figure on holding the line and not increasing the expenditures so that one gets gradually back to the trend. You can get something out of government expenditures in a slump, but they will have only a limited restraining impact in a boom.

When it comes to general monetary policy, I would say that if you are willing to apply it strongly enough, it certainly can have a powerful restraining effect. It is only a question of how much you want to do. At a 20% interest rate, you can stop everybody from doing anything. You can have the panic of 1907 again, if you have enough guts to do it. But on the whole, I think at present it works slowly in a restraining direction. I think there are a lot of things we could do which would speed it up, but I am not going to talk about them. In a slump, it seems to me that many of the things that monetary policy restrains in the boom are likely to be things that will not look so hot in a slump, and they will get voluntarily restrained, so I do not think it is really a two-way reversible street.

HOUSING CEILINGS VERSUS DIRECT CONTROLS

As far as housing controls are concerned, it seems to me that if they are worked through the ceiling kind of gadget that we have been using, they work relatively slowly. On the other hand, if we took off the ceiling and imposed direct controls on terms, maturities and down payments, which we varied administratively, we could sharpen the impact and make it work a good deal faster, and it would be a major weapon of monetary policy and cyclical stabilization. I shall not tell you what the optimum policy mix is, because it varies with the circumstances. But I think it is considerations of this general type that you want to employ in making policy decisions about cyclical stabilization.

Let me say a final word on this point about housing ceilings. It seems to me that what we have done in the postwar period is to have in effect something very much like a kind of direct regulation of down payments and terms, but we have proceeded in the rather weird way of introducing an interest rate ceiling on insured and guaranteed mortgages and then of playing monetary policy and the ceiling itself at times so as to make insured and guaranteed mortgages either attractive or unattractive. This has had about the same kinds of effects we would have had if we had had no ceiling but had used administrative regulation of minimum down payments and maximum length of term for insured and guaranteed mortgages. And we would have had a much more rational choice of what we were doing if we had done this explicitly by limiting the ceiling and using the controls directly. Also, we would have had better timing, because there is a lag between the time you make the decision to have higher interest rates and the time they actually get higher, and a still longer lag before they have their full impact on the lender's policy. It must be said that in 1950 there was a considerable lag in the lender's policy even when we did use direct regulation, but certainly it would be a shorter lag. But that is, so to speak, a technical point. If you are going to use nonmarket regulations, and that is essentially what this is, then you ought to use them in a sensible and consistent manner.

My more general proposition is that when we think about monetary policy in relation to housing, we want to think about it not as a matter of housing and housing policy first. We want to think about it as a part of the total set of decisions about the level of demand and allocation of resources.

Discussion*

JOHN O'DONNELL: I may be wrong here, but underlying this whole discussion is the presumption that the government can put certain variables where it wants them to be. Looking back over the last twenty years, there are probably two big events where the government tried to do this. In England, for example. Dalton tried to do it by pumping colossal sums of money into the system and holding money rates down because the Labour party felt that it could control these variables by such decisions. It failed miserably, with terrible consequences. In this country, I think we tried the same thing by pegging the interest rate. In the light of the attempts of the government to control these variables and put them where it wants them by fiat, do you think our experience has been particularly happy? Does all go well in this type of economic policy?

MR. DUESENBERRY: First of all, the implication you make about interest rate policy I would not take as correct. That is, I would not suppose that interest rate policy is, with respect to industrial investment, the major factor. On the contrary, it is a very second-rate matter. On the other hand, with respect to housing and commercial construction, I would think it was of greater consequence.

Now, I left out one section on feasibility. I do not really contend that it is possible to manipulate all these instruments over an indefinite range. The power of each instrument is limited by a number of factors. It is limited, first of all, by its own power, so to speak; I mean, by this, how much impact you get out of how much movement in the variable. Secondly, it is limited by political considerations; there are limits to how much you can push these variables. Thirdly, it may be limited in the sense that there are some natural limits to the variable itself.

* Proceedings of the Fourth Annual Conference, 1961, Excerpts from the Discussion, pp. 125–32.

When you cite these policies about the interest rate, part of the difficulty, for instance, in pegging the interest rate, is a matter of consistency. If it turns out that the basic structure of taxation, including business taxation, and the level of investment demand that is associated with the level of income, technical changes, population growth and so on, works out so that at a full-employment level of income and a 2% interest rate, you have more investment than can be financed out of the savings that you get at that level of income, then if you try to push the interest rate to 2% you are naturally going to get inflation. That is exactly what I meant when I said that when you think about these matters you must make a consistent decision on all fronts simultaneously.

It is possible to get the interest rate to 2% even in the face of strong investment demand, if you are willing either to repress consumption by sufficiently high taxation or to use other devices which will repress investment demand in some other way. But if you have a situation which makes the investment demand very high to begin with, and then try to push a monetary policy which gives you a 2% level of interest rate, then you will have inflation.

That is just an example of a policy which is internally inconsistent. You worked only on one front and did not work on the other fronts. Now, pegging of the interest rate is a kind of policy that arises out of the fact that some people were in the habit of thinking that there would not be enough investment to go around even if you had an easy-money policy, a relatively easy tax policy and so on. They were just concretely wrong.

This is not to say that you should not engage in these games because you may be wrong. You have to engage in them because you have an interest rate policy. It is very important that it be in a consistent manner. But you cannot go around not having an interest rate policy because you think you might make a mistake in choosing the policy. You have to have some policy, so you will have to make some mistakes. But you will make fewer mistakes if you think about the over-all picture and make it consistent.

I agree that those were bad experiences, but I do not agree they were inconsistent with what I was saying.

HARRY BLYTHE: On the comment you made favoring the trend of increasing government expenditures over reducing taxes, can you defend that position?

MR. DUESENBERRY: As to the question about tax rates and government expenditures, this is mainly a question of value judgment. The tax rates, incidentally, which are involved here are to a large extent low-income tax rates. High tax rates on high-income individuals are just political sand in the machinery because they do not produce any revenue and they do not restrain any expenditures. They are in there only because you cannot tax the poor unless you also tax the rich. They do not have anything economically to do with anything. If it turned out that there were extremely deleterious effects from those high income taxes, either in terms of incentive effects, which I doubt, or in terms of distortion of activity effects, of having everybody spending all his time figuring out how to beat the taxes, then of course there is some question in high tax brackets and it would be greatly desirable if we could work this game of plugging up loopholes and reducing the high-bracket rates.

I do not say there is no room for any tax cuts, but I do feel there is a great need for a large variety of government expenditures, and I am very much concerned, personally, as a matter of value judgment, about defense expenditures and about all kinds of other expenditures. I think those are good things. If we bring in the free market argument, I would say that the things that I want are either things which by their nature are collective goods or things where there are significant external economics or effects, such as education. This is not necessarily a collective good in the sense that you can educate an individual privately and not educate some other people; but I think there are significant effects on the whole community from the level of education, so you should not let it be a matter of free choice but a matter of collective choice. But that is not essentially an economic judgment.

GLENN BEYER: Last year [1960] was about the first time that housing starts did not respond. I should like to get some comments from you.

MR. DUESENBERRY: The pattern this time is a little peculiar in the sense that monetary policy began to ease somewhat earlier, so that the cyclical pattern looks a little different from what it did in previous recessions. It was a little less sharply defined pattern, so I think perhaps there was some net rise as a result of the monetary policy. But I think the major difference is probably that we are getting toward the trough of a population cycle where the number of people who are entering the labor force is now getting quite large, while the number of people at the ages at which houses are normally bought is somewhat smaller. We have worked off a number of backlogs. There was a big undoubling at the end of the war; the percentage of undoubled couples has fallen from 8% or 9% down to 3% or something like that. We had a good deal of splitting households and things of that sort, and that is a one-shot proposition. So I suppose the underlying demand is somewhat lower than it was a few years ago. Presumably this will rise again before very long when we get the bulge of family formation perhaps about six years from now.

Those are the major things that I can think of. There do not seem to be any difficulties about the mortgage credit position.

PART FOUR

Savings in the American Economy

In the United States, fairly elaborate institutional machinery has been established to channel financial savings into capital formation and investment. For potential users of capital, the problem is one of financing. For savers, the problem is one of investing efficiently and at an acceptable rate of return. For the nation as a whole, the problem is one of utilizing and allocating savings in a manner that maximizes economic growth and minimizes the risks of economic instability or depression.

Whatever savings are not channeled directly into capital formation must flow through the financial intermediaries. A host of such intermediaries exist — banks, life insurance companies, investment houses, savings and loan associations, credit unions, etc. Although the introduction of intermediaries complicates the picture, it also simplifies the problem, for intermediaries eliminate the need for each group of savers to seek out and choose among the wide variety of capital users. Equally significant, those seeking capital have an opportunity to gather funds from a wide variety of savers.

The readings selections in Part Four take up the question of savings and capital formation in three parts: The supply of saving in its broadest sense is explored at length in our first paper by Raymond W. Goldsmith. This paper is based on Goldsmith's definitive work for the National Bureau of Economic Research, published in *A Study of Saving in the United States* in 1955. An effort is made here to define the subject, both quantitatively and qualitatively. Next, the importance of institutions in the savings process and an evaluation of the current status of direct investing relative to the use of intermediaries is presented by Jules I. Bogen. The final paper, by Leon T. Kendall, looks into the decade ahead and examines the present status and posture of financial intermediaries for clues to the future development of such organizations.

14

The Supply of Saving*

Raymond W. Goldsmith is a member of the research staff of the National Bureau of Economic Research and the author of *A Study of Saving in the United States,* among other works. Mr. Goldsmith received his doctorate at the University of Berlin, and served as Ford Distinguished Visiting Professor at New York University in the spring of 1958. He was formerly director, Savings and Capital Market Study, sponsored by the Life Insurance Association of America; director, Planning Division, War Production Board; chief, Research and Statistics Section, Securities and Exchange Commission; economic adviser to the United States delegation at the Paris Reparations Conference and Austrian Treaty Negotiations; member, Currency Reform Mission to West Germany.

IT MUST BE EVIDENT TO EVERY ONE of you that it is not possible to present in less than one hour a well-rounded discussion of all the major problems of the supply of saving in the United States.[1] I have therefore limited myself to five questions, and even their discussion must be summary and to some extent superficial. These five questions are:

1. What have been the long-term trends in aggregate national and personal saving?

* Proceedings of the First Annual Conference, 1958, pp. 103–19.

[1] With few exceptions, the figures cited are from tables for the period before 1946 appearing in R. W. Goldsmith, *A Study of Savings in the United States* (Princeton University Press). Those for the postwar decade 1946–56 are from a study of the postwar capital market now in progress at the National Bureau of Economic Research.

2. How has the structure of personal saving changed since the turn of the century?

3. What has happened to the relation between home building and home financing and the supply of personal saving?

4. What role has the supply of saving played in the current business cycle?

5. What can we say on the basis of past experience about the outlook for the supply of personal saving and of home financing?

I will have to compress into half a dozen paragraphs what seem to me the main lessons of our past experience with the supply of saving, thus greatly oversimplifying the situation and sometimes risking misunderstanding.

Trends in the Level of Saving

1. National saving during the last half century has averaged 13½% of net national product if consumer durables are included in saving and 12% if they are excluded for what we may call "normal" periods omitting the two world wars and the Great Depression. From 1946 through 1954, a period which comprises two complete business cycles and is not too much affected by extraneous events so that it may be compared with normal periods of the past, the national saving ratio averaged 12% including and 9% excluding consumer durables. The same ratios most likely will also be obtained when we are able to include the next full cycle, which on a calendar-year basis will probably comprise the years 1953 through 1958.

I do not feel that the small difference in the national saving ratio including consumer durables between the postwar period and the first three decades of the 20th century justifies our assuming a downward trend in the ratio. The argument for a slight long-term decline, however, is stronger if consumer durables are excluded from national saving. The hypothesis of a slightly declining trend in the ratio of national saving to national product would be somewhat reinforced if closer analysis confirmed the view, now necessarily based on rather unsatisfactory evidence, that the national saving ratio was somewhat higher in the last three decades of the 19th century than during the following 30 years.

2. During the nonwar periods before the Great Depression, personal saving accounted for fully 70% of national saving while corporate saving contributed somewhat less than 20% and government saving, well under 10%. During the postwar period the share of personal saving has been slightly higher — upwards of 75% — while that of corporate saving has been slightly lower. It would seem too early, however, to conclude that a structural change in the distribution of total national saving among the main sectors has occurred, particularly if consumer durables, which are

mainly responsible for the increase of the share of personal saving during the postwar period, are excluded.

3. The personal saving ratio — the share of saving by nonfarm households and by agricultural and unincorporated business enterprises in total personal disposable (after tax) income — has during the postwar period averaged 12% if consumer durables are included and 9% if they are excluded. This compares with ratios of 10% including and 9% excluding consumer durables for nonwar periods before the Great Depression. There certainly is no evidence here of a downward trend in the saving ratio, even if consumer durables are excluded. However, the small increase in the saving ratio including consumer durables should not be regarded as evidence of an upward trend, particularly since the ratio for the postwar decade was not above that for the 1920s. In this case the argument for the existence of a trend would be weakened, not strengthened, if the ratio for the period 1870 to 1900 proved to be somewhat higher than that in the following three decades.

4. Even if we limit ourselves to annual data, the personal saving ratio has shown considerable short-term fluctuations that closely correspond to different phases of the business cycle. Thus, the ratio declined from 17% in 1905 to 8% in 1907; from 14% in 1912 to 8% in the following year; from 14% in 1919 to only 2% in 1921; from 14% in 1929 to the all-time low of minus 7% in 1932; and from 11% in 1937 to 6% in 1938. The correspondence between the movements of saving and the business cycle are even better if the comparison is based on the absolute volume of saving rather than on the personal saving ratio; it is also better if consumer durables are included in personal saving than if they are omitted from it.

In the postwar decade the fluctuations in the personal saving ratio have been much less pronounced, even if we now use quarterly figures that are not available for most of the earlier period. During the 1948–1949 recession, the ratio of personal saving to personal disposable income fell only by a few percentage points. During the 1953–1954 recession, a small increase in net saving through consumer durables partly offset a substantial decline in saving through intangible assets. For the current depression most of the figures are still missing. However, at least through the first quarter of 1958 the decline in the saving ratio was moderate, bringing the ratio down from about 10% in the first half of 1957 to between 6% and 7%.

5. We have so far dealt with the facts regarding aggregate saving of the nation or of all households taken together. A large body of statistical material, however, has also accumulated on the saving of sample groups of households, providing information not only on the total saving of such households but also on the forms in which their saving or dissaving

occurs. These data are not available year after year but only for a few benchmark periods. The most important sample surveys refer to 1935–1936, 1941 and 1950. No data of this type are available for a recent year. This is unfortunate, since sample savings provide needed information on the supply of saving that cannot be obtained from aggregate statistics, particularly the contribution made by different groups in the population to the supply of personal saving.

In all these sample surveys of saving it has been found that when households are grouped by income — usually income for one year — a family's saving increases as we move upward from the lower to the higher income groups. This increase occurs not only in the absolute amount of net saving but also in the ratio of saving to income.

It also has been found, and this is more novel and possibly more significant for deeper analysis, that this positive correlation between the level of income and the saving-income ratio is less pronounced if families are grouped on the basis of their average income over longer periods — ultimately on the basis of their lifetime income — and, secondly, if other influences likely to affect saving, such as age, family size and composition, occupation and ownership of assets, have been separately allowed for. In other words, as the reference period is lengthened and the influence on the saving ratio of the level of income is isolated, the influence of this factor is found to diminish.

The inequality of the saving-income ratio among households of different income levels, and the positive correlation between income level and the saving ratio, are found to be much smaller if permanent income rather than one year's observed income is used as the independent variable and if the influence of other relevant variables is separately allowed for. Indeed, one recent study, probably the most original and provocative one that has appeared in this field for many years,[2] claims that under such conditions the positive correlation between income level and saving ratio disappears entirely. In other words, the ratio of saving to permanent income is the same for households at all income levels provided they are similar in other respects. This conclusion, however, I would as yet hesitate to include among the established facts about the supply of saving.

STRUCTURAL CHANGES IN PERSONAL SAVING

In contrast to the stability of the ratio of aggregate saving to personal disposable income, very substantial changes have occurred in the forms of savings. These changes are indicative of shifts in the channels through which saving flows from the ultimate suppliers of funds to their ultimate

[2] Milton Friedman, The Consumption Function (Princeton University Press, 1957).

users. They are possibly brought out most clearly by a comparison of three periods: at the beginning of the century, in the 1920s and in the 1950s. Each of these periods is long enough to eliminate or mitigate the influence of business cycles and is not unduly affected by extraneous events and thus comes as close to reflecting a "normal" state of affairs as can be expected in this ever changing world.

Let us first look at the share of saving through homes. Here the differences between the net and gross approach — that is, the deduction or not of mortgage debt from expenditures less depreciation — is such that we must look at the two situations separately.

On a gross basis, net expenditures on one- to four-family homes (that is, the cost of construction and land of new homes less the depreciation on the entire stock of homes at replacement cost) represented about one-fifth of total saving of nonfarm households from 1897 to 1908, the first of the three periods; about one-fourth from 1922 through 1929; and again about one-fifth during the postwar decade 1946–1955. Thus, homes seem to have absorbed about the same proportion of total gross saving of nonfarm households in the three periods. The somewhat higher ratio in the 1920s is easily explained by the extraordinarily high level of home-building activity during that period.

If we now shift to a net basis, deducting the increase in home mortgage debt from net expenditures on homes — and, of course, similarly deducting increases in other forms of debt from the appropriate items of gross saving — we find a sharp decline in the share of homes in total net saving of nonfarm households. From 1897 to 1908, slightly less than one-fifth of nonfarm individual saving was attributable to homes. In the 1920s, this share declined to one-seventh. In the 1950s, net saving through homes virtually disappeared.

The reason for the difference in the two calculations, of course, is the relatively heavier reliance on borrowing in the postwar period. Early in the century the increase in mortgage debt offset only about one-quarter of net expenditures on homes. During the 1920s it canceled approximately two-thirds of net home expenditures, and during the postwar decade it offset them almost completely.

Quite a different picture is shown by the share of consumer durables in net saving of nonfarm households. It rose from less than one-tenth at the beginning of the century to almost one-sixth in the 1920s and retained that relatively high level in the 1950s. This was the result of a continuous increase in the proportion of expenditures on consumer durables in gross household saving — from one-eighth from 1897 to 1908, to more than one-fifth in the 1920s and almost three-tenths in the 1950s — an increase more than sufficient to offset the sharp rise in depreciation allowances on the stock of consumer durables.

Turning to intangible assets, we find that the share of deposits in financial institutions (including currency) was virtually the same — approximately one-fifth — early in the century and in the 1920s, but rose slightly to more than one-fourth in the 1950s. While the upward movement in the aggregate is modest, the rise in the share of deposits with savings and loan associations in the saving of individuals is spectacular: from less than 1% in the first decade of the century to 7% in the 1920s and to 12% in the 1950s.

Life insurance has accounted for a steadily increasing share in the total saving of nonfarm households — 7% in the beginning of the century, 10% in the 1920s and 16% in the 1950s. Still more pronounced has been the rise in the share of governmental and private pension funds. They were virtually negligible until the 1930s, but in the 1950s accounted for almost one-sixth of total saving of nonfarm households.

The share of saving in the form of long-term claims (bonds and mortgages) shows a declining trend, but at a lesser rate than might be expected, from not quite one-fourth at the beginning of the century to about one-sixth in the 1950s.

A sharp decrease, on the other hand, has occurred in the share of saving through stocks (adjusted for borrowing on them) in total net saving of nonfarm households. Compared to a share of about one-fifth, both in the beginning of the century and during the 1920s, common stocks accounted for less than one-tenth of net saving of nonfarm individuals during the 1950s.

TRENDS IN PERSONAL SAVING

For economists, several rearrangements of these individual forms of personal saving are possibly of greater interest. The following trends then emerge:

1. The share of the most liquid forms of saving (deposits with financial institutions and United States government securities) was considerably higher in the 1950s, with over one-third of the total, than in either of the two earlier comparison periods. Similarly, the share of the least liquid forms of saving (consumer durables and pension funds) increased from one-tenth early in the century to almost three-tenths. Sharp declines, on the other hand, were shown between the two earlier periods and the 1950s in saving of an intermediate degree of liquidity — securities, mortgages and life insurance.

2. While total net saving was divided approximately equally in the first two periods between claims and equities, which include not only stocks but also real estate and consumer durables, claims accounted for three-quarters of total net saving of nonfarm households in the 1950s and equities for only one-fourth. Little change, on the other hand, occurred

in the distribution of claims saving between short-term and long-term claims. In all three periods, approximately two-fifths of total claims saving had the form of short-term claims while three-fifths was made in the form of long-term claims.

3. As is well known, one of the characteristics of saving in the postwar period has been the increasing importance of contractural saving. If it is defined to include only saving through life insurance and pension reserves, the share of contractual saving increased from less than one-twelfth early in the century and about one-eighth in the 1920s to three-tenths in the 1950s.

If the term is interpreted more broadly to include saving in the form of contractual repayment of mortgage and consumer debt, the change is even more spectacular. In that case it may be estimated that the share of contractual saving in total of net saving of nonfarm individuals rose from only about one-tenth early in the century to one-fifth in the 1920s and well over one-half in the 1950s.

4. From the economist's point of view, possibly the most interesting classification by forms of saving is that between saving used in the saver's own household, saving made available directly by the saver to the ultimate user and saving transmitted by the saver to a financial intermediary, which we may call "indirect" saving. On the gross basis, where the liabilities attaching to certain forms of saving are disregarded, indirect saving increased its share from one-quarter earlier in the century and in the 1920s to about two-fifths in the 1950s. The share of direct saving, on the other hand, declined from over two-fifths to less than one-fifth. Finally, saving for self use stayed at around two-fifths in the 1920s and 1950s compared to less than one-third earlier in the century.

HOME BUILDING AND LENDING AND THE SUPPLY OF SAVING

At least three sets of aggregative figures are of interest in assessing the connections between home building and financing — generally limited here to one- to four-family homes — and the supply of saving. The first and simplest of these figures is the share of home building in national investment, gross or net of depreciation allowances. The ratio of gross or net expenditure on home construction to national gross or net investment indicates the proportion of resources not used in current consumption that has been devoted to increasing the stock of homes. The ratio of the value of the stock of homes to reproducible, tangible wealth measures the same relation, but cumulatively as the result of saving in the past rather than as a reflection of current saving.

The second measure is the share of saving through homes in total personal saving. Here as many as three ratios need to be distinguished for adequate analysis. The first ratio relates gross expenditures on homes to total gross personal saving. The second ratio compares net expenditures on homes — gross expenditures less depreciation allowances — to net personal saving. The third ratio relates net expenditures on homes less the increase in home mortgage debt, which may be called net saving through homes, to total net personal saving. All three ratios reflect one aspect of the relative importance of homes as direct or indirect outlets for personal saving.

The third measure is the share of homes and home mortgages in the total holdings of assets of financial institutions. These ratios show the relative importance of homes as an outlet for funds of financial institutions and indicate their standing relative to other competing outlets.

SHARE OF HOME BUILDING IN NATIONAL INVESTMENT

Let us begin with the share of homes in national investment and national wealth, using estimates in constant prices to eliminate the effect of valuation changes. There we can go back well into the 19th century and we shall for a moment indulge in this luxury.[3]

We then find that between 1805 and 1929 net investment in residential real estate — this is very close to net investment in one- to four-family homes alone — accounted for between 20% and 30% of total national investment. The ratio rose from only a little over 20% between 1805 and 1880 to close to 30% for the half century between 1880 and 1930. This increase probably reflects, among other factors, the urbanization of the United States during this period.

The next two decades — taken up mostly by the Great Depression and its aftermath and by World War II — present the unprecedented picture of the stock of residential structures failing to grow, if appropriate allowance is made for depreciation, while the increase in total reproducible tangible wealth was still substantial, although relatively much smaller than in the preceding periods. In the postwar decade, however, net investment in residential real estate again has accounted for slightly over 20% of total national investment, which in turn reverted to approximately its former level in relation to national income.

These movements are reflected in the share of residential real estate in reproducible tangible wealth in current prices, although changes in the relationship between the cost of construction of homes and of other components of reproducible tangible wealth also affect this share. Our statistics, not too reliable in the early periods, show that the share of

[3] The figures before 1897 were derived from R. W. Goldsmith, *The Growing of Reproducible Wealth of the U. S. A. from 1805 to 1950* (*Income and Wealth*, Series II) [Bower and Bower, 1952].

residential structures in reproducible tangible wealth rose from less than one-fifth during the 19th century up to 1880 to over one-fourth between 1900 and 1930. After a temporary dip, the share recovered and even exceeded its former level. Throughout the postwar decade, residential structures have accounted for about 30% of reproducible tangible wealth in current prices.

The record of the past 100 to 150 years thus would seem to indicate that if fairly long periods are taken, residential real estate has absorbed between 20% and 30% of the national supply of saving. No long-term trend in one direction in the ratio is evident from the figures, although long swings possibly may be detected.

SHARE OF NET SAVING THROUGH HOMES

We have already had occasion to discuss the second set of measures when reviewing the structural changes in personal saving since the turn of the century. We may, therefore, limit ourselves to recalling that there has been no visible trend in the share of gross expenditures on homes in gross personal saving or in net expenditures on homes in net personal saving, but that the share of net saving through homes, which makes allowance for increases in home mortgage debt, has declined sharply.

It may be well to dwell for a minute on this point in order to make clear its significance and its relation to the trend in the ratio of owners' equity in homes in current prices. At the beginning of the century, owners' equity was equal to about 85% of the then current value of residential real estate, including both structures and land. Until 1950 this ratio was never substantially lower, except during the Great Depression. Even in 1956, owners' equity was still in excess of 70% of the market value of residential real estate.

The explanation of the apparent discrepancy between the level trend in the share of net residential construction in national investment, the sharp decline in the share of net saving through homes in total personal saving, and the very moderate reduction in the share of owners' equity in the market value of homes is, of course, provided by the upward trend in the price of residential real estate. Realized and unrealized capital gains have been large enough through the period as a whole to offset the effect of increases in mortgage debt on the debt-to-value ratio. Although new residential structures start, on the average, with a debt ratio between 50% and 70% — the ratio increasing as we get closer to the present — contractual monthly repayments of mortgage debt, irregular repayments particularly on occasion of change of hands of homes, and the rise in real estate values have combined to hold the increase in the debt-to-value ratio to modest proportions and have left owners, in absolute terms, with vastly increased equities, rising in the postwar period alone from approximately $125 billion to $250 billion.

SHARE OF HOME MORTGAGES IN FINANCIAL INSTITUTIONS

Finally, then, the third measure: the share of home mortgages in the portfolios of financial institutions. Here some interesting trends appear.

Home mortgages, of course, have always, barring only war periods, accounted for most of the assets of savings and loan associations. Other institutions, however, have experienced substantial changes in the proportion of their portfolio represented by home mortgages. These changes represent the combined result of numerous factors such as interest rate differentials, the phases of the home-building cycle, and changes in legislation such as the government guarantee of certain types of home mortgages. Among these, probably the most important single factor has been the relative urgency of demand for home building compared to that of the other customary outlets of financial institutions, that is, primarily the demand of business and government for short-term and long-term financing, a factor which finds expression in the size of interest rate differentials.

Among mutual savings banks, the share of home mortgages has risen from approximately one-fourth at the turn of the century to two-fifths before the Great Depression. At the end of World War II the share was down to not much more than one-tenth, but in one decade it had recovered to more than one-third, almost reaching its previous high mark. The fluctuations in the share of home mortgages were similar in the case of commercial banks, though all movements were on a much lower absolute level. During the postwar decade the share has risen from 2% to 7%, thus exceeding the 1929 peak of 5%. Home mortgages absorbed a relatively stable proportion of the total assets of life insurance companies from 1900 to 1930 — approximately one-tenth. During the postwar decade they have advanced rapidly from the low level of 5% at the end of the war to 20% in 1956.

There is only one group of financial institutions for which home mortgages have represented a declining outlet of funds — the personal trust departments of banks and trust companies. Rough estimates indicate that at the turn of the century about one-fifth of their funds were kept in home mortgages, but that this share had already declined to not much over 5% by 1921 and that it remained almost negligible — on the order of 2% — during the postwar decade.

This rising share of home mortgages in the portfolios of most financial institutions finds its reflection in the increasing share of the total home mortgage debt that is held by institutions, including personal trust funds, rather than by individual savers. This share has risen during the postwar decade from fully 70% to almost 90% and is now considerably above the level of three decades before the Great Depression.

SUPPLY OF SAVING IN THE CURRENT BUSINESS CYCLE

It may be worthwhile now to test the findings derived from the record of the past 50 years against our experience with the supply of saving in the current cycle which started in the summer of 1954 and will end its downward phase, if we can believe the majority of forecasters of today, sometime late this year or early in 1959. If it does, this cycle will have lasted just about as long (somewhat over four years) as its two immediate predecessors, which, you will recall, stretched from the fall of 1945 to the fall of 1949 and from then to the summer of 1954, respectively.

Let us look first at the course of personal saving — or, more correctly, saving of nonfarm households — during this cycle. Saving through intangible assets, often rather erratic in its movements, was fairly stable from the middle of 1955 to the end of 1957 at an average of slightly over $7 billion a quarter, or one-ninth of disposable income, after a definite increase over the level prevailing for the preceding one and a half years. Net saving through homes has shown only small positive or negative figures, while net saving through consumer durables has had a tendency to decline from 1956 on, at the same time exhibiting the usual sharp seasonal fluctuations. As a result, total net saving of nonfarm households shows no clear nonseasonal movements during this cycle. We may, however, distinguish two segments of saving. On the one hand, we have saving in the form of deposits with financial institutions, life insurance, and pension and retirement funds which has fluctuated only little from year to year in the cycle. On the other hand, we have saving through securities and through tangible assets (homes and consumer durables), the components of which have shown considerable though not synchronized variations.

Probably the most interesting question is whether or not the extreme tightness in the money and capital markets which characterized the later part of the boom of the current cycle — say, from early 1956 to mid-1957 — and the rapid loosening during the year following, much more pronounced in the short-term than in the long-term market, have been due primarily to changes in the supply of saving; and if so, whether these changes differed from our usual cyclical experience.

To anticipate, my answer to both questions is "no." In positive language, the movements in the capital and money markets — in particular, the up and down of interest rates — reflected primarily changes in the demand for funds and not in the supply of saving; and they entirely conformed to the usual cyclical pattern. There has been, to repeat a conclusion which I tried to justify a little more fully before the San Francisco meeting of the National Industrial Conference Board in March of 1957, no "shortage of saving" such as many observers then professed to see — at least not if that term is used in a reasonable sense and is not simply treated as equivalent to the absence of a borrower's market for funds, some difficulty in obtaining money for every project that appeared to promise a profit, and a rise of interest rates beyond the level of the preceding decade.

In this group, I do not have to dwell on the difficulty of disentangling the effects of supposed changes in supply and demand on observed changes in the volume of business and in interest rates in the various sectors of the capital market. But if we are willing to use the economist's armory of supply and demand curves, there are at least some presumptions that can be established. The presumption, particularly for short-period analysis, is that if both volume of transactions and interest rates rise or fall together, a change in demand may be regarded as the cause of the observed movement in rates while the supply schedule may be presumed to have remained unchanged. On the other hand, if interest rates and the volume of transactions move in opposite directions, we may look for the cause in a shift in the supply schedule for funds.

If we take this approach, there can be little doubt that the capital market tightness of 1956–57 was primarily the result of an increase in demand and not of a shortage of supply, since market rates rose to the accompaniment of an increase, rather than a decrease, in the volume of business in the capital markets, that is, in the volume of new offerings of securities and of new loans made.

Should we want to be more specific, we might even pinpoint the prime responsibility for the upward surge of demand and thus for the rise in the level of interest rates. The figures are fairly clear in pointing to the sharp rise in business expenditures on plant, equipment and inventories as the last straw that broke the back of low interest rates.

To drive the point home, let us use the mathematician's indirect proof. From the middle of 1956, when the period of real tightness in the capital market started, to the middle of 1957, the volume of residential construction and expenditures on consumer durables tended downward. This was accompanied, not astonishingly, by a decline in the growth of mortgage debt and consumer loans. The U. S. Treasury during this period actually returned funds to the market instead of absorbing them. Capital expenditures and new borrowing of state and local governments continued to increase, it is true, but the amounts involved were too small in the framework of the entire capital market to have initiated or decisively supported the upward movement in interest rates. This leaves nonfarm business. This, indeed, is the spot where we find a substantial increase in capital expenditures and a relatively still more pronounced increase in the absorption of outside funds.

For nonfinancial corporations, capital expenditures (plant, equipment and inventory) rose — to use the figures of the Bankers' Trust Company[4] — from an annual rate of $20 billion in 1954 by leaps and bounds to $29 billion in 1955 and $38 billion in 1956, then declined to $34 billion in 1957 and are expected to fall more rapidly during the current year to a level of about $25 billion — not much more than in 1954. While internal sources increased only insignificantly after 1955, the absorption of outside funds (net security issues, mortgages and bank loans) jumped from only $4 billion in 1954 to $16 billion in each of the years 1955 and 1956; still held at $11 billion in 1957 due to a high level of outside financing in the first half of the year; but are expected to fall to not more than $5 billion in the current year, again returning to the level of 1954.

To explain the increasing tightness in the capital markets between the middle of 1955 and the middle of 1957, we must thus explain, first, why business capital expenditures increased as much as they did; and, secondly, why the increase fell virtually in full on outside funds.

The run-up in business investment may be regarded as the combined effect of a continuation of rapid technological progress; of everybody's desire not to be left behind in expansion of capacity; and of increases in inventory values due to expanding volumes of business and accelerating price rises. The increasing share of expenditures that had to be financed from outside funds, on the other hand, reflected the stagnation of business saving — itself not unconnected with generally declining profit margins; the inability of depreciation charges to keep step with capital expenditures; and the using up of the excess liquid assets accumulated during World War II.

These developments in the face of a supply of personal saving keeping in step with the growth of personal disposable income but not much exceeding it, and of tight reins on the expansion of the money supply, would seem sufficient to explain quite satisfactorily the tightness, and finally the squeeze, in the capital markets from mid-1955 to mid-1957.

Similarly, the sharp decline in the absorption of funds by nonfinancial corporations and, secondly, by other sectors of business, since the middle of 1957 in the face of a well-maintained supply of personal saving is quite sufficient to explain the easing of the market, particularly if we remember that movements of this type will often be reflected in an accentuated fashion in interest rate movements, particularly on short term, as a result of anticipatory actions by borrowers and lenders.

[4] Investment Outlook for 1958, Table 2, p. 35.

Outlook for the Supply of Saving

I am quite sure that our sponsors, and possibly also most of you, are more interested in discussing the future than the past — in the supply of saving during the next decade than during the last 50 to 100 years. Since the customer is always right, I shall at least briefly consider the outlook for the supply of saving and the share of residential real estate in it, even if only to provide a target for discussion.

In view of the remarkable stability of the ratio of personal saving to personal disposable income, particularly if consumer durables are included, that we can observe since the beginning of this century and possibly back to the middle of the 19th century in the face of so many changes in the economic structure of the United States, in financial organization and technique and in economic attitudes, the burden of proof would seem to be on those who argue that in the near future the ratio will be significantly different from its accustomed level of one-eighth — say, lower than one-tenth or higher than one-sixth, once averages over full business cycles are taken. I am not willing to shoulder that burden.

This uninspired and uninspiring evaluation of the outlook — that the personal saving ratio is likely to be about what it has been — can be defended on two levels. The first is crude empiricism, not always to be rejected out of hand, notwithstanding its obvious limitations. The other is the theoretical analysis, mostly of recent vintage and to a large extent due to economists from the Chicago school, which leads one to doubt sharp changes in the ratio of saving to permanent income.

This analysis, it is true, implies that the saving-income ratio is likely to be influenced, if not by the level of real income per head itself, then by factors such as the ratio of asset holdings to income, the interest rate, the retirement age, and the length of life. However, none of these theorists has specified exactly how each of these factors is likely to influence saving, singly or together. We simply have not yet arrived at the point where we could insert the expected values of clearly defined independent variables into these complicated formulae — even granting their exact form derived from the past to hold in the future — and to read off the answers.

If we assume that the ratio of personal saving to personal disposable income will be stable at around one-eighth, we implicitly also assume that the absolute volume of personal saving will increase in step with the growth of income per head, the increase in population and the movements in the price level. You certainly do not expect me to discuss the outlook for these three variables in a minute or so. One only needs to recall the debacle experienced with what might seem a very easy variable to forecast — the rate of population growth — to discourage anyone from rashly undertaking such forecasts or from believing them.

The reason for assuming that the distribution of total personal saving by main forms will in the next decade or so be similar to that of the postwar decade is certainly less persuasive. However, there seems to be little evidence to expect substantial changes.

The share of saving through life insurance and pension and retirement funds is likely to remain at least at the level it had during the postwar decade and may even increase slightly. The proportion of saving kept in liquid form is, of course, in part determined by monetary policy. Again, however, it is difficult to see convincing reasons why the proportion of liquid assets in total personal saving, which has been reasonably stable in the normal periods of the past, should change considerably in one direction or the other.

The relatively high share of net saving through consumer durables similarly does not promise to be substantially reduced. Whether or not one expects some further increase is probably a matter of judgment. This means that the proportion of total personal saving, and hence of personal disposable income, that is represented by saving through residential real estate or through securities is not likely to exceed its level during the postwar period. How this share will be divided between net expenditures on residential real estate, increase in mortgage debt and net purchases of securities remains the main question.

Finally, let me say a few words on a related topic, where I may be a little more positive — the level of interest rate that we can expect. I feel that I am free to prognosticate here, since for five or six years I have committed myself on the subject and am just reiterating what I have said, until convicted of error or justified.

There is a good deal of evidence that there are long swings in interest rates — swings where each of the phases, upward or downward, take something like twenty years. We had a clear swing of this type in the first half of this century. We started with low rates around 1896, reached a high in 1921, and then came down until the next trough in 1946.

The evidence is not as clear, but still suggestive, it seems to me, that there was one earlier swing of similar duration in this country, while in western European countries we can follow two such swings running back throughout the 19th century, although not with perfect clarity. These long swings in interest rates of course do not exclude minor ups and downs in between. If you believe in these swings, you must conclude that we are in the upward phase of one which started in 1946. In our previous experience, we have hardly ever seen one of these upward or downward phases terminate in less than about two decades. We therefore have to count on an upward long-term trend in interest rates until the middle 1960s. If we deal with the next decade or two, I would say, judging from past experience, that a basic tendency toward increased interest rates for most of that period must be expected.

Of course, not all interest rates behave exactly alike; but, as you know, long-term movements are quite similar. I have not made a special study of the long swings in home mortgage rates. But from what little material we have — and you are well aware yourselves that once we go back beyond the 1920s the data are tenuous — these long swings also seem to dominate the movement of home mortgage interest rates, although of course the movements in that rate are much less pronounced, particularly over short periods, than is the yield in corporate bonds or government securities.

Let me close here. This is the right spot for a good deed. I have tried to emphasize several times — if I have not done it, I shall do so now — that the supply of saving is a subject about which we still know very little, notwithstanding the accumulation of a considerable amount of new data in the last decade, a subject which calls for further improvement in the statistics. There is even more need for a careful analysis of the great mass of material that we have accumulated but by no means digested. Such an analysis will require the collection of additional material in several fields, material tailored to help us in providing answers to our specific questions.

Discussion*

JAMES GILLIES: Have you made any study of the interest elasticity of savings?

MR. GOLDSMITH: In the aggregate, we are pretty sure it is not high. We deduce this both from intertemporal and from interspatial comparisons. The countries with the highest interest rates are the countries with the lowest saving ratios. However, there is no doubt that there is a considerable interest elasticity in relation to interest rate differentials, particularly on a narrow scale. It has always been found that, in one locality, between forms of saving that are basically similar the interest rate differential undoubtedly is a factor and the interest rate elasticity is quite substantial. But interest rates do not seem to be crucial in deciding how much a man spends on consumer durables or saves in the aggregate or puts into securities. It is a micro-phenomenon, apparently, but it is not effective or at least cannot be traced on a macro-scale.

MR. GILLIES: Just to follow it up, does this mean that, in your prediction that interest rates are going to be higher for the next fifteen years, you don't think this is going to have any effect on the volume of savings?

MR. GOLDSMITH: No, not much, at least.

LELAND PRITCHARD: Do you include all demand deposits in commercial banks as savings?

* Proceedings of the First Annual Conference, 1958, Excerpts from the Discussion, pp. 119–23.

MR. GOLDSMITH: Yes. I think I know what the question aims at. The argument is that increased bank deposits are not true and voluntary saving. If someone will tell me how to distinguish between true and voluntary savings and those that are not, I will then think about how to amend the statistics accordingly.

MR. PRITCHARD: I don't think you can measure it statistically. But wouldn't it be useful, perhaps, to recognize that only part of these demand deposits are savings?

MR. GOLDSMITH: You can go as far as to say that none of them are saving because they ultimately are all created by the lending capacity of the banks. Either all demand deposit increases are in or they are all out. To go further, you have to give me operational distinctions between those that are saving and those that are not. This is a famous problem that always comes up in discussing saving, and I wish I could answer it more satisfactorily. Nobody has taken the trouble to define what true savings are, except that there is one definition that you can very easily frame. This is that all saving other than demand deposits represents true saving, because demand deposits in principle are bank-created. However, here we get into problems which have now been brought to the surface, namely, whether such a distinction can really be made between demand deposits of banks on the one hand and all the other types of liabilities of financial institutions on the other.

In the last three years we have been presented with two very interesting theoretical challenges in this field. One is the Gurley-Shaw theory, which ultimately denies the specific difference between money and other liabilities of financial institutions. The other one is Milton Friedman's theory that there is no correlation at all between the level of income and the saving ratio.

We will have to wrestle with both these theories for several years and will have to come to some decision one way or the other. I expect that the Monetary Commission will spend a good part of its days on hearing numerous witnesses on both sides and will, let us hope, come up with some illuminating conclusions. Thus the situation is much more stimulating now than it used to be when there was very little general theoretical interest in the field. We cannot complain about the absence of theoretical problems now, not until we have solved these problems as we have solved what appeared to be the problem of creation of deposits by banks. In the 1920s, and maybe even in the 1930s, you were a black sheep among the bankers if you held that those honest men could create deposits.

Now, I think, most commercial bankers have learned to distinguish between what a single bank and what the banking system can do. This problem is no longer intellectually interesting, and you can hardly get any discussion of it going except in an undergraduate class. But the two other problems, I think, are still well beyond the undergraduate level.

CARL ARLT: In your projection of an upward swing in interest rates through the 1960s, are you projecting that swing on the basis of past swings or are you making certain specific assumptions as to monetary policy?

MR. GOLDSMITH: What struck me is that long swings in interest rates have been basically similar over the last 100 years, although there have been very considerable changes in monetary and banking policy during the period. The current upswing started in 1946, at a time when what you might call an easy money policy was still predominant — not only in the United States. You may feel satisfied that the forces of nature finally overthrew the money managers and they had to give in, beginning with Belgium and finally all over the world. Or you may put another interpretation on the movement.

To assume that the current upswing will continue for at least another decade — with interruptions, of course — is quite frankly an empirical extrapolation mitigated only by the consideration that the same relation prevailed in the past, although many factors that you think would have affected them did change. Nevertheless, these factors apparently did not disturb this basic pattern of interest rate movements. But as to the exact timing, I would not want to be held to past precedent.

There have been substantial differences in the length of long swings in interest rates before. I think there has not been any of less than fifteen years, so I would be in trouble if rates turned down for good before 1961. In the past, the upward swing has been shorter than the downward swing, and so far each successive peak has been lower than the preceding peak, and each successive trough lower than the preceding trough. Whether this pattern will persist — we have had only three swings in each direction — I do not want to say. There is some reason, I think, to assume that the present upswing will terminate before we reach the rate level of 1921, which was the previous peak. That would be my guess.

15

Trends in the Institutionalization
of Savings and in Thrift
Institution Policies*

Jules I. Bogen was, in 1960, professor of finance
at New York University; editor of the *Journal of Commerce;*
economic consultant, Savings Banks Trust Company; member of
executive committee, American Management Association. He is
the author of *Anthracite Railroads, Analysis of Railroad Securities* and *The New Tax Problem;* co-author of *Investment Banking* and *Money and Banking;* and editor of *Financial Handbook.*
Mr. Bogen earned his bachelor's, master's and doctoral degrees
at Columbia University. He is a former technical adviser to the
Senate sub-committee on Banking and Currency, and former
vice president in charge of Finance Division, American Management Association.

FEW SECTORS OF OUR DYNAMIC ECONOMY are undergoing such vast and
rapid changes as the field of personal savings. We can gain insight into
these dynamic changes by doing four things:

First, determine the broad pattern of personal savings during the
decade of the 1950s, for the more we know of the personal savings
pattern that developed during that momentous decade, the easier it
becomes to orient our thinking to changes in the pattern as these occur.

Second, isolate the economic forces that are affecting the savings
pattern and giving it new forms.

* Proceedings of the Third Annual Conference, 1960, pp. 101–10.

Third, look closely into the behavior of personal savings in 1959, because it throws a good deal of added light on the factors that affect both the volume and distribution of the flow of personal savings.

Finally, project the likely pattern of the savings flow for the next five years in the light (1) of the economic forces that are affecting the flow of savings and (2) of the particular experience of 1959, which provides a suitable laboratory for the study of the savings flow.

THE SAVINGS PATTERN OF THE 1950s

The pattern of personal savings in the 1950s had three main characteristics.

First, there was a high and stable rate of savings, as indicated by the savings estimates of the Department of Commerce, which are a suitable rough measure of relative volume. Savings averaged 7.3% of the disposable personal income of the American people during the decade, and fluctuated surprisingly little from year to year. In only two years — 1950 and 1955 — was the ratio materially below 7%. These were years in which there was a temporary bulge in personal consumption expenditures. This occurred in 1950 because of the Korean War and in 1955 because of a great increase in the buying of homes and durable consumer goods on credit. Otherwise, year after year, savings held a little above or a little below the 7% level.

This stability of savings at a high level is very significant, because many economists and others have been predicting a reduced propensity to save. One basis for this prediction has been Social Security and private pension plans. Another has been the government program to stabilize the economy, which has lessened the threat of unemployment. A third has been the unprecedented use of consumer credit, which many predicted would reduce the pressure to save because people can borrow to buy and then pay off a loan, instead of saving in advance the funds needed to buy durable goods and homes. Growing concern with inflation contributed to the belief that savings in fixed-dollar form would be affected adversely.

All of these gloomy predictions about personal savings have been without justification to date. In the light of the record of the 1950s it is clear that the craving for personal financial security and personal liquidity has caused people, despite all temptations, to maintain the level of personal saving at 7% of disposable personal income. This compares with 4% in the late 1930s, and indicates how significant the lever of personal income is in determining how much people will save.

People talk inflation. Yet they put the bulk of their savings in thrift institutions that repay a fixed sum in dollars.

The second characteristic of the savings pattern of the 1950s was a marked preference for saving through financial institutions.

Personal financial savings during the 1950s totaled $220 billion. Of this total, $90 billion, or a little over 40%, flowed into deposit-type savings accounts. The deposit type of savings service is provided by banks, savings and loan associations, credit unions and, to a minor extent, the Postal Savings System. Another $90 billion, just about the same percentage, flowed into contractual forms of institutional savings, which include life insurance policies, corporate pension plans, and state and local retirement plans.

I leave out Social Security, because that is tied to public debt management and fiscal policy much more than to the flow of personal savings. Net additions to the Social Security funds are invested in federal debt obligations and thus affect the Treasury's cash budget. The other forms of contractual savings — life insurance, corporate pension plans, and state and local retirement funds — are free to channel savings into a number of private investment media.

The remainder of about $40 billion of personal financial savings in the 1950s flowed directly into securities, without the mediation of either deposit-type or contractual-type institutions, with the one exception of mutual funds, which accounted for nearly a fifth of the direct investment in securities. I am including them in direct investment in securities, as does the SEC in its savings series.

Of the $220 billion of financial savings of individuals in the 1950s, a little over two-fifths went into deposit-type financial institutions; a little over two-thirds went into contractual institutional forms of savings; and the balance of less than a fifth went directly into securities, to a fractional extent through mutual funds.

A third characteristic of savings during the decade of the 1950s was the occurrence of two great changes within the institutional savings pattern.

One has been a massive shift in the flow of funds from banks — commercial and savings — to savings and loan associations. In 1949, before the decade began, associations held 17% of the deposit-type savings; in 1959, when the decade ended, they held over 35%. They more than doubled their proportion of the total of this type of savings during the decade.

The second great change that occurred in the institutional savings pattern has been among contractual-type institutions. Life insurance has lost its relative position, and pension and retirement funds have greatly increased their proportion of the total. In 1950, corporate pension trusts and state and local retirement funds accounted for an insignificant fraction of the flow of funds into contractual-type savings. At the present time, the increase in corporate and state and local retirement funds is very nearly as large as the increase in assets of life insurance companies. State and local retirement funds this year are expected to gain over $2 billion in assets; and corporate pension funds, as much as $3½ billion. Life insurance companies will gain something short of $6 billion. Thus, pension and retirement funds are growing nearly as fast as life insurance companies, and this comparison leaves out the Social Security funds.

That has been the savings pattern of the 1950s. Let us now look at the economic forces that have been affecting the flow of savings and that promise to influence the flow of savings to an increasing extent during the 1960s.

Three broad economic developments have had a particular impact upon the flow of personal savings.

DEMAND FOR FUNDS OUTRUNNING SAVINGS SUPPLY

One has been that the economy is generating a demand for funds that outruns the supply of savings. This tendency for the demand for funds to exceed the flow of personal savings is indicated by the public and private debt statistics of the Department of Commerce. Outstanding public and private debt in the United States has increased more since 1945 than during the entire period from the War for Independence to 1945. In other words, public and private debt outstanding more than doubled in the fourteen years from 1945 to 1959.

The increase in debt outstanding in 1959 was greater than in any other year in our history, including 1944, when the federal government alone increased its debt by $52 billion. The increase in debt in 1959, as shown in the President's Economic Report, was $57.4 billion. This was almost four times the increase in debt in 1949, at the threshold of the decade of the 1950s.

MAJOR SHIFT IN THE DEMAND FOR FUNDS

A second basic economic development affecting the flow of personal savings is that the demand for funds has been shifting increasingly from the business sector to the personal sector of the economy. Business — corporate business particularly — is financing its requirements, great as they are, increasingly from internal sources, so that the need for funds from external sources has tended to shrink.

The chief source of corporate funds by far has become depreciation allowances. In 1960, depreciation allowances of all business corporations will approximate $22 billion. That is nearly three times what it was at the beginning of the decade. And depreciation allowances increase every year as plant and equipment spending goes on at a very high rate. The latest McGraw-Hill estimates indicate that plant and equipment expenditures for 1960 will reach $38 billion, exceeding even the 1957 peak. Also, more and more corporations are adopting accelerated methods of depreciation. In the declining balance method, the first year's depreciation of a new asset is double what it would be under the straight-line method. Thus, high-priced assets now being acquired are depreciated at a rapid rate, while assets being retired were generally acquired at a low cost level and were depreciated at a low rate.

For a number of years to come, American business will be charging off more and more for depreciation. It is a fallacy to say, as some accountants have done, that accelerated depreciation merely defers taxes for a time. Faster depreciation effects a permanent reduction in a corporation's tax payments if we assume a level or rising stream of capital expenditures over an indefinite period of time. Deferring taxes by faster depreciation of fixed assets every year is to defer them until Judgment Day.

This high level of depreciation is going to produce some striking side effects. Corporate profits will fluctuate widely and erratically, for example, with even a moderate decline in sales. Heavy depreciation allowances act like fixed charges — like interest charges of the railroads. As such charges increase, when sales decline the reported profits can drop like a plummet, as they did in 1958.

But these are side issues; we are concerned primarily with the effect of the heavy internal corporate cash flow upon the demand for savings. The essential point in this connection is that American business, after an interval marked by a great increase in capital requirements, is once again relying mainly upon internal sources of funds for its new capital needs. Corporate spending for plant and equipment will exceed $32 billion this year. But depreciation alone will provide $22 billion of funds for financing these outlays. Retained earnings will provide maybe $11 billion or $12 billion more. And since utilities will always finance part of their needs on the outside, it means that the rest of the corporate structure is spending considerably less on plant and equipment than its cash flow from internal sources.

On the other hand, the demand for mortgage loans is increasing by leaps and bounds. The cost of new homes and much other building is financed almost entirely from external sources. There is no internal cash flow, because the increase in mortgage debt is computed as the net figure after amortization of outstanding mortgages.

Business capital requirements and home building capital requirements thus have very different impacts upon the demand for personal savings. One is financed primarily from internal cash flow, the other must be financed in the capital market out of personal savings.

Consumer debt also is increasing rapidly. Last year it increased by

$6½ billion, which was an all-time peak somewhat above 1955. And that was more than twice the increase of 1949, the last year before the decade of the 1950s. Consumer credit is provided in large part through the commercial banking system. Hence, it is a matter of bookkeeping as to whether you consider it to be coming out of savings, representing savings deposit gains of commercial banks, or out of demand deposit expansion.

With business borrowing limited in volume and with mortgage borrowing on so large a scale, the credit demands of our economy are increasingly for long-term as against short-term credit. The shifts in demand to personal as against business credit and to long-term as against short-term credit have profound effects on the personal savings flow.

THE IMPACT OF HIGH INTEREST RATES

A third economic development that affects the flow of savings has been the rise in interest rates, to the highest level of the century for some rates. And relatively high rates of interest will persist if our economy continues to generate huge demands for credit and if the central banking system, as I think it must, refuses to allow an expansion of bank credit that would be sufficient to balance such demand with an adequate supply of funds.

Even if a large-scale expansion of demand deposits should be favored by a new administration that has politically criticized high interest rates, which is conceivable, it will soon become evident that this is not an economically feasible policy because it would necessarily lead to an acceleration of the rise in prices. It would then become evident that in an economy of heavy credit demands, there must be a choice between higher interest rates and relatively stable prices. Confronted with this choice, a responsible administration of either party would have to decide in favor of price stability, as has been the case in virtually every economically advanced country in the world.

Interest rates have increased generally as the demands for funds have risen. At the same time, the relationship between interest rates for the several kinds of borrowing has reflected shifts in the demands for funds. As mortgages and consumer borrowing have been heaviest, mortgage interest rates and interest rates on consumer debt have held at a high level sufficient to attract the very large volume of funds required to satisfy the demand.

Bond yields represent the marginal group of interest rates which are quite sensitive to changes in demand. They went up sharply in 1957 when corporate bond financing rose to a peak, and they dropped quite sharply in 1958 when demand fell and credit policy eased. They ran up very sharply again in 1959 because the Treasury had to finance belatedly the huge deficit incurred during the recession of 1957–58. With the budget balanced and the Treasury even making a small reduction in its debt, yields are dropping once more. A widening spread between mortgage yields and bond yields is thus developing again as in past periods of lower bond yields.

THE LESSONS OF 1959

The experiences of 1959, often confusing at the time, provide an excellent laboratory for studying the impact of borrowing demands upon interest rates and the impact of interest rate changes on the flow of savings.

One point that is demonstrated by the statistical record is that high interest rates greatly increased the volume of personal financial savings. The accompanying table shows that there was a 25% increase in the volume of personal financial savings in 1959. This appears to disprove the oft-heard generalization that the volume of personal savings is not sensitive to the rate of interest. The figures indicate distinctly that it was extremely sensitive to interest rates in 1959.

Table 1

The Changing Pattern of Personal Savings
(billions of dollars)

TYPE OF PERSONAL SAVINGS	1958	1959	1960
Savings accounts:			
Savings and loan associations	$ 6.1	$ 6.6	$ 7.0
Commercial banks	7.1	2.7	1.8
Mutual savings banks	2.3	0.9	1.2
Credit unions	0.4	0.5	0.6
Total	$15.9	$10.7	$10.6
Contractual savings:			
Life insurance	$ 6.3	$ 6.0	$ 6.2
Corporate pension funds	2.8	3.1	3.4
State and local retirement funds	1.7	1.9	2.1
Social Security funds	0.4	1.0	1.5
Total	$11.2	$12.0	$13.2
Direct investments:			
U. S. government securities	$–2.9	$ 8.5	$ 2.3
State and local obligations	1.2	2.5	2.6
Corporate bonds	1.0	–0.1	0.3
Investment company shares	1.6	1.7	1.7
Other equities	–0.2	–0.7	0.5
Total	$ 0.7	$11.9	$ 7.4
All personal financial savings	$27.8	$34.6	$31.2

Yields of 5% and more on government obligations attracted a flood of individual funds, as well as corporate and foreign bank funds, into direct purchases of government obligations. Individual holdings of government securities, after deducting the cashing of savings bonds, increased by $8½ billion, according to the latest SEC estimates for the entire year 1959. Individual holdings of tax-exempt obligations increased by $2½ billion. Individual holdings of all obligations increased by $11 billion. This compares with a net reduction of such holdings of $700 million in 1958, when interest rates declined sharply.

A second point shown by the statistical record is that contractual savings not only held stable during 1959, despite the fact that these institutions do not compete on a rate basis, but actually showed a slight increase. The growth of pension and retirement funds is a secular trend making for a slow but steady year-by-year rise in the volume of contractual savings.

Deposit-type savings, on the other hand, were very sensitive to the high yields offered individuals in the bond market, as the table clearly shows. Deposit-type savings declined by a full third between 1958 and 1959. The decrease, however, was entirely in bank savings. Savings and loan associations increased their gain in 1959 over 1958, as you know, by 8%; they reported an all-time record gain of $6.6 billion in savings accounts.

Therein, it seems to me, is a lesson that all deposit-type thrift institutions can learn to advantage. Savings and loan associations in 1959, pursuing a formula that they have adhered to for a number of years, demonstrated that they are far more successful than their competitors in attracting funds from savers. They concentrated on securing a higher return on their earning assets, not only through interest but also through fees, commissions, and charges. Having increased their earnings, they were able to raise the rates of return paid savers and thus outbid other thrift institutions in attracting savings. Price competition, contrary to what some bankers have contended, is quite effective in the savings account field; the large volume of funds California associations have been drawing from the East is a clear case in point.

At the same time, an objective appraisal points to the conclusion that savings and loan associations, by doing the most aggressive job for the saver, did the best job for the borrower, too. The borrower is much more interested in availability of funds than in the interest rate, particularly since interest is a deduction from taxable income; an extra ½ of 1% or an extra fee becomes a secondary consideration if the funds wanted are obtainable. Home building has been held back in the last year or so, primarily by unavailability of funds and not by unwillingness to pay higher interest rates. So the institution that does the best job for the saver, and thus attracts loanable funds in volume, also does the best job for the borrower.

PERSONAL SAVINGS PATTERN PROJECTED TO 1965

In the light of the experience of 1959, the broad outlines of the personal savings pattern for the next five years or longer come into focus. The assumptions are:

First, that there will be sustained economic growth subject to moderate cyclical recessions. Economic growth will be sustained by population increases, technological progress, and rising living standards.

Second, that a growing economy will generate a very large demand for funds. But the demand will be in the areas of mortgage and consumer, rather than business, debt. The federal government will be in and out of the market; its role as a borrower will be largely cyclical.

Third, the wage push, which evidently will continue although it will meet increasing resistance, will not have the same inflationary effect upon prices as during the 1950s because of increasingly intense competition, foreign as well as domestic. When competition is not intense, a wage push becomes a price push, too. That is what we saw in the 1950s. But a wage push with intense competition becomes a profit squeeze, since it gets to be harder and harder to pass along an increase in labor cost to the buyer. And when an increased labor cost per unit of output comes out of the profit margin, resistance to the wage push becomes correspondingly greater on the part of the employer.

Under these conditions, the 1960s should see a lessening preoccupation with the inflation threat, which will be favorable to fixed-dollar forms of investment of savings.

Based on these assumptions, personal savings could average 7% or a little more of a rising disposable personal income in the period ahead. Direct investment of savings in fixed-income securities, a striking development of 1959, should be a cyclical phenomenon. When the demand for funds by the federal government expands due to a large budget deficit, and when other demands for funds are heavy, savings institutions can expect to encounter intense competition from security offerings like the Treasury's "magic fives" of last October. But when, as in the spring of 1960, the volume of government security offerings declines, direct investment will be much less competitive with institutional investment. In other words, what can be called the "deinstitutionalization of savings" — the most striking development of 1959 in this sector of our economy — is a cyclical, not secular, development. It is already on the wane, as the 1960 projections in the table of the pattern of personal savings indicate.

The 1960s appear certain to witness a gradual further rise in contractual savings. Some think it will be accelerated by the authorization of sales of variable annuities. I doubt that this will occur if inflation pressures lessen, as is probable. But there is nothing to stop the rise in corporate pension plans. Their growth is aided by the increased stress by labor unions on fringe benefits as against take-home pay, and liberalization of pensions is very high on the list of fringe benefits.

The annual net flow of funds into savings accounts should recover from the slump of 1959 because there will be a diminished attraction in direct investment. I see no evidence that the American people have shown any lessening of attachment to the savings account as the favored medium of investment, because of its liquidity, safety and flexibility, except when substantially higher yields are offered by short- and inter-mediate-term government obligations. A substantial decline in stock prices could, as it did in the 1930s, swell the flow of personal savings into deposit-type savings institutions.

Among savings account institutions, intensified competition is inevitable in the 1960s. Because savings and loan associations have had such conspicuous success in attracting savings by resorting to aggressive price and other forms of competition, they must expect "the sincerest form of flattery" — imitation — from commercial and mutual savings banks. These institutions lean toward increased mortgage investment in par-ticular, since this policy has proved so important a part of the savings and loan success formula. To satisfy the huge demand for new homes, it is necessary to channel the larger part of personal financial savings into mortgage investments. Mortgage borrowers must pay a higher rate of interest than other classes of long-term borrowers, to attract so large a proportion of savings. To perform this function, savings institutions as intermediaries must pass along to the savers the higher rates that mort-gage borrowers are paying for the funds they want.

Credit unions undoubtedly will become a more important competitor for personal savings. They have a setup which is hard to beat. They invest personal savings in consumer loans at rates that average close to 12%. With aggressive management, they could attract a steadily growing proportion of savings, even though their share is relatively small today.

In the decade of the 1960s, therefore, savings accounts and deposits should continue to be the chief channel through which personal savings will flow into the several sectors of investment. Deposit-type savings institutions will provide a very large part of the credit needs of the American economy, and their role will be all the more important as demand-deposit expansion continues to play a restricted role as a source of new funds for the economy.

Discussion*

ERIC LAWSON: You made the statement that the shifts in the flow of personal savings between 1958 and 1959 prove conclusively that savings respond to interest rate changes. I should like to have a little more support for that. I am not sure that the 1959 experience was exactly a laboratory experiment.

MR. BOGEN: I welcome the question. I did not make the statement lightly. If I am wrong, it is because of factors other than those reflected in the personal savings statistics I have used, and it is not clear to me what these factors can be.

We are not concerned here with the personal balance sheet definition of personal savings as used in the SEC series, since increases in personal debt are there deducted from the total. Personal savings are personal savings to the student of the capital market, regardless of whether these savings are loaned to corporations and governments or to other individuals who are using the savings to build houses or buy automobiles. From the capital market point of view, financial savings did rise, as the table shows, by 25% between 1958 and 1959. The burden of proof, it seems to me, is on those who question these statistics that measure the flow of personal savings through financial institutions and the security markets.

Individuals put $34.6 billion into savings institutions and directly into securities in 1959 and only $27.8 billion in 1958, the best available statistics I know of indicate. This is not a shift in savings, but an increase in the total amount. If the conclusion is wrong, some of these statistics must be shown to be wrong.

JAMES LEONARD: Do you not think that the higher interest rates themselves, to a great extent, activated former idle balances?

MR. BOGEN: I think so, but you are describing the monetary mechanism for saving, not the volume of savings.

MR. LEONARD: From one point of view, this is not necessarily an increase in savings, but did it attract funds into savings and loan associations?

MR. BOGEN: It seems to me that an idle bank demand-deposit balance that is shifted to a savings and loan association account to earn more interest becomes activated as it is used to make a mortgage loan on a new home, and so has the same effect as any other form of savings. So far as the economy is concerned, increased velocity of deposits has the same effect as an expansion of the volume of deposits. Velocity increased by

---

* Proceedings of the Third Annual Conference, 1960, Excerpts from the Discussion, pp. 110–19.

over 7% in 1959, partly because higher interest rates activated idle demand deposit balances in many cases.

MR. LEONARD: But of course this does not shift anything away from the banks — I mean from the banking system — does it?

MR. BOGEN: It does very much, because the restrictive Federal Reserve policy holds down the volume of demand deposits, which did not increase at all last year. Hence, if savings deposit increases go largely to other institutions, commercial banks will gain only in velocity of turnover of deposits as the economy grows — and there is very little nourishment in velocity for a financial institution.

Project that trend for ten or twenty years and tell the commercial banks, "Please don't worry, because when money is taken out it comes back, but you won't grow." I do not think the commercial banks will get much comfort out of your reassurance.

DAVID FAND: I was surprised to hear you say that if, in the 1960s, there is going to be high employment, a strong demand for capital and rising interest rates, savings and loan associations will be in an advantageous position. It seems to me that you can make just the opposite case for an institution that specializes in long-term assets — where the average life of assets is, say, ten years. That means it gets a cash payback of only about 10% on top of growth of, say 5%, and comes into the market each year with only 15% of its portfolio. So it would be at a relative disadvantage as compared with an institution that has short-term assets and can capture the higher interest rate each year.

MR. BOGEN: What you say is persuasive, but the experience of the past decade shows that savings and loan associations can cope with this problem quite successfully. Certainly interest rates rose quite rapidly from the low levels of the "pegs," ended in 1951. The 1960s, I think, will be more an era of sustained relatively high interest rates than of a new rise comparable to that of the 1950s. The savings and loan associations displayed a remarkable ability to adapt themselves to the rising level of interest rates in the 1950s, and increased earnings and rates paid.

MR. FAND: If interest rates continue to rise — I know they may not, but if they do — would the savings and loans be at a disadvantage?

MR. BOGEN: Let me cite a few statistics that are pertinent. I have seen one compilation for California savings and loan associations which indicates that 40% of the loans made by the associations are to the builder, not to the home buyer, so they are on a relatively short-term basis because they are to be refunded once the homes are sold. Builders pay substantial fees on such loans, so that the net return is substantially higher than on an FHA mortgage with a 30-year maturity. Loans of this kind also involve a rapid turnover. In view of such lending, I do think that the turnover of a savings and loan portfolio is considerably greater than the percentage you indicated. Just how much greater it is, I do not know.

MR. FAND: But you are coming close to saying that savings and loan associations will be acting more like commercial banks and will go in for construction loans instead of mortgages.

MR. BOGEN: The test is not loan maturities, but the effectiveness of the job the institutions do for saver and borrower. In a decade of a very rapid rise in interest rates, savings and loan associations outdistanced their competitors with respect to earnings and the return paid on savings. When associations raised the dividend rates paid, I had misgivings as to what would happen to their ratio of reserves and undivided profits to savings capital. But during the last few years, despite the rapid rise in savings, that ratio has been rising. Savings and loan associations are not the lowest-cost savings institutions, since mutual savings banks have a little over half the operating expense ratio of savings and loans. But they have been the most aggressive savings institutions in taking advantage of opportunities, as they arise, to build up earnings, pay higher dividends, and spend money for advertising and promotion to attract funds. Last year's gain of $6½ billion demonstrates that savings and loan associations can adapt themselves quite successfully to a period of rising interest rates.

GEORGE HANC: I should like to ask you about your prognostications for the future. You have said that you do not see any secular deinstitutionalization of savings in sight and that you see a more or less constantly increasing desire for the type of liquid thrift medium that one has in a savings institution. Certainly it would be hard to predict these things without knowing more about savings habits; but could you not make a rather strong argument that with higher personal incomes, greater sophistication and greater education in the years ahead, there will be a tendency to diversify savings? Individuals will tend to place more of their savings than in the past among different types of media, and this would suggest a somewhat smaller share of the new savings for savings accounts than in the past.

MR. BOGEN: One advantage of being as old as I am — and there are many disadvantages — is that earlier experiences repeat themselves, and I then see current events in better perspective. In the 1920s we witnessed a great deal of investment sophistication. People drew money out of savings accounts in banks and savings associations to get 6% on Strauss bonds and guaranteed mortgage certificates, and above all to get the "growth" that only common stocks can give. At that time grave doubts were expressed as to how long the savings institution could continue to play the major role in directing the flow of savings in the American economy.

Then came the 1930s, and people developed doubts about their ability to invest their own money. When Strauss bonds and guaranteed mortgage certificates defaulted and the Dow-Jones industrial index declined from a high of 381 to a low of 41, the institutions that provided safety and liquidity looked awfully good, and a much larger proportion of savings flowed into them. The bulk of the financial savings of the American people were institutionalized as a result. Even in the 1950s, an era of great expansion and growth, 83% of personal financial savings went into thrift institutions, excluding mutual funds, and only 17% went directly into securities, including mutual funds.

Savings habits change slowly. Perpetual prosperity and inflation, were it attainable, would doubtless change these habits. But the decline in stock prices early this year already has caused a decline in the sale of mutual funds.

It may be that just *because* people are more sophisticated, they will want the liquidity and safety of an adequate savings account. With pension plans and other contractual forms of saving growing steadily in volume, and with the ownership of fluctuating equities more widespread, the desirability of a substantial savings account becomes greater than ever. That is sophistication of the highest kind. The savings account gives the individual liquidity, and liquidity is something neither contractual savings nor equities are designed to provide.

MR. HANC: Perhaps one of the disadvantages of being young is that one does not remember the depression as well as one might. But surely I hope you do not mean that the growth of savings accounts depends largely upon people's fear of a depression on the scale of the one in the 1930s? I am not talking about Strauss bonds either, but U. S. government five-year notes — things of that kind.

MR. BOGEN: But a depression does not have to be nearly so bad as that of the 1930s to make the point valid. I do not think the Dow-Jones average will go down an extreme of 89% again, for the causes of that extreme deflation of stock prices are not at all likely to recur. I should be quite surprised if the average were to undergo an extreme decline of 50%, but even 25% would be enough to demonstrate anew the advantage of a savings account. I agree with you that if the government were to keep on putting out what savings bankers called the "tragic fives," there would be a considerable shift from institutional to direct investment. But I do not expect this to happen. A 5% intermediate-term Treasury issue is at most a cyclical development. Certainly a balanced budget, which is the picture for 1960, precludes a repetition of such an offering.

You put it better than I did when you said that large-scale direct investment will be a cyclical and not a secular development in the flow of savings.

PAUL SAMUELSON: The questions keep returning to your analysis of the effect of interest rates upon savings. I think that is no accident, because of the many important and interesting things you have said. The most interesting to the economist is what you seem to be saying about this relationship. Of course, in any impromptu talk, nobody holds anyone to strict definition, but I do think it is desirable that we clarify exactly what is being asserted.

I am not thinking of particular problems of the capital market. I am not thinking of whether a changed interest rate or yield for one part of the capital market can attract funds to that part of the capital market. I know there are some people who claim that that will not happen, but I think most economists are quite prepared to believe, and have believed for a long time, that differential rates in one part of the whole capital market have an effect upon its share of the total.

However, from the standpoint of basic policy, if I believe, as I take it you do, that the decade of the 1960s is going to see a heavy demand for real resources and more capital formation, then the important economic problem would be this: How much resources will be released by consumers through changes in the structure of interest rates? That is the problem I think we were talking about in terms of heresies. I believe you went back and forth between financial saving and real saving. From the standpoint of the general economist, the question is: How much resources in our economy will be released from consumption purposes and be made available for capital formation?

In that connection, an extremely interesting question would be this: Does the experience of 1958 and 1959 throw new light, by means of a laboratory-control type of experiment or by means of a more difficult interpretation-judgment type of experiment, upon whether an increase in interest rates does cause the consumer, out of his disposable income, to release more real resources to capital formation? It is not a question whether the "magic fives" can cause the consumer to take his money out of a savings and loan association and put it into government bonds, but whether a rise in interest rates causes him to buy less at the supermarket.

I have reviewed your evidence, your statements and also the national income accounts, and I should like to ask you whether you disagree with me on this point. Do you conclude that the interest rate is perceptible in terms of the definition which I have set up?

MR. BOGEN: I am convinced that it is. I do not refer to shifting of funds from one part of the capital market to the other, but to shifts from consumption to investment.

16

The New Environment Facing Financial Intermediaries in the Next Decade*

Leon T. Kendall was, in 1963, economist for the United States Savings and Loan League and staff adviser to the League's Committee on Trends and Economic Policies and its Committee on the Federal Home Loan Bank System. He is the author of *The Savings and Loan Business: Its Purposes, Functions, and Economic Justification* and the co-author, with Miles Colean, of *Who Buys the Houses*. His research includes investigations into characteristics of savers and qualitative aspects of conventional home mortgage loans. Mr. Kendall earned his bachelor's degree at St. Vincent College and his master's and doctoral degrees in business administration at Indiana University. He was formerly an economist with the Federal Reserve Bank of Atlanta and a teaching associate at Indiana University.

IT IS MY FEELING THAT A PAPER with so imposing a title ought to be prepared and delivered by a senior statesman of the financial markets, not by a sophomore senator like myself. Qualitative forecasting, which is what this paper asks for, requires more than statistical projections or econometric models. It requires an understanding of what makes the world of finance tick. It requires a familiarity with, and working knowl-

* Proceedings of the Sixth Annual Conference, 1963, pp. 55–71.

284

edge of, the written and unwritten rules of financial markets. It requires a redefinition of the role of finance in the business community. Whether anyone or any committee possesses all these ingredients is difficult to say. Although I feel that any germ of an idea in this paper may well wither rapidly under the sunlight of other minds, Marshall Ketchum's demand that I do the work certainly proved worthwhile for the speaker.

STATUS OF INTERMEDIARIES TODAY

Defining what we are to consider as financial intermediaries is no easy task. Intermediaries, in the broadest sense, are financial middlemen. The term includes all the institutional arrangements or mechanisms designed to effect the flow of funds from suppliers to users. Their function is to facilitate the flow of goods and services in our economy. Generally, financial institutions have developed, not by legislative fiat of constituted authority, but as the result of relatively free relationships among individuals. This is true even though governmental agencies and governmental statistics focus the attention of analysts on aggregative operations. Banks and savings and loan associations are local, not global, entities. Hence, part of our problem, as I hope to demonstrate, results from economic theories developed from overaggregating financial institutions.

Under the broad definition, financial intermediaries would include all elements covered in a standard text on financial institutions. For our purposes, such a definition would be quite unwieldly.

Rather, we shall use a more restricted definition and shall concern ourselves with the major consumer-oriented savings intermediaries. Although the general premises are applicable to all institutions, our focus will be on nonmonetary functions of commercial banks, savings banks, savings and loan associations, credit unions (all of which are deposit-type institutions) and at times insurance companies (which have a specialized character from the deposit point of view). Also, we shall introduce another variable into the definition. The commercial and industrial corporation, by placing itself in the position of a mediator — a limited-service intermediary — between the consumer and the established intermediary, is assuming a new role as an active participant in the field of finance.

QUALITATIVE ASPECTS OF INTERMEDIARIES

One of the most widely noted changes in the financial structure of the United States has been the relative shrinkage of the commercial banking system in the total financial picture and the concomitant growth of other financial institutions. Raymond Goldsmith's work indicates that commercial banks held only about 50% of the assets of all financial institutions in 1950, as compared with about 70% in 1900. Insurance companies, on the other hand, increased their share from about 10% to almost 30% during that period. This trend continued through the 1950s — until 1960, when commercial banks became militant intermediaries.

Primary concern with this trend focused on monetary policy and the possible leakage in policy effects due to these shifts. In addition, strong feelings grew that monetary policy was inequitable as well as ineffective. It forced the commercial banks to bear the brunt of restraint, while other financial institutions had at their disposal various ways and means to ease the pain. Various kinds of reserve requirements were proposed for intermediaries.

Professors John Gurley and Ezra Solomon debated these points at the Conference in 1959. Two years later, in 1961, Professor Leland Pritchard of the University of Kansas and Professor Edward Edwards of Indiana University debated the question: "Should Commercial Banks Accept Savings Deposits?" Professor Haggott Beckhart, in 1962, spoke on "Criteria of a Well-functioning Financial System," dealing once again with the bank-intermediary controversy.

My purpose here, however, is not to catalogue or comment upon the banking vs. nonbanking debate. Rather, it is to point out that one basic, essential theme seems to pervade all these analyses. They are all based on the framework of what we shall call traditional money and banking theory. In spite of the decline in the relative importance of banks, the main stream of theory remains commercial-banking-oriented. The central position of commercial banks seems to have taken on a sacredness in the minds of many theoreticians, and they tend to evaluate the intermediary, its role and position in the economy, as adding to or taking away from the commercial banking function. One cannot deny the central position of the unique money creation function of the commercial bank sector, but whether commercial banking is the guideline against which we are to judge the intermediary and its ability to contribute to our economic well-being may well be more open to question than most of us thus far have been willing to grant.

My purpose is to suggest, to some of you at least, that we explore other approaches to explaining the role, purpose and function of financial intermediaries. Our findings might lead to a different set of policy recommendations and proposals.

The reason this point is important in this paper is that if one were to accept the continued commercial bank dominance of financial markets and deem this to be the appropriate and most efficient kind of financial structure, then one's forecast of the prospects for intermediaries in the next decade would be vastly different from that drawn up under other premises. In looking forward, I suggest that we explore the basic elements which make financial intermediaries function in a dynamic rather than a static model. Thus, we should re-examine the model, not in terms of laws and regulations, charters and branching powers, but rather in terms of the needs and desires of the American people in the market place.

DEVELOPING A THEORY OF INTERMEDIARIES

There is a substantial theoretical gap in our understanding of financial institutions. During the last five years we have seen a remarkable growth of interest in intermediaries, but thus far the interest seems to have expressed itself largely in descriptions of the sheer magnitude of the asset holdings of life companies, savings and loans and others. We seem to have bypassed some basic questions: Why are financial intermediaries in existence? Why did they come out of the past to such tremendous size today? Why did they flower precisely when they did and the way they did?

Certainly the answers are not to be found in the history of specific institutions. Here one gathers, at the one extreme, supersweet references to an imaginary altruism and, at the other, a naive acceptance of a notion that financial institutions get big when everything else does.

Intermediaries, like commercial banks or any other businesses, were launched because they provided a service and because they were profitable to someone. The concept that these institutions were promoted because the wise and good men of the community wanted to do something nice for people is in many respects a myth. Until profits, or prospects for gain, existed, directly or indirectly, the managerial effort would not be made. Sometimes it was a "moonlighting" job for a bookkeeper, sometimes a supplement to insurance or real estate activities.

Probing a little more deeply into the subject, one can come up with a theoretical framework which offers an explanation of why intermediaries came to be what they are today.[1]

The nonbank financial intermediaries that concern us are essentially consumer-directed. They render, with a few exceptions, some kind of service to the household unit. They serve as a go-between, linking household units to demanders of funds, which may be another household unit or a business. By way of contrast, commercial banks are schizophrenic. Although they are beginning to increase their retail and consumer appeal, their really important contact is with other businesses rather than with household units. To understand intermediaries, one must develop knowledge of the financial needs and desires and capacity of consumers.

[1] I am indebted to Professor Ross Robertson of Indiana University for developing this concept.

Building upon so elementary a premise, we can come to the point that until the consumer developed financial needs and desires and the capability or capacity to satisfy them, intermediaries could not exist or grow vigorously.

Let me cite another theory developed by Professor Robertson: "The growth of nonmonetary intermediaries is preceded and largely determined by an expansion of the money supply by the banking system; the non-monetary intermediaries serve the cause of total economic growth by dislodging idle bank balances and making them a part of the active money supply."

To be profitable, a financial specialty shop must operate in a market environment that includes:

1. A large number of potential savers or customers.

2. A growing and urbanizing economy.

3. Homogeneity of money forms. Savings and loan accounts, for example, have to be substitutes for bank deposits at an acceptable level and for a reasonable magnitude of consumers.

4. The ability of the intermediary to provide a ready supply of liabilities for sale, i.e., savings accounts, life insurance policies, etc. Turning the coin around, the intermediary must find assets for purchase in increasing volume at acceptable yields.

Such a climate developed in our country following World War II and accelerated during the 1950s. It is this period that marks the real birth and maturing of the financial intermediary. Those who would study intermediaries today and where they are headed tomorrow must concentrate on the postwar years.

Speaking in terms of evolution, there is a law that goes something like this: Certain characteristics develop in a species and continue to propagate themselves for many generations, yet remain below the surface. Then comes a time when the environment permits these mutations to push forth with vigor. To some degree, the bursting forth of inter-mediaries in the postwar years was such a phenomenon. The mutations of the late 1920s and the first half of the 1930s reached fruition. Perhaps what we are doing today — through the rash of inquiries such as the study of the Commission on Money and Credit — is building future mutations.

MARKET FOR FINANCIAL SERVICES

The 1960s have been a period of considerable ferment for financial intermediaries — in legislative bodies, in academic study groups and in the market place. Most of you are familiar with what has been happening in legislative and academic circles. Because I spend my time close to the market (perhaps too close, in the minds of some), I tend to favor the market approach to understanding intermediaries. The forces destined to shape the role of our institutions during the next decade are market forces; many of them are now at work and some can be identified. Let us look at the market place in the light of the conditions necessary for the success of financial specialty shops.

1. Large Numbers of Potential Customers

Who are the savers and customers of financial intermediaries? Financial intermediaries in some respects are unique in that their volume-producing customers are not the mass market per se, but rather select segments of that mass market.

The traditional image of savings and loan associations and savings banks is that these are "little people's" banks. Savings and loan associations are a type of self-help organization oriented toward home ownership. Savings banks were begun to help the "little man" by providing him with convenient savings plans and facilities. They would encourage thrift and develop attitudes toward money and capital that would be desirable. National thrift committees, Christmas clubs, school savings programs and payroll savings plans exemplify this concept.

Such an attitude or image continues to be held quite widely, even today, among casual and some not so casual observers. That image is not true, however, when one considers intermediaries in terms of dollars and cents. I say this even though many of our own savings and loan managers actually believe their institutions are the "little people's" banks. Facts in the area are scarce. It took us longer than Kinsey to leave the broad numbers and go to the people. The Federal Reserve and Census Bureau have undertaken a massive investigation in this area, costing a quarter of a million dollars. Harvard University, under Professor Lawrence Thompson, and the Capital Markets Research Group performed a similar but considerably more limited analysis. At the United States Savings and Loan League, thanks to the growing interest of our managers in market research, we are, through survey techniques, developing a considerable body of information regarding savers. I shall give you some of our facts to demonstrate what I mean.

Classifying Accounts by Size. Table 1 shows the results of the classification of savings accounts at selected associations in various parts of the country. Whenever such analysis is done, we find a distribution very similar to what you see here. The largest accounts, relatively few in number, provide the bulk of the dollars. At our Indiana association, accounts of $9,000 and over, 6.2% of total accounts, provided 33.7% of the savings dollars. At the other end of the range, the smallest 54% of accounts, those with balances under $1,000, produced only 6.4% of the savings dollars. Available evidence indicates that similar analyses per-

Table 1

Classification of Savings Accounts at Selected Associations
(percentage distribution)

ACCOUNT SIZE INTERVAL	INDIANA		OHIO		CALIFORNIA	
	NUMBER OF ACCOUNTS	SAVINGS DOLLARS	NUMBER OF ACCOUNTS	SAVINGS DOLLARS	NUMBER OF ACCOUNTS	SAVINGS DOLLARS
Under $100	22.7%	0.4%	34.2%	0.4%	20.0%	0.2%
$100 to $ 999.99	31.3	6.0	27.0	5.8	30.7	5.0
$ 1,000 to $ 1,999.99	13.1	8.0	17.5	16.6	29.8	29.0
$ 2,000 to $ 2,999.99	8.1	8.7				
$ 3,000 to $ 3,999.99	5.2	8.3	7.6	15.8		
$ 4,000 to $ 4,999.99	3.8	7.6				
$ 5,000 to $ 5,999.99	3.6	8.3	5.6	17.2	12.3	34.0
$ 6,000 to $ 6,999.99	2.4	6.5				
$ 7,000 to $ 7,999.99	1.2	3.9	4.2	19.0		
$ 8,000 to $ 8,999.99	2.4	8.6				
$ 9,000 to $ 9,999.99	2.3	13.8				
$10,000 to $10,999.99	3.9	19.9	3.9	25.2	5.6	22.2
$11,000 and Over					1.6	9.6
Total	100.0%	100.0%	100.0%	100.0%	100.0%	100.0%

formed at savings banks and commercial banks would produce comparable findings. The customers of intermediaries, then, are a relatively select group. It is my judgment that the growth of intermediaries has come in the form of larger account balances. The motives of greatest interest to these people are rate of return and convenience. The typical association will find 65% to 75%, perhaps more, of its savers within two to four miles of the association offices. This tends to be true in California as well as in other parts of the nation.

Survey of Large Savers. Because we have identified large savers as so important, we ought to find out a little more about them and where their funds come from. During January of 1961, the United States League attempted to determine the characteristics of savers moving large amounts of money through our institutions. January is a high activity period. In 1961 the stock market was moving upward. Banks were paying 3% and not 4% at that time. Questionnaires were sent to 44,000 savers at 77 associations in 27 states and 46 cities, and 17,000 questionnaires were returned. The consistency of the results from one association to another and from one part of the country to another lends considerable confidence to the data which is summarized in Table 2.

Table 2

Characteristics of Savers Adding to or Withdrawing
$1,000 or More from Savings and Loan Associations
(January 1961)

1. OCCUPATION		2. AGE	
Professional	20.5%	1–18 years	0.5%
Executive, manager or		19–24 years	1.5
merchant	26.9	25–34 years	9.4
Skilled or semiskilled work	9.5	35–44 years	17.9
Clerical or sales work	9.8	45–54 years	22.5
Retired	22.7	55–64 years	23.1
Housewife or widow	5.8	65 years and over	25.1
Farmer	1.4		100.0%
Other (student, minister,			
etc.)	3.4		
	100.0%		
		4. FAMILY INCOME IN 1960	
3. EDUCATION		Under $1,000	2.8%
Grammar school (1–8 years)	13.3%	$1,000–$3,999	14.0
Some high school		$4,000–$4,999	8.9
(9–11 years)	13.9	$5,000–$7,499	20.3
High school graduate	16.8	$7,500–$9,999	16.7
Some college	22.2	$10,000–$14,999	16.4
College graduate	33.8	$15,000 and over	20.9
	100.0%		100.0%

5. REASONS FOR SAVING AT A			
SAVINGS ASSOCIATION*			
Convenience	27.8%	6. SAVINGS ACCOUNTS PER FAMILY	
Higher return	72.5	Number with us	1.5
Friendly staff	14.8	Number at other savings	
Safety	30.1	associations	1.2
Premium or gifts	3.1	Number at banks, credit	
Save-by-mail plan	9.6	unions, etc.	0.9
Other	2.8	Total	3.6

* Most savers gave more than one reason.

Occupationally, the professional and executive categories rank very
high, along with retirees. In terms of age, savers tend to be quite heavily
concentrated in the older groups. Educationally, college training tends
to be a real plus factor in savings performance; 56% indicate some
college, and one out of three identifies himself as a college graduate.
Relating education to age, one might conclude that our institutions
attract a very high percentage of individuals who went to college in the

prewar years. Incomewise, savers tend to be concentrated relatively more heavily in the $10,000-and-over category.

The reasons for saving are, first, rate of return, followed by convenience and safety. As the size of transaction (and, we assume, size of account) increases, transfers between banks and savings associations and among savings associations become more frequent. Current income and bonus become relatively less important as reasons affecting the transaction totals. The number of accounts a family holds increases as transaction size increases.

Income Patterns. What is happening to the households in the category most likely to be heavy users of savings intermediaries? The income data indicate that this sector of the economy is growing relatively more rapidly than are other sectors and that the broad trends here are extremely favorable to intermediaries.

The income data in Table 3 show what has happened to the number of consumer units in the upper income brackets. In 1947, 2 million families out of a total of 44.7 million could be found in these categories. In 1962, 10.9 million families out of 58.6 million were found here. On a percentage basis, 19% of our families are in this potentially heavy user category now, compared with 5% in 1947.

On a dollar basis, income received by the $10,000-and-over category in 1947 amounted to $36.4 billion, or 20% of total earnings. In 1962, $182.5 billion, or 44% of total dollars, was in the hands of families in this group. Since markets cannot be developed profitably until they reach the size necessary to overcome certain break-even costs, intermediaries could not have been successful until large numbers of potential savers or customers were available. Such a condition was not met until 3 million to 4 million families were in the top income classes.

Savings Life Cycle. We need to begin to concern ourselves with the life-cycle aspects of American families and their demand for financial services. Philip Hauser said something recently to a savings and loan group that gave me some pause for thought on this matter. He pointed out that we are the first nation with a controllable birth rate. Its ups and downs with depressions and wars can produce baby booms, college booms and all kinds of problems relative to stability. Dr. Hauser asks: "Is our national economy elastic enough to absorb changes in the reproductive habits of the American people?" I do not know the answer. I do know that these same factors can and will play a vital role in the future of intermediaries during the years ahead. In the late 1970s, the population curve will not be ideal for saving. The number of persons in the heavy-user age brackets, 45 to 65, will decline. Whether income and education, both of which will continue to improve, can overcome the life cycle effect requires further investigation.

Table 3

Distribution of Consumer Units and Their Income by Family Income Level, 1947 and 1955–62

FAMILY PERSONAL INCOME (before income taxes)	1947	1955	1956	1957	1958	1959	1960[1]	1961[1]	1962[1]
FAMILIES AND UNATTACHED INDIVIDUALS *Number (in millions)*									
Under $2,000	11.1	8.2	7.7	7.6	7.7	7.5	7.3	7.2	7.1
$2,000–$3,999	17.1	13.3	12.2	11.9	12.1	11.4	11.1	11.1	10.9
$4,000–$5,999	9.2	13.6	13.6	13.0	13.0	12.4	12.2	12.4	12.2
$6,000–$7,999	3.8	8.5	8.8	9.3	9.4	9.9	10.2	10.5	10.8
$8,000–$9,999	1.5	3.7	4.5	5.0	5.1	5.7	5.9	6.2	6.7
$10,000–$14,999	1.2	3.1	3.8	4.3	4.7	5.3	5.9	6.3	6.9
$15,000 and over	0.8	1.8	2.2	2.5	2.6	3.1	3.5	3.6	4.0
Total	44.7	52.2	52.8	53.6	54.6	55.3	56.1	57.3	58.6
PERCENTAGE DISTRIBUTION									
Under $2,000	25%	16%	15%	14%	14%	13%	13%	13%	12%
$2,000–$3,999	38	25	23	22	22	21	20	19	19
$4,000–$5,999	20	26	26	24	24	22	22	22	21
$6,000–$7,999	9	16	17	18	17	18	18	18	18
$8,000–$9,999	3	7	8	9	9	10	10	11	11
$10,000–$14,999	3	6	7	8	9	10	11	11	12
$15,000 and over	2	4	4	5	5	6	6	6	7
Total	100%	100%	100%	100%	100%	100%	100%	100%	100%
AGGREGATE FAMILY PERSONAL INCOME *billions of dollars*									
Under $2,000	$ 13.2	$ 9.3	$ 8.7	$ 8.6	$ 8.6	$ 8.4	$ 8.2	$ 8.0	$ 7.8
$2,000–$3,999	51.2	40.7	37.4	36.2	37.1	34.8	33.8	33.8	33.3
$4,000–$5,999	44.5	67.7	67.5	64.6	64.8	61.6	60.7	61.8	61.1
$6,000–$7,999	26.0	58.2	61.0	64.3	64.9	68.5	70.5	72.8	74.6
$8,000–$9,999	13.3	32.5	39.7	44.3	45.1	50.5	52.5	55.0	59.5
$10,000–$14,999	14.3	36.9	45.6	51.9	55.9	63.2	71.1	75.1	82.8
$15,000 and over	22.1	48.9	57.5	64.7	66.9	78.8	85.1	89.7	99.7
Total	$184.6	$294.2	$317.4	$334.6	$343.3	$365.8	$381.9	$396.2	$418.8
PERCENTAGE DISTRIBUTION									
Under $2,000	7%	3%	3%	3%	3%	2%	2%	2%	2%
$2,000–$3,999	28	14	12	11	11	10	9	9	8
$4,000–$5,999	24	23	21	19	19	17	16	15	14
$6,000–$7,999	14	20	19	19	19	19	18	18	18
$8,000–$9,999	7	11	13	13	13	14	14	14	14
$10,000–$14,999	8	12	14	16	16	17	19	19	20
$15,000 and over	12	17	18	19	19	21	22	23	24
Total	100%	100%	100%	100%	100%	100%	100%	100%	100%

[1] Includes Alaska and Hawaii.
Source: U. S. Department of Commerce, Office of Business Economics.

Discretionary Income. Saving and investing are discretionary uses of income; i.e., they come from income over and above the basic requirements. The National Industrial Conference Board's continuing study of discretionary income indicates that about half of the entire increase in family income over the past ten years has been discretionary. Thus, the nation's market for consumer-oriented savings services not only is growing larger, but very likely is becoming significantly different. This trend is likely to continue — at an accelerated pace — in the coming years.

Households with discretionary income tend to be headed by persons between the ages of 35 and 55, the peak earning years. (Close to 60% of optional expenditures are made by this group, although they represent only 45% of all households.) Younger households, with the head of the household under 35, represent 25% of total households but have less than 15% of discretionary resources. These demographic findings, plus the educational attainment and occupation of the growing group, dovetail perfectly with our findings regarding our savings customers.

2. A Growing and Urbanizing Economy

Intermediaries are essentially urban institutions. They need relatively high concentrations of population — consumers — in contrast to commercial banks, to support their activities and operations. This environment is needed not only from the savings accumulation side, but from the lending side as well. Between 1950 and 1960, the population of the United States increased from 150 million to 180 million persons. Over 100% of the increase was in urban areas and 60% of it was in the twenty largest urban places. Rural areas registered a decline in population. Looking ahead, such trends are expected to continue and even accelerate, thus supporting the expansion of specialized intermediaries and intermediary-type services.

3. Homogeneity of Money Forms

In the over-the-counter savings markets, the substitute products have gained great acceptance relative to the standard product, bank deposits, during the past decade. In fact, we are now at a point where substitutability is very close to perfect. Why? The reasons include (1) insurance of accounts; (2) promotion and advertising; (3) experience of savers and investors in finding they can get their money when they want it; (4) a new generation of savers without direct personal experience in the 1930s.

Image. There was a time when the word "bank" meant much to savings and loan association managers. They desired strongly to incorporate this term in their operations. Now, I find more and more of them developing a conviction that the time when they needed this word is past. The industry's contribution to the local economies, its physically attractive buildings, its growing prestige in community after community are gaining for associations a place in the sun that makes the appeal of "bank" shrink. Among the general public and customers, differences between the words "bank," "deposits" and "shares" have become just about academic and legal. Credit unions and other intermediaries offering a substitute money form to savers are making equivalent progress, even though they work in limited markets.

The basic point seems to be this: The financial age of Americans is rising. There is an increasing acceptance among all socioeconomic groups that money can in itself be a source of additional income. Money can work for its owner. If you can envision a continuum of money movement, with one force pulling toward greater security and, at the other pole, a force pulling toward greater reward and growth, I think the pattern will be clear. Figure 1 presents such a concept schematically.

There is a need for some group to assume the role of finance counselors to American families, to help them understand how to manage the funds now in their possession. Evidence that this has started is indicated in the mass media magazines. *Better Homes and Gardens,* with a circulation of over 6 million, has inaugurated a monthly family finance feature. It does this for dollars and cents reasons: because its advertisers, corporate executives, think it makes sense.

The very high levels of participation in the stock market last year by individual investors also indicate that some movement up the ladder in the world of finance is underway. I find a good bit of significance in the fact that individual investors took a real beating without their losses being reflected in consumer spending to any significant degree. In other words, I am impressed with the way in which the individual investor took his losses and capital adjustments last year. This could not have happened under a different income schedule — à la 1929.

4. Ready Supply of Investment Outlets

Walter Morton of the University of Wisconsin, while attending one of our earlier conferences, stated this principle of finance: Financial institutions buy those assets available to them. During the 1950s, the desire for funds from institutions of all types was great. Demand for business loan funds, for long-term corporate financing in the form of public bond issues and private placements, and for state and local financing all proved quite high. In fact, just about every type of financing except railroad bonds was in rising demand. In the consumer sector, the asset being

Figure 1

Zones of Financial Sophistication*

*Pull toward Greater
Reward and Growth*

Zone of High Sophistication			
Demand for Management Decisions by Individual	Business investments Real estate Speculative stocks Speculative mutual funds Blue-chip stocks Corporate stocks	↑	Minimum security Maximum reward Minimum availability Speculative
Zone of Moderate Sophistication			
Demand for Decision in Principle (at least initially)	Balanced diversified mutual funds Credit unions Savings and loan associations		Medium security Medium reward Medium availability Considered slightly speculative
Zone of Little or No Sophistication			
No Demand for Management Decisions (or very minimal)	Mutual savings banks Commercial banks Government savings bonds† Cash box‡ Mattress/drawer/socks‡	↓	Maximum security Minimum reward Maximum availability Not speculative

The Continuum of Money Movement

*Pull toward
Greater Security*

* As ranked by Institute for Motivational Research, based upon various tests and interviews.

† Government savings bonds are seen as possessing only medium reward and availability, but they are regarded by many in the upper-lower classes and the lower-middle classes (by the less financially sophisticated) as even safer than the richest, most completely protected banks.

‡ Our subsequent tests revealed that the "cash box" and the "mattress or drawer at home" represent maximum security only to the most financially unsophisticated elements in our population. For the more educated, well-informed and financially sophisticated members of all socioeconomic classes and subgroups, "saving money at home" is regarded as one of the riskiest and most unreliable ways of handling surplus cash.

offered by the economy in greatest volume was mortgages and home mortgage debt. Between 1950 and 1960, home mortgage debt grew from $45 billion to $141 billion. Institutions set up to purchase and hold mortgages found that they could take in savings in exchange for their shares or savings accounts quite readily.

For savings and loan associations the postwar decade could not have been better. Single-family houses were in tremendous demand, and associations could put to use quickly just about all the dollars they could get for savings accounts. There was practically no cycle in this demand. Rates on both savings accounts and mortgages moved only in one direction. Other institutions with a lesser concentration of assets found, through hindsight, that their attitudes toward diversification hindered them and tempered their willingness to buy the assets the economy offered Perhaps their growth was at sufficiently satisfactory levels so that any further effort did not seem necessary.

A quick review of the 1960s indicates rapid changes taking place in our financial markets. Suddenly, savings associations, savings banks and commercial banks find themselves with an excess of funds seeking acceptable assets. The reasons for this shift include (1) the slow rate of economic growth; (2) attractive yields offered to savers and investors by intermediaries relative to the return on other assets; (3) stickiness of rates offered by intermediaries; (4) internal problems of size, including (a) mounting repayments and (b) extension of terms to the end of the line (mortgages of 30 years and beyond); (5) the question of a profits squeeze on intermediaries and financial institutions — in sum, heightened competition. Looking ahead, the key question becomes whether savings institutions will be able to find sufficient outlets for funds at rates that will enable them to expand their liabilities or shares aggressively.

THREE TRENDS OF NOTE

Scrambled Finance. The fact that consumers can generate savings funds relatively more rapidly than individual intermediaries can invest these funds has produced a condition in the financial world similar to one found in retailing, namely, scrambled merchandising. Perhaps we can call the new tendency in the financial world "scrambled finance." The traditional pattern whereby personal loan companies lend on personal notes, mortgage lenders lend on mortgages and commercial banks lend on business loans is breaking down quite rapidly. Old labels now provide minimal enlightenment and may well prove quite misleading.

Among virtually all institutions the earnings squeeze has produced a desire for diversification. Customary compartmentalization and specialization are breaking down. One class of institution seeks to skim the cream from another's operations. Auto financing firms enter the personal loan business. Small loan-type operations extend their efforts to college education and larger loans. Savings and loans seek consumer credit powers. Commercial banks seek the right to make competitive mortgage loans. Such trends cause great problems for the supervisory and regulatory authorities. The traditionalists see the trends distorting their definitions, regulations, and controls. Scrambling seems destined to grow.

Through diversification, individual intermediaries may well be able to attract a sufficient volume of investments and have available a ready supply of liabilities for savers. The trends, however, are merely a manifestation of something even more fundamental at the consumer level.

Financial Packaging. Consumers are accepting readily the combining of various types of separate institutional offerings into one financial contract. Financial packaging probably has reached its highest stage of development in the automobile business. Here, as you know, the profit on the sale of the car, the financing of the car, the casualty insurance and the credit life insurance are folded into one contract. You could not make money in the sales finance business alone today; you have to have your own life company and your own casualty company as well. Dealers and finance companies seek to maximize by considering all these components. Beginning at another point, the financial institutions like State Farm Mutual and Allstate offer low-rate car financing in a package to secure the car insurance.

In the housing field, some prefabrication companies have their own mortgage banking operations and there is a report that United States Steel owns more mortgages from its housing activities than 90% of the individual savings and loans in the country. At a savings and loan you can secure a package today which might include a mortgage loan, property insurance, mortgage protection life insurance and MGIC insurance or a casualty contract to insure against your defaulting. In addition, if the mortgage is written on an open-end advance basis, you can get various kinds of consumer loans from the association during the life of your mortgage. The other day one of my insurance friends read me a circular describing a program the Morgan Guaranty Bank has for correspondents and is offering to savings and loan associations. This is a package group life insurance program for officers and employees of banks and savings associations who are customers of Morgan Guaranty.

Any number of similar proposals can be identified. One-stop finance seems to be a very live trend and a trend gaining consumer acceptance. The time when you secure insurance from insurance companies, mortgages from mortgage lenders and consumer loans from consumer lending companies seems to be passing. Competition within finance is producing changes affecting the assets available to individual intermediaries and, thus, their ability to supply liabilities for sale.

Corporations and Finance. A most significant change on the horizon is the shift in the attitude of the major American nonfinancial corporations toward finance and financial functions. As users of financial services, major corporations are considerably more adroit today than they were through the 1950s. Bankers will tell you their toughest customers are their biggest customers; they demand the most in terms of services and are the toughest in terms of compensating balances and rates.

It is on the selling side, however, that the greatest underlying changes are taking place. More and more corporations are finding that financing and control of financing are very important elements in the sale of their product. Corporate officials more and more are becoming convinced that the financial institution is a middleman that can be either eliminated or controlled. The growing pool of corporate funds or savings available for finance services provides, for the first time, the means which make circumvention of financial middlemen possible. The packaging of financial transactions more closely with the selling transaction and the putting together of as many finance elements as possible strengthen the conviction of corporate executives that the financial institution is a middleman that can be eliminated.

Corporations like Alcoa, Reynolds, Union Carbide, Du Pont and Kaiser are researching home building as a ripe field for their funds and managerial talents. In financing their operations, chances are they will not use savings associations or savings banks as these institutions are currently established. They may even bypass the mortgage instrument. In the insurance field, the great risk to insurance companies rests in the growth of wholly owned companies. Caterpillar Tractor self-insures its employees, reinsuring all losses over $200,000 a year. Swift, Kroger and HFC have captive insurance companies.

The greater portion of existing intermediaries may well find themselves doing business on a wholesale and indirect basis, as nonfinancial corporations carve out a place as mediator between consumer and financial intermediary. To the degree that this takes place, intermediaries will find the spread between savings rates and portfolio returns squeezed. The existing body of rules and regulations governing intermediaries will be greatly strained as some institutions attempt to gain part of the growing market. This is not to say that the intermediaries will not continue to finance consumer transactions. The intermediary can fight back by enlarging the scope of financial services it offers the consumer, by scrambled finance, by financial packaging. Holding companies and syndication may be one answer. An active and alert commercial banking system is another.

Therefore, competition among financial institutions may not determine the future course of intermediaries so much as will competition among financial institutions and entities that we do not now consider as such. The role that intermediaries play in the economy will change greatly as consumers accept and encourage changes in the way financial services are provided by corporations. Goethe once said: "The greatest difficulties lie where we are not looking for them."

RECAPITULATION

Let me try to summarize my comments relevant to the environment for financial intermediaries during the years ahead.

1. The consumer will play a new and growing role as a supplier and user of financial services.
2. Urbanization will continue to favor the intermediary.
3. The financial age of the population is rising. We get closer and closer substitutability of various money forms and movement up the money continuum.
4. Looking ahead, the most critical and controversial point concerns the ability of intermediaries to find acceptable assets for investment in volume to permit continued growth.

Points 1, 2, and 3 tend to favor the growth of intermediaries in the frames of reference we hold today. Point 4 indicates that trends such as the drive of present-day intermediaries to diversify, consumer acceptance of the finance package and the active entry of major corporations into the business of providing financial services will alter greatly the institutional framework through which financial services are provided to the American public. Competitive pressures characteristic of the economy generally are not bypassing the finance field. In fact, they are, if anything, growing more intense here.

Public Policy Implications. The public policy issues raised by the kinds of shifts the future may bring are many: Should financial institutions be permitted to scramble? How far should such a trend be permitted to go? Who is to control nonfinancial corporations that begin to offer financial services in volume? Or, more fundamentally, need we control them at all?

Questions centered on monetary policy will be particularly critical to many of you in this room. What will the impact of growth in nonbank and nonfinancial corporations in finance be on monetary policy? On stability in the economy? On the price of financial services to the consumer? Each of you must be "Marlboro men" and think for yourself on these issues.

For what they are worth, I offer these contentions: The system I envision is not a throwback to earlier times or to comparable situations in other economies. The American financial system has reached a size and stage in its evolution that are unique. I view the work of the Commission on Money and Credit, the Saxon Committee, the Heller Committee, and similar efforts as manifestations of this fact. The challenge will be to design monetary controls so as to fit the new conditions without destroying the vitality and innovation the new elements promise.

Efforts to squeeze the modern financial intermediary into preordained molds run real risks. Policies to maintain full employment, price stability, and the world value of the dollar can be better programed on the global level if some of us take the time to make certain that our "global thinkers" have an understanding of the market effects of their policies. Time expended in studying the meaning of the new forces on the financial scene — the American consumer and the nonfinancial corporation — will be time well spent. An enlarged role for intermediaries is predicated in part on the enlightenment such investigation will bring.

Discussion*

MARSHALL KAPLAN: You started by pointing out that the commercial banks are oriented toward businesses and not toward consumers. Presumably this was a breech into which the intermediaries stepped. But later on, when you developed your theory of one-stop financing, it seems to me that the commercial banks really do have tremendous advantage. They start out with checking accounts and have certain other advantages, too. I wonder if this means that maybe the commercial banks are coming into their own again.

MR. KENDALL: That is a very good point. In the kind of environment I envision, the commercial bank, potentially, could be the favored institution; it could enjoy the best of both worlds. In addition to its service to business, it could function quite aggressively as an intermediary in savings accumulation, in trust departments, etc. Banks could become great retail financing institutions.

But I do not think they are going to do the job. Why? First, the intermediaries will continue to be aggressive politically and in the market place; they will give the banks no quarter. Second, the corporate treasurers with their sharp-pencil, money-management techniques will circumvent banks as readily as any other intermediary. The price of competition is going to be high.

The problem also is one of attitudes. The commercial bank is a schizophrenic kind of institution. Bankers want to finance business primarily, and will move in and out of consumer markets depending on money conditions. If they separated the demand deposit function from their activities as intermediaries — if they ran these things somewhat on the General Motors principle — I think they could do the job. As I said, the issue is one of attitudes.

I used to accept the premise that intermediaries would not exist if commercial banks had done their job, that there would be no sales finance companies if the banks had taken on the sales financing business back in the 1920s, that there would be no savings and loans of any consequence if the banks had taken on the home mortgage business after

* Proceedings of the Sixth Annual Conference, 1963, Excerpts from the Discussion, pp. 72–78.

World War II. I no longer hold this view. There is something about bank operations that seems to give bankers a tremendous blind spot on this particular point.

CHARLES PARTEE: Lee, you accuse the banks of having a blind spot, but I think your answer to Marshall indicates that you have a blind spot, too. It seems to me that all the evidence of the last few years on commercial bank activity in a variety of matters is that the banks are slowly becoming aware of the situation and are being pressured into moving more competitively into these fields and that, given the same level of managerial ability to move broadly and with vision, they can do very well not only in savings competition but in the mortgage loan field as well.

For example, the early postwar period up to 1955 was marked by a very rapid expansion in sales finance company importance, but since 1955 the sales finance companies have declined rapidly in relative importance. In the last two years, it seems to me, the commercial banks have been more vigorous in attracting savings and have again shown that they can attract savings if they work at it. If the commercial banks were as aggressive in the mortgage field as savings and loans, I think they would have an advantage in making that type of loan.

I am saying this to support Marshall's point of view. I do not mean to be an apologist for the commercial banks, but I wonder whether it still is not true that the central institution in the financial sector is eventually the commercial bank and whether we might not see a return to that position by the commercial banks in the decade ahead.

ARTHUR MEYERS: I have often thought something different from what you have been saying here today. I have gone so far as to accuse the bankers of being more than schizophrenic and uncertain, as you express it, and of being positively antagonistic. In other words, in driving away the consumer who wanted to borrow, because they thought the risk was too great, and in driving away real estate loans, they actually had antagonism. I have accused them of spawning all these other agencies and then of coming to their senses belatedly and suddenly realizing that they were the creator of some of this other activity.

MR. KENDALL: Here we have a contrasting philosophy of specialty shops and department-store-type operations. Department stores at the executive management level tend to spread their talents over a number of fields; discount houses, on the other hand, have a more restricted focus, concentrating on relatively low-overhead, high-turnover items — originally noncredit, nondelivery, etc. Discounters generally produce a better value for the consumer and caused a competitive reaction on the part of the department store operators that was desirable. Now, in finance, we have the chief executive officers of savings and loan associations, credit unions and other specialty shops, who are adequately compensated, working constantly to solve problems in their own areas. Here, I think, we tend to get certain innovations from these people that we do not get from department-store-type thinking.

I have talked to advertising men, and they say, "You know how much time commercial banks think about you? Fifteen minutes a day. You know how much time savings and loan people think about commercial bankers? Twenty-four hours a day!" I have not checked the accuracy of their judgment, but I think the answer is somewhere in this area.

MR. WINNICK: In arraying the factors which explain the growth of the savings and loan business, you make no attempt to give relative weights to them. But, if I understood you correctly, you seem to play down a bit the impact of higher interest rates on savings as a factor. You quote one statistic that in a whole array of towns, savings and loans, matched against savings banks or commercial banks, did not have higher interest rates. Yet there are at least four or five statistics in your tables which imply the opposite — for example, the large account which is a natural part of savings growth. California stands out by quite a bit as the receiver of large savings deposits, and California is the prime competitor on savings rates. Another table shows a reversal to commercial banks in the last two or three years, and I would say that interest rates were a very heavy factor here.

MR. KENDALL: Of all the factors causing people to overcome the attitudinal barriers to savings and loan investment, I think the high dividend rate has been number one. Thus, you are correct in that rate is of prime importance. But let us go further. Until late in the 1950s, most managers held the view that savings and loans had to pay 1% more than commercial banks. The record of 1962 and 1963 is relevant here. What did savings and loans do when the commercial banks went from a top rate of 3% to 4%? One might expect the first reaction to be, "Let's go up another 1%." But in most communities the differential is ¼ of 1%, and in some big and medium-size cities there is no differential at all. The tendency has been for the spread to shrink, as people accept the savings and loan account as a substitute for the bank account, to where one can name probably twenty significant cities where there is no differential. Yet growth continues at the savings and loans; it is slower, but it continues.

MR. WINNICK: I am fully satisfied that this situation exists. But if the large deposit is the dynamic element, I could argue that this narrowing of differential is due to the fact that the large account is becoming more sensitive than the small account to slight differentials in the return available on savers' funds. I would want to be satisfied that the locations which had no differentials had something like a representative number of big accounts and I would like to know something about comparative growth rates.

JOHN STAFFORD: On the question of rate in attracting savings, it is pertinent to recall that despite low dividend rates, savings banks and savings associations in the East have been successful in attracting large accounts. In these institutions, accounts of $10,000 and over represent about one-third of all savings held by the individual bank or savings and loan. This is close to the usual distribution one finds as one moves from the East to the West, even in the high-rate West Coast area. Large accounts hold about 30% of the total savings in the average savings institution. Generally there appears to be only a moderate difference in this regard between the East Coast and the West Coast.

SHERMAN MAISEL: I have a great deal of difficulty reconciling your paper today with your monograph for the Commission on Money and Credit. There it appeared that savings and loans are unique institutions because they are concerned only with the mortgage borrower and not with the saver or anybody else having any financial interest except the home owner.

MR. KENDALL: Concentrating on the savings markets, as I did today, does not change my view of the basic function of savings and loans as intermediaries. I would say that the savings and loans today continue to see their function basically in the home ownership sector of the economy. In broadening this concept, they would move to include those things that go into making a house a home. This would mean package financing of draperies and furniture and the like. I think the sensible way for them to do this financing is through various techniques which tie such purchases to the mortgage contract.

If you should tell me that the housing and real estate markets are going to be unattractive, I would say that savings and loans have a relatively bleak outlook and are in a relatively poor position in my model because of the corporation moving into the housing field. Reducing the number of home builders from 25,000 to closer to 1,000 means that many of them will be multimillion-dollar operations and they will not want to work with financial peanut stands.

So what will savings associations do? A relatively large association will get together with some others and will service these larger builders as they move around the country. If they work with General Mills, for example, it will be in the shelter field, through trade-in housing, housing for corporate executives, etc.; their function will not be financing the plants or inventory of General Mills. I think I would be sufficiently consistent in saying that associations live and die with the shelter and shelter-related needs of American families.

PART FIVE

Housing

The demand for shelter on the part of Americans has generated more debt than any other single force. An examination of the record indicates that mortgage debt grew from $33 billion in 1946 and $59 billion in 1950, to $238 billion today. The growth has been more than double that of consumer installment debt and more rapid than corporate or government debt. Looking toward the future, the population trends seem to indicate that demands for residential financing will continue to grow.

Housing is now and into the future should continue to be an important source of investment to financial institutions. The expected growth in the demand for dwelling units indicates that by 1970, more and more types of institutions will have larger portfolio positions in mortgage debt. As a consequence, the focus of Part Five is forward-looking rather than a review of the past. It seeks to explore the yet uncharted territory to be traveled during the years ahead by mortgage finance and its institutions. It is in such a dynamic context that housing and shelter demands of the American public and the financing that will be tied to these demands becomes most meaningful for financial institutions, their managing officers and students of the subject.

Moving from the general to the specific, the first selection examines the characteristics of the home-buying and mortgage-borrowing customer, the second, the nature of the homebuilding industry and the third and fourth, the demand for single-family and for rental facilities and the financing arrangements under which these demands will probably be met during the years ahead. The calibre of the authors, Messrs. Colean, Rogg, Hoadley and Winnick, speaks for the quality of the presentations that are made.

17

Who Owns the Houses*

> *Miles Colean* is a consultant on building finance
> and construction to trade associations, manufacturing and con-
> struction firms, financial institutions and government agencies.
> He is an adviser to *Architectural Forum, House and Home,* and
> *House Beautiful.* He is the author of numerous research studies
> in the field of residential housing. Mr. Colean has a bachelor
> of architecture degree from Columbia University. He was
> formerly vice president, Starrett Brothers and Eken; director,
> Twentieth Century Fund Housing Survey; technical director
> and assistant administrator, Federal Housing Administration; and
> member, President's Advisory Committee on Government Hous-
> ing Policies and Programs. He is a member of the Conference of
> Business Economists; member, Business Research Advisory
> Council, Bureau of Labor Statistics; trustee, Urban Land Insti-
> tute; and chairman, Advisory Committee on 1960 Housing
> Census.

I AM HERE, I MUST CONFESS, under false pretenses, for a number of reasons.
For one thing, I have no academic prestige or even pretensions. The
only advanced degree I ever got was given me by the doorman of the
Cosmos Club. So what you are getting here is strictly what I have been
able to pick up in a nonacademic way.

I have another confession to make, particularly in reference to Mr.
Hauser's comment on Frank Lloyd Wright. Obviously, economists hold

* Proceedings of the First Annual Conference, 1958, pp. 69–85.

architects in very low esteem. I have been told that the lowest form of intellectual life is an architect or engineer turned economist. I have done that, and coming back to this building brings it very close to home, because I was the chief draftsman in the architectural firm that did this building back in 1923 and 1924. This floor always gives me distinct discomfort, for a reason that I shall explain briefly.

If you have been down the corridor on this floor you have seen some niches with statues. Mr. Potter Palmer had some statues he wanted to put in niches, and that seemed like a good place to do it. So we put in the niches. Then lo and behold, when they started to build the vault in the lobby down below, those niches stuck right through the vault, so we had to come in with jackhammers and cut off half of each niche. Mr. Palmer never knew that, but it added a little to the cost of this fine building.

Another reason that I am here under false pretenses is that I gave you an outline. The outline of what I am going to say will be related to the outline I gave you only by coincidence, owing to the fact that I had hoped, when this Conference was organized, to have the results of the housing inventory that was taken last December. It would have given me a very neat and easy out by allowing me to compare what the situation was in 1950 with comparable data in 1956.

Well, the Census let me down. I do not have that material. So what I am going to say has only a coincidental relationship to what I had in mind saying. I preserved the title just because I thought I ought to preserve something, and it may have something to do with what I am going to say.

I am talking about home ownership and changes in home ownership and the prospects for home ownership.

Home-Ownership, Home-Building Relationship

I want you to bear in mind, as we go along, that this has really, again, only a remote relationship to the amount of home building. The two — home ownership and home building — do not necessarily coincide. As you know, during the war, when we had a very low rate of building, we had a very high rate of increase in home ownership. This home ownership growth does not necessarily relate itself to growth in building, and the factors that influence one do not necessarily influence the other. But as things go in this world, we are a nation of home owners; and with few interruptions, the most serious of which occurred between 1930 and 1940, the trend has been toward an increase in the number of nonfarm families who live in houses to which they hold title. If you have a 90% mortgage, some may argue as to whether or not you really own the house, but at least theoretically you have title to the property.

Unfortunately, this generality must rest on observations of an imprecise sort for most of our history. We just do not know a lot back of 1890, but since 1890 the record is clear. In that year about 40% of all occupied nonfarm dwellings were owned by their occupants. The ratio dropped slightly between 1890 and 1900, due, no doubt, to the troubled business conditions in the midpart of that decade. It then rose decade by decade until the economic disaster of the 1930s, when the ratio fell from 46% in 1930 almost to 41% in 1940. It was probably lower in some of the intervening years.

In other words, in that one decade we lost almost all we had gained from 1890. But from 1940 the recovery was very rapid. By 1945 the ratio was already nearly 51%. By 1950 it was well over 53%. In 1956 it approached 60%. In other words, in less than twenty years, since 1940, the ratio of home ownership grew three times as much as it had grown during the forty years from 1890 to 1930.

A number of special influences played their part in this dramatic development. Important institutional changes had taken place and were making themselves felt by 1940. Among these were the stabilization of the shattered mortgage market by the Home Owners Loan Corporation and the creation of an integrated system of home finance through the Federal Home Loan Bank System, including provision for federally chartered savings and loan associations and the insurance of share accounts.

Through FHA mortgage insurance, an effective means was established for channeling life insurance and bank funds into home mortgages in a way that had never been done before. During World War II, and for some time after, a stimulating influence on home buying was one of the results of controlled rents. During the postwar years, the main motivating forces appear to have been the rapid growth in the number of families, rising incomes, and extremely generous financing terms, especially for former servicemen.

When Mr. Hauser was giving you all the figures about family formation, population, income and so on, I began to feel like an actor playing Shakespeare's King Richard III.

At a very high point in the proceedings a messenger came in and said, "My lord, the Duke of Buckingham has been taken."

The king replied, "Let him be executed at once."

One day a new messenger came in and announced, "My lord, the Duke of Buckingham has been taken and executed."

The king, having his punch line taken away from him, said, "Well, I'll be damned."

Some of what I am going to say may sound a little warmed over. But you can always bring variety into this business by just quoting somebody else's statistics. You can take your choice.

Main Factors in the Home-Ownership Equation

The influences that have been particularly motivating here are a rapid growth in families, rising incomes, and varying credit terms. It is very hard, for me at least, to tell just what specific part each of these influences has played. Since in our science — if we may presume to call it that — controlled laboratory experiments are not possible, we can only surmise what values to give the factors in this home-ownership equation.

For example, the sentiment for home ownership may be so strong and persistent an underlying influence that it can be considered a constant. The institutional factors I mentioned are now so firmly established that they may be bracketed in with the general influence of credit. The FHA now is really part of the system, I assume even the U. S. League will admit. This appears to leave us with the three principal variables I have mentioned: growth, income, and credit.

During the years of greatest increase in the home ownership ratio, from 1946 to 1950, all three of the forces were in the ascendant. The number of new families was increasing very rapidly. Family incomes, especially in the lower and middle ranges, were mounting at an unprecedented rate. Mortgage money was available at the easiest terms on record.

After 1950, the rate of family formation fell off rather sharply; and from 1950 through 1953, mortgage credit was less easy to obtain than it had been in the previous four years. Then in 1954 and 1955, credit was as easy as, or easier than, it ever had been; and in 1956 it became rigorously restricted, especially in the areas of insured and guaranteed financing, where the greatest growth had taken place earlier. Family income through 1957 continued on the uptrend.

Irrespective of these crosscurrents, the ratio of ownership continued its spectacular rise during the first six years of the decade.

What do we make of this? We are probably safe in concluding that the ownership ratio can increase in a period when the rate of family formation is falling but when, at the same time, income is rising and credit generally is easy to obtain. But how can we separate these latter two forces?

Although direct information on changes in the ownership ratio are not available for intermediate years, we may judge from changes in the number of new houses built and the number of new mortgages made that at least the rate of increase in ownership is retarded when credit is stringent.

We have now entered a period in which credit is to be easy, family formation neutral or less as an influence for expansion, and changes in family income at least washed out temporarily as a positive influence. This is a configuration not yet experienced, since, as you will recall, when family income was falling in the 1930s, mortgage credit remained fairly tight through the first half of the decade, and by the time the effect of the government's efforts to ease credit were becoming effective, incomes were also on the rise.

THE EASY-CREDIT INDUCEMENT

So now we have an equation in which we seem to have more constants than variables. The question this raises is: Can easy credit itself, under such circumstances, offer a sufficient inducement to assure an increase in the home-ownership ratio? This is, of course, a matter apart from an increase in the number of new houses built. It is probable that easy credit will provide a spur to house building, and that around 85% of the new units will be built and sold for owner occupancy. This could happen, however, without an increase in the ownership ratio if a sufficiently large number of presently owner-occupied houses were transferred to rental status. A rise in the number of new houses built, therefore, does not automatically mean an over-all increase in the ownership ratio.

Probably the greatest source of our additions to rental housing comes from the sale of formerly owner-occupied housing. That, I think, is generally true. Such additions could be made in a period like this, even though we still had a very high percentage of new houses sold for owner occupancy.

The problem, however, is not alone that of judging the effects of easy credit in the face of an otherwise static or negative situation. For one thing, the static factors may change. While the likelihood is that a notable upturn in the rate of net new family formation will not occur until some time early in the 1960s — and apparently it will be a little later, about the middle of the decade — I am optimist enough to believe that, before long, the rise in family income will be resumed, putting more substance into the push exerted by easy credit.

OTHER FACTORS IN THE HOME-OWNERSHIP RATIO

At the same time, some added factors that have not been of serious consequence up to the present time may have to be taken into account in estimating the future of the home ownership ratio.

One of these is the cost of housing. While the statistics are far from conclusive, there is evidence of some slippage in the normal relationship, if we may call it that, between family income and the price of new houses. A recent study by the Bureau of Labor Statistics, which was published in the *Monthly Labor Review* in February, 1958, shows that current building trends have resulted in the construction of more houses than can readily be absorbed by a matching number of families with enough income to buy at a ratio of price to income of about two and one-half to one. The Bureau's study skeptically concludes:

"It seems likely that the new housing market will be expanded and housing standards will be improved appreciably only if ways are found to hold down construction costs and, at the same time, maintain a quality product."

The First Federal Savings and Loan Association of Chicago has just taken a look at what has happened to the annual cost of owning the average-priced house built in the Chicago area between 1947 and 1957. On the assumption that the average family can afford to budget about one-fifth of its income for housing purposes, the First Federal finds that, while the average family's annual housing budget has risen 53% during the ten-year period, the annual cost of buying a house (that means paying for it — mortgage, interest and amortization, taxes and so on) on the basis of a twenty-year mortgage has risen 97%, due to increases all along the line from land to interest and taxes. It might have noted that there also has been an increase in the cost of transportation between the home and work and in the cost of home maintenance.

While we need not concern ourselves too much with the preciseness of these figures, I think we may grant that it has become harder, even with the encouragements of better income and easy credit, to buy a house now than it was ten years ago.

There is also the matter of convenience. Especially in the moderate to lower price ranges, the choice of a house gets more or less down to a choice of an obsolete house close in or a new one in areas increasingly remote from the centers of urban activity. With the old house, there is the inconvenience of the accommodations or the cost of modernization. With the new one, there is likely to be the inconvenience of getting to and from work, shopping facilities, and places of worship and recreation. Faced with such choices, many families, otherwise able, may defer or drop the decision to buy.

Has Home Ownership Reached Its Peak?

Here is another matter for speculation. Has the home ownership ratio perhaps been pushed close to the limit under any circumstances? A 60% ratio is an historical anomaly. So far as I can determine, it is something that has never occurred before at any time in any country. May not a reasonable provision for mobility and for differences in living tastes and housing requirements imply that the present availability of rental housing is close to a minimum? I do not know.

Our vacancy statistics do indeed indicate more slack in the rental than in the ownership market. But since we have almost no information about the characteristics of the vacancies as to price, quality or location, it is impossible to judge whether the slack is a real one or one composed of dwellings no one will live in so long as he has a choice.

Fortunately, the Census is going to be able to give us more information on that crucial subject. As you may know, the Census Bureau issues a quarterly estimate of housing vacancies — one of the very important additions to our statistical information during the last few years. I understand that the next report, covering, I think, the first two quarters of this year, will be able to give us some information, at least, on characteristics of rental vacancies, and perhaps something more.

So far, I have raised more questions than I have given answers. In fact, I can't recall having given any answers. Nor is it likely that I shall do much differently as I proceed. Maybe what I am doing, and I hope this is true, is to demonstrate to you how fruitful a field we have here for study and research, how fascinating a field it is to study, and how helpful to our knowledge of the economy it would be if more answers could be found. If I can incite you to work in this field which too few are presently plowing, I consider my effort here worthwhile, despite its shortcomings in a more definitive sense.

As I have said, I had expected to be able to shed some light on some of the questions I had raised by looking into changes, if any, that occurred between 1950, when the last comprehensive census was taken, and the 1956 interim inventory. As a result of delay in completing the tabulations, however, the only clue we have to the post-1950 composition and performance of home buyers must be found in scattered material.

The surveys of consumer finances made each year by the Federal Reserve Board, though based on a very small sample, are valuable. And one volume of the special tabulations made by the Board in its recent study of consumer installment credit — a monumental work done at the request of Congress a year ago — contains a great deal of information from which I am going to draw.

Direct comparison, however, between the Census and Federal Reserve data is very hazardous because of the differences in coverage, definition, size of samples and so on. Some insight into the characteristics of home buyers may also be obtained from the Veterans Administration and the Federal Housing Administration in respect to homes purchased with guaranteed or insured financing; but since they comprise a great deal less than the majority of purchases, it is difficult to judge how typical these transactions may be. Except for data recently compiled by the U. S. Savings and Loan League, we are almost wholly in the dark as to the characteristics of recent buyers using conventional mortgage financing.

Mr. Strunk might have mentioned that one of the really important works that this organization does is in the research area, and I consider that this study, *Who Buys the Houses*, is really something of a milestone in our knowledge.

BORROWER CHARACTERISTICS

In spite of certain limitations, a few assertions may dependably be offered and a few assumptions may at least tentatively be made. As might be expected, most home owners are married couples and most of these home-owning couples have children.

In 1950, about 75% of the home owners were officially described as "male head, wife present." That is, I may say, strictly a Census euphemism; wherever there is a male present, he is considered to be also a male head. That is one of the questions they never ask when they come to the door.

Of these families — male head, wife present — 70% had related persons in their households, mainly children. The other classes of home owners had a varied composition, but it is especially interesting to note that about 4% of home-owning households were composed of single men and women more than 65 years old, each as a single-person household, indicating the persistence of home ownership even into advanced years and widowhood.

That also relates to the point Mr. Hauser made this morning about undoubling. People do maintain their households — their independent households — much longer now than they used to, due to the generally prosperous conditions that prevail and to increased pensions, savings, social security and the like.

As also might be expected, most married couples are home owners — 54.8% of them in 1950 — although Federal Reserve data show that about 65% of the married couples were home owners in 1956. That figure, however, is on a very small sample basis, and there may be some margin of error there; but it indicates again the rapid growth of home ownership during the last few years.

The relationship between marital status and home ownership is thus clear. In 1950, close to 85% of males between 35 and 64 were married. In 1930, the corresponding figure was 82% and in 1940 it was 81.6%. So there has been an increase in the proportion of married men. If, in the decades ahead, men can be persuaded to maintain this pace, the future of the ownership ratio may be safe. It is probably a reasonable conclusion that they will, since only a severe depression could provide an upsetting factor.

We have noted, of course, a decrease in the marriage rate this year and probably a decrease in the birth rate as well. These shifts have been attributed to the so-called present recession, but I think maybe it may also be due to the change in the style of women's dresses. If you recall, the last time women appeared in anything like the things you see in the windows today was during the twenties, and we also had a drop in the marriage rate and a very low birth rate. So I think that is a subject for study among you sociologists; the influence of women's styles on these deep and profound matters ought to be given a little more attention.

But be that as it may, Dr. Joseph Davis, the elder member of the Council of Economic Advisers, and a man very wise in these things, considers that all these influences are ephemeral and that the upward growth in marriage rate and birth rate will be resumed as soon as the temporary setback in business conditions has passed, which we hope will be soon.

The point here, however, may not be the over-all marriage rate so much as it is the age at which home buying customarily takes place. The FHA and VA data on the subject generally agree that the median age of the husband at the time of purchase is around 34, and that the greatest concentration of purchases is within the range of 30 to 34 years. For buyers of single-family houses with conventional financing, the median age appears to be about four years higher. There is, to be sure, an accumulation of purchasers in higher age brackets. Thus, while only 17% of household heads less than 25 years old were home owners in 1956, according to the Federal Reserve, 49% of those between 25 and 34 years of age were home owners. Above that group, owners substantially outweighed renters, moving from 63% of the 35 to 44 group steadily up to 68% of the group 65 years and over, and indicating much additional purchasing after the peak years for buying. Much of that purchasing no doubt was for a second house.

AGE RANGE OF BORROWERS

Nevertheless, the crucial purchasing age has been from 25 to 34 years, a matter of some importance when we look ahead toward the rest of this decade and to the next. From 1955 to 1960, we shall be having a growing deficit of males in the age group most prone to marry or to buy houses, because of the war and the low birth rate of the 1930s. There will be some increase in the 35 to 39 bracket, but only about three-fifths enough to make up the other deficiency. Much the same situation will prevail from 1960 to 1965. By 1965, the 25 to 29 bracket will be showing a slight pickup, but much less than needed to make up the accumulated deficit in the range from 30 to 39 years. Not until 1970 will the increases in the 25- to 34-year bracket be well ahead of the lingering deficit in the 35- to 39-year group.

These figures may be interpreted as forecasting a drop in the ownership ratio, or at best a halt in its advancement if buying patterns in the decade ahead do not change. In any case, they indicate that those who are interested in selling and financing houses should be thinking more about potential buyers who are either younger or older than those with whom they have been accustomed to dealing. New appeals and different motivations may have to be considered; and the effects on price, design, and location may be substantial.

There is still more to note in the data that we have at hand. According to the latest Census estimates, published in 1956, the highest likely net increase in the number of new households from 1956 to 1960 is expected to be in the neighborhood of 4 million. You can check these with Dr. Hausers' figures. They are not quite the same. Between 1960 and 1965 there will be an increase of about 4.3 million new households, or annual averages ranging from 800,000 to 860,000. At any rate, irrespective of the magnitude, you will see that the trend is the same.

These increases may be compared with the annual average of 1,275,000 net new households created between 1945 and 1950 and of 885,000 between 1950 and 1956. On their face, taken along with the complications already mentioned, these figures indicate some difficulty ahead in keeping up the proportion of home ownership, unless it becomes possible to make home owners of a larger proportion of newly formed households than is now the case.

The factor that I want to go into particularly is that of income. But before I do I may also insert another factor, which I have not alluded to in any of the material I have given you: that is the factor of race, which Dr. Hauser mentioned this morning. I have not covered it simply because we have no statistics since 1950 as to what has happened to home ownership among Negroes. But there we have a very important reservoir of potential buyers.

In 1950, if I recall correctly, something like 35% of Negro families living in cities or rural nonfarm areas were home owners. Part of the reason for the low ratio is the segregation problem; probably more important is the fact that Negroes still are pretty much concentrated in the lower income range. To the extent that this is so, what I have to say about income will apply to them as well as to the market as a whole.

INCOME RANGE OF BORROWERS

High income is not a critical characteristic of home ownership generally. In spite of what I have said, home ownership is, in fact, spread well over the whole range of incomes. For 1950, the Census shows that over half of the owner-occupied units were occupied by husband-and-wife families with incomes of less than $5,000 and about 40% of them by husband-wife families with less than $4,000 of income. If all types of

families — widows with children, single persons, unrelated individuals —
are taken into account, these ratios are increased to over 70% and nearly
60%, respectively. These high ratios among the lower income ranges
undoubtedly represent numerous cases of older persons living on savings
and annuities in houses purchased years before. Some of the Federal
Reserve Board figures show how large a percentage of the older persons
bought their houses prior to 1954, the cutoff date.

So we have attained a pretty wide distribution of home ownership
throughout the income scale. Nevertheless, there is a very considerable
amount of buying — new buying — by persons of moderate income.

According to Federal Reserve estimates, half of the home buyers between 1954 and 1956 had incomes of less than $5,000. Around 35% of the
recent buyers had incomes in the $3,000 to $5,000 range, and 15% had
incomes of less than $3,000. The range of $5,000 to $7,500 accounted for
31% of recent buyers, and the ranges of $7,500 and above accounted for
only 19%. Almost as many families with incomes of less than $3,000
bought houses as did families with incomes of $7,500 or more! The recent
compilations by the U. S. Savings and Loan League, which I mentioned,
tell much the same story.

In 1957, a third of the houses financed with conventional savings and
loan mortgages were bought by families with incomes between $4,000 and
$6,000. Nearly two-thirds of the purchasers had incomes of less than
$8,000, and nearly three-fourths of the mortgages were made in amounts
less than $14,000.

The bulk of the recent buyers has been in the middle income ranges,
where it may be noted that government-sponsored mortgage programs
were most active. But the fact remains that home ownership — whether
viewed in respect to all owners or to recent buyers, or to government-
sponsored or conventional financing — is by no means distinctly a class
phenomenon. Certainly without the under-$5,000 income buyers, we
would not have much of a home-buying market or home-ownership
ratio.

At the same time, the data of both the Census and the Federal Reserve
show that the proportion of home owners in any income group varies
directly with the level of income. Breaking the total at $1,000 income
intervals, the Federal Reserve figures indicate that in each group below
$3,000 the proportion of home owners is about 50% of all households in
those classifications. As we move to groups above the $3,000 level, home
owners outweigh renters until, for families with incomes of more than
$10,000 a year, the home ownership ratio is well over 80%.

This circumstance provides ground for another assumption about the
future of the market. If the number of families in the higher income
ranges increases relative to the total and if the present ownership ratios

in these ranges persist, then we might expect some increase in the over-all ratio of home ownership.

Indeed, this could happen even under conditions of a decline in the rate of the total net increase in the number of households. Actually, this is what appears to have been happening over the past several years.

INCOME UPGRADING AND THE HOUSING MARKET

Throughout the postwar period there has generally been, year by year, an upgrading in income. Each year has brought a large number of families for the first time to the point where they could buy a house. It has carried many others, who were already home owners, to a point where they could contemplate buying a better house than the one they already owned.

This situation has given the market a new and great fluidity. It has proved an enormous stimulus not only to home buying, but also to home building. And it has made it possible for the so-called and much-abused filtering-down process really to serve as a means of increasing the supply of good housing for lower income families. The importance of this is shown by the fact that the proportion of buyers who purchase new houses varies directly with each step up in the income scale.

The extent of the phenomenon of income upgrading is revealed by estimates of the Department of Commerce, published in the *Survey of Current Business* for April, 1958. According to these figures, during the three-year period from 1953 through 1956 the total increase in the number of nonfarm families — individuals living alone or with unrelated persons excluded — is put at 2.6 million, or an average increase of about 860,000 a year. With that total, however, we find over the period a decrease of 450,000 families with less than $5,000 annual incomes on a constant-dollar basis and an increase of 3 million in the number of families with incomes of $5,000 or more. The average increase was about one million a year in the number of families with $5,000 or more of income.

Thus the increase in the total number of families in the "most likely to buy" segment of the housing market was actually 17% higher than the increase in the total number of families. Here, it seems to me, may be the main key to the future. It does seem possible that rising income, especially if it is accompanied by a substantial upgrading from the lower reaches of the scale, can prove to be in itself a force of sufficient strength to outweigh the effect of a static or even a declining over-all rate of growth in household formation. This circumstance, as I have said, may be the main key to the expansion of the demand for ownership in the period ahead, but it is not the only key. The process of upgrading has still another element of vital bearing on the market.

In a situation such as we have witnessed, and as we hope to continue to experience, families find themselves in a status where their desires, like their incomes, have been upgraded faster than their savings have increased. They find themselves in a position to maintain a higher standard of housing, but they may lack the wherewithal to launch it, at least in terms of ownership. In short, if they are to own as good a house as presumably they might afford on a rental basis, they must borrow — and they must often borrow substantially.

According to the Federal Reserve, 84% of recent buyers incurred mortgage debt in connection with the purchase of their houses. This situation does not seem to vary much from one income range to another. If anything, families in the upper income ranges may more often purchase subject to a mortgage than those in the lower brackets. However, this fact may reflect, more than anything else, the greater difficulty incurred by lower income families in meeting the credit or property requirements imposed by the lender of the mortgage insurance agency.

I may note that another of the facts revealed by the Savings and Loan League study is that a conventional lender is more apt to take care of the low-income and very small house buyer than is the lender who is using the FHA or VA program.

It also appears to be true that differences in family incomes are not strikingly reflected in differences in the ratio of debts incurred to the value of the property bought. The most outstanding exceptions are at the extremes on the income scale where, for the very low, credit is harder to get and, for the very high, it may be needed less. Data on these matters are far from satisfactory; but all that we have adds to the conclusion that while credit may not be the motor in the home-ownership machine, and while it may not even be the fuel for the motor, it certainly is at the least the oil that makes it possible for the wheels to turn.

The Question of How Much Credit

How much credit may be needed is another matter. We could debate at length whether it takes an 80% or a 90% mortgage to produce an optimum market; or whether it takes the 100% loan to value ratio now possible with the veterans' guaranteed home-loan plan; or something in between. There is no settled answer to this, and in the course of the argument we are apt to get into the morality as well as the economics of the situation and that confuses the issue even more.

Whether or not people ought to borrow as heavily as many do, the fact remains that they pay off their debts whether or not they borrow heavily. Losses to date under the veterans' guaranteed home-loan plan, where the loan to value ratios have been the highest, have been only 0.06% of the amount of mortgages guaranteed. The same figure is true for the FHA one- to four-family mortgage program, although the figures are on a different basis. The FHA loss ratio is calculated after all possible recovery is made through resale, and the VA ratio is calculated before such recovery. While it may rightfully be said that neither of these systems has faced a severe test, the lesser tests of 1948 and 1954 did not greatly affect the rate.

Plainly, the tendency is to pay and not to default, irrespective of the meagerness of the buyer's monetary stake. And with regular amortization now practically universally established, it will undoubtedly take a most violent and prolonged recession to produce a mortgage disaster even remotely resembling that of the 1930s.

As evidence of the strength of the ownership structures as a whole, we may observe that although nearly 85% of those who bought houses between 1954 and 1956 incurred mortgage debt, only 42% of those who had bought prior to 1956 were still making mortgage payments. About half of all owner-occupied houses carried no mortgage debt of any kind.

I shall not try further to reduce whatever qualms you may have over the size or incidence of the mortgage debt. If the system is not as safe as it reasonably needs to be, we should of course devise means for avoiding unnecessary difficulty. But when all is said and done, we remain face to face with the apparent fact that generous credit has played an essential part in the rapid expansion of home ownership since 1940. I leave you with the strong presumption that generous credit will be required to produce a further expansion, or perhaps even to maintain the ownership ratio at its present record level.

To me the data which are available to us, and which I have sketchily displayed here, support my thesis that a rising level of income and a liberal infusion of credit provide the elements most necessary to an increase in home ownership. It seems obvious, too, that these elements can be effective only up to a point unless basic growth is also taking place. I wish to emphasize that what I have said is thesis and not fact, and again I solicit your further explorations.

Future of the Home-Ownership Ratio

In fairness to you, I presume it would be appropriate to tell you how I put together the elements in this equation, the result of which will be the future of the home-ownership ratio. I assure you that any effort of mine to do so will not be in the form of a neatly arranged mathematical symbol carrying precise values and leading up to a precise answer. There will be none of what Mr. Hauser referred to as high positive correlation. What I may offer will be a judgment based on an analysis of insufficient and not wholly dependable data, mixed with a distillation of such experience as I have had in the business.

First, I think we are safe in assuming that a reduction in home ownership is unlikely, either in the present economic situation or, say, during the next ten years. Historically, a reduction has occurred only in company with a severe depression and has resulted mainly from forced selling, either in fear of or actually under mortgage foreclosure.

Today, the universality of the practice of regularly amortizing mortgage debt diminishes greatly the prospect of forced liquidation even in the midst of a fairly severe business decline. So far, the present recession gives no indication of being severe enough to disturb very markedly the steady flow of mortgage remittances. According to the latest reports, delinquencies on home mortgage payments as yet have not shown a noteworthy increase. This is almost as true for a community of high unemployment, such as Detroit, as it is for more happily situated areas.

The Mortgage Bankers Association, if I may refer to another notable trade association, produces a delinquency study correlation — which is one of the few studies of this sort in the field — broken down by conventional loans on one- to four-family houses, by FHA loans and by VA loans. The last report was for the first quarter of this year. It did show a slight upturn since December, but it still showed a lower rate of delinquencies than was true in 1954. In the conventional area the payments were still just as they had been, and the same was essentially true for the FHA area. Most of the increase in delinquency — and, as I said, it was still very small — was in the VA sector.

There is, moreover, no change in immediate prospect that would tend to modify consumer attitudes toward home ownership. The urge for suburban living, where home ownership is especially concentrated, is still strong. And the current highway program will greatly augment the amount of land available for suburban development.

Both credit and tax structures are biased in favor of ownership as compared with rental occupancy and of building for sale as compared with building for rent. Of the approximate million new dwellings to be built in 1958, the great bulk, probably at least 85%, will be built for sale to home buyers. And it may be noted that of the half-million dwellings likely to be demolished, probably the greater number will have been rental units.

Looking further ahead, some changes in the composition of metropolitan areas which would affect the ownership-rental relationships are possible. It seems inevitable that in time suburban dispersion will reach its practical limits and that a new recentralization may get underway. Such a movement is likely to have its greatest first appeal to childless couples in both the lower and upper ranges of the age scale. This circumstance, combined with the obvious difficulties of building houses for sale in close-in locations, may eventually tend to turn the balance toward more rental accommodations. Or it may result in the development of other types of ownership than a single dwelling or an individual plot of ground.

Already the cooperative ownership of apartment buildings has made considerable headway. While we have no information about the number of cooperative units, we do know that in 1950 there were about one million owner-occupied units in structures built for three or more families. This group, of course, included the cooperatives and is probably much larger today than in 1950. Even in the close-in areas, therefore, there may be a countervailing force working to maintain the ownership ratio.

Nevertheless, as I said earlier, a 60% ratio is high and we may be reaching the feasible limits for expanding home ownership. Certainly we must expect the rate of increase in the ratio to decline far below the dramatic trend it followed from 1940 to 1957. Furthermore, if continued expansion is to take place, we must contemplate some changes in the characteristics of the families who will be the future purchasers. As pointed out, there will be a diminishing number of heads of households in the age groups that up to now have provided the most active group of buyers.

My present conclusion is that, all things considered, we shall continue to have a moderate increase in the ownership ratio over the next several years. I doubt, however, that the total will rise much, if any, over 65% by 1965.

I leave to your critical review the questions of whether or not my analysis holds water and of how much water it holds. I want to repeat to you my invitation — indeed, my earnest plea — that you interest yourselves and your students in this area of study. The field is open. The workers are far too few and can consider themselves little more than pioneers. The opportunities for original contributions are numerous, and I hope you will find the area alluring.

Discussion*

THEODORE SMITH: Is it your statement that our annual housing budget had increased 53% and our cost of housing about 95 or 97%?

MR. COLEAN: Yes, except that the study referred to an estimated "annual housing budget" rather than to "income."

MR. SMITH: What impact will this have if that ratio continues and even

* Proceedings of the First Annual Conference, 1958, Excerpts from the Discussion, pp. 85–88.

becomes more pronounced in the future? Are we pricing ourselves out of the market, and has this liberal credit made it possible for these prices to get distorted?

Mr. COLEAN: There is no question in my mind but that the exceptionally easy credit in the early postwar period contributed to the price rise. It was an extremely inflationary thing. It did get a lot of houses built, but it got them built faster than the industry really could supply them without an inflationary impact on both labor and material costs. I think there has been some change in that; at least we brought it to a halt.

WILLIAM ROSS: In this same connection, would you not agree that the key to the future of housing — the housing industry — is going to be in large part whether or not it can produce the house that a broader group of the population can afford to buy?

A second part of the question: Is there any valid implication in certain developments that the public is now ready to accept a product that is perhaps of reasonable quality but with far less space and with less chrome plate than they had dreamed about? The average American had the idea of a 100-foot lot and a house that was to have ample space and all of the gadgets and so forth. Is there any implication for housing in the present market for the imported small automobile — for example, the Volkswagen? Can we say that the market for homes may also be changing and that there may now be a real place for the manufacture of prefabricated houses?

Mr. COLEAN: I don't think the answer is in the prefabricated house. For some reason or other, prefabricators are having their cost problems, too, and many follow this same process of upgrading quality. Many builders this year are apparently testing the market for lower-priced homes.

There will be a survey published by the Home Builders Association in the next week or so which will give the views of what builders' plans are for this year, and that is one of the things we will find out.

Mr. ROSS: You don't think the prefab house still has potentiality?

Mr. COLEAN: I think it has potentiality, but so does the trailer, for that matter.

RICHARD RATCLIFF: If prefabs have no great promise, in your opinion, are there any other changes in technology in terms of materials that appear to have promise in the reasonably near future?

Mr. COLEAN: Don't misunderstand me. I don't want to write off the prefabs. I don't really feel competent to answer that.

Mr. RATCLIFF: Shifting to another subject — to the subject of trading in older houses on new ones — this is a practice to which the industry has given a lot of attention. Do you think that this will be a factor having any impact?

MR. COLEAN: I think it is a spreading device, and one of the proposals in the housing legislation yet to be enacted this year is a provision that would facilitate the trade-in process by eliminating one set of closing costs.

JAMES LONGSTREET: During the last eight years the cost of carrying consumer credit has gone up from 10% of personal income to 15%. What effect do you think this will have on the willingness and ability to assume mortgage debt?

MR. COLEAN: I think home buying has been under very serious competition with everything else that people wanted. Particularly in this early postwar period, when there was a great demand for all kinds of things and many new products were being introduced, there was competition. I think, however, today we have the reverse of that. The amount of installment credit is declining. I think it is a great opportunity, as a matter of fact, for the builders and for those who are interested in remodeling and refurbishing older houses to get in and take advantage of the vacuum that is being created.

ROLAND STUCKI: Over a period of years we have been gradually lengthening the life of our mortgage contracts. How far can we go in this direction? The law permits mortgages up to as high as thirty years. Have we reached the maximum?

MR. COLEAN: I don't know. Eddie Edward's great statesman from Indiana, Senator Capehart, once made the remark that he saw nothing wrong with a 50-year mortgage. But neither Eddie nor the Senator has been able to achieve that yet.

EDWARD EDWARDS: The trend is in that direction, sir.

MR. COLEAN: However, the average pay-off, even on the thirty-year mortgage, is in the neighborhood of ten to twelve years.

JAMES GILLIES: There is a great concentration of population in our metropolitan areas which will send prices of land up. What makes you think that housing prices are going to stay the same?

MR. COLEAN: I am talking about this year.

MR. GILLIES: To generalize, don't you have to put a statement regarding housing costs into your equation that rising levels of income plus an infusion of credit mean more home ownership? This will be true only if housing prices stabilize.

MR. COLEAN: Don't forget that, as Professor Hauser outlined for you this morning, there is a lot of available land that can come into use as a result of a new highway program, land that could not be reached by rail commutation. That land is still virgin and can be serviced fairly economically.

18

Another Look at Some Factors in Determining Housing Volume*

Nathaniel H. Rogg is director of the Economics Department of the National Association of Home Builders. Mr. Rogg earned his bachelor's and master's degrees at New York University; he also holds a doctor of laws degree from George Washington University. He is a member of the Business Research Advisory Council, Bureau of Labor Statistics, and a member of the Housing and Construction Statistics Advisory Committee, Bureau of the Census. Formerly he was an economist and statistician with various agencies of the federal government.

MY OBJECTIVE TODAY IS QUITE SIMPLE. I want to emphasize the need for re-examining the traditional thinking in the field of housing markets. I should like to suggest that a reappraisal of the factors involved in an analysis of these housing markets is essential, not only in the light of many changes that have already taken place, but also in the light of changes that are in the making today.

In recent years I have worked closely with home builders — or, more accurately and less romantically, with men in the business of building homes. I had many preconceptions about them when I first went to work with them. Some of these, time has strengthened; others, experience has eroded; and some, common sense has led me to dispense with completely. Later, I shall tell you something about builders which a recent survey has disclosed.

Anyone who deals with housing ends up fascinated, even obsessed, with the subject. Its fundamental importance to society and the economy,

* Proceedings of the Third Annual Conference, 1960, pp. 31–49.

and its political appeal, invest it with a mystic attraction from which few observers ever recover. I have had a wonderful vantage point from which to watch, participate in, and mull over the happenings in one of the really important industries in our country; and I hope to share with you some of the things I have observed. While I plan to try to be objective, I do not claim to have been completely unaffected by participation in these events.

Housing economics is a frustrating business — as frustrating as it is rewarding. There are no ready answers, and we have more experts — more or less — over less solid data than in almost any other area of our economy. This is perhaps why they venture to be experts. The inadequacy of the data gives everyone an excuse for being unacquainted with what little there is, and the inadequacy of our vocabulary in the field makes for all kinds of semantic confusion.

In the last generation probably no industry in America, outside of politics — which I now classify as a kind of industry — has spawned more conferences and fewer solutions than have housing and home building. Sharing the confusion seems to be a major product of most of these conferences. In fact, most of us in the field are like the blind man and the elephant. Each of us speaks with absolute authority on the minor part of the beast which we have been privileged to touch. So it is a rope, a tree, a wall, a fan, a snake.

Basically, American home building today is really an industry in flux, set out against an economy in a high stage of development and of mass consumption. Both the supply side and the consumption side of the equation have undergone vast changes; and even greater ones, in my opinion, are in the making. Much of the analytical framework we have used to discuss housing markets in the past seems to have missed the point, because it is pegged to a situation no longer existing.

Originally it was suggested that I talk on the subject of housing demand. That is a rather broad topic, so I have narrowed it down somewhat. I am going to concern myself with some of the factors which influence the volume of new construction and to concentrate on certain of them with which I have had particular and specific experience in recent years. Although I shall touch on the broad secular movements, I shall necessarily concentrate on the shorter-term movements.

TRADITIONAL FACTORS IN HOUSING DEMAND

The factors affecting housing markets which we usually think of as vital in the field are:

Population and changes therein.

General economic conditions, consumer income and assets.

Housing prices and costs.

State of the existing supply, vacancies and removals from supply.

Credit availability and cost, and, within this, government actions affecting housing directly and indirectly, including those affecting credit availability.

Consumer preferences.

The building industry.

Others can be added, but all of them in some form or another make up everyone's "best-item list." Let us examine just a few of these items.

First, our population, its composition and changes. Over the last forty-five years, as Chart 1 shows, new home building volume has very closely paralleled year by year the net change in our population. Let the demographers make the guesses on population, this chart seems to say, and the problem is solved; there is no need to worry about residential construction any more.

Actually, part of the problem in using population figures is that of definition. For example, by definition a household is an occupied dwelling unit. So, in the sense that as population change seems to forecast household formation over a period of time, it is in essence also forecasting the gains in housing supply. Yet, even within the population factor, there

Chart 1

Nonfarm Housing Starts and Population Trends

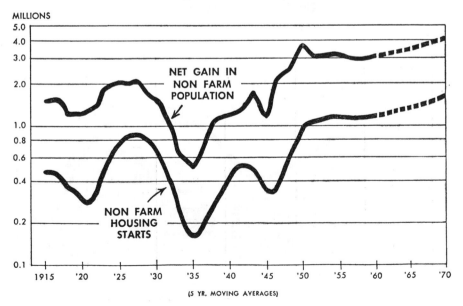

(5 YR. MOVING AVERAGES)

are many variables. Along with such factors as internal migration, changes in family size and so on, there are other factors in the next decade's population itself which are pitfalls in depending upon a forecast of housing related solely to population.

Chart 2 carries the population projection over the next ten years. This shows a mixed-up kind of increase in population as the low birth rate of the depression years has its effect upon the number of people who will be reaching the ages of 35 to 45 years in the next decade. In fact, despite large increases in population, there will be fewer people 30 to 45 years of age at the end of the decade than there were at the beginning. These are the people who are basically in the home buying market. So population increase alone, particularly in the next ten years, is going to generate serious problems and will offer some real difficulties in our housing analysis.

One of my missions in recent years has been to attempt to disabuse home builders and related industries of the widely held belief that the population explosion of the 1960s is a guarantee of automatic prosperity. It is going to be hard to do, because everybody in the business has been sold on the notion that the "sizzling sixties" are going to be years of automatic prosperity. I think economists have something to atone for in much that we have said during the years leading into the 1960s.

Chart 2

The Housing Ages of Man

Age Distribution, 1960 and 1970

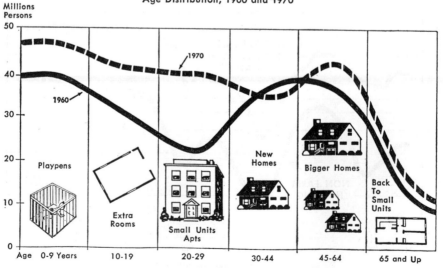

*Source: Bureau of the Census

The Bulk of the Homebuyers

Let us turn to another factor — interest rates. Chart 3 compares non-farm housing starts with interest rates; one adjustment we made here was to advance the interest rates by five months. This chart would seem to say that all you have to do is to forecast interest rates for the period ahead and your housing volume estimate falls pretty much in line. This is more easily said than done and is, in its own way, self-defeating; as you

Chart 3

Housing Production and Money Market Rates

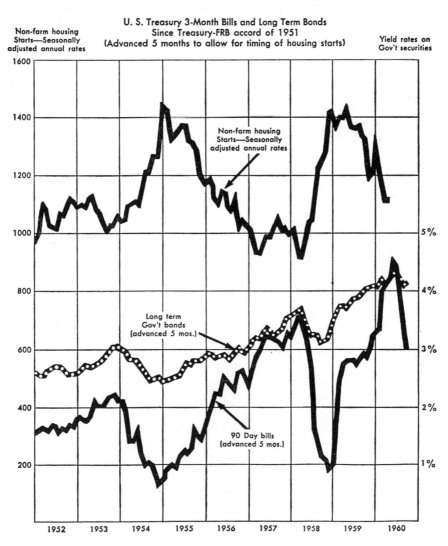

all know, one would fare better trying to forecast housing volume than trying to forecast interest rates.

Another theory holds that the use and price of the existing inventory play a vital role in the level of new building — that when the inventory is used intensively, charges for that use rise and we then get factors favorable for building. Oddly enough, some local market studies have indicated rather high vacancy rates in localities which have had a high volume of home building, and particularly high vacancy rates in the lower-priced, less desirable types of housing. This is an inverse picture: A high volume of home building makes it possible to have a high disuse, if you will, of the inventory.

Others have examined the role of government housing programs.

I am not going into any more detail about these individual factors, except the three I want to concentrate on. The great plethora of factors, however, that undoubtedly play some part in the housing market inevitably brings us again to the blind man and the elephant. Most people analyzing the great "beast" report on it in terms of their own experiences, not to say biases. I suspect, too, that the "animal" is changing faster than we can accumulate and digest our knowledge of it. Nevertheless, I shall discuss the "elephant" as my own sense of touch enables me to know it.

INADEQUACIES IN THE HOUSING DATA

Before doing so, I want to comment on the data we have in the housing field. They are among the poorest of all our major national statistics.

Fortunately, the best known series, *Housing Starts,* is now being recast at the Bureau of the Census. Census has finally obtained from the Congress more funds for its statistical compilation than has hitherto been available. Also, the Bureau will soon announce a new housing series which will probably raise the over-all housing level by 10% to 20% — somewhere close to the level of understatement suggested by the Housing Census of 1950 and by the National Housing Inventory of 1956.

On credit flows into housing we get some pretty good figures from the Federal Home Loan Bank Board, but they are not adequate because they do not cover the whole field. We know very little about some of the other areas — construction loans, household formation and removals from supply.

All the data we have are subject to considerable discount in terms of coverage, accuracy, and timeliness. But in all fairness I should hasten to make it clear that in my opinion the data inadequacies are not the fault of the agencies charged with their compilation. They stem primarily from an unwillingness on the part of all of us engaged in the field, and of the Congress as well, to make funds available for the collection and compilation of data on a sound basis. As a matter of fact, it is rather surprising, under the circumstances, that so much good work has been done with such poor data. And I suppose it really is not quite so bad as I say; otherwise we would know somewhat less than nothing about the field.

I want to examine in particular the importance of three of the factors I enumerated earlier as affecting home building volume: the role of the government, changing consumer preferences and the role of the industry. None of them is independent of the others; they all have some effect on one another. And they all need to be considered in the light of major postwar changes in our economy.

The Federal Government's Role

At the same time, very great changes have been taking place in housing. Prior to the 1930s, the federal government played practically no role in the housing field. States played some role but their responsibility was limited largely to regulating certain types of mortgages and lenders. The 1930s saw major legislation providing for the Federal Home Loan Bank System, the insurance of savings and loan accounts and FHA mortgage insurance, followed by the VA program for returning servicemen, major changes in the secondary mortgage market, the establishment of the Housing and Home Finance Agency, a vast undertaking in the field of urban renewal, and a whole conglomeration of other programs.

Certainly the housing scene could never again be the same. Moreover, the Congress made a commitment in the Housing Act of 1949, reaffirmed in somewhat different language in the Act of 1954, to involve itself in housing thenceforward.

How many of you know the preamble to the 1949 Act, which states very simply: "The Congress hereby declares that the general welfare and security of the nation and the health and living standards of its people require . . . the realization as soon as feasible of the goal of a decent home and a suitable living environment for every American family. . . ."

This commitment has on numerous occasions run head on into other government policies concerned with fiscal and monetary problems and has frequently not come off too well. The years 1955–1956 are fair examples of that, I believe.

Chart 4 compares housing starts and the general level of economic activity for the past decade, as reflected in the industrial production index. It seems to make a classic demonstration of the fact that housing is a lead industry, that it precedes the economy on both the downswing of recession and the upswing of recovery, and that it fluctuates more than economic activity generally. This is a textbook picture of the

Chart 4

Industrial Production and Housing Starts

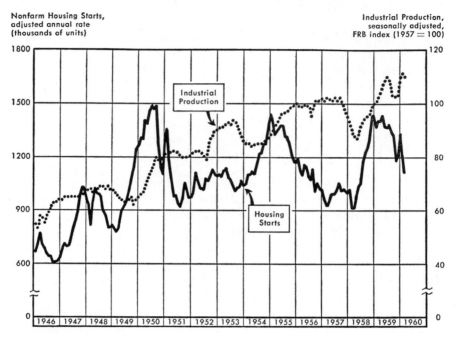

Nonfarm Housing Starts,
adjusted annual rate
(thousands of units)

Industrial Production,
seasonally adjusted,
FRB index (1957 = 100)

industry; yet it is rather misleading, I think. Most of the important movement of the housing starts line is traceable, not to any fluctuations which seem to be inherent in the free-market nature of our home building economy, but to some action of the government which resulted in depressing or raising the level of housing starts — some action by Congress, by the executive branch, by the fiscal and/or monetary and fiscal authorities.

CONVENTIONAL VERSUS GOVERNMENT-UNDERWRITTEN LOANS

One of the concepts gaining hold in recent years is that the government programs are the main source of instability in housing. Chart 5 would seem to support this contention; it indicates that the conventionally financed sector of home building starts shows relatively little fluctuation, while the FHA and GI sectors show relatively great fluctuation. For example, in the housing recession of 1956-57, practically all the loss was in the GI program, which declined by close to a quarter of a million units in two years, plus some decline in FHA starts. Ergo, the conclusion that follows is: Kill these programs and there will be some stability in the

Chart 5

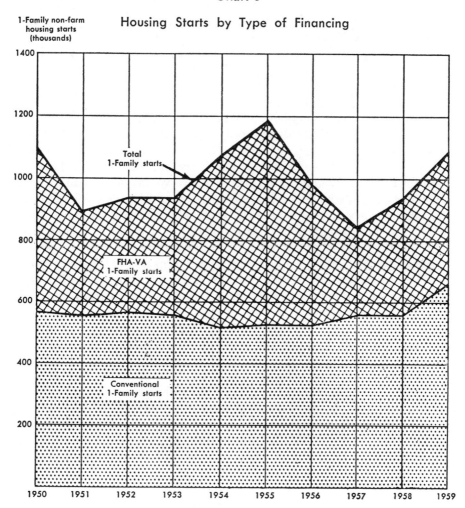

1-Family non-farm
housing starts
(thousands)

Housing Starts by Type of Financing

housing. Well, maybe. We had stability of that kind in the early 1930s, but it was more like the stability of the grave. I think none of us here would want to see that kind of stability again.

Actually, as we move into the decade of the 1960s, it is apparent that the government programs of mortgage insurance and guarantee have been playing a far less prominent role in the housing field. In 1955 the FHA and GI programs accounted for about half of all housing starts, and by 1958 they had dropped to about 27%. They were up somewhat in 1959, reflecting largely the Fanny May Special Assistance Program, which was a one-year emergency program; but I think they will be down again in 1960. In fact, much of the anticipated decline in 1960 housing starts will be in the moderate-priced sales-type units built particularly in the South and West under these government programs.

There are a number of reasons for the decline of the FHA and GI programs. They worked very well in stimulating construction in the immediate postwar period and in periods of credit ease, when there were large sums of investable capital to be put to work. Conditions are changing, however. Throughout much of the 1960s it is likely that capital funds will be in relatively short supply. In their present form, the FHA and GI programs, particularly with fixed interest rates, will be considerably less attractive to investors; I think the recent record bears that out.

So far as these programs are concerned, we would do well to explore other methods of stimulating home ownership and housing volume than the familiar ones of lengthening the term and lowering the down payment. The additional benefit of lower monthly payments to be obtained from lengthening the term is small. The difference between the monthly payment per $1,000 at 6% on a thirty-year term and a forty-year term is only 49 cents a month. Putting another ten years at the end of a forty-year contract cuts only an additional 24 cents a month from the total monthly payment per $1,000.

The increasing volume of conventional loans in recent years points up this fact. In 1959, over 900,000 units of housing starts were financed through conventional means — nearly 50% more than the volume of five years earlier and an increase of about 160,000 over 1958. That is fine, except for one thing, which I shall mention and pass over quickly: I am afraid there may have been recourse in some of this conventional lending to unsound financing practices. A movement toward second mortgages, contracts for deed and the like, which are subject to tremendously high discounts in the market and which have in many cases much higher interest rates than the first mortgage itself, is not good.

It is a mistake to assume that the government programs are going to stay in their present form. In the next few years I think we can expect some concerted efforts to modify them. Senator Sparkman has introduced legislation which may involve the government much more deeply in housing than it now seems to be under the FHA and GI programs. So I think any effort to maintain these programs in their present form is going to run into solid political and economic realities.

THE INCREASING ROLE OF LOCAL GOVERNMENTS

So far, much of this discussion has been confined to the changing role of the federal government. There is a very large role in the making by local governments, a role which arises because of limitations inherent in our present forms of local government, as well as in the manner in which they operate on the housing scene. The forms of local government which served so well in this country from the founding of the republic are simply inadequate for the problems ahead in the second half of the 20th century. One of the major problems we face as we go ahead in the housing field arises from the frustrating limitations of the current forms of local government.

Local actions affect local home buying in the fields of zoning, planning, community facilities, taxation and building codes, to say nothing of the more direct programs such as urban renewal and highways. In many cases they decide what can be built, where it can be built, what price classes will prevail, and whether there will be any building at all in some areas. Because of the shortage of usable land, these actions of local governments throughout the nation are of prime importance in any local home building market. We could profitably spend an entire session on this particular problem. However, I can merely indicate here that they are going to be increasingly important factors in the whole determination of housing volume in this country.

Consumer Spending and Prefaces

What about the consumer and his preferences? Studies by Grebler, Blank and Winnick, in their invaluable *Capital Formation in Residential Real Estate,* show a secular decline in the proportion of consumer expenditures going for housing. While the authors suggest that some of the decline may represent a transfer of expenditures from shelter to household operations, and thus may reflect problems in definition of terms, at the same time they conclude that the long-term trend in housing expenditures has been downward.

In Chart 6 we have endeavored to depict that trend. In 1909, about one-fifth of every consumer dollar went for housing; in 1959, only about one-eighth. There has been some improvement in the past decade — about a 20% gain since 1949. This undoubtedly reflects the high volume of single-family postwar home building. If the industry, in its over-all competition for consumer spending, can do as well to improve its position in the 1960s as it did during the 1950s, we may well see a volume of new housing far in excess of the volume needed merely to meet our shelter needs, and a higher proportion of the consumer dollar going into housing.

One of the problems, as we move into the field of consumer expenditures, is whether it is important that we spend as much for our housing in a more highly developed society as we spent in much earlier periods.

One theory holds that in the early stages of economic development most of the consumer income is spent for basic necessities. The figures for the early 1900s bear this out. At that time about two-thirds of our con-

Chart 6

Housing's Share of the Consumer Dollar

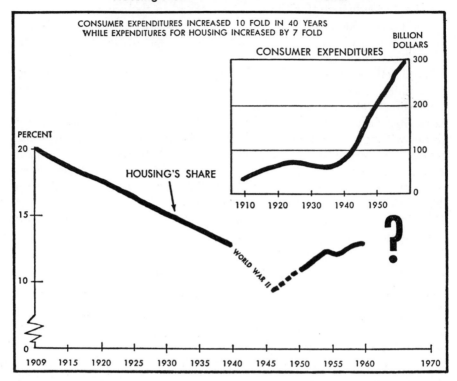

CONSUMER EXPENDITURES INCREASED 10 FOLD IN 40 YEARS
WHILE EXPENDITURES FOR HOUSING INCREASED BY 7 FOLD

sumer spending was for food, clothing, and shelter. Today about half of it is for these essentials. This may well be a reflection of basic changes on the American scene rather than a reflection of housing's failure to get what some people call housing's "fair share" of the consumer dollar — a concept I do not particularly care for.

Further changes in housing expenditures lie ahead. The trends of the last ten years should have a definite effect: the trends toward home ownership, toward additional equipment in the home and the acceptance of "built-ins" in the home mortgage package, and toward two-bathroom homes. In 1950, nine houses out of ten had one bathroom; today, only one house in three is built with one bathroom. The increased use of air conditioning, the development of garden and patio amenities, better design and better materials are all symptomatic of an emerging change that is affecting the volume of consumer dollars going into the house.

Another factor, and one that I think is very much underrated at the moment, is the possibility of developing a second-house or seasonal-house market. According to some estimates we have made, if in the next decade only one family per year out of fifty in the $10,000-and-over income bracket obtained a second house, it could increase the market by 100,000 units a year.

To the economic forces we must add the fact that housing is much more than simply an economic concept. It has psychological and social meanings which, in turn, affect its economic importance. Some years ago the Survey Research Center, in an examination of the housing motivations, concluded: "In brief, there now exists upgrading needs of such magnitude that they represent an important additional element in the housing market." Their study revealed that one-third of all home owners and two-thirds of the renters were dissatisfied with their current homes. In short, one of the important elements in the housing markets of the future is the desire of the American people to have a better place to live.

Dr. Robert Turner of Indiana University, in speaking to this group last year, put it very well: "For many men, the instinct for creativity and the desire for recognition both find their expression in a house — a man's monument to himself. . . . People become much more emotionally attached to a house than to any other object of ownership. They will make investments of time and money in a house that are uneconomic by any rational standard."

NATURE OF THE BUILDING INDUSTRY

Let us turn now to the home building industry itself and what it can do to affect these consumer preferences.

Unfortunately, most of the theoretical work in the field of housing demand has examined housing from the viewpoint of the role of the ultimate consumer — the so-called demand side of the equation. Relatively little attention has been paid by economists to the industry which produces the product and the industry's effect on its own market. By and large, it has been assumed that production capacity will be there to meet the housing demand which a mysterious set of forces has somehow or other generated among puppetlike consumers who respond to temperature changes in the demand climate.

Now, I do not mean that the decision-making process by the industry is ignored in these theories of demand. But usually it is examined as the responses of the industry or of builders' organizations to their estimates of demand changes and prospects for profit, rather than on the basis of what the industry can do to change those markets. Actually, it comes as a shock to anybody who deals with the day-to-day problems of this industry that so little attention is being paid to what the industry itself can do to affect its market.

Let me make it clear that when I talk about the industry I am not talking merely about the people who put the house together. I am referring to the whole complex of factors engaged in providing that house, and I include in this concept the material producers and distributors and the financing institutions in addition to the builders. In fact, the builder is increasingly becoming an end-product assembler. He puts together a package, including the land and the materials — which more and more are being factory-produced, and then assembled on that land, according to plot and plan, by labor forces. He may also arrange the financing. This is the package you have to visualize.

In essence, this complex process is not yet fully understood, even by those engaged in putting the package together — the builders themselves. They play what I call a major market-generating role, the full potential of which is barely understood today but which will be even greater in the housing markets of tomorrow. It may seem inconsistent to emphasize the market-generating role of the industry in an era in which admittedly the choices will be made by a consumer who has many discretionary choices, who may already be adequately housed and who has no major compulsion, in terms of shelter alone, to spend more for his housing. To me this is not an inconsistency, for what I am talking about is the industry's role in influencing that consumer to modify his preferences.

It is impossible to analyze the housing market intelligently without recognizing the part played in helping to make that market, not only by builders, but also by lenders such as the savings and loan folks.

The savings and loan business finds its main outlet in the housing market. This particular financing group has grown from $6 billion in savings capital in 1930 to some $55 billion in 1960, and has its sights set on double that amount in the next ten years. A vital factor in that growth has been a trade association under very vigorous leadership; make no mistake as to the power and influence of that combination. It has not been supremely passive to outside forces, but has had much to do with shaping both the public acceptance and the legislation which have made this growth possible. And in the process of achieving that ninefold growth, savings and loan leaders have unquestionably had some influence in shaping and expanding the markets in which they operate.

The home building industry has changed vastly in the postwar decade and is going to change even more in the next ten years. We are, in effect, getting poised for a take-off as the results of research, new financing developments and the cooperative interest of all the segments of the industry become focused on common problems. In recent years, builders have begun to think of themselves in these broader terms.

Look at the industry as it was twenty-five or thirty years ago. It was essentially handicraft, and dominated by small-scale builders. The financing came from local small-scale lenders, and very frequently the buyer arranged his own financing. Major suppliers and producers had little concern with housing as a major natural market. Even by the end of the war the industry had changed very little. In 1946, *Fortune* magazine called home building the "industry that capitalism forgot." I think it was a fair charge.

You are well acquainted with some of the postwar changes in the financing area. Many of the postwar studies, including excellent ones by Klaman, Saulnier and Ratcliff, have dealt with them. Now, how about the suppliers and material producers?

Perhaps the most significant change in the last few years has been the awakening of large industrial corporations to the markets that could be available for them in housing. Companies such as Du Pont, Alcoa, Kaiser, Reynolds, Weyerhauser, American Standard, Owens-Corning, U. S. Plywood, and many others exemplify this recent and major revolution in the American understanding of the significance, actual and potential, of home building as a major market for their products.

It is this awakening of interest on the part of such industries that makes me most hopeful of major changes in the next decade. Bringing their vast corporate resources to bear on research into the problems of better and less expensive ways to build, to utilize land and even to finance, adds a much-needed dimension to the home building picture. In seeking a profitable outlet for their productive resources, they cannot but help to increase the home building market potential.

PROFILE OF THE HOME BUILDER

Now, what of the builder in this changing picture? As I have mentioned, the builder has changed markedly in the last decade. He is becoming more of a businessman; he has moved away from the role of a small-scale artisan building one or two houses a year and has become interested in merchandising and in market development — major revolutions, as anyone who has watched the industry for years can attest. Through his trade association, he is investing money in research, in cooperative marketing, and in merchandising ventures with manufacturers. Going further, his trade association has also taken an active interest in problems of housing abroad and in the legislation which shapes the industry's markets.

We have just completed a major study of builders. Although it was undertaken to check the NAHB association services in relation to the members' needs, its by-products were immensely valuable. It is the most

comprehensive study ever made of builders, and we believe it to be
rather representative. Over 7,000 builders responded to our questionnaire, a 42% response from a mailing to 16,000 NAHB members. Chart
7 summarizes our findings.

Chart 7

Home Builders and Their Scale of Home Production

In 1959, NAHB members, over 16,000 of the nation's professional
home builders, built an estimated 950,000 housing units

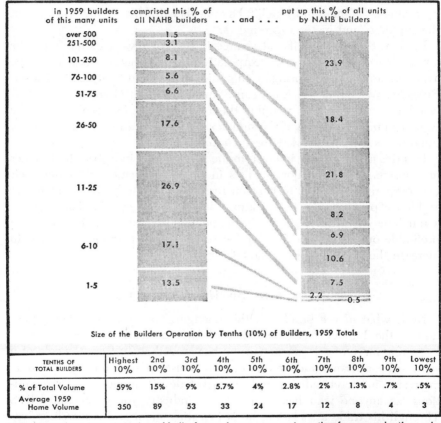

Size of the Builders Operation by Tenths (10%) of Builders, 1959 Totals

TENTHS OF TOTAL BUILDERS	Highest 10%	2nd 10%	3rd 10%	4th 10%	5th 10%	6th 10%	7th 10%	8th 10%	9th 10%	Lowest 10%
% of Total Volume	59%	15%	9%	5.7%	4%	2.8%	2%	1.3%	.7%	.5%
Average 1959 Home Volume	350	89	53	33	24	17	12	8	4	3

Note: Values have been derived graphically from a Lorenz curve and are therefore approximations only.

As businessmen, the builders are relatively young, with a 41-year
median age; the largest single group is between 30 and 39 years of age.
The typical builder had his homes professionally designed. He built
twenty units in 1959, and used model homes and other merchandising
measures to sell his houses. Three-quarters of the builders build in
subdivisions of their own; one-fourth build on scattered lots.

One of the most interesting, though not unexpected, disclosures was that most of the building was done by relatively few builders. For example, although the median builder put up twenty units, the arithmetic mean was sixty units per builder. About two-thirds of all the units were built by 20% of the builders. Half of the group accounted for 92% of the total; the other half accounted for only 8%.

As a group, the more than 7,000 builders who answered our questionnaire accounted for over 900,000 new units in 1959 and produced some $15 billion worth of sales and rental housing. The larger the builder, the lower the price class in which he operates.

One fact that fascinated us was that the builders reported their major problem as an industry to be the lack of suitable land. Many of us had believed it to be financing.

Through their trade association, the builders take considerable interest in legislation. They take a very large interest, as some of you know, in monetary and fiscal policy, in the operations of the government agencies, in other trade associations in the field, in research and in community planning. In their trade association, they have departments working on the problems of merchandising and marketing. They work with planning groups, for they have come to realize that sound planning can mean better markets. They also are interested in better statistics and in education for home building, and are working with some of the universities on setting up courses leading to degrees in home building.

These interests are all a part of a decided interest in what I have called the builders' market-generating function; they are all a part of the new dimension in the home building markets. Much of this new dimension is still in the formative stage, but it is evident now and will be more so in years to come.

BETTER DEFINITION OF TERMS NEEDED

I should like to make a few suggestions as to definition of terms in the building field, for this is a real problem.

A while back I was asked to make an analysis of the home building potential in the years ahead. The first hurdle was one of definitions. We started with "housing needs," which in effect are estimates of basic requirements for adequate shelter and which involve figures, not only on population and households, but also changes in the housing supply at various time periods in the future, making allowances for removals as well as for renovation of older housing.

The next concept was "housing demand." We defined this term as estimates which modify the "needs" estimates by analyzing them in terms of projected available income and which result in estimates of the market demand which would exist at various income and housing price levels.

It was soon evident that these terms were barely adequate for any kind of analysis. So we tried to formulate another definition, a concept of what we called "housing market." We described this as a modification of "housing demand" by applying to it the qualifying factors of the price and terms at which housing is or could be made available, as well as the relative preference consumers give or can be influenced to give to housing in their personal consumption expenditures.

SHELTER NEEDS VERSUS MARKET POTENTIAL

In the immediate postwar period, housing need was in effect the outside limit in the market. For example, the so-called Taft Subcommittee on Housing and Redevelopment of the Senate Banking and Currency Committee made some studies toward the end of World War II and concluded in its report of August 1, 1945, that our shelter requirements were in excess of a million new units a year. No one thought the industry would quickly reach that level, so the figure was the outside limit of the total volume of home building to be expected. By the early 1950s, however, the problem had changed, because housing shortages were no longer a national factor. We have not satisfied all the housing needs in the country, particularly among the low-income and minority groups, but the housing markets today and in the foreseeable future can pretty well assume that need and shelter requirements are not an outside limiting factor as they were right after the war, but are really the market floor.

I think it is important to get away from the shelter-needs concept and to deal with housing as a market for businessmen. The housing market can vary not only with the basic shelter requirements but also with the importance one can persuade the consumer to place on the way he lives and with the kind of product the industry can produce to influence the consumer and with the terms on which that housing can be made available.

I do not mean to suggest that we can ignore the basic factors in housing markets, such as population, income, housing inventory, prices, and so on. My purpose today has been to focus attention on some factors which have not been given sufficient importance in appraising housing markets and their potential — specifically, the changing role of government, the problem of consumer preferences, the changes in the industry, and the interaction of these changes on the markets. I simply do not think we have yet developed a really usable theory of housing markets.

I have tried to avoid the term "demand" because I consider it inadequate to describe the housing complex in the American economy at its present advanced stage of development. It is for this reason that I urge talking about housing markets rather than about housing needs or demand.

Experience with the postwar housing markets has cast strong doubts on much of the accepted theoretical approaches and has pointed up in high relief the need for a more basic understanding of the market forces which are actually at work and which will be even more important in the housing field in the years ahead. Business economists ordinarily have little time to do the basic research and analysis out of which a satisfactory theory can be developed. But you people in the universities can do a great deal to enlarge our understanding of these processes. This is the challenge I leave with you.

Discussion*

HAROLD FRAINE: The cost of housing can be affected by whether or not we have intelligent building codes or, let us say, intelligent restrictions by labor or by the public. Is there any evidence that that is a factor today? If it is, has it improved over the last several decades or is it worse?

MR. ROGG: The problem of building codes, I think, is one of the knottiest problems in the building field, primarily because it is a problem that goes to the thousands of local governments all over the country. Considerable progress has been made in developing better model codes, but considerably less progress in getting them adopted.

For example, in a nearby state a uniform building code was developed and virtually all forty-one municipalities in one metropolitan area wanted to adopt it. It turned out, however, that under state law they could not adopt a building code by reference. They would have to print it, and this would cost somewhere in the neighborhood of $10,000 per printing. So they cannot go ahead with their plan unless they can get the state law changed.

There are handicaps all along the way. We know what a good code should be: we know that it should be basically a performance code rather than a specification code. So, in terms of theory, a great deal of work has been done; but in terms of adoption, relatively little progress has been made.

NATHAN BAILEY: Many of us assume that the building of residential housing is one of the few areas where a young man, with either guts or lack of common sense, whichever viewpoint you take, can borrow money and get ahead. Now, in terms of your survey, and recognizing that many people just getting started do not belong to the builders' association yet,

* Proceedings of the Third Annual Conference, 1960, Excerpts from the Discussion, pp. 50–56.

is this a fiction or is it true? Does a little man really have an opportunity to flourish in this business?

MR. ROGG: Yes, I think so. He might be out of his mind for going into the business, but the opportunities are there.

MR. BAILEY: Do you have any more detailed figures on builders that can be tied either to experience in the business or to the size of operation?

MR. ROGG: The only figures we have been able to put together on the subject are from the usual statistics at Dun and Bradstreet. They do not ordinarily separate out home building, but in one special analysis they concluded that the rate of bankruptcy among home builders is much greater than among the business population at large. The basic reason, in their very staid language, is "competitive weakness." I am not sure exactly what that means.

SHAW LIVERMORE: Is there any sentiment in your association for buying and scrapping the very worst housing, such as occurs in the automobile market and the appliance market, and not waiting for urban renewal to get rid of the worst fringes of bad housing? Could this be done cooperatively among the builders?

MR. ROGG: I wish it could. I think it would be an interesting move. Your question applies to cooperative ventures in local communities, which they have not been undertaking. It is an interesting idea.

LAWRENCE THOMPSON: Mr. Rogg, in speaking of the role of the builder as a packager, you mentioned his activities in putting together the ultimate financing for the home owner. He has also the problem of obtaining construction financing for himself. Many of us have thought that over the cycle one of the major problems the builder faces is obtaining financing — interim financing commitments, construction money, and ultimate financing for the purchaser.

Did your study take account, or raise the question, of the availability of funds to the builder in varying periods of monetary ease or tightness? In other words, did it bring out the pattern or shift in the availability or movement of funds from one source to another?

MR. ROGG: We did not go into any questions of availability of funds, but we did get into questions as to how builders do their financing. We found that 37% of our builders use commercial banks for construction financing and that this accounts for about 49% of all units. This means that typically the role of commercial banks is to provide the short-term production credit.

Savings and loan associations account for 40% of construction financing for builders, but they account for a smaller percentage of the total volume. Typically, when a builder finances with a savings and loan, he gets both his construction financing and his permanent financing there.

The patterns have not been very definite. There have been periods when long-term mortgage financing was not easy to get and other times when it was available but when builders found themselves unable to get construction financing. By and large, they tend to vary together, but at times during the last several years construction financing has been a sticky problem despite the fact that builders had permanent take-outs on home mortgages.

Mr. THOMPSON: So sticky that it affected the rate of construction?

Mr. ROGG: Yes, sir.

HAROLD FELDMAN: You have indicated that the building business is a very different business these days — that it has come a long way. Yet I am quite surprised that the offsite fabrication of major parts and erection of factory-built homes is such a small percentage of the total construction. Would you not say that the building industry on the whole has been rather slow in promoting associated research and development activities, as many other industries have done?

Mr. ROGG: May I answer your questions in inverse order? Yes, it has been very, very slow. This is the reason I emphasized the significance of a trade association. We are only fifteen years old as a trade group; that is the length of time builders have worked together as a group. We started our first research house only two years ago.

Large corporations suddenly realized that building is an outlet for their productive resources. This is a welcome development and there is a great push behind the movement. For example, I know full well that the large aluminum companies moved in on the aluminum markets in housing about three years ago with the notion that they would sell no appreciable amount of aluminum until maybe 1963 or 1964 and that until then they would be going through a research and development phase. But, unexpectedly, they are already selling aluminum in housing markets and are beginning to put even more money into research.

On the other question that you asked, in our survey 75% of the builders said they were using conventional construction methods generally. These builders put up 57% of the homes. This means that 43% of the homes are constructed using factory methods of some kind. I think it is phenomenal that as much as 43% of the houses were built using some fabricated components. This indicates a lot more than slow acceptance of this sort of thing.

One of the problems here, if I may conclude with this, is that of definition. Thirty or forty years ago the builder built practically everything on the site, even the doors and the kitchen cabinets. Now, he does not even think of such methods. He gets these components elsewhere as fabricated units; they have become so standard that they are stock items, bought from specialized companies that have developed good businesses out of them.

19

The Housing Market in the 1960s*

Walter E. Hoadley is vice president and treas-
urer of the Armstrong Cork Company; a member and deputy
chairman of the Board of Directors, Federal Reserve Bank of
Philadelphia; and an author and lecturer. He is a periodic adviser or consultant to the U. S. Department of Commerce, President's Council of Economic Advisers, Joint Economic Committee
of the U. S. Congress and other governmental agencies. Mr.
Hoadley earned his bachelor's, master's and doctoral degrees at
the University of California. He was formerly president, American Statistical Association; senior economist, Federal Reserve
Bank of Chicago; and member of or consultant to various governmental and private agencies.

UNFORTUNATELY, I WAS NOT ABLE TO BE HERE yesterday, but I have been
told you had some very interesting and significant discussions on many
of the subjects related to what I am going to talk about this morning. And
earlier today, Jim Duesenberry gave you, I think, a very significant back-
drop as to the problems associated with determining policy.

What I should like to do this morning is to consider with you some of
the broad implications of the housing market to see if we can penetrate
a little more deeply and understand the situation better than if we looked
at it just on the surface. We shall consider the question of growth and

* Proceedings of the Fourth Annual Conference, 1961, pp. 134–47.

348

some of the longer-range problems that confront the housing industry. Finally, I wish to comment on the attitude of the government at the moment, and the implications of the future government policies which are now in the process of formulation.

I think it is important at the outset to remind ourselves that in appraising any market, and certainly the housing market, we must go beyond the narrow sense of what we might define as supply and demand. We must go very definitely into the realm of government policy. Certainly few industries are subject to more government influence and control than the housing industry. I believe we must dare to go even further and consider some of the psychological problems associated with today's market.

These latter areas are, of course, difficult; and for anyone interested in economics to probe into them is perhaps extremely shortsighted, because the answers are not very clear. Nevertheless, we cannot appraise the market for housing unless we look at the house from the inside out, from the outside in, and from the standpoint of the scars that people have from previous policy decisions which they themselves have made or which other people have made for them.

Market Forecasting Is Precarious

In most industries it is difficult to project what is going to happen. Forecasting is indeed precarious. In the housing field the situation is compounded. We cannot even be sure where we have been, let alone where we are going. The statistical problem in housing, with which I am sure you are familiar, has been the source of great consternation for years. You will recall that in the middle of the last decade there was undertaken a housing inventory which suggested that the official statistics had understated the volume of postwar home building in the country by perhaps 20% or more. A little later, at the close of the decade, there were suggestions that the whole housing start series should be revised. Last year a revision did take place, and it confirmed the view that there had been an understatement of the volume of new housing. There was an increase of better than 10% in the adjustment from the old series to the new series.

When the 1960 housing census came through in something approaching a final form, the gap between the reported figures and the now official figures was narrowed still further. This may reflect a change in statistics, it may reflect simply the human tendency to round in the direction of previous error, or it may be simply the fact that the science of statistics is still far from accurate. In any event, we do know that a great many houses have been built in the last decade; and in all probability, because there was undercounting, more houses were built than were officially reported.

Many other areas of discrepancy exist. This is a common complaint of anyone appraising any market. We know very little about the size of the home improvement market; yet there are very interesting indications that this market is of enormous proportions. It may well provide the basis for a very high level of housing activity over the next several years, in contrast to a forward surge of any significant proportions in new housing construction.

We know very little about costs. Many of the financial figures are suspect because of incompleteness and matters of definition.

All this is important, because here is an industry where people are making decisions, presumably on the best information available. Yet, small changes in official statistics have in the past been considered the basis for making major decisions in policy. The industry as a whole does not seem to be terribly concerned about the data deficiencies because the people in it are not statisticians. They are concerned primarily that there simply be more housing of whatever type anybody wants. That this may not always be the best public policy, I am sure you will agree.

There is, of course, a very close relationship between the housing market and the financial market. We may not have too high a level of economic literacy in many parts of the country, but the average house-holder knows that money and housing go together — and, I might add, the average politician knows that, too. These are inseparable, and for that reason any discussion of the market must necessarily hinge to a very large degree on financial considerations. I assume, however, that because of your previous discussions on financial matters, we can today pass over lightly the purely financial side. I recognize that this may be a glaring omission.

One final observation as we develop the approach to this subject. In looking at housing, most people somehow tend to feel that the trend is a pretty relentless one. Basically there are cyclical problems, of course, but the industry is not likely to be subject to drastic changes, dramatic changes. I, personally, have a suspicion that we are going to see a great many changes affecting the housing market over the next decade or two, perhaps much more profound than generally might be suspected at the moment. But what are the dimensions of the housing market at the moment?

How Big Is the Housing Market?

In some of the comments earlier, the suggestion was made that the market has changed and caught up with some of the backlogs of demand. Housing is a very big market, variously estimated statistically in the neighborhood of $20 billion annually against a GNP in the neighborhood of $500 billion. You can take out of the blue any figure you want for repair and modernization; it is my feeling that such work amounts to a minimum of perhaps $10 billion and may even go as high as $20 billion. Add this to the housing total and you get another dimension on the market. Or you can take the housing market in its overall and broadest sense, and include the costs not only of new houses and maintenance, but all the equipment, furnishings, services, and so on. This way you can get a figure well over $100 billion, and housing begins to be quite a factor in the national economy. You might even compare the housing expenditures in the United States with the total economy of Great Britain and Germany, in order to get a perspective.

This is indeed big business. It is not surprising, therefore, that it is fraught with all sorts of public policy questions. It is also, I think, because housing appears to be so large that many people are concerned about it. It is a very dynamic market. Home ownership, of course, has been moving up, somewhere in the neighborhood of 60%. Yes, most people have a keen interest in housing. But it is very important that we recognize the distinction between quantitative measures of housing and qualitative measures.

In many respects we can say we have now reached a balance quantitatively between the units of housing available in the United States and the number of families needing something in the general nature of shelter. To stop the discussion at that point, however, is misleading. We have not, I think, any serious housing shortage quantitatively, but we certainly have a very distinct shortage qualitatively in America today.

When we consider the housing market, we ought to remind ourselves that we tend to think of new housing. Most of the public policy decisions concern the volume of housing starts, new home building. Yet in all probability we have fifty to sixty older houses or older housing units for every new house being built. This may be an important perspective quantitatively, but I think it is exceedingly important to look at the quality of that housing. From the recent census we have gained some information that confirms suspicions that the quality of American housing has improved quite definitely in the last ten years but that, by some generalized definition with which you may agree or disagree, there still was some physical deterioration affecting perhaps 20% of the housing stock of America.

THE "LIFE CYCLE" IN HOUSING

In looking at the current market, I believe it is extremely important to draw attention to what we call the life cycle in housing. Historically, families in all sections of the United States have tended to live in a

limited number of structures in their lifetime; but over the past generation, the mobility of the American population has increased tremendously.
All of us or most of us have been participating in this trend to some
degree.

People are now more inclined — by no means overwhelmingly inclined, but more inclined — to look upon a house as an investment for a
period of limited duration as opposed to an indefinite duration. Life cycle
takes on the connotation of the newlyweds moving, typically, not into
a new single-family home, but moving in with the in-laws — step number
one. As income rises, this undesirable state changes quickly or is avoided.
Next, the interest in individual housing rises very sharply in the year or
two years preceding the date when the first child enters kindergarten.
Then, except for mobility of employment and other considerations, there
is an element of stability as far as housing is concerned until the children
reach early teen-age. At this point there is a new demand for housing,
more specifically in terms of space and also of quality. Many families
across America are in this stage right now; queuing up for the bathroom
behind several daughters is a bit of a problem.

THE DO-IT-YOURSELF MOVEMENT

The do-it-yourself movement has taken on enormous dimensions over
the years. In our business, for example, if we can convince one of you to
put in a new floor or ceiling, the neighborhood wives will have such a
discussion about it that several other men in the block will be working
on a new project within a matter of weeks. This is a contagious thing,
giving emphasis to the problem of quality and status, I suppose. We
find the do-it-yourself movement at a peak during the age brackets up
to about 40; then it tapers off and picks up again at age 55. This may
be a matter of economic necessity or it may be that, having tried it a few
times you and I decide, "Let's lay off for a while and let somebody else
do it." The urge, however, recurs later on when retirement approaches
and we need a hobby. Some say this apparently is important to lengthen
life — it may shorten it in some circumstances, instead.

Notice that the housing problem then changes again. Along through
the late 40s and the 50s that momentous decision has to be made as to
whether the house should be larger as a reflection of rising income and
importance in the community, or smaller for practical reasons as mobility
of the parents increases to the extent that they are free of the immediate
responsibilities of children. Later on, at retirement, smaller quarters
become more important.

My comment on the life cycle is merely to give you a dimension, rather
obvious perhaps, of the changing housing structure. We do not have a

single uniform demand of people of all ages for the same kinds of units
to the degree we may have had previously.

The idea of owning a house has certainly caught on. I suspect that as
far as the decade of the '60s is concerned, the immediate requirement
may well be as much to find inexpensive rental units — I say inexpensive
as opposed to new skyscraper apartments — for the young married
couples, because they may not be interested in living in suburbia; we
find indications they are not, to the same degree that some other age
groups are. In short, we must question some of the obvious generalizations and trends, based on our postwar experience.

So I think we can say that we have had a change in the structure of the
market. At the moment we have a rather significant kind of situation that
perhaps documents some of the things that underlie the comments that
Jim Duesenberry made as to why some earlier normal developments do
not bring about the same public response today.

Insofar as we can determine, about 90% of the homes in America are
now occupied; ten years ago, the figure might have been 93% or 94%.
Let us compartmentalize the remaining 10% of unoccupied homes.
There are those that are used just seasonally and not all year round.
Then there is a significant group of perhaps one-third of the unoccupied
10% that are rental units. Then there is a rather interesting group of
houses, perhaps 2% or 3% of the unoccupied 10%, that represent homes
held off the market for various and sundry reasons. We can, in short,
find no more than ½ to ¾ of 1% of all the houses in America vacant and
for sale. Add in dilapidation, and we have accounted for the 10% of
unoccupied dwellings.

MILLIONS LIVE BEHIND "FOR SALE" SIGNS

These are the obvious implications of the housing market. I think the
less obvious point is that millions — unnumbered, but millions — of
families all across America are living behind a "For Sale" sign. Based on
our sample analysis, many more families are living behind "For Sale"
signs than there are empty houses behind "For Sale" signs. In short, we
have a minimum, I would think, of 5 million families in America (some
say it may be double that) who want to get out, not because of a threat
of unemployment or because of economic necessity, but because they are
concerned about the quality of housing. This is, I think, another new
dimension in the market.

Let me move ahead with a few observations with respect to the structure of buyers and sellers. The buyers are people who already typically
own a house; they have learned something about the housing market and
their psychological attitude is different. The sellers are in many respects

the same people; if they are not — if they are builders or others with new houses — they are conscious of the changing dimensions of this market. So there has to be a significantly different sales approach to moving houses today.

Curiously enough, the price of new housing continues to edge up, at least statistically, and the price of older houses is beginning to edge down. This poses many questions to families who want to get out but frankly do not know how. It has been estimated that three-quarters of the people living behind "For Sale" signs want a house that is larger because of their life cycle stage, and one-quarter want a house that is smaller because of their life cycle stage. Thus, housing is a very dynamic market, far from the staid and prosaic one that might show up in some aggregate statistics.

With this background we can, I think, look ahead into the growth potentialities of the housing market. I should like to ask this group, if you will, whether in your opinion the housing market, however you want to define it, is a growth market, however you want to define it. More specifically, the question before us is whether housing per se will contribute to the growth of the American economy in the decade of the '60s. How many of you would classify housing as a growth industry for the decade of the '60s? [Show of hands.]

Ketch, what do we have? A little more than half?

CHAIRMAN KETCHUM: A little less.

MR. HOADLEY: All right, 50–50. This is a good, balanced group.

How about the decade of the '70s? May I see the hands? [Show of hands.] About the same.

If you polled a group of financial analysts across America on this same question, you would be struck by the lack of hands, the feeling that housing is not a growth industry for the decade of the '60s, and you would get a smattering of hands on the '70s, perhaps as many as here.

Is Housing about to "Take Off"?

In short, we have a very curious situation in that in many discussions there is a feeling that housing is about to "take off" because of family formations, yet the financial analysts are not looking at the market this way and do not see anything too dramatic. Is it because they know more about it or because they feel there may be growth in sales but no growth in profits? It is a very, very interesting question.

If you look at the rather easily obtainable figures on population, now that we are in the decade of the '60s, you get an impression that the soaring '60s, populationwise, are not quite as vibrant as perhaps they looked from the standpoint of the '50s. The projections call for a gain in population of perhaps 18% over all; but in the age brackets where most of the housing is likely to be needed, ages 22 to 44, the increase will be perhaps 3% in this decade. This is the kind of information which is filtering back into the financial community. This is the kind of information which I have a suspicion reached Washington long ago, and it may account for some of the rather interesting twists in the new housing legislation. You can also find evidence of a rise in older families.

Certainly there is nothing in the statistics of population that suggests housing is about to collapse. But certainly as to timing, it may be that the decade from 1965 to 1975 is the real decade from the standpoint of population and family formation; some people would say '68 to '78. Not that more housing will not be needed, but what kind of housing does make a difference from the standpoint of real stimulation to the economy, particularly if home improvement takes place. Nevertheless, this is a debatable question.

QUALITY IS THE BIG DIMENSION

It might be stated again that the big dimension in housing is quality. Space requirements are important because, as income rises, there is a very strong desire to get more space, quality space. Insofar as we can, we often ask our Armstrong consultants to check the psychology of the American public. Although this is very tenuous and dangerous, we are of the impression that quality space is a major goal of families in America. It is, however, a goal which they may lose after a while. Many a family that has put a house on the market with the expectation that it would sell at a very nice price within a week, six months later look upon the idea of getting out of the house in a different light; the quality space in terms of a new dwelling has lost its appeal. Thus we find them asking: What can we do about the older house?

We know a little bit, of course, about the income relationship to the market. We know that the most significant dissatisfaction with housing today in terms of economic ability to do something about it lies in the families with incomes over $7,500. They now represent 20% of the total, so far as we know, and income projections over the decade suggest that this figure may actually double. Depending upon inflation and so on, however, this may not be too accurate a measure. In any event, the ability, incomewise, for people to make good on their quality space requirements is likely to improve rather markedly.

This does not take care of the suburban people or solve our urban slum clearance problems. I think we can very easily generalize about suburbia to the point where we become almost too dramatic. I can hardly go anywhere in America today that someone does not ask, "Is it true that there is a net migration back to the city?" Illustrations of John or Joe, who got tired of mowing the lawn and said, "The kids are gone, let's get back to town," are often mentioned. I only wish I could give a definitive answer. We know there has been a net in migration of certain minority groups. This is a reflection of social and economic conditions in various parts of the country, indeed of the world.

Basically, so far as one can compartmentalize the market, it falls into three categories. We have suburbia, which in our judgment can only grow, because of sheer physical, geographical space requirements as the population increases. Stop for a minute and consider where you are going to put the people who are going to be born, as well as those who are currently alive, and visualize what would be required physically to put them in the center city. I think you will rapidly conclude that suburbia will grow. It may not grow in the sense that it has grown in the last ten or fifteen years, but we are going to use more land for housing. That seems to me to be an inescapable conclusion. We have, then, suburbia.

Then we have the center core, the older part of town. This is a problem all over America. Some attention is being given to it, and I hope a great deal more will be. This is a specialized kind of problem where the financial requirements are fantastic if we hope to do the job by bulldozing down and building new. Various estimates are that it would cost $50 billion to $70 billion a year for at least a decade, in order to catch up; and by that time we would be in trouble again. This is a fantastic job of rebuilding; yet in many communities there are plans, blueprints, price tags that are pretty vague, which result in hope on the one hand and frustration on the other.

Finally, we have an enormous gray area that is neither downtown, metropolitan center core nor suburbia. Here we find the bulk of the housing of America. In many respects it is basically deteriorating and not likely to get better unless something is definitely done to give people there incentive and encouragement. This is the focal area of the housing quality problem for the decade ahead.

SINGLE VERSUS MULTIFAMILY DWELLINGS

We do not have a great deal of time to dwell on any of these problems, but I do think we have to call attention to the fact that the metropolitan core is now being populated to an increasing extent by multifamily structures. Now 20% to 25% of all the housing units being started are two-family and up, in contrast to half this figure just a few years ago. Such construction is in anticipation of the family formation bulge.

Unfortunately, the rental on these multifamily units is usually so high that it is obvious they were not built for the younger generation about to marry. So we have a beautiful case in the postwar period of building the wrong size house — it has been too small for current family needs — and now of overbuilding too large and too expensive apartment type dwellings for the families which have been formed or are being formed. The market indications of this are apparent in the high vacancy rate in various sections of the country for these types of dwellings.

There are real problems in connection with finding ways and means of reducing costs and many longer-range problems we could dwell on. Let me just say that gaining acceptance of something new in the building industry is a frustrating problem in itself. So long as people feel that a structure has to look as if it were built of some old-established, conventional material, so long as they feel it has to look sturdy, we are going to have difficulties in selling them on a house that is strong but looks less strong than something with a masonry type wall. The research that is going on in the building industry is very encouraging from the standpoint of ability to come up with new materials and new ideas, but rather frustrating in terms of acceptance. I might add that the financial leaders in the country are probably as conspicuous as any others in saying, "Well, we wonder about that structure because it doesn't really conform to what we consider to be a house." Acceptance problems take time to overcome, but there is some gradual progress being made.

As to the other longer-range problems of cost, Norman Mason, former head of HHFA, put his finger on land. He polled a great number of building specialists asking what one factor would make the greatest difference in bringing the costs of home building down. Land seemed to be the consensus of the replies. Land has been perhaps the most important factor contributing to cost increases over the past ten or fifteen years. It has been said, I suspect with some reason, that there has been at least as much speculation in land since the end of the war as there has been in the securities market. There have also been a great many road blocks because of legal and financial red tape that add materially to the final price.

THE PSYCHOLOGICAL FACTOR IN HOUSING COSTS

Slowness in adopting component construction and other labor-saving techniques is a significant road block to lower prices in homes. Labor restrictions come up constantly. These, I suspect, will be subjected to enormous pressure as this decade unfolds. It may well be that we shall see inquiries into the building industry in the decades of the '60s and '70s to demonstrate in some conclusive fashion whether component construction is phantom or real. I think it is safe to say there is already indication on the part of most of the parties interested, including labor, that a fresh approach is necessary. When there has been a lot of discussion about the inflationary consequences of wage settlements in such major industries as steel, always keep in mind that construction workers vastly outnumber the steel workers and their increases in pay per year have been significantly higher. So we face problems of wages here, too.

Of all the factors involved in cost, perhaps the most significant is the psychological one. The American public, for reasons that are in part understandable, fails to recognize the depreciation and obsolescence costs in home use; there is great reluctance to admit that money invested in a home does not necessarily have to earn a capital gain. This is what has frozen the housing market in America. Families cannot get out of the house; they do not know how to get out of the house. The trade-in market is practically nonexistent in most communities, certainly as far as old house for old house is concerned. It exists only to a moderate degree among builders of new homes taking houses in trade.

The establishment of a trade-in mechanism would remove one road block and would get fluidity into the housing market. There has been relatively little interest in achieving such a market; but, perhaps more important, in order to make it economically feasible, there has to be an appraisal. Because of the cost of the trade-in, an individual must take something less than the full appraised price, and people are reluctant to do this. The psychology of trading an automobile will some day come in the psychology of trading a house. I expect some progress in the decade of the '60s, although I am not so strong in my belief as to feel that we will have a vigorous trade-in market in the immediate future.

There are, of course, innumerable financial problems, and these I said at the outset I would skip over. We have a problem of liquidity in the country. As we look ahead, it is not going to be easy to finance housing. On the other hand, I am hopeful that funds will be available. I could never forget that housing in recent years has had the largest claim on the savings of America. Nobody — not even those who believe the share has not been large enough — can say that housing has not had the biggest share.

This leads me to a quick appraisal of the new administration's housing program and a comment or two on the immediate housing outlook.

THE ADMINISTRATION'S HOUSING POLICY

Government has had an enormous influence on the housing industry over the years. Some of it has been very constructive. A great deal of it, though, actually has been harmful rather than of help to the housing situation. The net effect of pumping in enormous amounts of credit has been to inflate the cost of housing, because it has been largely a matter of credit first and everything else second. Where have the incentives been in the building industry to reduce costs? The answer has always been: "Pump in the money, and we shall go on doing pretty much what we are doing now, because you can finance it." The problem is to take a fresh look, an extremely difficult point to get across.

Nevertheless, the role of government has to be a tempered role, in my judgment. It also should be a positive role. For that reason I am quite encouraged by some of the "fresh thinking" of the Kennedy administration in its approach to housing. There is probably something in the package for almost every stage of the life cycle I have talked about, with a tremendous dramatic appeal for certain groups — but also with inflationary overtones.

There are, of course, provisions for open space, a very interesting factor. Funds are also available for experimental housing. You know, more money has probably been lost in prefabrication than has been made so far. Experimental housing has been difficult to finance, because you do not play around in a test tube with a house; you must sink millions of dollars into research in the housing field. This provision, I think, has some very definite merits.

HOME IMPROVEMENT A SOUND PROGRAM

The most important provision, in my humble opinion, concerns the role of home improvement. In the Democratic platform of a year ago, you recall the feeling of urgency which was repeated in certain task force statements, such as: "We need 2 million houses. If we don't need them now, we are going to need them in the relatively near future. Let's build them." Common sense economics suggests that if you were to build 2 million homes in the kind of market we have at the moment, particularly with the present lack of trade-in facilities, you would do nothing but bring utter chaos. The market could not absorb these units without drastic implications on finance and folks in the market. But in the housing message of six weeks ago, the impression I got was quite different: "We'll need 2 million housing starts per year by the year 1970." This is common sense. This squares with my analysis of the market. Therefore, as Neal Hardy, the new housing administrator, has said, "We have the opportunity to improve the quality of American housing." Home improvement has always been an important factor in the economy, but it can be a significantly important one if the leaders of government and the related business and financial organizations will get together and figure out answers to the road blocks.

The principal road block to home improvement can be removed by finding a way of handling the old mortgage relatively inexpensively. If the old mortgage can be turned into a new one or something related thereto, home improvement can be financed without piling a large monthly payment on top of an already significant mortgage payment. There is equity in these houses, and yet somehow we have the feeling that home improvements must be financed like an automobile, through consumer credit. I, personally, cannot see the merit in this. I would say improvement financing represents a near mortgage, a semi-mortgage, or interim-type loan-financing opportunity. I would simply add that because of the administration's dramatic emphasis on it (I use "dramatic" advisedly, because the headlines have all been "low-cost housing"), the word has gotten through to people all over the country and there is much interest in the home improvement package today. We are going to see hundreds, if not thousands, of home improvement contractors come alive in the next few years; we will also encounter difficulties, for many of them will be "suede shoe operators" and the public will have to have its guard up. People of high integrity, however, are looking at home improvement as a sound way to improve the quality of American housing.

THE NEAR-TERM OUTLOOK FOR HOUSING

As we sit today and look at the housing market of America, and look forward to the remainder of 1961 and at 1962, we can from an economic standpoint say there is little basis for any significant change from the level of activity that we now see. From a political standpoint, there will be increases by virtue of legislation calling for further funds or special arrangements of one type or another. We will get an increase in terms of units, not because of economic need so much as because of political pressure. Hopefully, from many standpoints, the home improvement bill will be adopted. I think this is the soundest part of the 1961 proposals.

Psychologically, the public is sitting watching Washington. In fact, we have checked in recent weeks many people who are completely and utterly frustrated. They do not know whether to try to go for a new house, assuming they can get a long-term mortgage, or whether to fix up their old house because there is an attractive deal here. Other people are considering a second house and are wondering whether mobile homes will be included in the new legislation. The housing message and its innuendoes have the public confused. I hope that within the next sixty to ninety days some decision will be made to clear the air.

On balance, new home building may increase a modest 3% to 5% over the next twelve months. We may also see the liquidation of older unsold inventories, plus a vigorous upturn in home improvements, over the next eighteen to twenty-four months.

In short, the housing market is dynamic in its potential; it is static in its reality. The opportunity is for quality improvements for the next several years; then, later in the decade, for quality and quantity. At that point I think there will be little question that we have a growth industry. Finally, remember that the people in the industry have been scarred by previous government decisions, and they will not react the same to the same kind of policy decisions again.

Discussion*

SIDNEY ROBBINS: I was most interested in your comments about lack of marketability of the house, for I have been wondering about this for some time.

It occurred to me that the government may be making a mistake fooling around with interest rates, amortization, and all the traditional ways of trying to solve the housing problem. A much more direct solution would be along the following lines: Why, for example, could there not be some federal agency doing what corporations are doing — having objective appraisals, assuming the house for a temporary period of time and shifting it back and forth? Or, if not the federal government, some combined financial group that could take over this kind of responsibility?

If this is not done, what will be done, since the problem is there and is clearly one of the more significant ones? If the solution that has occurred to me quickly is not the feasible one, what will be done by those concerned in this industry?

MR. HOADLEY: It is perhaps because corporations are concerned about this and do feel that it is necessary to have mobility that they are giving attention to this problem. A great many companies are in the real estate business; there is just no question about it, and they do not like it. This encourages employees' wives, for example, to go out and buy old historic mansions and build them up and really live high and expensively because the corporation is there to bail them out later. There are all sorts of tax problems, too.

But you have put your finger on the critical question: How do we solve this mobility trade-in problem? It is going to be solved just because people are beginning to show the interest you have indicated. In other words, we now have a better chance of getting government people, business people, finance people, lawyers, and builders to look at this matter in more realistic terms. We may get them off high-level policy — and I am not deprecating high-level policy — and down to the specifics. We must work on a trade-in mechanism the people generally can understand.

Let me outline what some keen people in the building industry are now thinking. This is how they plan to tackle the problem. First of all, they recognize that they must have a strong and effective new builder organ-

* Proceedings of the Fourth Annual Conference, 1961, Excerpts from the Discussion, pp. 147–56.

ization; secondly, crews that specialize in the repair and modernization of old houses; thirdly, a sales organization (in the building industry the amount of selling that has been done in the real sense has been at a minimum); then, finance people who can see the opportunity, not only for mortgage loans and construction loans, but for inventory loans on a temporary basis as well. This takes big money.

Then what happens? As Mr. and Mrs. America walk onto a builder's site and see a display home, the salesman comes to the door, introduces himself and says, "The odds are that you already own a house," almost before the people have crossed the threshold. Of course, they are flattered. We estimate that 70% to 75% of all the people looking for new houses already have a house; so the odds are three out of four, which is pretty good. The salesman says, "If you are interested in this house, let me take away any concern about your old house; we'll take it in trade. You just look at the new house." The enormous change that comes about following that statement is reflected in tape recordings which have been made of such conversations.

What happens next? "You get two appraisals, we'll get two and we'll average them — split them down the middle," the salesman explains. "Then we'll build this house for you. You sell your house if you can get more than 80% or 90% of the appraisal." The result is that people get excited and begin to realize, "Yes, we'll take a little licking on our old house, but we'll update our equity in this new house."

I dwell on this point just to illustrate that it can be done in local areas by certain builders.

JOHN KENDRICK: In the longer-term growth potential of the housing industry, do you not think that the mix between intangible investment to improve technology and the tangible investment is important? I mean, not just research and development with respect to quality, new items and so on, but also to reducing costs? How much growth we get will depend to some extent on how much the industry we conceive interests itself in this kind of investment.

MR. HOADLEY: John, your point is very important. It bears on the psychological approach to the market. A great many people have said that what we need is austere, rapidly produced industrial-type housing. In practice, this is not popular housing for the average American. The approach, then, has to be, as you point out, to build the intangibles and tangibles together. I have a feeling we are going to get a great deal more of this, because many of the builders now see limitations to their market if they just reproduce the 1947 house that has been updated gradually. They have to do something really new.

MR. KENDRICK: Is the industry planning to spend an increasing amount on research?

MR. HOADLEY: The amount of research which is being done in the building industry, if we really knew, is probably quite small. It is, however, accelerating rapidly, not only because some of the "old-line" companies are doing more of it, but also because a great many companies that are looking for growth outside their conventional fields — chemical companies and so on — are now moving into the home building area. They think, contrary to financial analysts, that building and specifically housing offer, internationally and nationally, one of the greatest long-range potentials of anything they can visualize. So, the amount of research in the development of buildings will mushroom.

There is a great limitation in this area, however. When you start doing research, you get into the problem of whether you will research pieces of the house or the total house. You find that you must eventually go into the total house concept, and when you reach this point you are not talking about peanuts but about fantastic sums of money. Relatively few organizations can afford the outlays, since the chances of return, in view of all the road blocks to acceptance of newness, seem to be minimized.

SYLVESTER FRIZOL: To what extent will real estate taxes and high commissions be a retarding factor? We are talking about stretching out amortization and lowering interest rates, and then someone comes along and raises the real property tax about 10%. In some cases, especially in the suburbs, the taxes are terrific.

MR. HOADLEY: Jim Duesenberry stated very pointedly the alternatives here. It is pretty obvious that the average American taxpayer is much more concerned about the millage on his property tax than he is about income tax. The real estate people are quite concerned in many communities because of the high level of taxes. This is a chronic problem all over the country.

You raise the basic idea: What do we want the local government to provide? Now, insofar as there is inefficiency there, or there is a way of getting more for your tax dollar, the public has to put a lot of heat on the local tax authorities. More hidden is the feeling that if you reach a limit in the local community beyond which you cannot go, somehow you can make up the difference from Washington, and that when you get it from Washington, somehow the other guy is going to pay. This gets back to the fundamental thought: What is it that people want from the government?

Now, the philosophy of the present administration is that there are enormous needs and that the public wants them met. This is something the public either accepts or rejects; but the one thing we have not fully understood, I think, in terms of economic literacy, is that any plan costs money. So if you end up with a tax policy locally that is a deterrent to housing, then, as Jim pointed out, you have killed the deal by one method. If you maneuver it to the federal level, you may find a temporary offset, but in the end you cannot bury the problem of costs.

I do not want to give the impression that we can go through these problems one after the other and end up with nothing but net frustration and can do nothing. There are probably thousands of reasons why nothing will ever be done, but I am convinced that something will be done because eager people will see the opportunity and recognize that the greatest need in America today as far as we can determine is quality improvement in housing, better quality space.

EDWARD EDWARDS: Walter, will you say a little more about the inadequacy of the statistics, especially since we here represent most of the states of the Union and have graduate students who might be doing some work in this area?

MR. HOADLEY: Eddie, you knew you were hitting a soft spot. For many years I have been personally concerned about the inadequacy of statistics in the construction field — long before I joined Armstrong. It seemed to me that here was an enormous industry being influenced by public and private policy to a large degree on the basis of very inadequate data. When I think of Regulation X days in which the seasonally adjusted nonfarm rate of house starts determined whether you turned the regulation on or off, I cringe. Nobody in Congress really understood the inadequacies and the extent to which there were frankly just plain guesses. This is not criticism of the people who put the statistics together; you simply could not sell anybody on the need to do anything better.

In the housing starts field we have had problems. Anybody who has looked at the housing start series in the last six months [November, 1960 to April, 1961] cannot help but be profoundly disturbed by the severe fluctuations in the series. The seasonal adjustments used just do not seem to be reliable. We had a horrible December, a surprisingly good January, we fell out of bed in February, yet March made us look like heroes.

You are not only estimating what has happened to housing, but you are trying to outguess the buys who are guessing what it is. The fellows in the Census Bureau are now trying desperately to improve this situation. The internal battle in Washington as to who was going to put out what housing statistics went on for years, but that problem, I think, has been resolved and improvements should come. In the series on construction put in place, we have only the phasing out of contracts by an estimated average duration of contract. Thus, if there was a steel strike, nobody knew what happened, because the contracts for a certain type of structure, for example, normally requiring six months to build, were simply phased out, one-sixth per month as if no strike had occurred.

20

Rental Housing: Problems
for Private Investment*

Louis Winnick is program associate, public affairs, The Ford Foundation; director, Citizens' Housing and
Planning Council; and consultant, Bureau of the Census. He is
the author of *Rental Housing and Opportunities for Private Investment* and *American Housing and Its Use* and the co-author
of *Housing Choices and Constraints, Capital Formation in Residential Real Estate* and *Housing Market Analysis.* Mr. Winnick
earned his bachelor's degree at Brooklyn College and his master's
and doctoral degrees at Columbia University. He was formerly
a faculty member, Brooklyn College, Rutgers University, and
Columbia University; research associate, Institute for Urban
Land Use and Housing Studies, Columbia University; director
of research, New York City Planning Commission; and executive
director, Temporary State Commission on Economic Expansion.

OF ALL THE IMPORTANT DEVELOPMENTS in the real estate markets of the
postwar period, I would single out three as having the most significance
for capital investment. First has been the massive intervention of the
federal government in the residential mortgage market. As everyone
knows, this resulted in substantial gains in the volume of home building;
in the emergence of the large-scale builder; in advances in building technology; in shifts in the location of metropolitan jobs and population; and
in the formation of something like a national mortgage market.

* Proceedings of the Sixth Annual Conference, 1963, pp. 101–12.

The second notable development has been a dramatic strengthening of investor preferences for urban real estate, partly because of new depreciation rules, but mainly because of a favorable demand picture which resulted in rising before-tax earnings plus bright prospects for capital gains. Among the consequences of a new investment climate for real estate, we can count the following: a substantial increase in the flow of equity capital; a deepening of the investment base which brought in, via syndicates and public issues, many thousands of small investors; an expansion in the geography of investment to truly international proportions; a sharp reduction in the yields required by equity investors; new flows of money into mortgages, which lessened dependence on government insurance and guarantees and which gave rise to a growing market for second and third mortgages plus various schemes for private mortgage insurance.

The third major real estate development has been the continuing trend toward the apartment house. This is the subject of this morning's lecture. Although the apartment house boom does not have the same fundamental significance for the capital market as does the revolution in mortgage and equity investment, I have added it to my list for two reasons. One, the volume of investment in apartments has by now reached sufficient dimensions to make worthwhile a thorough examination of its implications: how it may alter the pattern of urban development; the extent to which it will bring about new sources and flows of mortgage capital; and whether or not it will influence the construction cycle, creating, perhaps, more pronounced instability than was the case when the one-family home was king.

THE APARTMENT BOOM: ASTONISHING TURNABOUT

What makes the apartment boom of the past six or seven years doubly interesting is the fact that it came as something of a surprise to most people, a humbling reminder that there are no inevitabilities in the American economy. More accurately, we do not know enough about the determinants of consumer demand for housing to speak with total confidence about the future. To many or most of us in the '50s, the triumph of the single-family home seemed complete.

In fact, in 1956 a citizens' group asked me to do a book on why the construction of new rental housing had almost disappeared and what we should or could do about it. In that year, fewer than 100,000 units were started in multifamily structures, something less than eight out of every 100 units built. There were actually more apartments produced in 1905 and 1906 — a half-century earlier — when the urban population of the United States was one-third as great. I then made the statement that it would be hard to find many other consumer goods whose markets were actually smaller in the '50s than at the beginning of the century; even the output of snuff was twice as great in 1956 as in 1900.

Today, if one were asked to do a similar study, he could rightly ask: What ever has happened to the market for new one-family houses? We have been witnessing one of the most astonishing turnabouts ever recorded in the annals of construction statistics. The inconsequential 82,000 private apartment starts in 1956 grew to more than 215,000 in 1959, to nearly 300,000 in 1961, and to more than 400,000 in 1962. Now, I have reason to remember that last figure, for though I do not place too much confidence in forecasting, my book concluded on the note that rental housing had a promising future. And a little later, I was reported in *Fortune* magazine as making what then seemed a rash statement — that the decade of the '60s would see an annual average of 400,000 apartments.

The decade is still very young and, as I have said, in the housing market there are no inevitabilities. Nonetheless, factors that were already observable in the second half of the '50s, which foreshadowed a wave of apartment construction in the '60s, are still very much with us, as strong as ever.

These factors include a shortage of land; changes in consumer tastes; some disillusion with the suburbs; a remarkable surge of funds into equity apartment investment; and, finally, the broader market brought about by the changing demographic composition of the American people. All these explanations have validity, and I shall have something to say about each.

But I would single out the last factor — the demographic — as having a significance greatly exceeding all the rest combined. It was close attention to historical trends in the age structure of the population, so importantly related to birth and marriage rates and so importantly influenced by wars and the business cycle, that led to insights as to why apartment construction was so relatively strong in the '20s, so weak in the mid-'50s, and was likely to become strong again by the end of the '50s and for an indefinite period thereafter. In other words, whatever the aggregate volume of construction may be, the way in which new housing is divided between the one-family and the apartment-house market seems to be greatly affected by the shifting proportions of population who are in the various stages of the life cycle, chiefly the relative proportions of child-bearing families and non-child-rearing couples and individuals.

The Role of a Changing Age Structure

By now so much has been written and spoken about the impact on the housing and other consumer markets of changes in demographic composition that almost nothing new can be added. But allow me to review again some of the underlying data looking ahead to the 1970s.

Between 1960 and 1970, the number of persons aged 20 to 24, from which group will derive the young households so important to rental housing, will increase by 6 million. To indicate the magnitude of this growth, let me point out that the net gain in the present decade will exceed the full net gain in the whole eighty years between 1880 and 1960. From this young group will spring between 2.5 million and 2.75 million additional households, of which upwards of 80% are likely to be renters. Likewise, there will be a gain of 2.7 million in the age group 25 to 29, whose preference for renting appears also to be quite well developed. Most of the latter individuals will be in already established households and, judging from past experience, more than half are likely to remain renters until the husband turns 30. It was the sluggish growth of the 20 to 29 age group during the early '50s — a reflection of the low birth rate of the '30s — that produced such a drop in the contemporary rental market. The rate of growth in young households became brisker toward the end of the '50s, pulling up with it the marriage curve and contributing importantly to the upturn in rental construction.

By contrast, there will be a net loss in the child-rearing, home-ownership age groups. The 30 to 39 group, whose very fast growth after World War II (a reflection of the high birth rate during the '20s) was such a powerful influence in the home ownership boom and suburban migration of the late '40s and early '50s, will actually shrink in numbers by more than 2 million. Indeed, this shrinkage in the age group which buys its first home has apparently already left its mark. I regard this deficit of first-time home buyers to be the most fundamental reason for the comparative stagnation in the one-family home market of recent years, evidenced by a lack of vitality in home construction, an apparent check to the rise of existing house prices and an increase in foreclosures. It is a failure to take account of these demographic factors which causes many observers to overrate the income effect on one-family construction. In most local housing markets, an overwhelming majority of home purchasers must sell a house to buy a house. No matter how much the appetite for a new house may be whetted by rising income, the transaction cannot be completed unless some other family is willing to take the old house at an acceptable figure. Few consumers will hold two houses, and the imaginative devices invented by dealers to allow trading up do not work very effectively when the demand for existing homes weakens.

LARGER NEW RENTAL MARKET FORESEEN

But will the home ownership market not expand and the new rental market diminish as the bulging number of young households moves into the child-rearing, home-buying ages? The answer is "yes," the new one-family market is likely to expand in the latter half of the decade, and "no," the new rental market certainly will *not* shrink. For each individual who will leave the 20 to 29 age group after 1970, one and a fraction individuals will take his place; that is, the 20 to 29 age group will be larger in 1975 by another 3.7 million. And, barring a very sharp drop in the birth rate, it is virtually certain that the 1985 cohort will be larger than the 1980. Rental builders and mortgage investors will be dealing with a market whose potential will be increasing long into the foreseeable future. In other words, the rental market will be supported not merely by a temporary increase, but by a sustained increase in one of the most important sources of its demand.

Now, in addition to these gains in young households, the changing age structure holds forth other promises to the apartment investor. The number of persons aged 50 or more will grow by more than 8 million to 1970 and by 13 million to 1975. The growth in these age groups will be accompanied by very large gains in the number of single individuals living alone — a gain of perhaps 3 million. Single adults, particularly with rising incomes, have a very marked propensity toward rental housing and constitute an important demand factor in the central city apartment market.

PREFERENCES OF THE POST-50 AGE BRACKET

More important, however, will be the behavior of the much larger number of married couples in the post-50 age bracket. The market potential of this group for the rental builder is enormous, because older people are at the peak of their income and asset accumulation cycle. Nevertheless, the fact remains that persons over 50, particularly in the higher income groups, traditionally have shown a strong affinity for home ownership. The home ownership rate of higher-income families aged 50 or over is nearly 80%. Having acquired a home to rear their children, older people have not been inclined to re-enter the rental market in great numbers.

But housing market surveys have noted that there has not been a marked increase in the ownership rates of older people during recent years. The upsurge in ownership was chiefly among young or maturing married couples. Should ownership rates among persons over 50 stabilize, the rental market is likely to capture by 1957 one-third of an increment of 13 million persons, or over 1.5 million households, the actual number depending on economic growth and differential death rates of men and women.

OTHER FAVORABLE DEMAND FACTORS

Although these population factors deserve the fullest attention, there is no iron law of demography. Younger or older couples may have a love for renting and couples with children for owning, but love can be a fickle thing. What can we say about changing preferences, as between owning and renting, and as between suburban and city locations? The two questions, of course, overlap, because a substantial proportion of the recent increase in apartment starts has occurred in suburban areas.

Although we can speak only with diffidence about how consumer tastes will change in the future, there are at least two reasons for a tendency to shift a little away from ownership and a little toward renting. First, it seems that some disillusionment with the suburbs may already have set in, although there are few facts upon which to base an assured judgment. Current surveys of families moving into new apartments show that between 7% and 12% come from suburban areas. However, similar ratios were uncovered in 1957–58, so that the return trek must be considered a trickle rather than a genuine counter-migration. In my opinion, the return from the suburbs is less likely to be accompanied by large numbers of people moving *back* to the city than by smaller numbers moving *out* to the suburbs.

SCHOOL TRANSFERS, USED HOUSE PRICES

Judging from the data on school transfers in New York City and from the trend in comparative rates of new construction between the central city and its environs, some abatement in the rapid rate of exodus seems already to have occurred. We must also remember that the heavy rates of outmigration of population from the city to the suburbs was not accompanied by comparable outmigrations of households. Thus, New York City lost over 100,000 people, but gained 250,000 households. Similar trends were observed in other large cities. The explanation is that outmigration was far commoner among families with children than among childless adults. That is, a husband, wife and three children leave the city for a house in Levittown, but their place may be taken by one childless couple and two childless individuals. Although population goes down by 20%, the demand for central city housing then goes up by two units. Another consequence is that jobs and income in the central city also tend to increase. This simplified example helps explain why household size in the central city has maintained its historic decline; why per capita income has been rising so sharply in places like New York, despite the influx of large numbers of low-income minority groups; and why the resident labor force has increased, despite the loss in population.

A second factor that may weaken, at least to a degree, the preference for home ownership is the apparent slowdown, if not cessation, in the rise of used house prices. The exuberance of the young home buyers of the postwar period who took it for granted that they could always resell at a profit is giving way to a more cautious attitude, to a realization that the estimated costs of home ownership will have to be enlarged by an allowance for depreciation rather than reduced by an anticipated capital gain. The rising rate of foreclosures seems to me to be a clear symptom of static or declining prices. There is little need for mortgagees to foreclose when house prices are rising.

Let us now turn to the supply side of the residential market. What about the increasing land shrinkage and the continuing rise in land costs? Now, it is sometimes said that the increased price of land causes builders to shift from one-family houses to apartments. I think this view somewhat mixes up cause and effect. Apartments are built only if a market for apartments can be foreseen, no matter how expensive land is or may become.

I myself think that land shortages in the suburbs may play a somewhat different part. As home builders find large tracts of inexpensive land increasingly scarce in and around centers of employment, they will become less able to build on a mass scale. Because in many metropolitan areas they will forfeit the economies of mass construction, which have been estimated to be as much as 15%, the price of new one-family houses will tend to rise more sharply than building costs. That is, what might have been a $15,000 house might cost $16,000, solely because of rising land prices, but would have to be priced at $17,000 because of the loss in efficiency involved in small-scale construction. The first-time home buyer, having fewer new Levittowns from which to choose a bargain, may elect to stay a little longer in his apartment or to buy an existing home from an older family who in turn will shift to rental housing.

NET EFFECT OF URBAN RENEWAL

The subject of land naturally brings to the forefront the question of urban renewal. To what extent will the federal Title I program increase the future volume of apartment construction? Here, again, I think that the net effect will be comparatively small. Although new apartments are a major element in past, present, and future urban renewal projects, it seems to me that Title I and the Section 220 mortgage will do much more to alter the geographical distribution of apartment construction than to increase its over-all amount. To be sure, the Title I program has some potential for demand stimulation, both by reducing rents and by improving the quality of the final product.

But the rent reductions attributable to Title I have not proved very significant. The main importance of land write-down, at least until recently, has been to make a site marketable, not to subsidize the incoming tenants by way of submarket rents; in effect, government write-downs defray the costs of getting rid of slum buildings, the costs of creating more open spaces around apartment houses than are required by zoning controls, and the costs of the long waiting time involved in urban renewal projects. Despite the heavy write-down in Title I, final land cost per rental room is not much lower in urban renewal sites than it would be elsewhere in the city, making allowances for differences in locational quality. Likewise, Section 220 mortgages can bring about minor rent reduction compared to conventional mortgages; but this would not necessarily be true in favorable mortgage markets such as the present, particularly if allowance is made for the extra time costs of dealing with FHA. Title I may also stimulate apartment demand by the power of land assembly, which tends to increase the scale of individual apartment projects, thereby achieving some rent-reducing economies in construction and operation, or by supplying some demanders, such as businessmen and professional people, who prefer to be in certain neighborhoods where no private builder will operate. But, all in all, the rents of Title I projects have not proved vastly lower, and indeed are frequently higher, than what unaided developers charge for a comparable unit.

Although the proposition is endlessly debatable, I myself think that most of the families who become tenants in Title I projects would have been tenants in other new apartments if Title I did not exist. For example, under existing Title I rules, Third Avenue in New York, which is now undergoing an astonishing apartment house boom, might easily have been designated an urban renewal area. Urban renewal officials would now be claiming credit for a huge volume of private apartment construction that is coming about without federal assistance.

RESTORED CONFIDENCE OF INVESTORS

Still speaking of the supply side of the market, the apartment boom has also been fed by the resurgence of confidence on the part of investors, particularly the equity investor whose incentives were further sharpened by favorable depreciation rules. Let me quickly say that I dissent — and vigorously so — from a prevalent view, given wide circulation in an article in *Harper's* a couple of years ago that syndicates and depreciation are *the* causes of the urban real estate boom. I do not even think them to be among the most vital causes. With a long-lived, immobile asset such as real estate, it is the demand side, not the supply side, that dominates new construction.

As already stated, families do not move into new apartments just because someone has some expensive land to develop. Nor do families move into apartment buildings just because they were built by a syndicate seeking fast write-offs. Apartments and other income properties are built because there is thought to be sufficient demand to fill them up, and they will stop being built when the demand falls off. Even if an occasionally irrational equity or mortgage investor is indifferent to demand factors, the errors are swiftly punished by excessive vacancies. No acceleration in depreciation rates can benefit an equity investor if there is not enough occupancy to create a cash flow after meeting all outlays. I do not think that many would now quarrel with this view. The recent shakeout in syndication and the sharp drop in the prices of real estate stocks can be traced to an insufficiency of demand at rents high enough to support the incredible capitalization upon which many public offerings have been based.

I do not wish to overstate my case by dismissing investment factors altogether. Obviously they have at least this much importance. First, the investor's restored confidence, together with the newer depreciation rules, have brought about a measurable reduction in the price required by equity capital. Equity capital which might have required 12% to 15% in a given apartment investment in the '50s could by 1960 be obtained at 9% to 10%. If we assume a typical division between equity and mortgage of 15% and 85%, respectively, a reduction in the return required by equity of one-third would, under competitive conditions, reduce the rent of new apartments by something like 6%; that is, a new apartment that would have required a rent of $200 a month under previous conditions could now be priced at $185 or $190. Such a reduction in rent would surely draw in many extra tenants to a particular building, but not a very large number over all if all investors are pricing down at the same time.

A second expansionary influence of the new investment climate is a greater willingness to take risks, to probe new or unseasoned market areas. Now, some of these experiments will not pay off, but so imperfect is the flow of market information and so rudimentary is the art of market analysis that ofttimes a hitherto undisclosed demand can be tapped if risk-taking investors are willing to test every possible submarket.

I have attempted thus far to delineate a series of factors favorable to a high volume of apartment investment in the 1960s. But what about the other side? Are there no unfavorable factors? Indeed there are; but, major war or depression aside, I do not think that they will have lasting significance.

Unfavorable Factors

Foremost among the unfavorable factors may be a tendency for apartment construction to move in a cyclical pattern. That is, rather than an even expansion over the decade, we are likely to witness a fairly sizable downturn by 1964, to be followed by renewed advance. I have something more in mind than the present shake-out in syndicates and public issues, as these may prove to be. I am referring to a more basic tendency to overbuild, which is virtually a chronic disease in the apartment sector — more so than in the one-family home market or even in the case of other income-producing property. This is so, first, because of the very much longer lag — two to three years — between the time the decision to build a new apartment is irrevocably committed and the time the actual demand can be ascertained. Most other types of construction, including one-family homes, office buildings and shopping centers, have at least some safeguards in the form of advance leases and contracts. It perhaps is not surprising that the vacancy rate in New York City's postwar apartments is much greater than the vacancy in postwar office buildings.

A second reason is the "lumpiness" of investment; unlike the one-family builder, the apartment developer, once his foundation is in the ground, can do little to change either the scale of his project or the size and layout of individual units, no matter how much market preferences are shown to be changing. Add to these market imperfections the herd instinct of investors in general (e.g., one successful apartment building can touch off a whole wave of new construction in the same area), plus an over-supply of mortgage credit which causes lenders to compromise the quality of loans, and the condition is set for at least a temporarily oversaturated market.

Further, in New York City, the citadel of new apartment construction, a new zoning law has touched off a tide of new building, far in excess of any visible demand. So large is New York City's share in the national total that a severe downturn there is almost certain to produce at least a statistical recession in official construction data. But as long as basic demand factors remain strong, most of the excess supply will sooner or later be absorbed. There will of course be some quite adverse repercussions for investors — the equity investor in particular, although mortgage lenders also will not be spared.

Rising Building Costs a Threat

A continuing threat to the future of apartment construction is the persistent and apparently accelerating rise in building costs. True enough, there have been a few innovations in construction methods which may offset some of these rising costs. But most of their impact will be reflected in rent increases. Since prospective tenants for new apartments are usually occupying fairly satisfactory housing and are not under undue pressure to move, large price increases may diminish the potential rental market.

Let us note also that the main test of the depth of the apartment market is yet to come. The huge apartment figures we all talk about are still largely in the form of permits. Although we lack good statistics on permit lapses and lags, it is safe to say that the attrition rate will be greater than is usually recorded for one-family houses. Nonetheless, even when full allowance is made for permit lapses and indefinite deferrals, the volume of completions will still be rising. The avalanche of 1961 and 1962 permits may not be felt until 1963 and 1964, with severe consequences in a number of local markets.

NEW TYPES OF FINANCING

A final comment on new types of financing such as cooperatives and condominiums on the equity side and new sources of mortgage funds on the debt side. About the condominium no one knows a great deal, although a great many words have been uttered. Despite the barrage of publicity that heralded FHA Section 234, I do not share the view that it will revolutionize the middle-income housing market. In fact, it will not contribute very much to total apartment construction. To the occupant of a multifamily structure, a condominium offers little advantage over a straight cooperative. So much of the typical apartment investment is in the form of joint facilities (roof, land, corridors, lobby, heating plant, etc.) that each tenant is almost as much a prey to his neighbor's behavior as in a cooperative. On the other hand, the cost of mortgage financing for individual apartments can be greater than for a single mortgage against a cooperative, and the transfer of property rights can be far more complex and expensive.

About cooperatives I feel more optimistic; indeed, I think that mortgage lenders frequently tend to underestimate their potential. To be sure, the cooperative apartment is still very much a New York City specialty, although it is now spilling over into two of its closest suburbs, Miami Beach and Los Angeles. My observation of the New York City cooperative — luxury, FHA's 213s and subsidized — is that while it usually is more difficult to attract initial tenants, the long-term investment prospects may be superior to a straight rental job. This is because the cooperators form a much more stable tenancy; are much more concerned with, and willing to pay for, good maintenance; and take an active role in trying to preserve or uplift their community. An adverse trend in a given neighborhood or school may quickly bring the downfall of a rental building but not, in my experience, a cooperative; the individual stake of the tenant is much too great to risk. I know that some mortgage investors are suspicious of cooperatives; the tenants tend to sue at the drop of a lawyer's fee and in general can make life perfectly miserable for everybody, including the mortgage lender. Nevertheless, in a city where changing neighborhoods are among the more critical investment risks, the mortgage lender may well reconsider whether the added safety of a cooperative mortgage does not more than make up for its irksomeness. When all is said and done, however, the cooperative will remain, quantitatively, quite unimportant. Even in New York City it accounts for less than 5% of the apartment inventory; outside of New York City the percentage is entirely negligible.

New Sources of Mortgage Credit

Concerning new sources of mortgage funds, I can suggest only these: First and most obvious is a clear trend for savings and loan associations to take a much larger role in apartment finance than has historically been the case. The demand for residential mortgage capital is the lifeblood of the savings and loans. If the demand shifts away from one-family homes to apartments, savings and loan associations will surely have to follow, or accept a slowing down in growth and earnings.

A second new source of apartment mortgage credit is likely to be government. New York state is already a direct lender to private apartment builders and is likely to be followed by New Jersey and other states. A program like New York's has recently been recommended to the governor of California. And the federal government's program for direct lending under Section 221(d)3, housing for the elderly and college housing, is likely to be further expanded.

This, then, is the long-run picture for rental housing: a generally high and rising trend of new construction with some interruptions, one of which appears imminent. Needless to say, there are many subjects which I have not covered or have covered inadequately. But let me stop here. It is more than time for some discussion from the floor.

Discussion*

ARTHUR MEYERS: You made no mention of, and I am interested if you have some reflections on, what is happening in cities of over 500,000, where population loss is also the consequence of an influx of poorer families, white and colored, from other areas of the country. When the

* Proceedings of the Sixth Annual Conference, 1963, Excerpts from the Discussion, pp. 112–25.

Census-takers asked people in St. Louis where they lived prior to January 1959, it was found that over a third of them had lived someplace else. The great boom in single-dwelling building was a consequence of these poorer groups moving into areas where white families tended to live; when the white families moved, they had to go out and get other single-family dwellings. This might be a very substantial continued stimulus to single-home building in the '60s.

MR. WINNICK: There is no doubt, I think, of this basic trend of substitution for higher-income families in the city by lower-income groups moving in. I agree with you that this trend is likely to continue.

MR. MEYERS: But they are not moving into apartments.

MR. WINNICK: There is a real question in my mind whether the exodus away from neighborhoods of change, while continuing, will continue with the same force as before. We know that exodus takes place most frequently, earliest, and most sensitively among families with children, because the school problem tends to be foremost. The less mobile tend to be the families without children. I suggest that as the age distribution moves in the direction of the childless couple the exodus will slacken, not because of any change in preference, but because there will be a larger number of people having less reason to move.

MR. MEYERS: In other words, the steam is out of this thing. It was a '50 to '60 phenomenon.

MR. WINNICK: I might add, too, that of the people who do move, the age factor again being involved, a larger portion may take apartments in some inner ring; or it may be in some suburb, or in the outer ring of the city itself. As I said, the apartment boom has gone way beyond the city limits now, and very considerably into the suburbs of all large cities.

GERHARD COLM: I am interested in how far there is a basic change in consumers' preferences from single-unit to apartment houses. In Washington I have heard the observation, not based on any scientific authority but from people close to the business, that particularly in the suburbs the people who are moving into apartment houses largely are the people with temporary jobs, and the impression is that they still eventually want homes of their own. This is not the same with the people who move into downtown apartment houses; they prefer that way of living. I think it would be interesting to find out whether any surveys have been made on motivation, particularly with respect to apartments downtown and apartments in suburban areas.

MR. WINNICK: Some work has been done on this. Let me say that you are referring to two separate things, Gerhard. With respect to military personnel and so on, you are talking about the apartment preferences of a very mobile segment of the population. This I did not mention, but it has always been a prominent element in any discussion of the market for

apartment houses. The question is whether the proportion of people in
the mobile group will increase or decrease in the future. I hesitate to
answer that question.

About changing preferences, I shall not make any flatfooted forecasts
of my own. You will recall that my own argument was merely in terms of
the change in the base figures among certain groups. If we applied to
these figures historical ratios of owning versus renting, this would feed a
much larger number of renters into the market. In other words, the
apartment sector will grow without even allowing for any increase in
preferences for apartments, defined to mean an increase in the proportion
of some age or life-cycle group that wants apartments over home ownership compared to some comparable group in the past. This, I think, is
the exciting, dynamic part of the future and it also is the part that cannot
be forecast with any degree of reliability.

Some work has been done on motivation and preferences. I think
Chester Rapkin has been involved in a considerable amount of this. He
might like to comment.

CHESTER RAPKIN: Yes. As a matter of fact, I am highly impressed with
the high degree of segmentation in this market. When we studied the
characteristics of the occupants of the more distinguished apartment
houses in Philadelphia, by which I mean the more expensive and newer
apartment houses, we found a very close grouping of characteristics.
Most of the families were very small — one- or two-person households
and only 6% had children. Incidentally, that is a figure I see in many
cities around the country. It is almost a magical number; I find it all the
time — 6% had children. Virtually all of them worked in the downtown
area, many within walking distance. They were all in the upper echelons
of the income distribution — $10,000 a year or better — and they were all
in white-collar occupations. As a matter of fact, when we took all four
characteristics together, we found that they represented 80% of all the
households in these apartments.

We wondered, too, about where they came from. To our astonishment
we found that very few came from the suburbs. Those who did were
only in part home owners; most of them had been renters. But the predominant grouping came either from adjacent apartment houses which
had moved down in the quality scale or from the inner ring in the city
where changes in the demographic characteristics of the population had
begun to occur.

We also wondered about the contrast between the occupant of the
suburban apartment and the downtown apartment. There, too, we were
astonished. We found that their income characteristics, household characteristics, and occupational characteristics were very much the same.

There was one major difference, however. Occupants of suburban apartments had previously been suburban residents, and many of them had been home owners. They liked the suburbs and wanted to stay there. There was also a differential of from $5.00 to $15.00 a month in the apartment rental; that may have accounted in part for the preference, but my personal feeling is that there was a predisposition to the outdoors, the fresh air, the spinach, and all the other salubrious elements which people are supposed to prefer.

I wonder, too, about something else you said, Lou. We found that virtually all the families were elderly. When we looked at the other segments of the rental market — the older apartments, the rehabilitated apartments, those lower down in quality — that is where we found the younger families, the people just starting out in life, the few families with children that wanted to brave the rigors of central city living. This is the area where we will not be able to produce many new houses at rents that the families with lower incomes can afford. This is particularly important in Philadelphia as well as in other cities. I am very much concerned about Philadelphia because we are now constructing over 3,000 new dwelling units in the central city alone, aside from the garden apartments being erected in the suburbs. Some years ago we estimated a market of about 400 units a year, and this has proved to be accurate. Now, we suddenly find a surge of eight times that number being poured into the market within a period of approximately one year. We are very fearful about what will happen. I cannot see this number being absorbed very rapidly. The market may be saturated for the better part of a decade.

MR. WINNICK: Chester, it would be hard to quarrel with anything you have said, but I should like to return to one point you made, because it is important. Young couples, newly formed households, are not a prime factor in the market for new central city apartments. Chester's figures for Philadelphia are, with some differences, confirmed in New York. We do find young couples to be a more important factor in the market for the less expensive apartments outside of the central ring. Also, as Chester said, they become the market for existing apartments.

Now, I would argue that this is just as important a factor in the trend of the apartment market of the 1960s as new construction is, because — to repeat Chester's figures — something like 85% to 95% of all families that move into a new central city apartment or any other kind of apartment come from a rather small geographical area around that building. Typically, they vacate other apartments when they move and, unless their places are taken by people lower down the income ladder, the build-up of vacancies in existing rental apartments will be simply too great to allow the new construction movement to continue. So I do not distinguish too sharply between these two important sources of demand. They both contribute to the aggregate apartment rent bill of the nation, which is the underlying support of all investment in rental housing.

ERNEST WALKER: You emphasized the manufacturers as primarily influencing the boom, and in fact you looked somewhat with contempt on the supply side. So I should like to know, from the standpoint of continuation of this boom, whether these supply factors act as deterrents or whether you see them as a continuing secondary force.

MR. WINNICK: I think their main role is such that I do not hold them in contempt; I hold them in the greatest respect and awe. But I would not attribute the same importance to them as some generalists have done. In other words, depreciation can get a great many apartment houses built or a zoning law can get a great many apartment houses built in New York or any other city. Then if there are no customers around, the next wave of construction will not take place until those have been absorbed. So, over a long period the total quantity built will be more or less in conformance with the over-all demand picture. But there are short-run build-ups of inventory. Those inventories have to be worked off, and then a new wave of construction may take place. The classical theory of inventory in the capitalist economy is that it accentuates the amplitude of the cycles.

PART SIX

Focusing on Institutions

The changes in business and consumer demands for financial services provides a never-ending challenge to the nation's network of financial institutions and their managers. Each year brings with it its share of knotty issues. Questions such as Regulation "Q" on savings, unit versus branch systems and the merger trend, and the ability of institutions to shift funds from capital surplus areas like the East Coast to capital deficit areas like the West Coast have both practical and theoretical implications. The questions are important and deserve careful attention on the part of students of finance. Yet, a review of the current literature of finance indicates that they receive inadequate treatment relative to their importance.

The purpose of this section of reading selections is to focus precisely on three key issues and to provide for the student some insight into the dimensions and complexities of the problem. The issues are:

1. Can institutions stimulate savings?

2. What is the status of competition among financial institutions?

3. How well do financial institutions serve in allocating capital?

The thoughts presented here on these topics represent the consensus of the considered judgments and attitudes of groups of conferees rather than a well-rounded and carefully drawn position of the spokesman on each point. Such an approach may well be appropriate, for in the real world the character and effectiveness of institutions more often reflects intuition and considered judgment than factual and definitive analysis. If the student gains nothing else from this section, it will be an appreciation of the complexity and the indefiniteness of the issues at hand.

21

What Economic Policies Are Needed

to Stimulate Saving*

Arthur M. Weimer, Moderator

SPOKESMEN FOR DISCUSSION GROUPS

Martin Bronfenbrenner, Department of Economics, University of Minnesota

Douglas A. Hayes, School of Business Administration, University of Michigan

Paul F. Wendt, Graduate School of Business Administration, University of California

MODERATOR WEIMER: This is a panel endeavoring to determine what broad economic policies are needed to stimulate saving; I suppose this assumes that saving needs to be stimulated. I am going to ask Martin Bronfenbrenner to report for his group first, and we shall go in alphabetical order to Douglas Hayes and then to Paul Wendt.

The need for savings is being heralded as one of the outstanding challenges of the 1960s. Whether our economy can produce the capital funds required to support consumer, business and government investment has been a subject of national and international conferences, academic debate, and editorial comment. What economic policies are needed to stimulate saving? How can thrift

* Proceedings of the Third Annual Conference, 1960, pp. 83–90.

385

institutions best aid in this cause? Will their role grow in importance during the years ahead? Will the trend toward the institutionalization of savings that we have observed in the past continue?

REPORT OF GROUP 1

MARTIN BRONFENBRENNER: In our group we divided the topic into six general headings: (1) the desirability of an increase in savings; (2) the effectiveness of interest rate policy; (3) the effects of fiscal policy, meaning taxes and expenditures; (4) the effects of monetary policy, meaning changes in the quantity of money; (5) the effects of wage policy; and (6) the effects of price policy. Each of these was to be considered, insofar as possible, within the framework of conventional economics. As you can very well understand, we did not get very far toward completing our rather long agenda.

With regard to the desirability of saving, we got into a disagreement. I shall indicate what the main arguments were. The argument in favor of increasing the rate of saving ran mainly along the lines of playing our part in the growth of the world economy. It was believed generally, with some exceptions, that additional saving by the United States would mean more capital available for use abroad for development of the world economy, and that the United States might benefit from this.

Objection No. 1 was that perhaps capital is not what the world needs. Objection No. 2 was that it is not at all certain that the development of the economy of the rest of the world would necessarily react favorably on the United States. If we saved instead of consumed, and sent the money abroad to finance sputnik plants in Lithuania, the net result might be unemployment in the United States, if not destruction. Objection No. 3 was the point which is associated with Professor Milton Friedman of the University of Chicago. Why do we want to raise the rate of growth above what people want it to be? The rate of growth should be determined by the decisions of individuals as to spending and saving, and why have we any moral right to influence this decision any more than we should attempt to influence any other decision?

So much for the desirability point.

Then, instead of discussing the effect of all these various policies upon saving, we got sidetracked into a discussion of the meaning and validity of Denison's Law. Mr. Fand, a member of our group, was a member of the Committee for Economic Development, along with Mr. Denison, at the time Denison's Law was developed. There may be some of you whose familiarity with Denison's Law is less than Mr. Fand's, and perhaps even less than Bronfenbrenner's, so I had better tell you what it is.

Denison's Law is the principle that, come what may, total private savings, individual and corporate, is a fairly constant percentage of GNP. The percentage turns out to be 14.63, plus or minus a very small standard deviation. Thus, it really does not make any difference what the rate of interest is, what government spending is, what taxes are, what wages are, what prices are, what the income distribution is or what the level of prosperity is. This seems to be one of the broad uniformities that the economy gets into.

If Denison is correct, there is really nothing we can do about the economy except beat our gums. If we encourage individual saving, perhaps all we are doing is discouraging corporate saving. That is to say, suppose individuals save more. This makes money more available for the corporate sector. Therefore, the corporate sector increases its payout ratio and saves less, and not very much is accomplished by any of these devices.

We discussed how valid Denison's Law is, how limited the cases to which it has been applied and what it all means anyway. One of the most interesting discussions of its possible significance was this: If it is true that private saving is a relatively constant proportion of GNP, then if we are going to save more and contribute more to the economic development of the underprivileged 90-odd per cent of the world population, the additional saving must come from the government sector. This means either lower government expenditures elsewhere or higher taxes, or both, in some combination. And higher taxes or lower government expenditures elsewhere imply lower incomes. Thus, we are operating somewhat at cross purposes, lowering GNP and thereby lowering private saving in our own economy.

We got into a certain amount of difficulty relative to the old argument between the economists and the business administration people, with the business administration people represented particularly by Professor Edwards. He took the position, I believe, that the economists expect everything to be done by the government, whereas market forces have a way of adjusting things themselves; the important thing is the economic climate. I do not think any of the economists really replied to this, so I shall stick my own neck out and say that, in general, what distinguishes an economist from other forms of social scientists is that the economist at least likes to consider what might happen as a result of a free market, so that the charge of undue reliance on the government is not one of our professional biases.

That is as far as we got, as I see it. It is not presented as being satisfactory. It would have been much better if we had had more time to cover some of these other subjects in detail, although I am not sure we would have had any more in the way of a consensus to report. Mr. Chairman, this is the best I can do.

MODERATOR WEIMER: This gives me a chance to comment on Denison's Law. It simply means that things are a lot more complicated than most people think they are. Probably this applies to saving.

What about your group, Professor Hayes?

REPORT OF GROUP 2

DOUGLAS HAYES: The general conclusion of our group was that the issues are very complex. As a consequence, there was considerable diversity of opinions on the question. I must admit that our meeting resembled a brainstorming session rather than a carefully thought out, logical framework of analysis. Therefore I am sure that there are a number of holes in the ideas presented.

In the first place, the premise was questioned as to whether the outstanding challenge of the 1960s is to increase savings. It seemed to be the consensus of the group that this hypothesis had arisen from the fact that the rate of growth of the Russians has received prominence in recent years, and reports have been widely disseminated to the effect that we are falling behind in the rate of growth in this country. As a consequence, it is argued that the rate of capital formation should be increased in the United States. It follows that in order to do this without severe inflationary consequences it will be necessary to increase the flow of money and real savings available for investment in productive resources. It was also felt that this premise may be based on our recent experience which has been marked by tight money conditions in the capital markets. It is sometimes held that these conditions are symptomatic of an inadequate supply of savings relative to the demand for them. But the question was raised as to whether savings could not be excessive under certain circumstances. In this connection, we thought of Professor Samuelson's statement this morning to the effect that perhaps a model can be constructed with a negative rate of interest. The possibility of such conditions would certainly not suggest the need for additional savings but would suggest that perhaps savings could be excessive, at least on a temporary basis. Perhaps we are here going back to the economic circumstances of the 1930s, but nonetheless it should be reported that some in the group questioned the need for strong stimuli for saving.

But, accepting the premise that capital formation should be increased, what can be done about it? One of the first comments was by Mr. Livermore, who suggested that the percentage of individual savings to the total amount of personal income has been reduced greatly in the last forty-five or fifty years. The opinion was expressed that the very heavy progressive income tax has been quite largely responsible for this fact. In brief, it was suggested that the income tax has greatly reduced the relative flow of income to wealthy individuals who formerly saved a large proportion of their incomes. Such individuals can no longer save at the same rate they could before.

As a result, one brainstorming idea was that if you really are serious about increasing savings in relation to consumption, what might be done from the tax policy standpoint would be to replace the progressive income tax with a sales tax on consumption items. One must admit that a revision of taxation along such lines is an interesting idea. To summarize, the theory is that this type of tax reform would discourage consumption and make it possible again for high income receivers to save larger portions of their incomes. The result, it is felt, would be an increase in the total supply of savings.

The question quickly arose as to whether such a means of stimulating saving would tend to reduce the relative share of savings flowing through institutions. There was some opinion expressed that if a greater proportion of savings accrued to wealthy individuals, this would mean a reduction in the relative flow through institutions, since such large savers would be more inclined to make direct investments of one kind or another.

Another interesting idea, at least to me, was suggested by an article in yesterday's *Wall Street Journal* on the very heavy growth in the sale of mutual funds and the tremendous pressures that have been brought to bear to increase their sale. The article pointed out that in the last ten years, through intensive merchandising of mutual funds, the industry has shown a tremendous rate of growth. The idea was expressed that perhaps more stress could be laid upon advertising and merchandising of the savings function to income receivers, using the ideas that the Madison Avenue boys have been employing to stimulate greater outlays on consumption items. Perhaps savings institutions should engage in heavier merchandising activities to stimulate saving by trying to tone down the idea that we need a new car each year with a higher tail fin.

We also discussed the point that savings arise when individuals pay on residential mortgages. In other words, the building up of equity in consumer durables and housing is a form of saving. With this fact in mind, the idea was expressed that possibly total savings could be increased by encouraging individuals to prepay their commitments to lenders. Along this line it was suggested that institutions might consider removing penalty rates on prepayment. There was even the wild suggestion that selective credit controls might be introduced to cause the rate of loan pay-off to be more rapid by reducing the maximum maturities of mortgages and possibly consumer loans; increasing original down payments would be part of such controls as well. Perhaps it is more accurate to say that such measures would tend to limit consumer dissaving rather than increase the total supply of savings. We did not explore fully the possible drawbacks to selective controls, so this view is not presented in the guise of a recommendation.

Finally, some attention was directed to the question of the relationship of the apparent inflationary bias in the economy to the rate of saving. Here we got into a chicken-and-egg kind of argument. Does an inadequate rate of saving encourage inflation, or does inflation tend to discourage saving? In other words, if you accept the premise that more saving should be encouraged, does an inflationary bias reduce the flow of savings that would otherwise occur? But some in the group held the view that an inadequate rate of saving might be partially responsible for the inflationary bias. However, the cause-and-effect problem here was not well worked out by us.

The inflationary problem would seem particularly troublesome to thrift institutions offering fixed-dollar returns of both principal and income to savers. If the general attitude or expectation of the general public became one of inflation, this might affect adversely the amount of savings placed with such thrift institutions versus other forms, such as equities and real estate. It was suggested that if this were regarded as a problem, thrift institutions might give careful consideration to the fact that perhaps the danger and risks of inflation in the last few years have been greatly exaggerated. Perhaps the mutual fund salesmen, who use the inflation argument to direct individuals into the funds, are overselling their product. It was noted that the rate of inflation has not been rapid in the last five or six years and that forecasts of continued creeping inflation have by no means been vindicated by our recent experience in the economy.

These were a few views that were expressed by our group. Once we accepted the premise that more savings are desirable, then saving might be stimulated by actions along the following lines: (1) national economic policy directed toward a high level of business activity without inflation; (2) merchandising by thrift institutions to encourage individuals to increase savings in relation to consumption; and (3) reorientation of the tax structure to encourage saving, such as shifting from a progressive income tax to sales taxes.

The question was asked: What national policies could conceivably be adopted to achieve the goal which was premised? The above were some ideas that were expressed as to what could be done. It was not necessarily agreed that these actions would be wise public policy in other respects, but only that they might increase the amount of savings in relation to total disposable income.

MODERATOR WEIMER: Thank you very much.

Professor Wendt, you also have a major contribution to make.

REPORT OF GROUP 3

PAUL WENDT: Our group made the Herculean assumption that it *is* desirable to stimulate savings. After hearing Mr. Bronfenbrenner's experience, I am pleased that we made this decision fairly early.

We endeavored first to decide what we meant by "savings." It soon became apparent that if we defined savings in the very general way in which most of us have defined it thus far in these discussions, we might set up a different set of policies for stimulating saving in that sense than we might set up for stimulating the flow of funds into a certain type of financial institution, for example. So some of our policies or recommendations are directed to the latter objective. A few of the more erudite members appeared to be familiar with Denison's Law, but we did not allow them to confuse us on this subject — we went right on.

We discussed three types of policies to stimulate saving. I have classified one of them under "general economic policy." It appeared to us that governmental policies which tended to control inflation — tended to stabilize the purchasing power of money — would have the effect of stimulating saving. Attention was called to the fact that in some countries which have been more successful in this respect, the volume of savings has been higher than in others. This is one set of general economic policies which we felt might be appropriate in terms of stimulating saving.

A second was the idea, possibly not entirely consistent with the first premise, that if incomes could be raised substantially, savings would be increased. It is, of course, real incomes to which I am referring.

Now we turn to a group of suggestions that I am calling "specific legal instruments." Here we spent a little time in discussing tax exemptions. One member of our group called attention to West Germany's highly successful experience in the postwar period in stimulating the flow of funds into savings institutions through a variety of tax exemptions, including exemptions for funds deposited in savings institutions, accelerated depreciation for tax purposes for persons investing funds in housing, and corporate tax exemptions for enterprises placing desposits at no interest with mortgage loan institutions. The record is impressive in terms of results.

The same questions that were raised a moment or two ago were raised in our discussion: Is the cure worse than the disease? What happens to the distribution of incomes? Will the patterns of corporate concentration or financial control in a country be altered through the employment of the tax exemption feature?

Several persons took rather a strong exception to the use of tax devices in this manner. Under the heading of specific legal instruments, we talked about forced savings on the part of the government. Most of the group were agreed that forced savings, in the sense that they occur in wartime, were not particularly palatable. However, this apparently would not exclude in the minds of many of us specific types of controls such as Regulation Q and Regulation X, which would require higher down payments or regulate borrowing and, hence, reduce the demand for savings as well as stimulate greater saving by certain groups. The point was raised, in a somewhat negative fashion, that perhaps some of the efforts of the government to aid the aged would have an adverse effect on savings for this particular group.

Then we explored a number of mechanical stimuli, including the promotional aspect of encouraging saving.

It seems to us, if I may summarize briefly, that this is a highly complex problem and that once you undertake to stimulate saving it is not altogether certain that there may not be some other adverse effect upon the economy so that in some over-all sense it may be less desirable than the current level of saving, if this is considered inadequate. I, personally, have been impressed with the technical success of the West German experiment in the use of tax incentives. With respect to general economic policy, we talked about raising incomes and in the same breath we talked about controlling inflation; this is a trick that none of us has mastered yet, but if we could do it I think it would have a salutary effect on savings. We did not discuss the point in detail, but it seemed to be the consensus that there are few good reasons for government control of interest rates. I might add, parenthetically, that I am not wholly satisfied with the argument that FHA and VA fixed rates have greatly restricted the total flow of funds into housing and the mortgage markets; they may have restricted them somewhat but, in my judgment, not to any substantial degree.

That is, I think, our summary, even though it probably goes somewhat beyond the views of some in our group.

Discussion*

SHAW LIVERMORE: There is one question that has been lost that I wanted to ask Woody after his talk. I do not know if anyone among us would try to answer this, but I am wondering where the free-economy people stand on removing all restrictions on the payment of interest? The one most familiar subject here is the restriction on commercial banks, which are not allowed to pay more than 3% on time deposits. Why not abolish that restriction and let each financial institution pay any interest rate it wants to? Where do we stand on the removal of this restriction in our economy?

* Proceedings of the Third Annual Conference, 1960, Excerpts from the Discussion, pp. 91–99.

MODERATOR WEIMER: Does anybody want to answer that?

MR. HAYES: I am willing to take a stand on this. In the case of commercial banks, I believe the Banking Act of 1935 also removed interest on demand deposits. It was apparent to many people at that time that many of the difficulties of the banking system in the late 1920s were a result of the undesirable repercussions of uncontrolled interest rates. If in some areas the government must step in, in the public interest, to regulate, then I suppose — and this premise was established way back in the time of the first and second Banks of the United States — that certain public control should be applied to banks that are given the authority to create and hold the money supply of the country. Therefore, I think we can make a case, even though we are in principle against undue interference with a free market, for such regulations as will promote the solvency and the soundness of the banking system. And I would stand, as a free-enterprise man, for at least some restrictions in this area, in view of the historical experience. My answer is purely historical, not theoretical.

MR. LIVERMORE: It always puzzles me why these people are against special limited interest rates for veterans or for the United States Treasury, which is trying to hold down the national budget by eliminating ceilings. Congress puts a ceiling on the rate at which the Treasury can borrow. You are in a tangle right away.

MR. HAYES: That is a different proposition, Mr. Livermore. The legislation limits the maximum amount the banks may pay.

MR. LIVERMORE: We are all aiming at the general welfare by these restrictions, are we not?

MR. BRONFENBRENNER: I am a free-market man. There have been some agencies of the federal government that have seriously doubted it, but I would go right along with Professors Gurley and Shaw and agree that these particular restrictions are obsolete and might very well be done away with, particularly since we have the Federal Deposit Insurance Corporation for the protection of depositors. They have explored this much more than I, and I am not going to propose this as my own view. But this is part of the gist of their thesis: that competition between commercial banks and other financial institutions would be made more equitable by removing the limitations on commercial banks.

I do not know whether the savings and loan business, which is sponsoring this Conference, would like this because it might be affected adversely by it. But I accept that general position.

MR. LIVERMORE: I simply feel that we are challenged by a past period of mismanagement of the banking system, that is all.

PAUL SAMUELSON: Denison's Law has been brought up. I should like to name a law which is not so well known because I have just formulated it. It is "Samuelson's Law," and it says that all laws like Denison's Law, Clark's Law and a number of others are false. To make this a noncontradictory statement, I append — with the exception of Samuelson's Law.

I do not mean that as a joke. Take Pareto's Law. A lot of income statistics can be plotted on double-log paper and there is some resemblance in the coefficient that occurs. From what Pareto concluded, there is not anything to do about anything. Actually, Pareto's Law is not a terribly good fit to the coefficient. It has changed. It may look like a small change, but that is just because you do not know what "small" is, once you are using double-log paper. Progressive — and by that I mean modern, developed — nations show a systematic difference in Pareto's Law from other nations. And if you confront Denison's Law with questions and statistics, and if you wait until people have looked into it more carefully, I think you will find that it will go the way of Colin Clark's Law and other laws.

My final word is about a numbers game which I used to study with respect to countries. It does not get you too far. One year, West Germany looks very good; it used to be Belgium that looked very good. But you can almost always, even in Western Europe, compare two countries which have quite different behavior patterns of their institutions and get almost the same result. You could not imagine two more diverse countries than Sweden and Switzerland, but I am told that they have grown at about the same rate in the last thirty years and that, while the differences have become more pronounced, the rate of capital formation has been about the same. Take Chile and Brazil, two countries with tremendous rates of inflation; in Chile you do not get capital formation, but in Brazil you are getting a lot of capital formation. Take West Germany and France, where you would not know which was which, if you just looked at the production index; France defied the textbooks by depreciating its currency and West Germany pursued its purpose through other devices, but both were going in the same direction.

DAVID FAND: I do not see why you want to repeal Denison's Law to get your policy conclusion, because actually his law goes directly along the lines you are suggesting. That is, if private saving is a fixed ratio of gross national product, the only way that you can get more capital formation is to have government savings so that you can buy surpluses.

MR. SAMUELSON: In the first place, I am sure that our hosts did not invite us here simply to say things they would like to hear, and I am not trying to sell any particular program. In the second place, I had not realized that Denison's Law refers to private savings. In any case, for the policy conclusion which I have been discussing, not recommending, it is not necessary that there be any constant coefficient or any specific monetary policy.

22

Freedom of Entry in Finance*

We hear increasingly the charge that certain metropolitan trade areas are "overbanked," implying that the number of institutions and the number of offices is excessive and that no additional charters or branches ought to be authorized. What criteria might be developed to aid supervisory authorities in their task of determining the validity of this claim? How far should we go in protecting existing institutions against entry by others? Looking ahead, what kind of a network of financial institutions, in terms of offices and facilities, seems most appropriate for the next decade?

ELMUS WICKER:[1] This topic is concerned primarily with problems arising out of the freedom of entry in finance. Our major question was: Does overbanking exist and, if so, what criterion or criteria might we suggest for use by the regulatory authorities?

I believe I can summarize in one sentence the deliberations of the group. The discussion was always interesting, frequently important and seldom decisive. But there was unanimous agreement, I think, among the members that there was need for much conceptual clarification.

First, the question was raised as to what we mean by overbanking. The retort was that maybe we have underbanking, and members of the group from New York and California stressed the differences which exist in the two states. The clarification that was needed arose out of the meaning of

* Proceedings of the Sixth Annual Conference, 1963, pp. 91–99, Report on and Discussion of Topic 3 in a panel entitled, "The New Environment Facing Financial Intermediaries in the Next Decade."
[1] College of Arts and Sciences, Indiana University, Bloomington, Ind.

overbanking. We did not take the question to refer only to commercial banks. We interpreted the terms of reference more broadly to include all financial institutions, and frequently our discussion referred to both commercial banks and nonbank financial institutions. The conclusions we reached and the analysis we undertook applied to both.

There was some merit, the group thought, in allowing the market test as a relevant criterion for freedom of entry into banking. Some individuals in the group expressed qualifications about the criterion, but I think there was widespread agreement on the necessity for a greater liberalization of existing legislation with respect to freedom of entry by both bank and nonbank financial institutions.

The question arose as to whether we were talking primarily about the proliferation of existing offices of a given number of firms or about the growth in the numbers of firms. The question also was raised whether there are economies of scale among both the nonbank intermediaries and the commercial banks. Needless to say, no conclusion was reached except that agreement was expressed that there are very little data at the moment to warrant any strong opinion one way or the other.

The major conclusion of the group, already expressed, was that there should be greater liberalization of existing legislation relative to freedom of entry. We directed ourselves specifically to the question of branch banking, and I gathered that most members of the group felt that branch banking should be inaugurated throughout the country. I also gleaned the conclusion that they would be favorable to the development of national branch banking for savings and loan associations as well.

Discussion

MODERATOR KETCHUM: Thank you, Elmus. Who has the first comment or question on Mr. Wicker's report?

JOHN BOWYER: On the matter of freedom of entry into the market, I think one should distinguish between financial institutions that are allowed to accept deposits of various types and the so-called nondeposit type of financial institution. The reason I make this distinction is that sales finance companies are now having a very difficult time because of the freedom of entry that certain financial institutions possess in their field. Because of this competition they have been forced, in order to obtain income, to accept marginal paper, a poor quality of loan. Now, if the same thing happened to commercial banks and savings and loan associations in their efforts to obtain more income, they would have to accept loans of similarly poor quality. I think the consequences in the deposit type of financial institution would be very grave as far as the general public is concerned. The operators of these institutions would also reach for marginal paper; and because of their fiduciary or quasi-fiduciary relationship with their depositors, someone would start losing money.

A second point on branch banking. At the time I studied under Professor Edwards, I was thoroughly indoctrinated — I do not recall whether by him or by Professor Cleveland — in the divine origins of branch banking. I have long since been disabused. One very good reason is that branch banking, with all its efficiencies, will foster, relatively speaking, inefficiency in the rest of the economy. Large branch banking organizations follow restrictive lending practices; that is, they tend to have a rigid lending practice for particular types of businesses. If they do not happen to have experience with that particular type of business, they just do not grant a loan. The fact that a business has been rejected goes on the teletype, or however they communicate, and then there is no freedom of entry. In unit banking, on the other hand, there are different personalities, different ways of looking at things. I think unit banking will tend to foster the over-all efficiency of the economy.

MR. WICKER: I will have to ask Mr. Grunewald to answer that, because I had to spend all my time listening and not talking, and that was very painful. But I think it was implicit in the group's discussion that there is a distinction between commercial banks and nonbank intermediaries with respect to the destabilizing effects of insolvency. I think the view was expressed very well by one member that perhaps there is less need to concern ourselves with the insolvency of a savings and loan association than with the consequences of insolvency of a branch bank.

DONALD GRUNEWALD: I want to make two points in this connection. First of all, we have bank examiners to see to it that banks are not making bad loans or taking weak paper. So there is that regulatory function to protect depositors.

On the second point, with respect to the making of loans, the problem comes in small unit banking towns where there is only one bank to go to, and no competition. With branch banks, there might be eight or ten different large banks. For example, in Canada there are only nine or ten banks, I believe, but every bank is in every city. The result is that if one bank does not specialize, for example, in garment trade loans, another bank will, so that there is much more competition and, I think, a much better chance of getting a loan than if one had to resort to one little unit bank in a town.

LEON SCHUR: When Mr. Wicker asked the group if anyone objected to the concept of branch banking, certainly on a statewide basis there were no objectors. Some may just have remained silent, but no one was willing to express that opinion at the time. Secondly, there was a feeling — certainly general if not unanimous — that we have no objective criteria today to support or deny entry into the banking field or the nonbank intermediary field. We all hope such criteria may be developed, but I think there was a healthy skepticism, at least on the part of some of us, that criteria ever can be developed. In the absence of such criteria, there was a feeling that we should move in the direction of free entry into both areas — the banking area and the nonbank intermediary area. We might, as a step, take the Shaw proposal in California that some sort of bidding for charters be used, but this is just a step in the direction of even greater entry into the field.

SHERMAN SHAPIRO: Mr. Bowyer has asserted things that are not facts. Unit banks behave in a specific fashion and branch banks in another — there is no use arguing about facts. It is a yes or no proposition, and I do not think his position is supportable. I do not think that virtue is completely on the side of the unit bank in that it behaves in a gentlemanly fashion as a community servant and so on. There are many myths connected with the unit bank. In our discussion we touched on the economies of scale and monopoly, but we came to no conclusion on these issues.

MR. BOWYER: I should like to ask Mr. Shapiro one question. You say this is a statement of fact. What is your support for this factual statement?

MR. SHAPIRO: You asserted that unit banks behave in a certain fashion. I do not think that statement is supportable.

MR. BOWYER: I have been engaged in some extracurricular activity for a number of years, making presentations to commercial banks on behalf of finance companies attempting to secure bank loans. I admit that my sample is small, but I have noticed that in the western part of the United States, where we have quite an extensive branch banking system, if a finance company of any size (I am not talking about a national company but about a regional chain) gets turned down by one or two institutions, it is hard put to expand very much.

Now, in reply to Mr. Shapiro, I have read in the annual report of one of the Canadian oil companies that a bank in Montreal which specializes in oil loans decided last winter that the oil market was not going to be the best in Canada, so it refused to advance funds to the company. Now, it is conceivable that if there had been another bank in Canada specializing in oil loans, it might have taken another view. If this conference is any indication of the possibility of differences in points of view, I am sure that would have been true.

MR. SHAPIRO: But no one in the group suggested that we develop a system in the United States identical to that of Canada. I think only the chairman suggested nationwide branch banking.

MR. BOWYER: I was not there, so it is difficult for me to establish what your group did say.

MR. SHAPIRO: I would say our group did an excellent job.

CHARLES PARTEE: May I ask Mr. Wicker what he meant when he said that freedom of entry should be determined by the market — whether he really meant through the test of failure. Secondly, in connection with your later assertion that there is a difference between the importance of a failure of a savings and loan association and a failure of a bank, does this imply that the group would also support the idea of extensive branching for banks only with freedom of entry for unit savings and loan associations, on the grounds that a branch is stronger than a unit?

PRESTON MARTIN: I think that our comments in the group meeting with regard to freedom of entry had to do with freedom of entry of new offices within market areas for financial services. The group was very heavily in favor of branch entry rather than unit entry.

MR. PARTEE: You are thinking only of profits rather than of failure, that is, if the branch proved not to be profitable?

THOMAS WOLFE: That is right. I do not think that failure was what we meant. If a branch were established and proved unprofitable, it would be a simple matter and there would be no cause for repercussions, whereas if a unit bank in the same town were to prove unprofitable, it would be serious.

MR. PARTEE: I think that is an important qualification.

MR. WICKER: I do not know whether it is proper, but I wish to enter a very strong minority report in the group. I distinguish sharply between the behavior of the banking system and the nonbank intermediaries, and I am not impressed with their alleged similarities. Shaw and Gurley have yet to produce the evidence that nonbank intermediaries are destabilizing. I know that their evidence is supposed to appear in the second volume, but I also understand that is why it is delayed. That is a very unkind remark and it may not be true, but I confess that I see no reason why one ought not to have complete, unregulated freedom of entry into the nonbank intermediary field.

RICHARD GOODE: You would get rid of the government insurance of savings and loan accounts, I take it? That is inconsistent. It is not a public function.

MR. WICKER: I have no government function ideology here.

MR. GOODE: No, this is a serious question. If it really is a matter of no public policy concern, I do not see how we can justify this government insurance corporation for savings and loans any more than we can for gasoline filling stations.

MR. WICKER: Mr. Goode, I maintain that it is still to be demonstrated what are the destabilizing effects of complete freedom of entry into the savings and loan business. If there is evidence that they can initiate an economic disturbance, then I am prepared to support greater regulation.

MR. GOODE: Oh, I am sorry. I have not made my question clear. I was not taking a position of destabilization. I was just asking whether you feel that is an implication of your position.

MR. WICKER: No, I do not.

MR. GOODE: Can you tell me what the difference is, then, between a savings and loan association and another kind of business, and why we ought to have insurance for one and not the other?

ARTHUR MEYERS: No one has said that we should not have insurance for the other.

MR. GOODE: Maybe that is the answer.

MR. SHAPIRO: Are you in favor of completely free entry for the savings and loans?

MR. WICKER: I am trying not to maintain any strong position. I do not know of any evidence which strongly supports free entry other than the fact that they have had it for quite some time.

MR. SHAPIRO: Let us assume away the problem of instability, at least temporarily. You suggest this may be all right. Now, if we have completely free entry and we have insurance of accounts, I think we have a real anomaly, because I know of no insurer that is willing to write blank checks.

MR. WICKER: The government seems to be prepared to do it.

MR. SHAPIRO: No, no! That is not so!

MR. WICKER: It comes close to being so, however.

MR. SHAPIRO: The FDIC and the FSLIC, while they may not have all the powers they would like — typical of a bureaucracy — nevertheless have some powers. From time to time they exercise these powers; they entice, encourage and exhort savings and loans and banks to behave properly. It is very difficult for me to conceive of these insurers existing without any power whatsoever.

MR. WICKER: In the absence of knowledge demonstrating to me that nonbank financial intermediaries are destabilizing, I support account insurance. The lack of evidence does not lead me to a positive conclusion that there should either be or not be account insurance.

MR. SHAPIRO: It seems to me that, as a taxpayer, I would object seriously to this arrangement. My tax dollars would be dissipated because the government is willing to insure anyone who wants to come in.

HUGH MACAULAY: Could insurance not be optional? Then those savings and loans that wished to insure could and those that did not would not, and the customers might be attracted or repelled by this optional feature.

PETER GRAY: On the subject of free entry, I think there was no suggestion that there be no capital requirements. Under a system of capital requirements the stockholders, or whatever you want to call them, are taking the prime risk. In other words, I envision that any insurance agency would require a certain capital deposit ratio or something of that nature, and I think this certainly would be comprehensible and compatible with freedom of entry.

MR. SHAPIRO: No, that is not compatible. If anything, it would be a restriction.

MR. MEYERS: I get bothered by the discussion of freedom of entry, where the position is that the insurance provision applies uniformly to everybody. Now, if we are talking about the savings and loan business in contrast to another business, I can see that the insurance might be an issue. But if we are talking about a savings and loan going into business in one place in contrast to another, then our position is that the same insurance provisions everywhere are a limiting factor to entry. This I do not get. I cannot see that the uniform imposition of insurance is a restriction of entry — maybe entry into the savings and loan business, but not of one savings and loan in contrast to another.

MR. PARTEE: I happen to live in Maryland. Maryland had, in effect, freedom of entry, yet the capital coverage did not seem sufficient to have an effect.

MR. GRAY: May I amend my statement? I think I implied, but I did not state that I would insist, frankly, after the Maryland debacle, on federal insurance.

JOHN STAFFORD: As a matter of fact, there is freedom of entry. It is not necessary to be insured to start a savings and loan now. Any group of people that meets the requirements of state law as to capital, experience and so on has freedom of entry. There is no requirement for a state-chartered savings and loan to acquire insurance.

MR. MARTIN: Unless the state regulatory authorities cause such a requirement to be installed, which some states do.

MR. STAFFORD: But that is not too common. In our discussion group I do not think we were envisioning the sort of freedom of entry such as you had in Maryland, where there were no regulations or requirements. I do not think we went that far.

MR. WICKER: May I ask Mr. Goode a question? Is there some concern, such as I gather Mr. Shapiro is expressing, about the guarantee of losses of savers in savings and loan associations when there is free entry? Is this a question of social loss to the community as a whole by allowing freedom of entry?

MR. GOODE: I think there are two questions here, if I may say so. There might be a social loss. There might also be the loss which Mr. Shapiro mentioned and which I as a taxpayer do not like — the tax for support of this kind of venture. But my question really was not directed to that solely. Rather, it was a reaction to what seemed to me to be a rather strong statement that we need not be very much concerned about the insolvency of savings and loan associations. It seemed to me that view implied that we had been mistaken when we set up the Federal Savings and Loan Insurance Corporation to insure their savings accounts. If one holds to that view, I think one ought to get rid of the thing as an unnecessary government activity.

MR. WICKER: I am sorry if I created that impression. I thought I qualified my statement by saying that there is an absence of knowledge of what are the destabilizing effects of insolvencies of savings and loan associations. I should like to see instances where deposit shifts between savings and loan associations and commercial banks have been in the past, other than perhaps in the 1930s, a serious source of destabilization.

JAMES EARLEY: My impression of our group discussion was that we were not discussing freedom of entry in any abstract sense but that we did feel that it was important to free from any state restrictions the freedom of entry of banks and possibly savings and loan associations so that the use of the market test would at least be practicable. This led up, I think, to the proposal that perhaps branch banking would permit a closer approach to a market test without the dangers of insolvency. But there was no idea, as I got it, that we should leave financial institutions entirely free and without various types of restrictions such as insurance.

MR. WICKER: I hope the Conference will distinguish between what happened in the group and this hornets' nest I just raised.

MODERATOR KETCHUM: We have time for one more comment. John Stafford?

MR. STAFFORD: On the conferees' preoccupation with the loss to the taxpayer because of the failure of an insured institution, Mr. Mortlock has just passed me the year-end statement of his association, mainly to emphasize that the FSLIC is supported by the savings and loan business, not by the taxpayers. If you care to contend with Mr. Mortlock, he spent $112,147.67 for insurance last year. I just thought I would close with a complete concrete fact about which there is no theory.

MODERATOR KETCHUM: On behalf of all of us, let me thank the participants on this panel for their splendid job in summarizing the continuities and discontinuities of the presentations of their respective groups. Thank you all.

OBJECTIVE STANDARDS FOR ENTRY INTO FINANCE BUSINESS*

LEON SCHUR: I should like to ask a question about entry into the finance business. Such terms as "economic need" and "harm to existing institutions" are pretty vague, and may mean all things to all people. Now, we have heard one objective standard, that is, whether a particular city

* Proceedings of the Sixth Annual Conference, 1963, Excerpts from a panel entitled, "The Savings and Loan Business," pp. 151–78.

comes up to a per capita asset structure for a county and for a state. Mr. Anderson, would you accept this standard? Do you have any other objective standards by which everyone in this room, for example, using those standards could arrive at the same answer?

ALLAN ANDERSON: I do not think there are necessarily any population standards except in metropolitan areas. In the city of Chicago, we once figured that there should be at least 35,000 people for each association and that no new institution would be chartered unless it was a mile or so from another association. But in the chartering of new institutions, one cannot get away from the employment of judgment. I have taken statistics and studied towns in Illinois, and have found in one town of 8,000 people one institution with assets of $4 million and in another town with an equivalent population I have found three savings and loan associations, each of them larger than the single institution in the first town. They all sell thrift and home ownership, and tend to contribute to one another's success. There are so many variables at work that it is impossible to get away from the matter of judgment. The answer cannot be reduced to cold statistics.

MR. SCHUR: If you are going to allow judgment, is there not an element of abuse? Let me ask this: What do you think would happen if there were free entry into the field, in the sense that you might demand certain character requirements (say, a character similar to Professor Edwards'), certain capital requirements and insurance protection but, beyond that, you were to allow free entry? What would be the consequence?

MR. ANDERSON: There is free entry into the clothing business. Every man in this room, if he wants to, can go to Kokomo, Ind., and open a clothing store; if he loses any money he will, in large part, be losing his own money or such amount as he may have borrowed. But we cannot let every man in this room go to Kokomo and open a savings and loan institution, because he is not using his own money; he is using the people's money, and therefore it is necessary for a supervisory authority to step in and say there cannot be absolutely free entry into the market place. The public has to be protected. Competition is necessary to protect the public against excessive loan charges, but the public also has to be protected against excessive risk. If too many financial institutions attempt to live off the same land in attracting capital and putting their funds to work, there will be abuses. I know whereof I speak.

WARREN HILL: I have lived with the branch office question in our state legislature for the last two or three years. We started with the basic principle that everybody who runs an institution wants the right to have a branch wherever he wants one, but does not want anybody else to have a branch near his. We dealt with existing things as we found them and tried to find some standards for determining whether or not a group should be given a license to apply for a charter. The criteria Mr. Anderson spoke of also have to be met. We maintained for a long time that commercial banks had no right to object to our branching. The converse was equally true, because we are not commercial banks and they are not savings associations. But the Supreme Court upset that point and told the New Jersey banking authorities that we have a right to argue in their cases and they have a right to argue in ours.

MODERATOR STRUNK: Let me just say, before moving on to another subject, that if you people could come up with some criteria, you would be the most popular professors around, so far as the supervisory authorities are concerned. This has been a major problem for them. Frankly, sometimes they look for an arithmetical guide so they can say "no" to the applicant who has a governor, senator, congressman or mayor on his side. The political pressures in this area are quite real at times. It would be wonderful if the supervisory authorities could find some objective criteria in this field.

23

Institutional Aspects of Saving*

What have been recent trends in the institutionalization of saving and can we expect these trends to continue? Does this institutionalization inhibit the proper functioning of the capital markets? For example, does the unequal accumulation of savings in certain institutions committed to mortgage investment distort capital flows? What are the implications of changing income distributions of American families for the volume and character of savings? Has the United States savings bond program outlived its usefulness?

JOHN CLENDENIN:[1] I am sorry to be stubborn, Mr. Chairman, but I do not think I can speak for Group 2. The group rode off on Mr. Eisenhower's white horses in all directions rapidly at once, and I am a bit at a loss to know what it did conclude. We had three questions, and I can give you some of our thinking, however, on each of them.

The first question: What changes are taking place in savings institutions, and will these changes continue? Since this was discussed rather extensively in a carefully prepared talk at lunch, our group devoted itself to making observations about some facets of the matter.

We considered, first, the apparent indication in the financial savings figures that equity investment, particularly in stocks by individuals, is declining. This occasioned some surprise, but the figures themselves are

* Proceedings of the Fourth Annual Conference, 1961, pp. 90–93, Report on Topic 2 in a panel entitled, "Savings in the American Economy."
[1] Graduate School of Business Administration, University of California, Los Angeles, Calif.

not particularly arguable, I guess, in spite of the increase in the number of registered shareholders we hear about. However, the group observed that internally generated business capital is adding rather substantially to the equities owned by individuals and that individuals are likewise accumulating real estate equities; and we guessed, without having the figures to be positive, that equity ownership by individuals is probably maintaining its position in individual programs as a percentage of the total. It was also observed that new personal savings which we know are going into stocks are quite possibly retiring, and in the past have retired, large holdings owned by other individuals, which holdings have doubtless gone into personally owned businesses, into real estate ownership, and into municipals and governments and various and sundry other investments. So we are not especially disturbed about equity holdings by individuals.

Secondly, in considering changes which might take place in institutions, and their continuation, the group observed that many factors attract funds into institutional portfolios. There is the matter of yield rates, which bulked rather large in the presentation we heard at noon, the matter of service, the matter of convenience, the matter of the habits of individuals — incidental features which come along with the savings. It is observed that certainly for a generation in this country individual savings went into life insurance in large amounts, not because people elected to save via life insurance, but because they were electing to buy life insurance. An agent sold them appropriate forms of life insurance and they built up savings equities. This happens, of course.

It was also observed that the sales effort being made by institutional investors influences the flow of individual savings into those institutions. Mutual funds were mentioned. I am under the impression, for example, that it is not the economic merit of mutual funds, but rather the 7½% loading charge, which causes them to grow so vigorously. Americans will buy anything that is sold effectively.

However, we concede that threshold changes in amounts of investment by individuals in various institutions on pretty solid economic grounds do take place. Some of these changes may be slow because habit and contractual commitments (I cite again life insurance) are strong within us, but the institutions can change, and changes are to be expected.

The changes that we are to find in the future in the size and scope of financial institutions may come as a result of the changes in the demand for their funds to the extent that they are committed to particular channels of funds; and when the demand for these funds diminishes, certainly the earnings of these institutions, their capacity to pay, and ultimately the use of their funds by savers will decline. And institutions may decline because the savers changed their minds. We would encounter here changes in the growth rates of institutions. We might also encounter new forms of institutions, and we probably will. Variable annuities, real estate investment, and tax-exempt mutual funds were mentioned in this connection. Life insurance was mentioned as losing ground for rather obvious reasons: the growth of group coverage, the growth of pension funds, and perhaps the growth of Social Security.

We next turned our attention to our second question: Does institutionalization inhibit the proper functioning of the capital market? I suppose this means the channeling of savings into appropriate economic uses and on terms which are acceptable to the users, so that they are economically effective. There was some hesitation among us on this point — some question as to whether the types of loans and investments available to institutions which might appeal to savers would quickly enough satisfy the users of the funds, some question as to whether shifts in savers' allocations of funds could appropriately serve long- and short-term markets. But the general consensus of the group ran to the effect that not too much distortion is observed in the availability of funds to appropriate users, that we have enough different institutions and they have flexibility enough so that, in the main, savings funds will go through our collective institutions more or less where they should, admitting that there may be lags and some lack of fluidity at times. We concluded, in this connection, however, quoting this morning's discussions, that desirable broader investment powers and fewer restrictions on banks and probably other institutions would be helpful.

Lastly, the question: Has the savings bond outlived its usefulness? We did not call for a show of hands, but I can report some positive "yeses" and some positive "noes." In the course of the discussion it was observed that when savings and loan dividend rates, some three or four years ago, broke firmly in some areas above or close to savings bond rates, the correlation of small savings bonds sales with payrolls throughout the country was broken and some disappointment on the part of those who sell them was experienced.

It was observed that rapid and frequent changes in the savings bond plan and yield rate to accommodate changes in the competition were not very feasible for various reasons that I have not time to relate to you. It was also observed that the U. S. government needs the funds and that it might be difficult to manage anything like the volume of term financing that would be desirable on the part of the Treasury if the savings bond program were dropped or greatly reduced.

It was also observed that savings bond sales raid local communities of funds and that these communities are largely served by banks whose sources of funds are local and are needed locally. Counter to that argument, it was observed that local communities ought to expect to contribute to the financing of the federal government through the savings bond program and that if this means some embarrassment in the availability of local funds the communities ought to reach into the national capital markets, through agencies which are known to us, and ought to live like other people.

This, Mr. Chairman, is substantially the discussion of our group.

24

Financial Institutions and the
Allocation of Capital*

*Savings and loan associations, small business companies, credit
unions, and similar institutional types are confined to specific capital
markets. Can such specialization be defended on economic grounds?
Can such institutions increase risks that capital will be misallocated?
Can we accept the judgment of the Commission on Money and
Credit that the lending and investment powers should be broadened
as much as possible and that specialization will result from the
competitive patterns which evolve?*

BION HOWARD: I am not sure that we arrived at a clear position on any
one of these points. We had some trouble with the problem of definition,
but I shall skip that for the moment. I shall simply make a brief statement of what I think the general position of the group was on each of
the three questions, and shall leave it to the members of my group to take
issue with me if I have misstated our position.

Before getting to the questions, I might say that there was some discussion of the basic statement: "Savings and loan associations, small business
companies, credit unions and similar institutional types are confined to
specific capital markets." The issue was raised whether we were talking
about types of investment or geographic capital markets. We discussed
both.

I think we had the most difficulty on question No. 1: Can such specialization be defended on economic grounds? Generally, I think the feeling

* Proceedings of the Sixth Annual Conference, 1963, pp. 80–85, Report on and
Discussion of Topic 1 in a panel entitled, "The New Environment Facing Financial
Intermediaries in the Next Decade."

was that specialization embodies certain special privileges, for example, minimum liquidity, tax savings, etc., in the case of the savings and loan association. Along with that is the necessity of meeting certain standards and responsibilities, and in that sense specialization could be defended in terms of maintaining these special privileges. In other words, historically these institutions came on the scene presumably to meet a special need.

On question No. 2 — Can such institutions increase risks that capital will be misallocated? — we probably took the clearest position. I think the feeling of the group was that the risk of capital misallocation is minimal. In each of these capital markets we have a number of institutions which do have the ability to shift funds quite readily. This is true of insurance companies, pension funds, etc.; and to the extent that savings and loan associations or other institutions are not free to shift funds, the funds themselves will flow, with perhaps some small time lapse. I think the group felt this was not a great issue.

On the final question — Can we accept the judgment of the CMC that the lending and investment powers should be broadened as much as possible and that specialization will result from the competitive patterns which evolve? — we had a little problem with the term "as much as possible." Eddie Edwards suggested that "as much as possible" means "as much as politically possible" and, if that were the case, we did not have to go too far. It was definitely felt, I think, that specialization would result from competitive patterns, even though generally we were in favor of extending permission to go into all these capital markets. The feeling was that specialization probably would result.

I shall be glad to have any member of my group clarify or take issue with me on any of these points.

Discussion

MODERATOR KETCHUM: Thank you, Bion. I think it would be a desirable procedure if, after the presentation of the panelist, we had comments from other members of the group or questions and comments from the floor about the topic before we move on to the next topic. Are there any questions?

MARSHALL KAPLAN: I almost feel as if I had attended a different session. I suspect that is more because of my particular prejudices, but it was my impression that there was considerable argument on the advantages of relaxing present specialization restrictions. For example, there seemed to be almost unanimous agreement that the geographical restrictions under which savings and loans operate should be relaxed. I think most of us also would agree that consumer lending should be allowed to savings and loans; there seemed to be a great deal of feeling in that direction.

MR. HOWARD: Are you not saying essentially what I said?

MODERATOR KETCHUM: Was there any discussion about the determinants? That is, what would determine what additional outlets or uses of funds each of these specialized institutions would endeavor to develop?

MR. HOWARD: Is Mr. Mortlock here? We put the question directly to him as to what he would do if these restrictions were eliminated tomorrow. Generally speaking, I think he was not about to enter all these capital markets.

EUGENE MORTLOCK: I did qualify my position by saying that we should expand the authority wherever necessary so long as it relates to, say, the shelter industry and that there are some areas in the capital market that I personally would be hesitant to enter at this time. I feel that the concept of shelter area as such should be broadened to make use of our type of capital. There are many areas in which this can be done.

PAUL DARLING: I think this question was in the purview of your group. What was the feeling of the group, or would anyone here comment, with respect to a potential danger through competition on the paying of interest to customers of these institutions? Would this put the institutions under heavy pressure to find the necessary income to pay depositors or shareholders, thus leading to a possible dangerous increase in risks that are taken — or, more generally, the misallocation of capital?

MR. HOWARD: Our group did not get into that question directly.

SHERMAN MAISEL: I think one of your stated conclusions — that the market is flexible, that there are enough national lenders to cause these markets to form one market — is a matter of fact, and therefore the question is only one of interpretation of the fact. However, I certainly do not agree that there is any indication that there is any kind of a national market. Each lender at the moment is so specialized that he cannot enter into many individual markets. Looking at mortgage lending for any particular area, it seems to me that there is every indication that this is far from a national market. Therefore I would go along with the previous statement that if the ability to lend on mortgages were spread over a wider geographic area for all types of institutions, as opposed to the few types of lenders which now can enter the national market, it would make a great deal of difference.

MR. HOWARD: I did not mean to say that we did not think there would not be some misallocation, but we thought it would be mitigated by the fact that there are other institutions in the market.

MR. MAISEL: But there just are not any. If you look at the refinancing of single-family homes, you will find that there is only one institution basically in this market. There are all sorts of specialized markets in the shelter program where, in any one locality, you will find only one type of institution. As I say, I think this is a fact.

REUBEN KESSEL: Are insurance companies not in the mortgage business?

MR. MAISEL: They are not in the mortgage business for houses more than twenty years old and of specific types. They limit very heavily the kinds of loans they will make. In the average market you will find that the insurance companies are not in 80% of the mortgage market in most areas.

MR. HOWARD: The commercial banks are coming in more heavily, of course.

MR. MAISEL: No, they are limited very severely in the types of loans they can make, except FHA and VA — and FHAs and VAs are very limited types of loans.

MR. KESSEL: What fraction of the housing stock can savings and loans, commercial banks, and insurance companies make loans on?

MR. MAISEL: On the basis of local market studies, I would say that it fragments very rapidly so that loans are made by only one type of institution on 50% or more of the market in an urban area.

MR. KESSEL: That is not the question.

HARRY GUTHMANN: When you get into a higher-risk loan, which is what older property means, an on-the-spot institution is likely to make such loans more readily than a life insurance company is, and yet I have not seen any evidence that the local savings and loans have suffered proportionate losses. Maybe that is the efficient way of handling the loan — through a specialized institution close to the property. Indeed, I think there are some data prepared by the League to the effect that savings and loans and other institutions have suffered increased losses as they have widened the area which they attempted to serve. The farther you go away from home, the less you know about property and the person behind it.

MR. MAISEL: Yes, but the less your portfolio risks are, also.

MODERATOR KETCHUM: It has not been true of life insurance companies, has it, that they have suffered more on mortgages written thousands of miles from the home office?

MR. GUTHMANN: I do not know that there are any data to answer your question with certainty, but I think the fact that they have attempted to hold higher standards is merely a part of the difficulty. When making loans through local mortgage bankers, as they do, it is very difficult to generalize.

MODERATOR KETCHUM: Life insurance companies have a different system of acquisition.

THOMAS WOLFE: Do I understand that in institutional lending, specialization in capital markets increases the risks that capital is misallocated?

MR. GUTHMAN: The answer seems to have been "no," or there was no appreciable dissent. It seems to me that the lending practices of financial institutions are almost an historical accident.

Let us consider pension funds. They have developed largely in the postwar period when the capital markets and equity securities have been generally sound, and they have gone very heavily into this type of investment. Insurance companies had all their investment practices hardened in an earlier period when equity securities were considered dangerous, and either by law or by custom they stay away. So a good deal depends on whether a pension fund is handled by a bank, an insurance company, or the institution itself. I think the rigidities in these investment practices really do present a risk. I mention pension funds as one example, because they do invest so heavily in equities. The experience they have had has been very good, and they are completely convinced of the value of equities as investments. I think that this sort of specialization might under easily conceivable circumstances result in a rather serious misallocation of funds.

CHARLES PARTEE: My problem is with the term "misallocation of capital." I think I would agree that there is enough fluidity in these markets and in the ability of some lenders to move about in them so that, except for possible regional difficulties, in nineteen out of twenty years there has not been much serious problem with the misallocation of capital. But if the term is extended to include the possibility that undue risks will be taken by some particular lenders reaching for a higher yield, it seems to me that there is a possibility of running into structural problems that would in turn result for a period in the misallocation of capital. The trouble, as I say, is with the term.

MR. HOWARD: Actually, we did not treat the misallocation quite in the sense in which you are speaking of it — of the risky loan and so on. We were thinking of the total flow of funds and we felt that that would correct itself as interest rates changed in the various markets.

A B C D E F G H I J – R – 7 3 2 1 0 / 6 9 8 7 6 5 4

Lewis and Clark College - Watzek Library
HG2481 .K53   wmain
Ketchum, Marshall D/Readings in financia

3 5209 00413 3381